Unreal
TOURNAMENT

WELCOME TO UNREAL TOURNAMENT 3

Unreal Tournament 3 has been a long time in coming, and for fans of brutal deathmatch, there is nothing better. *UT3* builds on past Unreal games; polishing, refining, and adding to games that have come before.

New to *UT3* is an entirely new set of vehicles, nanomachine-powered vehicles created by the Phayder corporation, and piloted by the Necris, humans infused with sentient Nanoblack.

Vehicle Capture the Flag (VCTF) has become a standard game mode, with six maps providing vehicular mayhem with the greater focus of capturing and defending the flag.

Warfare, an expansion of *UT2k4*'s Onslaught mode returns with the Node based combat, but this time, special objective Nodes and destructible barricades have been added, infusing Warfare with some aspects of the old Assault gametype.

Naturally, Deathmatch (DM) and Capture the Flag (CTF) are well represented. DM spans many maps, large and small, for large scale team brawls, or more intimate Duels. CTF now has a greater focus on tightly focused combat, with an adjusted Translocator and an emphasis on fast paced action.

All the weapons of destruction from previous *Unreal Tournament* games return, and this time, the Enforcer is back in place of the Assault Rifle. In addition, all the weapons have received a tune-up, and each has been tweaked and refined. There are also new toys to play with—deployable weapons and equipment that can be a great help in VCTF and Warfare. Paralyze your opponents with the Stasis Field, or disable their vehicles with the EMP Mine.

For information on the single player campaign, continue through this chapter— just watch out for spoilers! You may want to finish the campaign at least once before you come back and look over the details.

Chapter 2 contains all the information on *UT3*'s weaponry, with detailed stats, and plenty of advice on how to use the weapons to their fullest potential.

Chapter 3 has data on the vehicles, so you can get an idea on the crunchy numbers behind the scenes, as well as commentary on their basic usage, and their effectiveness against other vehicles and players on foot.

Chapter 4 has overviews of every map in the game, head there if you want to get a feel for a certain map or gametype. The single player campaign uses all of the various maps in this chapter, so if you want some information on the layout or contents of a map in the single player campaign, this is the place to look.

BACKGROUND OF THE NECRIS CAMPAIGN

Some of the corporations of the Unreal universe may be known to you from past Unreal games. This time around, they play a major role in the single player campaign.

The bulk of the single player campaign takes place on the planet Taryd, a *massive* source of the Tarydium that fuels so much of humanities voracious energy needs, and the planet that Tarydium was first discovered.

On Taryd, the Liandri and their robotic assistants, the Axon and their powerful weaponry, and the Izanagi with their sprawling assets all vie for control, periodically skirmishing with one another in hidden (and sometimes, not so hidden) conflict.

The New Earth Government (the N.E.G.) enforces a ceasefire over critical areas of the planet, such as the massive Tarydium seam that runs through the Alluvion river valley, near the Torlan Delta. The N.E.G. keeps the conflict between the corporations for resources from spilling into outright warfare. Because of the N.E.G.'s oppressive policies (at least in the eyes of the corporate board leaders), the various corporations have left N.E.G. controlled space to establish many remote mining colonies. Reaper, the main character of the campaign in *Unreal Tournament 3*, is from one such mining colony.

All the corporations recruit tournament champions as advisors on their military activities, and recently, both Lauren and Malcolm have been brought to Taryd to advise the corporations.

The Phayder corporation, a highly secretive company that specializes in genetic research, has developed Nanoblack, a nanobot infused substance that they have begun infusing into test subjects, creating the race known as the Necris.

The Nanoblack infusion heightens mental and physical capabilities, and more importantly for the Necris, the transformation has taken on a spiritual aspect, altering not just the minds and bodies of the denizens of their home planet, but also their society.

The Necris homeworld, Omicron 6, has been completely transformed by the Nanoblack, with Necris infection tubes running through the crust of the planet, even the oceans have been infused with Nanoblack. The Nanoblack itself has become semi-sentient, as the massive nanobot colonies grow and communicate.

Before the single player campaign begins, events set in motion by the Phayder corporation and the Necris get the story rolling. The Phayder company decides they want the Tarydium on Taryd, and they're going to invade and assault other mining colonies as well.

Reaper's home, the mining colony of Twin Souls, is attacked and invaded by the Krall, vicious mercenaries in the employ of the Necris. Left for dead, he is barely rescued and resuscitated by Izanagi medical techs.

As the game begins, Reaper burns with a desire for vengeance, and as the events of the campaign move on, he gets far more than he could have ever expected.

SINGLE PLAYER CAMPAIGN

SPOILERS!

Avoid the remainder of this chapter if you don't want to have the overall story spoiled for you.

Once you've gone through the campaign once, if you want to look this over, you can get a better idea of when and where the various missions branch, and you can come back and play through the game again, tackling different missions.

CAMPAIGN STRUCTURE

The single player campaign is straightforward, but surprisingly large. Between the missions, which are simply battles played out on the various maps in the game, you usually have a choice of what mission you want to tackle next.

While the overall story always proceeds down the same route, which missions you play is different depending on the decisions you make along the way.

If you go for a more brute force approach, you may wind up playing a TDM match where you are outnumbered by two players.

Or you might be up against Necris vehicles, but without the ability to actually hijack them!

Conversely, if you take a more indirect route, you may ease the mission difficulty, keeping the combat more balanced.

As you play through the campaign and complete certain missions, you unlock "Cards" that can be played to give you a one shot boost on a tough mission. If you're having trouble with the route you've chosen, don't hesitate to use cards.

You can also play through the campaign cooperatively, and adjust the difficulty each time you resume a campaign, so you should never run into an impossible situation.

CHAPTER I: RONIN

The Twin Souls clan was targeted by the Phayder in the first assault wave of the war. The Krall were led by Akasha, the ruthless Necris High Inquisitor. The Krall had overwhelming numbers, and the element of surprise, so the slaughter was swift. They attacked without remorse, and with no concern whether they were killing security forces or non-combatants. Reaper was able to rally the remnants of the Fist and stake out a defensive position, but it was clear there was no chance for survival.

Reaper's parents fell early in the attack, but he still hoped to get his sister safely away from the conflict. He asked his sister and Othello to power up a ship for escape, with Bishop providing sniper cover – and then gave Othello his true orders, to get his sister safely off the planet. Reaper falls in the ensuing combat, and his sister goes back to save him.

Reaper is badly injured. His sister decides to answer the Izanagi's call for mercenary soldiers, thinking that this will both get them access to medical facilities and get them a chance at revenge against Akasha and the Necris.

Reaper and Jester practice in a Deathmatch 1-on-1 setting, and get accustomed to the portable respawner technology.

Reaper's force is often referred to as the Ronin by the professional mercenary forces of the Izanagi, as a sometimes condescending homage to their having lost their clan in the conflict.

AVAILABLE MAPS IN THIS CHAPTER

Rising Sun: DM Tutorial - Completion unlocks *Chapter II*.

CHAPTER II: WITH CAESAR'S COIN

The New Earth Government (N.E.G.) has been trying to keep the peace on Taryd, but surprise Krall attacks are popping up across the globe, and each corporation is scrambling to protect its holdings. Due to a slight technological advantage, Axon forces have managed to slowly push their way into Izanagi territories in recent years. The Ronin are ordered to patrol the new demilitarized zone between Izanagi and Axon processing facilities [*Shangri La & Reflection*]. The number of unofficial skirmishes has been on the rise, and tensions are high. As a show of force, Malcolm advises that Izanagi forces push across the DMZ to regain control of the entire Tarydium-rich peninsula and its associated ports [*Tank Crossing*].

This bold move has put Axon forces in a defensive posture, but they're not going to give up with out a military response of their own. Sensing that full-scale war is about to break, the N.E.G. has pulled out of the hotly contested neutral territories of the Torlan Delta and is establishing a base of operations in orbit. They've vowed to remain neutral and won't step in unless absolutely necessary. Izanagi will continue their struggles with Axon along the mouth of the Alluvion River while simultaneously making a move into the Torlan delta as a target of opportunity. As an established filed commander, Reaper is given the choice of assignments.

Taking the Torlan path sparks a huge international incident, and Axon forces mobilize in the ports and send the full force of their military toward the delta [*Main Branch 1*]. Choosing to continue the power play will move the Ronin into established Axon territory to fight for control of the port-territories [*Main Branch 2*].

This is the first decision point in the campaign, and pops up after winning in VCTF-Kargo.

MAIN BRANCH 1

Reaper chooses to move into the Torlan Delta and establish control of the continent's main power plants. As a counter move, Axon forces have mobilized in the south and are moving their Leviathan super vehicle toward the delta to put an end to Izanagi's power grab. The Ronin can face this threat head on and confront Axon forces [*Serenity*] or continue to weaken their reserves by cutting off supply routes and setting up a siege around the Axon capital [*Suspense, Downtown, & Defiance*]. Unfortunately, Krall forces have moved into the area and are attempting to take control of the battle weary ports.

This is another big decision point that pops up after winning the CTF-Hydrosis mission.

- If the player chooses to take on the Axon forces in Serenity, they regain control of the Torlan Delta and Krall attacks remain at a minimum.

- If they decide to follow the river into Oxida Nova, they suppress Axon forces quicker, but leave the Torlan Delta open to increased Krall attacks.

MAIN BRANCH 2

Reaper chooses to continue the power play against Axon forces. Doing so continues the drive toward the Axon capital, Oxida Nova, but leaves Izanagi forces in the Torlan delta vulnerable. The Ronin are given one more chance to move in and protect those forces. [*This is after the CTF-Hydrosis mission, where the player can choose between Torlan and Suspense.*] With Axon forces cut off from their ports, the Axon have started moving along land routes, so the Ronin can alternatively opt to make a final blow to control their main supply route [*Suspense, Downtown, & Defiance*]. Moving forward definitely advances Izanagi goals, but allows an opening for the Krall to move in and launch a surprise attack on the now weakened port territories. [*Essentially, ignore the Krall too long, and you'll have to fight them after taking control of Axon territory.*]

INDEPENDENT OF THE MAIN BRANCH

There are a several paths now open to the Ronin, but they all revolve around maintaining the balance between advancing toward the Axon city and defending the rear guard from the threat of Krall invasion. The longer the Krall are ignored, the farther they advance into Izanagi territories, and the more the Ronin will need to fight their way back out. The Krall have also moved against the Axon rear guard, so both corporations are under the constant threat of Krall attack. The Krall vastly outnumber both Axon and Izanagi forces combined.

At some point, Axon will offer a treaty to the Izanagi, and Reaper must decide whether to agree to their terms [*and join forces with the Axon Iron Guard, lead by tournament veteran Lauren*] or push forward and crush the Axon entirely [*to take control of their tech and gain the use of advanced weapons and vehicles, such as the Leviathan*]. There are seven final branch points in this chapter, but all ultimately end in variants of one of the previously mentioned two outcomes.

Depending on how you reach them, Torlan and Serenity can all unlock Chapter III.

AVAILABLE MAPS IN THIS CHAPTER

Defiance: Can grant Iron Guard Reinforcement cards, depending on how you reach it.

Diesel: 2 different versions depending on how you reach the map. Axon version unlocks Lauren. Upgrades or the Iron Guard Reinforcement cards (or gives them to you if you don't already have them), and grants Upgraded respawner cards.

Downtown

Hydrosis: 2 different versions depending on how you reach it.

Kargo: VCTF tutorial - 2 different versions depending on how you reach it.

Market District: Orb tutorial

Reflection: CTF tutorial

Serenity: 2 different versions depending on how you reach it; may unlock the Iron Guard reinforcement card.

Shangri La

Sinkhole: Warfare tutorial

Suspense: 2 different versions depending on how you reach it.

Tank Crossing: Unlocks Tactical Diversion card upon completion.

Torlan: 4 different versions depending on how you reach it.

CHAPTER III: THE LIANDRI CONFLICT

For an assault against the Necris forces, Izanagi will need to control sufficient Tarydium resources (mines, refineries, technology, etc.) to fuel their war machine. In *Chapter III*, the conflict escalates and the Liandri send their robots into the mix. Axon has the vehicle/weapon tech, Liandri has the AI and Robotics, and both control significant Tarydium resources.

If the Ronin have been primarily focused on controlling Axon forces [*in Chapter II*], then the Liandri will have already sent a team into the Torlan Delta to oust the Krall. While that means that the Krall are set back for a while, it also means that Liandri controls the flow of all power resources in the region. The Ronin must regain control of the Torlan Delta if they want to move forward into Liandri territories. If Izanagi forces have secured Axon tech and have already maintained a foothold in the Torlan Delta [*in Chapter II*], then the Ronin are already prepared to make their move directly into Liandri territory. Regardless, their first move against Liandri turf will be an invasion of their factories [*Arsenal*] to disrupt production lines and weaken their infrastructure.

From there, Reaper must decide whether to follow the main battle path leading into Hyperion, the Liandri capital city [*Heat Ray & Main Branch 1*], or move toward a recently discovered Liandri Taryduim plant, an unprepared target of opportunity [*Dusk & Main Branch 2*].

This is the first decision point in this chapter, and pops up after winning in DM-Arsenal.

MAIN BRANCH 1

After reaching in the streets of downtown Hyperion [*Heat Ray*] the Ronin should realize that they're vastly outnumbered in an incredibly difficult fight. Malcolm advises taking out secondary targets instead of making a full frontal assault. Reaper has the choice of back-tracking to a valuable Tarydium mine [*Dusk*], or taking a forward observation point along the Liandri archipelago [*Islander*].

Choosing to assault the island recon base means that the Krall will move in to take over the Dusk processing facility and make an initial foray into controlling the Liandri city. The Ronin will have to fight them off later, and defeat them before making any headway toward the Liandri Robotic factories [*Power Surge & Heat Ray again, but this time vs. Krall forces led by a Necris commander, and with Darkwalker reinforcements*].

Choosing to assault the Dusk facility will break down Liandri resources and allow for a safer move into the city and toward the Robotic Factories. The Dusk fight will be more difficult, though, now that Liandri forces have had time to prepare their defenses. Regardless, the Krall will move in behind the Ronin, and must be held at bay while fighting the Liandri bots at the same time.

MAIN BRANCH 2

It was a wise decision to interrupt the Liandri resource chain, but they seem to have managed some small defenses before the Ronin's arrival. Regardless, they must take out the facility and the more fortified mines below [*Dusk & Power Surge*]. Once the mine is under Izanagi control, Reaper has the choice of entering the city or taking out the Islander Archipelago observation point. The Krall are taking advantage of the Liandri's weakened position and have already moved into the city, so the Ronin must deal with them [*Heat Ray again, but this time vs. Krall forces led by a Necris commander, and with Darkwalker reinforcements*].

INDEPENDENT OF THE MAIN BRANCH

Eventually the Ronin will work their way from the lower industrial depths of the city [*Arsenal & Heat Ray*] toward the more modern and tech parts of the city [*Coret & Carbon Fire*]. There are various paths that lead through the map tree, shifting while the Ronin maintain a balance similar to *Chapter I*, alternatively pushing deeper into enemy territory while keeping the Krall at bay.

At various points through the ladder the Ronin have the option to investigate a Liandri base that contains a captured Necris Darkwalker vehicle [*Containment*]. A successful assault on this base will give the Ronin the ability to hijack Necris vehicles in subsequent matches.

The Ronin will eventually make it to the Liandri mainframe [*Strident*] but must figure out a way to access the systems and take control of Hyperion. They can hold the city [*fighting Krall*] and fend off attacks while the Izanagi techs hack into the mainframe, or they can go after Matrix, the leader of the Liandri forces and sole keeper of the codes needed to access the mainframe [*Gateway*].

Depending on how you reach them, Gateway, Carbon Fire, Heat Ray, & Containment can all unlock Chapter IV.

AVAILABLE MAPS IN THIS CHAPTER

Arsenal: Unlocks the Heavy Armor cards.

Carbon Fire

Containment: 2 different versions depending on how you reach it. One has a contained Darkwalker, and the other has the Darkwalker free to roam about. Completion unlocks ability to hijack/drive Necris vehicles.

Coret

Dusk: 2 different versions depending on how you reach it.

Gateway: Unlocks the Upgrade for the Liandri reinforcement cards and unlocks Matrix.

Heat Ray: 2 different versions depending on how you reach it. The first has the Darkwalker and the other doesn't. If you have not yet completed Containment, you will not be able to drive the Darkwalker.

Islander: 2 different versions depending on how you reach it; unlocks the Advance Warning cards.

Power Surge: 2 different versions depending on how you reach it.

Strident: 2 different versions depending on how you reach it; unlocks the Liandri Reinforcement cards.

CHAPTER IV: CALCULATED LOSSES

The Necris forces make a massive surprise attack, dropping their infection tubes from orbit and corrupting all of Taryd with nanoblack. This marks the first large scale use of the Phayder Necris legion in conventional warfare, explaining their absence from recent tournaments as they built up forces for the war.

Ronin will have to hold on to the [*Islander*] observation point in order to maintain a forward staging area and establish a watch post to warn of incoming Necris attacks, but the islands have already been corrupted by nanoblack and the Necris have a strong foothold there.

Now the Izanagi are on the defensive, and must reclaim all the territories where the Necris have established a foothold across the globe. First, they must return to Izanagi's Tokaido territories and retake control of areas lost to Necris forces [*Market District, Shangri La, & Corruption*]. The Ronin fight their way through various new battlefields and revisit some old areas which have now been transformed by the Necris.

Axon and Liandri territories will also need protection, and some areas will need to be revisited to oust the Krall and Necris forces entrenched there. The Krall Chieftain will eventually be cornered in Oxida Nova, and Ronin will be given the opportunity to take him out and end the threat of further Krall attacks [*Deck*].

By this point the Ronin have made good progress moving toward the Phayder base of operations, but Izanagi resources are stretched thin and the Necris are showing no signs of slowing down.

By pooling their resources with the Liandri and Axon, the Izanagi manage one last desperate attack in the heart of Necris-held territory. The Ronin are chosen to smuggle a Leviathan super vehicle into the Necris power center and take over the large mine that is their main resource center, thus dealing a harsh blow to the Necris infrastructure [*Onyx Coast & Avalanche*]. With their Chieftain down, Krall forces are in disarray, and the Necris have been pushed back into a corner. Akasha recalls her forces, and retreats back to the orbital jumpgate in an attempt to cover her escape into Phayder controlled space [*Deimos*].

AVAILABLE MAPS IN THIS CHAPTER

Avalanche

Biohazard

Corruption

Deck: Unlocks Scythe character.

Deimos: Unlocks *Chapter V*

Defiance

Islander: Unlocks Damian, Kragoth, and Malakai.

Market District

Onyx Coast: Unlocks ability to drive Necris vehicles if you haven't already gotten it.

Shangri La

Suspense

Torlan

CHAPTER V: DISPOSABLE ASSETS

With the cooperative success along the Onyx Coast, an unsteady balance has been restored among the corporations, and the Big Four all find themselves weakened, battle weary, and vulnerable. Fearing a political and economic crisis back on Earth as the war on Taryd spirals out of control, the N.E.G. steps in to put an end to what will later be called the Phayder Wars.

The ever-uneasy peace has been restored. While map boundaries have definitely changed (in Izanagi's favor), each of the corporations has returned to their respective territories. Tarydium production has begun anew. Reaper and the Ronin are war heroes, but they're not satisfied. The Necris are still out there, and Reaper has yet to get his revenge on Akasha after she destroyed the Twin Souls colony.

In a blitzkrieg strike, the Ronin hijack a transport ship [*Deimos*] and take it into Necris-controlled space. They slip through the Jumpgate to reach Omicron, the Necris home world [*Omicron Dawn*].

Out of options (and patience), the Ronin abandon all pretense of stealth and make a frontal assault. Jester lands the ship in the Acidus Desert [*Sandstorm*], and the Ronin begin their push into Absalom, the Necris-controlled capital city. Akasha seeks protection from the Necris, but they're disappointed with her failures on Taryd, and excommunicate her. With no one left to turn to, she visits the holy land [*Sanctuary*] in search of asylum, but is unable to escape Reaper and his team.

They pursue Akasha and her forces into the Phayder headquarters [*Fearless*] when she attempts to steal an invulnerability prototype, and eventually back to the capital [*Necropolis*] and down into the subterranean maze of the old city [*Vertebrae*].

Back on Taryd, Malcolm has contacted the Phayder to inform them of Ronin's defection. He's sold them out in order to protect Izanagi profit margins.

Akasha's forces meet the Ronin in the underground maze of Old Absalom [*Floodgate*], but the Ronin defeat them and successfully disable the only remaining Respawner. With the Respawners down, Reaper faces Akasha in one final battle, seeking to avenge his friends and family [*Sentinel*]. Everyone is killed except Reaper, and he realizes he's been betrayed.

AVAILABLE MAPS IN THIS CHAPTER

Fearless

Floodgate

Necropolis

Omicron Dawn: Unlocks Loque.

Sanctuary

Sandstorm

Sentinel: Unlocks Akasha.

Vertebrae

CAMPAIGN FLOWCHART

While much of the structure is revealed in the campaign overview, if you *really* want to know how to get to certain missions, you can use this flowchart to choose your route through the campaign.

Different routes put you up against different challenges. You may be battling the Krall, the Liandri, or the Necris, all on the same map at different points in the campaign. Sometimes the matches are either slightly, or wildly lopsided against you.

Completing certain missions unlocks character models for your use in multiplayer.

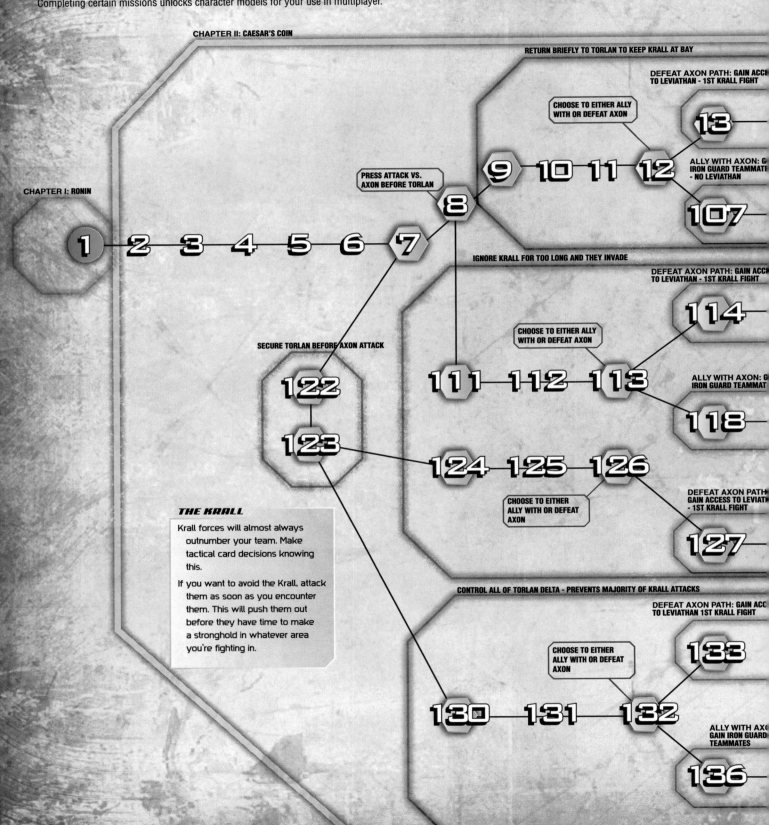

CHAPTER II: CAESAR'S COIN

CHAPTER I: RONIN

RETURN BRIEFLY TO TORLAN TO KEEP KRALL AT BAY

DEFEAT AXON PATH: GAIN ACCI
TO LEVIATHAN - 1ST KRALL FIGHT

CHOOSE TO EITHER ALLY
WITH OR DEFEAT AXON

13

9 10 11 12

ALLY WITH AXON: G
IRON GUARD TEAMMATF
- NO LEVIATHAN

PRESS ATTACK VS.
AXON BEFORE TORLAN

107

8

1 2 3 4 5 6 7

IGNORE KRALL FOR TOO LONG AND THEY INVADE

DEFEAT AXON PATH: GAIN ACCI
TO LEVIATHAN - 1ST KRALL FIGHT

114

CHOOSE TO EITHER ALLY
WITH OR DEFEAT AXON

SECURE TORLAN BEFORE AXON ATTACK

122

111 112 113

ALLY WITH AXON: G
IRON GUARD TEAMMAT

118

123

124 125 126

THE KRALL

Krall forces will almost always
outnumber your team. Make
tactical card decisions knowing
this.

If you want to avoid the Krall, attack
them as soon as you encounter
them. This will push them out
before they have time to make
a stronghold in whatever area
you're fighting in.

CHOOSE TO EITHER
ALLY WITH OR DEFEAT
AXON

DEFEAT AXON PATH:
GAIN ACCESS TO LEVIATH
- 1ST KRALL FIGHT

127

CONTROL ALL OF TORLAN DELTA - PREVENTS MAJORITY OF KRALL ATTACKS

DEFEAT AXON PATH: GAIN ACC
TO LEVIATHAN 1ST KRALL FIGHT

CHOOSE TO EITHER
ALLY WITH OR DEFEAT
AXON

133

130 131 132

ALLY WITH AX
GAIN IRON GUARD
TEAMMATES

136

AXON: ALLY OR ENEMY?

The decision of whether to ally with or beat down the Axon is basically a choice between getting a Lauren card, and getting the Leviathan in a couple key battles. If you're a vehicle player, it may be worth choosing the alternate route on Missions 12, 113, 126, & 132.

INVASION-STYLE: PLAYER HAS LEVIATHAN AT BASE TO START

14 — 15

TORLAN VS. LIANDRI

109   108   110

116   115   117

INVASION-STYLE: PLAYER HAS LEVIATHAN AT BASE TO START

IRON GUARD - NO LEVIATHAN

120   119   121

16 → TO CHAPTER III

INVASION-STYLE: PLAYER HAS LEVIATHAN AT BASE TO START

128 — 129

134 — 135

137 — 138

1

GAME TYPE	DM
MAP	Rising Sun
GOAL SCORE	10
OPPOSING TEAM	Twin Souls

TEAMMATES	OPPONENTS
	Jester
	Othello
	Bishop

2

GAME TYPE	DM
MAP	Shangri La
GOAL SCORE	40
OPPOSING TEAM	Iron Guard

TEAMMATES	OPPONENTS
Jester	Talon
Kensai	Kregore
Ushido	Drake
	Blain

3

GAME TYPE	CTF
MAP	Reflection
GOAL SCORE	3
OPPOSING TEAM	Iron Guard

TEAMMATES	OPPONENTS
Jester	Cain
Othello	Johnson
Bishop	Karag
	Wraith

4

GAME TYPE	Warfare
MAP	Sinkhole
GOAL SCORE	1
OPPOSING TEAM	Iron Guard

TEAMMATES	OPPONENTS
Jester	Talon
Othello	Kregore
Bishop	Blain

5

GAME TYPE	Warfare
MAP	Market District
GOAL SCORE	1
OPPOSING TEAM	Iron Guard

TEAMMATES	OPPONENTS
Jester	Cain
Othello	Johnson
Bishop	Karag
	Wraith

6

GAME TYPE	Warfare
MAP	Tank Crossing
GOAL SCORE	1
OPPOSING TEAM	Iron Guard

TEAMMATES	OPPONENTS
Jester	Johnson
Othello	Barktooth
Bishop	Harlin
	Cain

7

GAME TYPE	Vehicle CTF
MAP	Kargo
GOAL SCORE	3
CARD	Tactical Diversion
OPPOSING TEAM	Iron Guard

TEAMMATES	OPPONENTS
Jester	Slain
Othello	Johnson
Bishop	Talan
	Drake

8

GAME TYPE	CTF
MAP	Hydrosis
GOAL SCORE	3
OPPOSING TEAM	Iron Guard

TEAMMATES	OPPONENTS
Jester	Harlin
Othello	Slain
Bishop	Karag
Rook	Wraith
Kensai	Kregore
	Talan

9

GAME TYPE	Warfare
MAP	Torlan
GOAL SCORE	1
OPPOSING TEAM	Iron Guard

TEAMMATES	OPPONENTS
Jester	Cain
Othello	Karag
Bishop	Kregore
Connor	Drake
Harkin	Barktooth
	Harlin

10

GAME TYPE	Vehicle CTF
MAP	Suspense
GOAL SCORE	3
OPPOSING TEAM	Iron Guard

TEAMMATES	OPPONENTS
Jester	Johnson
Othello	Wraith
Bishop	Kregore
Ushido	Blain
Rook	Slain
	Barktooth

11

GAME TYPE	Warfare
MAP	Serenity
GOAL SCORE	1
OPPOSING TEAM	Iron Guard

TEAMMATES	OPPONENTS
Jester	Lauren
Othello	Slain
Bishop	Johnson
Hunter	Karag

12

GAME TYPE	Warfare
MAP	Downtown
GOAL SCORE	1
OPPOSING TEAM	Iron Guard

TEAMMATES	OPPONENTS
Jester	Lauren
Othello	Harlin
Bishop	Wraith
	Talan

13

GAME TYPE	DM
MAP	Defiance
GOAL SCORE	50
CARD	Iron Guard Reinforcements
OPPOSING TEAM	Iron Guard

TEAMMATES	OPPONENTS
Jester	Lauren
Othello	Barktooth
Bishop	Harlin
	Slain

14

GAME TYPE	Vehicle CTF
MAP	Kargo
GOAL SCORE	3
OPPOSING TEAM	Krall

TEAMMATES	OPPONENTS
Jester	Hellhound
Othello	Scorn
Bishop	Gnasher
	Cerberus
	Scar
	Worg

15

GAME TYPE	Warfare
MAP	Torlan - Leviathan
GOAL SCORE	1
OPPOSING TEAM	Krall

TEAMMATES	OPPONENTS
Jester	Hellhound
Othello	Scar
Bishop	Worg
	Lockjaw
	Claw
	Bargest
	Blackfang
	Gnasher
	Scorn

16

GAME TYPE	DM
MAP	Arsenal
GOAL SCORE	50
CARD	Heavy Armor
OPPOSING TEAM	Liandri

TEAMMATES	OPPONENTS
Jester	Aspect
Othello	Colossus
Bishop	OSC
	Raptor

107

GAME TYPE	DM
MAP	Diesel
GOAL SCORE	40
CARD	Respawn Upgrade Iron Guard Reinforcement
OPPOSING TEAM	Iron Guard

TEAMMATES	OPPONENTS
Othello	Lauren
	Barktooth
	Harlin
	Slain

108

GAME TYPE	Warfare
MAP	Serenity - Necris
GOAL SCORE	1
OPPOSING TEAM	Krall

TEAMMATES	OPPONENTS
Jester	Hellhound
Othello	Cerberus
Bishop	Gnasher
	Scar
	Worg
	Lockjaw
	Claw
	Bargest

109

GAME TYPE	Vehicle CTF
MAP	Kargo
GOAL SCORE	3
OPPOSING TEAM	Krall

TEAMMATES	OPPONENTS
Jester	Claw
Othello	Bargest
Bishop	Blackfang
	Scorn
	Cerberus

110

GAME TYPE	Warfare
MAP	Torlan
GOAL SCORE	1
OPPOSING TEAM	Liandri

TEAMMATES	OPPONENTS
Jester	Matrix
Othello	Cathode
Bishop	Enigma
	Entropy
	Aspect
	Colossus

111

GAME TYPE	Vehicle CTF
MAP	Suspense
GOAL SCORE	3
OPPOSING TEAM	Iron Guard

TEAMMATES	OPPONENTS
Jester	Cain
Othello	Johnson
Bishop	Karag
	Wraith

112

GAME TYPE	Warfare
MAP	Downtown
GOAL SCORE	1
OPPOSING TEAM	Iron Guard

TEAMMATES	OPPONENTS
Jester	Lauren
Othello	Barktooth
Bishop	Talan
	Kregore

113

GAME TYPE	DM
MAP	Defiance
GOAL SCORE	50
OPPOSING TEAM	Iron Guard

TEAMMATES	OPPONENTS
Jester	Lauren
Othello	Barktooth
Bishop	Harlin
	Slain

114

GAME TYPE	Warfare
MAP	Serenity
GOAL SCORE	1
CARD	Iron Guard Reinforcements
OPPOSING TEAM	Iron Guard

TEAMMATES	OPPONENTS
Jester	Lauren
Othello	Slain
Bishop	Johnson
	Karag

115

GAME TYPE	DM
MAP	Diesel
GOAL SCORE	50
OPPOSING TEAM	Krall

TEAMMATES	OPPONENTS
Jester	Worg
Othello	Cerberus

116

GAME TYPE	Vehicle CTF
MAP	Kargo
GOAL SCORE	3
OPPOSING TEAM	Krall

TEAMMATES	OPPONENTS
Jester	Hellhound
Othello	Scar
Bishop	Worg
	Lockjaw
	Claw
	Bargest

117

GAME TYPE	Warfare
MAP	Torlan
GOAL SCORE	1
OPPOSING TEAM	Krall

TEAMMATES	OPPONENTS
Jester	Scythe
Othello	Scorn
Bishop	Gnasher
	Cerberus
	Blackfang
	Lockjaw
	Hellhound
	Worg

118

GAME TYPE	DM
MAP	Diesel
GOAL SCORE	40
CARD	Respawn Upgrade Iron Guard Reinforcements
CHARACTER	Lauren
OPPOSING TEAM	Iron Guard

TEAMMATES	OPPONENTS
Othello	Lauren
	Barktooth
	Harlin
	Slain

119

GAME TYPE	Warfare
MAP	Serenity - Necris
GOAL SCORE	40
OPPOSING TEAM	Krall

TEAMMATES	OPPONENTS
Jester	Scythe
Othello	Hellhound
Bishop	Gnasher
	Worg
	Claw
	Blackfang

120

GAME TYPE	Vehicle CTF
MAP	Kargo
GOAL SCORE	3
OPPOSING TEAM	Krall

TEAMMATES	OPPONENTS
Jester	Cerberus
Othello	Gnasher
Bishop	Scar
	Worg
	Bargest

3 1833 05417 3114

121

GAME TYPE	Warfare
MAP	Torlan
GOAL SCORE	1
OPPOSING TEAM	Krall

TEAMMATES	OPPONENTS
Jester	Scythe
Othello	Scorn
Bishop	Gnasher
	Cerberus
	Hellhound
	Scar

122

GAME TYPE	Warfare
MAP	Torlan
GOAL SCORE	1
OPPOSING TEAM	Iron Guard

TEAMMATES	OPPONENTS
Jester	Lauren
Othello	Harlin
Bishop	Drake
	Wraith

123

GAME TYPE	CTF
MAP	Hydrosis
GOAL SCORE	3
OPPOSING TEAM	Iron Guard

TEAMMATES	OPPONENTS
Jester	Slain
Othello	Kregore
Bishop	Blain
Rook	Drake
	Johnson

124

GAME TYPE	Vehicle CTF
MAP	Suspense
GOAL SCORE	3
OPPOSING TEAM	Iron Guard

TEAMMATES	OPPONENTS
Jester	Cain
Othello	Johnson
Bishop	Karag
	Wraith

125

GAME TYPE	Warfare
MAP	Downtown
GOAL SCORE	1
OPPOSING TEAM	Iron Guard

TEAMMATES	OPPONENTS
Jester	Lauren
Othello	Barktooth
Bishop	Cain
	Johnson

126

GAME TYPE	DM
MAP	Defiance
GOAL SCORE	50
OPPOSING TEAM	Iron Guard

TEAMMATES	OPPONENTS
Jester	Lauren
Othello	Barktooth
Bishop	Harlin
	Slain

127

GAME TYPE	Warfare
MAP	Serenity
GOAL SCORE	1
CARD	Iron Guard Reinforcements
OPPOSING TEAM	Iron Guard

TEAMMATES	OPPONENTS
Jester	Lauren
Othello	Slain
Bishop	Johnson
	Karag

128

GAME TYPE	Vehicle CTF
MAP	Kargo
GOAL SCORE	3
OPPOSING TEAM	Krall

TEAMMATES	OPPONENTS
Jester	Scorn
Othello	Gnasher
Bishop	Cereberus
	Hellhound
	Scar
	Blackfang

129

GAME TYPE	Warfare
MAP	Torlan - Leviathan
GOAL SCORE	1
OPPOSING TEAM	Krall

TEAMMATES	OPPONENTS
Jester	Blackfang
Othello	Bargest
Bishop	Claw
	Lockjaw
	Worg
	Scar
	Hellhound
	Cerberus

130

GAME TYPE	Warfare
MAP	Serenity
GOAL SCORE	1
OPPOSING TEAM	Iron Guard

TEAMMATES	OPPONENTS
Jester	Lauren
Othello	Slain
Bishop	Johnson
	Karag

131

GAME TYPE	Vehicle CTF
MAP	Suspense
GOAL SCORE	3
OPPOSING TEAM	Iron Guard

TEAMMATES	OPPONENTS
Jester	Barktooth
Othello	Johnson
Bishop	Kregore
	Talan

132

GAME TYPE	Warfare
MAP	Downtown
GOAL SCORE	1
OPPOSING TEAM	Iron Guard

TEAMMATES	OPPONENTS
Jester	Lauren
Othello	Barktooth
Bishop	Drake
	Cain

133

GAME TYPE	DM
MAP	Defiance
GOAL SCORE	50
CARD	Iron Guard Reinforcements
OPPOSING TEAM	Iron Guard

TEAMMATES	OPPONENTS
Jester	Lauren
Othello	Harlin
Bishop	Barktooth
	Slain

134

GAME TYPE	Vehicle CTF
MAP	Kargo
GOAL SCORE	3
OPPOSING TEAM	Krall

TEAMMATES	OPPONENTS
Jester	Scorn
Othello	Gnasher
Bishop	Scar
	Worg
	Lockjaw
	Claw

135

GAME TYPE	Warfare
MAP	Serenity - Necris
GOAL SCORE	1
OPPOSING TEAM	Krall

TEAMMATES	OPPONENTS
Jester	Scythe
Othello	Cerberus
Bishop	Blackfang
Ushido	Bargest
	Worg

136

GAME TYPE	DM
MAP	Diesel
GOAL SCORE	40
OPPOSING TEAM	Iron Guard
CARD	Iron Guard Reinforcement
RESPAWN UPGRADE	
CHARACTER	Lauren

TEAMMATES	OPPONENTS
Othello	Lauren
	Barktooth
	Harlin
	Slain

137

GAME TYPE	Vehicle CTF
MAP	Kargo
GOAL SCORE	3
OPPOSING TEAM	Krall

TEAMMATES	OPPONENTS
Jester	Scar
Othello	Hellhound
Bishop	Claw
Kensai	Bargest
	Blackfang

138

GAME TYPE	Warfare
MAP	Serenity - Necris
GOAL SCORE	1
OPPOSING TEAM	Krall

TEAMMATES	OPPONENTS
Jester	Scythe
Othello	Scorn
Bishop	Gnasher
Harkin	Cerberus
Connor	Scar
	Lockjaw

INSTAGIB

The Instagib card is unique in that it must be played immediately (CTF-Vertebrae), or it will be lost forever.

HIJACKING NECRIS VEHICLES

You won't be able to hijack or use Necris vehicles at the start of the campaign. You must complete the Containment mission, so choose it as soon as it comes up. The last thing you want is to be trapped on Heatray, outnumbered, playing vs. Loque, and unable to use the Darkwalker.

DIRECT ASSAULT VS. LIANDRI FORCES

FIGHT VS. MATRIX TO CONTROL LIANDRI

PLAYER FIGHTS ON VEHICLE SIDE

24

22 — **23**

KRALL ATTACK HYPERION - LOQUE LEADS ATTACK

52

21

PLAYER FIGHTS ON VEHICLE SIDE VS. KRALL

55

RETREAT TO BORDERS TO WORK IN SLOWLY

53 — **54**

18 **19** **20**

FIGHT VS. MATRIX TO CONTROL LIANDRI

56

KRALL ATTACK HYPERION - LOQUE LEADS ATTACK - EXTRA KRALL IN PLACE

PLAYER FIGHTS ON VEHICLE SIDE

IF VICTORIOUS, CAN DRIVE DARKWALKER

60

57 — **58** — **59**

61

62

FIGHT VS. MATRIX TO CONTROL LIANDRI

MEASURED ATTACK VS. LIANDRI MEANS KRALL HAVE MOVED IN

IF VICTORIOUS, CAN DRIVE DARKWALKER

70

67

PLAYER FIGHTS ON VEHICLE SIDE

65 — **66**

69

68

71

KRALL ATTACK HYPERION - LOQUE LEADS ATTACK

FIGHT VS. MATRIX TO CONTROL LIANDRI

16 — **17** — **63** — **64**

KRALL ATTACK HYPERION - LOQUE LEADS ATTACK

75

73 — **74**

76

FIGHT VS. MATRIX TO CONTROL LIANDRI

77

72

KRALL ATTACK HYPERION - LOQUE LEADS ATTACK

80

IF VICTORIOUS, CAN DRIVE DARKWALKER

78 — **79**

81

82

FIGHT VS. MATRIX TO CONTROL LIANDRI

SLOW APPROACH ON LIANDRI FORCES TO WEAR THEM DOWN - KRALL ADVANCE

83

17

GAME TYPE	DM
MAP	Heat Ray
GOAL SCORE	65
OPPOSING TEAM	Liandri

TEAMMATES	OPPONENTS
Jester	Aspect
Othello	Colossus
Bishop	Enigma
	Entropy
	Monarch
	Raptor

18

GAME TYPE	Warfare
MAP	Dusk
GOAL SCORE	1
OPPOSING TEAM	Liandri

TEAMMATES	OPPONENTS
Jester	Evolution
Othello	Mihr
Bishop	Syntax
	Torque
	Monarch
	Raptor

19

GAME TYPE	Warfare
MAP	Power Surge
GOAL SCORE	1
OPPOSING TEAM	Liandri

TEAMMATES	OPPONENTS
Jester	Aspect
Othello	Colossus
Bishop	OSC
	Monarch
	Mihr
	Torque

20

GAME TYPE	CTF
MAP	Coret
GOAL SCORE	5
OPPOSING TEAM	Liandri

TEAMMATES	OPPONENTS
Jester	Cathode
Othello	Raptor
Bishop	Syntax
	Evolution

21

GAME TYPE	DM
MAP	Heat Ray
GOAL SCORE	50
OPPOSING TEAM	Krall

TEAMMATES	OPPONENTS
Jester	Loque
Othello	Scythe
Bishop	Scorn
	Gnasher
	Cerberus
	Lockjaw

22

GAME TYPE	Warfare
MAP	Islander
GOAL SCORE	1
OPPOSING TEAM	Liandri

TEAMMATES	OPPONENTS
Jester	Evolution
Othello	Mihr
Bishop	Syntax
	Torque

23

GAME TYPE	CTF
MAP	Strident
GOAL SCORE	5
CARD	Liandri Reinforcement
OPPOSING TEAM	Liandri

TEAMMATES	OPPONENTS
Jester	Matrix
Othello	Cathode
Bishop	Enigma
	Entropy

24

GAME TYPE	DM
MAP	Gateway
GOAL SCORE	40
CHARACTER	Matrix
KEY	Liandri Upgrade
OPPOSING TEAM	Liandri

TEAMMATES	OPPONENTS
Othello	Matrix
	Entropy
	Cathode
	Enigma

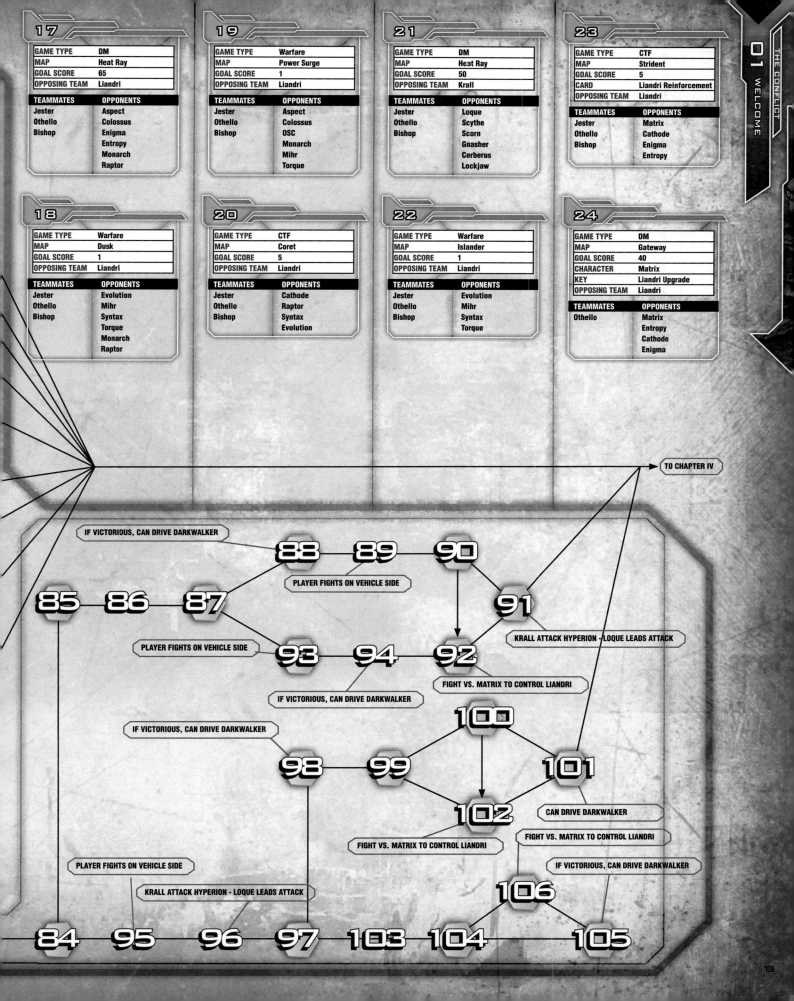

TO CHAPTER IV

IF VICTORIOUS, CAN DRIVE DARKWALKER

88 — 89 — 90

PLAYER FIGHTS ON VEHICLE SIDE

85 — 86 — 87

91

KRALL ATTACK HYPERION - LOQUE LEADS ATTACK

PLAYER FIGHTS ON VEHICLE SIDE

93 — 94 — 92

IF VICTORIOUS, CAN DRIVE DARKWALKER

FIGHT VS. MATRIX TO CONTROL LIANDRI

IF VICTORIOUS, CAN DRIVE DARKWALKER

100

98 — 99 — 101

102

CAN DRIVE DARKWALKER

FIGHT VS. MATRIX TO CONTROL LIANDRI

FIGHT VS. MATRIX TO CONTROL LIANDRI

IF VICTORIOUS, CAN DRIVE DARKWALKER

PLAYER FIGHTS ON VEHICLE SIDE

KRALL ATTACK HYPERION - LOQUE LEADS ATTACK

106

84 95 96 97 103 104 105

52

GAME TYPE	Vehicle CTF
MAP	Containment
GOAL SCORE	3
KEY	Necris Vehicles
OPPOSING TEAM	Liandri

TEAMMATES	OPPONENTS
Jester	Evolution
Othello	Monarch
Bishop	Mihr
	Torque

53

GAME TYPE	Vehicle CTF
MAP	Containment - SP
GOAL SCORE	3
KEY	Necris Vehicles
OPPOSING TEAM	Krall

TEAMMATES	OPPONENTS
Jester	Scythe
Othello	Lockjaw
Bishop	Cerberus
	Gnasher

54

GAME TYPE	CTF
MAP	Strident
GOAL SCORE	5
CARD	Liandri Reinforcement
OPPOSING TEAM	Liandri

TEAMMATES	OPPONENTS
Jester	Matrix
Othello	Cathode
Bishop	Enigma
	Entropy

55

GAME TYPE	Warfare
MAP	Islander
GOAL SCORE	1
OPPOSING TEAM	Krall

TEAMMATES	OPPONENTS
Jester	Scorn
Othello	Hellhound
Bishop	Cerberus
	Hellhound

56

GAME TYPE	DM
MAP	Gateway
GOAL SCORE	40
CHARACTER	Matrix
KEY	Liandri Upgrade
OPPOSING TEAM	Liandri

TEAMMATES	OPPONENTS
Othello	Matrix
	Entropy
	Cathode
	Enigma

57

GAME TYPE	DM
MAP	Carbon Fire
GOAL SCORE	50
OPPOSING TEAM	Liandri

TEAMMATES	OPPONENTS
Jester	Aspect
Othello	Colossus
Bishop	OSC
	Raptor

58

GAME TYPE	Vehicle CTF
MAP	Containment
GOAL SCORE	3
KEY	Necris Vehicles
OPPOSING TEAM	Liandri

TEAMMATES	OPPONENTS
Jester	Matrix
Othello	Evolution
Bishop	Mihr
	Syntax

59

GAME TYPE	Warfare
MAP	Islander
GOAL SCORE	1
OPPOSING TEAM	Liandri

TEAMMATES	OPPONENTS
Jester	Torque
Othello	Monarch
Bishop	Aspect
	Enigma

60

GAME TYPE	CTF
MAP	Strident
GOAL SCORE	5
CARD	Liandri Reinforcement
OPPOSING TEAM	Liandri

TEAMMATES	OPPONENTS
Jester	Matrix
Othello	Cathode
Bishop	Enigma
	Entropy

61

GAME TYPE	DM
MAP	Heat Ray
GOAL SCORE	65
OPPOSING TEAM	Krall

TEAMMATES	OPPONENTS
Jester	Loque
Othello	Scythe
Bishop	Scorn
	Gnasher
	Cerberus
	Claw

62

GAME TYPE	DM
MAP	Gateway
GOAL SCORE	40
KEY	Liandri Upgrade
OPPOSING TEAM	Liandri

TEAMMATES	OPPONENTS
Othello	Matrix
	Entropy
	Cathode
	Enigma

78

GAME TYPE	Vehicle CTF
MAP	Containment
GOAL SCORE	3
KEY	Necris Vehicles
OPPOSING TEAM	Liandri

TEAMMATES	OPPONENTS
Jester	Enigma
Othello	Entropy
Bishop	Evolution
	Aspect

79

GAME TYPE	DM
MAP	Heat Ray
GOAL SCORE	50
OPPOSING TEAM	Krall

TEAMMATES	OPPONENTS
Jester	Loque
Othello	Scythe
Bishop	Hellhound
	Scorn
	Worg
	Gnasher

80

GAME TYPE	DM
MAP	Carbon Fire
GOAL SCORE	50
OPPOSING TEAM	Liandri

TEAMMATES	OPPONENTS
Jester	Aspect
Othello	Evolution
Bishop	OSC
	Syntax

85

GAME TYPE	DM
MAP	Heat Ray
GOAL SCORE	50
OPPOSING TEAM	Liandri

TEAMMATES	OPPONENTS
Jester	Aspect
Othello	Colossus
Bishop	OSC
	Raptor

86

GAME TYPE	CTF
MAP	Coret
GOAL SCORE	5
OPPOSING TEAM	Liandri

TEAMMATES	OPPONENTS
Jester	Entropy
Othello	Cathode
Bishop	Evolution
	Mihr

87

GAME TYPE	DM
MAP	Carbon Fire
GOAL SCORE	50
OPPOSING TEAM	Liandri

TEAMMATES	OPPONENTS
Jester	Evolution
Othello	Monarch
Bishop	Mihr
	Syntax

88

GAME TYPE	Vehicle CTF
MAP	Containment
GOAL SCORE	3
KEY	Necris Vehicles
OPPOSING TEAM	Liandri

TEAMMATES	OPPONENTS
Jester	Matrix
Othello	Monarch
Bishop	Mihr
	OSC

89

GAME TYPE	Warfare
MAP	Islander
GOAL SCORE	1
OPPOSING TEAM	Liandri

TEAMMATES	OPPONENTS
Jester	Aspect
Othello	Colossus
Bishop	Torque
	Raptor

90

GAME TYPE	CTF
MAP	Strident
GOAL SCORE	5
CARD	Liandri Reinforcement
OPPOSING TEAM	Krall

TEAMMATES	OPPONENTS
Jester	Scythe
Othello	Scorn
Bishop	Gnasher
	Cerberus

91

GAME TYPE	DM
MAP	Heat Ray
GOAL SCORE	50
OPPOSING TEAM	Krall

TEAMMATES	OPPONENTS
Jester	Loque
Othello	Scythe
Bishop	Gnasher
	Hellhound
	Worg
	Claw

96

GAME TYPE	DM
MAP	Heat Ray
GOAL SCORE	50
OPPOSING TEAM	Krall

TEAMMATES	OPPONENTS
Jester	Loque
Othello	Scythe
Bishop	Blackfang
	Bargest
	Claw
	Lockjaw

101

GAME TYPE	Vehicle CTF
MAP	Containment - SP
GOAL SCORE	3
KEY	Necris Vehicles
OPPOSING TEAM	Krall

TEAMMATES	OPPONENTS
Jester	Scorn
Othello	Gnasher
Bishop	Cerberus
	Hellhound
	Worg
	Lockjaw

106

GAME TYPE	DM
MAP	Gateway
GOAL SCORE	40
KEY	Liandri Upgrade
OPPOSING TEAM	Liandri

TEAMMATES	OPPONENTS
Othello	Matrix
	Entropy
	Cathode
	Enigma

92

GAME TYPE	DM
MAP	Gateway
GOAL SCORE	40
KEY	Liandri Upgrade
OPPOSING TEAM	Liandri

TEAMMATES	OPPONENTS
Othello	Matrix
	Entropy
	Cathode
	Enigma

97

GAME TYPE	CTF
MAP	Coret
GOAL SCORE	5
OPPOSING TEAM	Liandri

TEAMMATES	OPPONENTS
Jester	Aspect
Othello	Colossus
Bishop	OSC
	Raptor

102

GAME TYPE	DM
MAP	Gateway
GOAL SCORE	40
KEY	Liandri Upgrade
OPPOSING TEAM	Liandri

TEAMMATES	OPPONENTS
Othello	Matrix
	Entropy
	Cathode
	Enigma

LEVIATHAN OVERWHELMS

The Torlan battles where you have a Leviathan vs. bots are insane fun, but pose a significant challenge at higher difficulty settings. This is probably the #1 place to use cards in the campaign. (Missions 15, 117, 129)

93

GAME TYPE	Warfare
MAP	Islander
GOAL SCORE	1
OPPOSING TEAM	Liandri

TEAMMATES	OPPONENTS
Jester	Entropy
Othello	Colossus
Bishop	Raptor
	Mihr

98

GAME TYPE	Vehicle CTF
MAP	Containment
GOAL SCORE	3
KEY	Necris Vehicles
OPPOSING TEAM	Liandri

TEAMMATES	OPPONENTS
Jester	Matrix
Othello	Enigma
Bishop	OSC
	Syntax

103

GAME TYPE	DM
MAP	Carbon Fire
GOAL SCORE	50
OPPOSING TEAM	Liandri

TEAMMATES	OPPONENTS
Jester	Mihr
Othello	Syntax
Bishop	Torque
	Monarch

BOSS BATTLES

Boss battles are optional (Lauren in Diesel, Scythe in Deck, & Matrix in Gateway) and you'll be outnumbered for sure, but they yield high rewards.

94

GAME TYPE	Vehicle CTF
MAP	Containment - SP
GOAL SCORE	3
KEY	Necris Vehicles
OPPOSING TEAM	Krall

TEAMMATES	OPPONENTS
Jester	Scythe
Othello	Scar
Bishop	Lockjaw
	Bargest

99

GAME TYPE	CTF
MAP	Strident
GOAL SCORE	5
CARD	Liandri Reinforcement
OPPOSING TEAM	Liandri

TEAMMATES	OPPONENTS
Jester	Matrix
Othello	Cathode
Bishop	Enigma
	Entropy

104

GAME TYPE	CTF
MAP	Strident
GOAL SCORE	5
CARD	Liandri Reinforcement
OPPOSING TEAM	Krall

TEAMMATES	OPPONENTS
Jester	Scythe
Othello	Scorn
Bishop	Gnasher
	Cerberus

95

GAME TYPE	Warfare
MAP	Islander
GOAL SCORE	1
OPPOSING TEAM	Liandri

TEAMMATES	OPPONENTS
Jester	Entropy
Othello	Raptor
Bishop	Torque
	Monarch

100

GAME TYPE	DM
MAP	Carbon Fire
GOAL SCORE	50
OPPOSING TEAM	Liandri

TEAMMATES	OPPONENTS
Jester	Aspect
Othello	Colossus
Bishop	OSC
	Raptor

105

GAME TYPE	Vehicle CTF
MAP	Containment - SP
GOAL SCORE	3
KEY	Necris Vehicles
OPPOSING TEAM	Krall

TEAMMATES	OPPONENTS
Jester	Scar
Othello	Worg
Bishop	Lockjaw
	Bargest
	Blackfang
	Claw

NECRIS INVADE TARYD WITH INFECTION TUBES

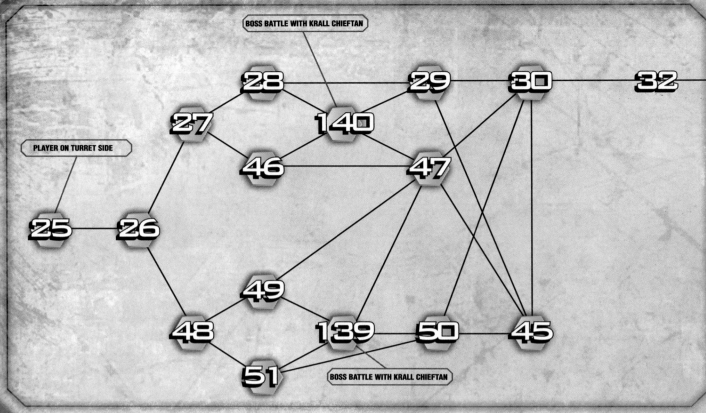

BOSS BATTLE WITH KRALL CHIEFTAN

PLAYER ON TURRET SIDE

BOSS BATTLE WITH KRALL CHIEFTAN

25

GAME TYPE	Warfare
MAP	Islander - Necris
GOAL SCORE	1
CHARACTERS	Damian, Kragoth, & Malaki
OPPOSING TEAM	Necris

TEAMMATES	OPPONENTS
Jester	Loque
Othello	Kragoth
Bishop	Malakai
	Damian

26

GAME TYPE	Warfare
MAP	Market District
GOAL SCORE	1
OPPOSING TEAM	Necris

TEAMMATES	OPPONENTS
Jester	Scythe
Othello	Nocturne
Bishop	Samael
	Bargest

27

GAME TYPE	DM
MAP	Shangri La
GOAL SCORE	50
OPPOSING TEAM	Necris

TEAMMATES	OPPONENTS
Jester	Grail
Othello	Hellhound
Bishop	Scar
	Worg
	Lockjaw

28

GAME TYPE	DM
MAP	Shangri La
GOAL SCORE	50
OPPOSING TEAM	Necris

TEAMMATES	OPPONENTS
Jester	Scythe
Othello	Nocturne
Bishop	Judas
	Scorn
	Gnasher
	Cerberus

29

GAME TYPE	Vehicle CTF
MAP	Suspense
GOAL SCORE	3
OPPOSING TEAM	Necris

TEAMMATES	OPPONENTS
Jester	Thannis
Othello	Pagan
Bishop	Harbinger
	Samael

30

GAME TYPE	Warfare
MAP	Onyx Coast
GOAL SCORE	1
OPPOSING TEAM	Necris

TEAMMATES	OPPONENTS
Jester	Loque
Othello	Harbinger
Bishop	Pagan
	Thannis
	Samael

32

GAME TYPE	Warfare
MAP	Avalanche
GOAL SCORE	1
OPPOSING TEAM	Necris

TEAMMATES	OPPONENTS
Jester	Loque
Othello	Akasha
Bishop	Harbinger
	Pagan
	Thannis
	Samael

JUMPGATE IN ORBIT

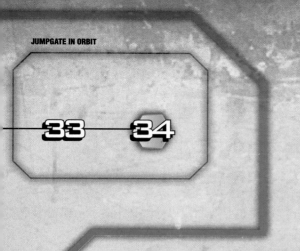

33 – 34

TEAMMATE ADVANTAGES

Use your teammates where their skills lie: Bishop is a good sniper, and a good CTF base guard. Othello is tactical and aggressive; give him attack orders. Jester is a little unpredictable, but tactical; as a wildcard, she's good to freelance.

LAUREN

Lauren has much better tactics, aim, and movement skills than almost all other players. Beware when fighting her, and rejoice if she's fighting at your side.

SCYTHE

Scythe is more tactical than most, although not as much as Lauren. He's a bit more unpredictable with his movement, and prefers the Link gun to burn the flesh from your bones.

AKASHA

Akasha is very skilled, and highly accurate, but doesn't jump around so much. She stays grounded because she likes to shock combo. She will make a point of going for the UDamage, so listen for it and you can trap here there in Sentinel.

LOQUE

Loque is incredibly accurate, and deadly with a Sniper Rifle.

MATRIX

Matrix isn't the most accurate of opponents, but he thinks out combat scenarios like a chess computer. Expect the unexpected.

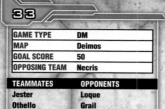

33

GAME TYPE	DM
MAP	Deimos
GOAL SCORE	50
OPPOSING TEAM	Necris

TEAMMATES	OPPONENTS
Jester	Loque
Othello	Grail
Bishop	Nocturne
	Thannis

34

GAME TYPE	CTF
MAP	Omicron Dawn
GOAL SCORE	3
CHARACTER	Loque
OPPOSING TEAM	Necris

TEAMMATES	OPPONENTS
Jester	Loque
Othello	Damian
Bishop	Kragoth
	Malakai

45

GAME TYPE	DM
MAP	Biohazard
GOAL SCORE	40
OPPOSING TEAM	Necris

TEAMMATES	OPPONENTS
Othello	Kragoth
	Thannis
	Scorn
	Cerberus

46

GAME TYPE	DM
MAP	Defiance
GOAL SCORE	50
OPPOSING TEAM	Necris

TEAMMATES	OPPONENTS
Jester	Scythe
Othello	Malakai
Bishop	Gnasher
	Scorn

47

GAME TYPE	Warfare
MAP	Torlan - Necris
GOAL SCORE	1
OPPOSING TEAM	Necris

TEAMMATES	OPPONENTS
Jester	Loque
Othello	Nocturne
Bishop	Claw
	Bargest
	Blackfang
	Lockjaw

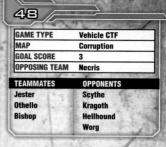

48

GAME TYPE	Vehicle CTF
MAP	Corruption
GOAL SCORE	3
OPPOSING TEAM	Necris

TEAMMATES	OPPONENTS
Jester	Scythe
Othello	Kragoth
Bishop	Hellhound
	Worg

49

GAME TYPE	Vehicle CTF
MAP	Suspense
GOAL SCORE	3
OPPOSING TEAM	Necris

TEAMMATES	OPPONENTS
Jester	Harbinger
Othello	Lockjaw
Bishop	Claw
	Bargest
	Blackfang

50

GAME TYPE	DM
MAP	Defiance
GOAL SCORE	50
OPPOSING TEAM	Necris

TEAMMATES	OPPONENTS
Jester	Grail
Othello	Damain
Bishop	Lockjaw
	Worg

51

GAME TYPE	DM
MAP	Shangri La
GOAL SCORE	50
OPPOSING TEAM	Necris

TEAMMATES	OPPONENTS
Jester	Pagan
Othello	Claw
Bishop	Scar
	Bargest

139

GAME TYPE	DM
MAP	Deck
GOAL SCORE	40
CHARACTER	Scythe
OPPOSING TEAM	Krall

TEAMMATES	OPPONENTS
Othello	Scythe
	Cerberus
	Scorn
	Gnasher

ROGUE MISSIONS - RONIN SEEKS REVENGE

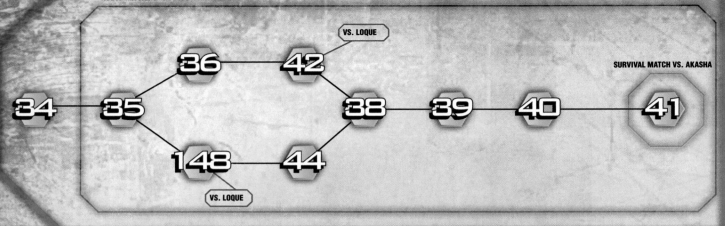

VS. LOQUE

 36 — 42

VS. LOQUE

SURVIVAL MATCH VS. AKASHA

 34 — 35 — 38 — 39 — 40 — 41

148 — 44

35

GAME TYPE	Vehicle CTF
MAP	Sandstorm
GOAL SCORE	3
OPPOSING TEAM	Necris

TEAMMATES	OPPONENTS
Jester	Nocturne
Othello	Judas
Bishop	Grail
	Samael
	Harbinger
	Pagan

39

GAME TYPE	CTF
MAP	Vertebrae
GOAL SCORE	3
OPPOSING TEAM	Necris

TEAMMATES	OPPONENTS
Jester	Akasha
Othello	Thannis
Bishop	Samael
	Grail

42

GAME TYPE	DM
MAP	Fearless
GOAL SCORE	40
OPPOSING TEAM	Necris

TEAMMATES	OPPONENTS
Othello	Loque
	Thannis

148

GAME TYPE	DM
MAP	Fearless
GOAL SCORE	40
OPPOSING TEAM	Necris

TEAMMATES	OPPONENTS
Othello	Akasha
	Thannis

36

GAME TYPE	DM
MAP	Sanctuary
GOAL SCORE	25
OPPOSING TEAM	Necris

TEAMMATES	OPPONENTS
Jester	Akasha
Othello	Damian
Bishop	Kragoth
	Malakai

40

GAME TYPE	Warfare
MAP	Floodgate
GOAL SCORE	1
OPPOSING TEAM	Necris

TEAMMATES	OPPONENTS
Jester	Akasha
Othello	Loque
Bishop	Damian
	Kragoth

44

GAME TYPE	DM
MAP	Sanctuary
GOAL SCORE	50
OPPOSING TEAM	Necris

TEAMMATES	OPPONENTS
Jester	Akasha
Othello	Malakai
Bishop	Harbinger
	Pagan

38

GAME TYPE	Vehicle CTF
MAP	Necropolis
GOAL SCORE	3
CARD	Instagib
OPPOSING TEAM	Necris

TEAMMATES	OPPONENTS
Jester	Akasha
Othello	Malakai
Bishop	Judas
	Pagan
	Thannis
	Grail

41

GAME TYPE	DM
MAP	Sentinel
GOAL SCORE	20
CHARACTER	Akasha
OPPOSING TEAM	Necris

TEAMMATES	OPPONENTS
	Akasha

140

GAME TYPE	DM
MAP	Deck
GOAL SCORE	40
CHARACTER	Scythe
OPPOSING TEAM	Krall

TEAMMATES	OPPONENTS
Othello	Scythe
	Cerberus
	Scorn
	Gnasher

UNLOCKABLES

CARDS

Tactical Diversion unlocks after Kargo
Respawn Upgrade unlocks after Diesel
Heavy Armor unlocks after Arsenal
Instagib unlocks after Necropolis
Iron Guard unlocks after defeating either Defiance, Diesel, or Serenity

CHARACTERS

Damian, Kragoth, Malakai unlock after Islander - Necris
Lauren unlocks after Diesel
Matrix unlocks after Gateway
Scythe unlocks after Deck
Loque unlocks after Omicron Dawn
Akasha unlocks after Sentinel

KEYS

Ability to drive Necris vehicles unlocks after Containment, or after
Onyx Coast Reinforcement Liandri unlocks after Strident
Iron Guard Upgrade unlocks after Diesel
Liandri Upgrade unlocks after Gateway

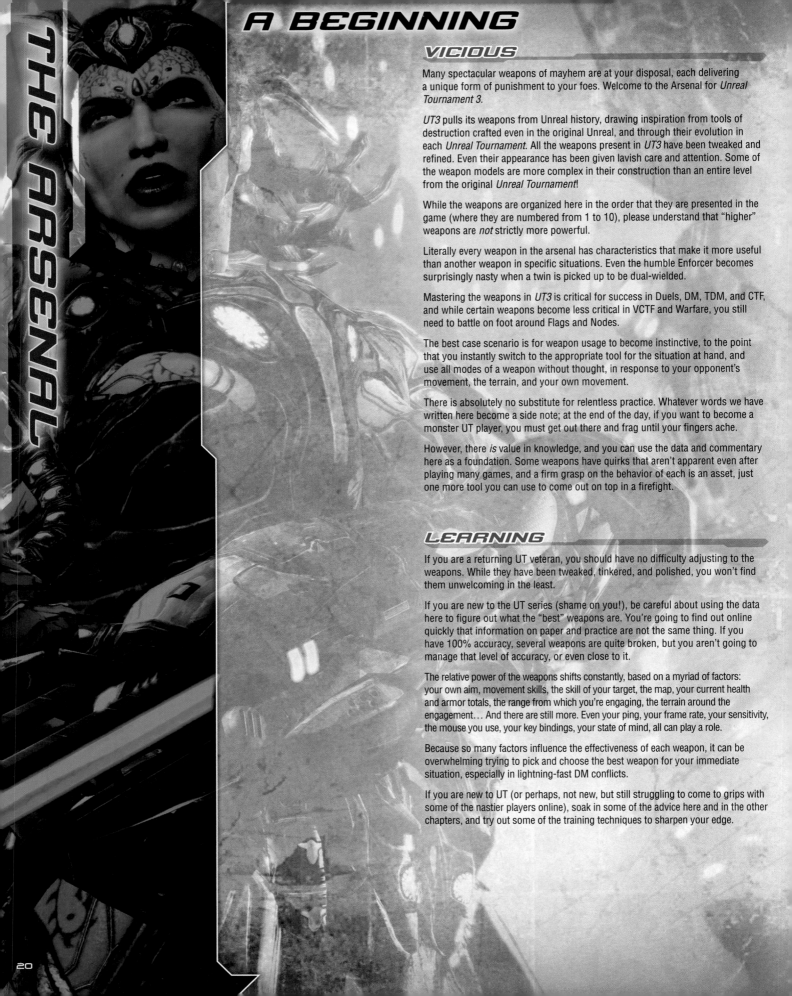

A BEGINNING

VICIOUS

Many spectacular weapons of mayhem are at your disposal, each delivering a unique form of punishment to your foes. Welcome to the Arsenal for *Unreal Tournament 3*.

UT3 pulls its weapons from Unreal history, drawing inspiration from tools of destruction crafted even in the original Unreal, and through their evolution in each *Unreal Tournament*. All the weapons present in *UT3* have been tweaked and refined. Even their appearance has been given lavish care and attention. Some of the weapon models are more complex in their construction than an entire level from the original *Unreal Tournament*!

While the weapons are organized here in the order that they are presented in the game (where they are numbered from 1 to 10), please understand that "higher" weapons are *not* strictly more powerful.

Literally every weapon in the arsenal has characteristics that make it more useful than another weapon in specific situations. Even the humble Enforcer becomes surprisingly nasty when a twin is picked up to be dual-wielded.

Mastering the weapons in *UT3* is critical for success in Duels, DM, TDM, and CTF, and while certain weapons become less critical in VCTF and Warfare, you still need to battle on foot around Flags and Nodes.

The best case scenario is for weapon usage to become instinctive, to the point that you instantly switch to the appropriate tool for the situation at hand, and use all modes of a weapon without thought, in response to your opponent's movement, the terrain, and your own movement.

There is absolutely no substitute for relentless practice. Whatever words we have written here become a side note; at the end of the day, if you want to become a monster UT player, you must get out there and frag until your fingers ache.

However, there *is* value in knowledge, and you can use the data and commentary here as a foundation. Some weapons have quirks that aren't apparent even after playing many games, and a firm grasp on the behavior of each is an asset, just one more tool you can use to come out on top in a firefight.

LEARNING

If you are a returning UT veteran, you should have no difficulty adjusting to the weapons. While they have been tweaked, tinkered, and polished, you won't find them unwelcoming in the least.

If you are new to the UT series (shame on you!), be careful about using the data here to figure out what the "best" weapons are. You're going to find out online quickly that information on paper and practice are not the same thing. If you have 100% accuracy, several weapons are quite broken, but you aren't going to manage that level of accuracy, or even close to it.

The relative power of the weapons shifts constantly, based on a myriad of factors: your own aim, movement skills, the skill of your target, the map, your current health and armor totals, the range from which you're engaging, the terrain around the engagement… And there are still more. Even your ping, your frame rate, your sensitivity, the mouse you use, your key bindings, your state of mind, all can play a role.

Because so many factors influence the effectiveness of each weapon, it can be overwhelming trying to pick and choose the best weapon for your immediate situation, especially in lightning-fast DM conflicts.

If you are new to UT (or perhaps, not new, but still struggling to come to grips with some of the nastier players online), soak in some of the advice here and in the other chapters, and try out some of the training techniques to sharpen your edge.

PICKING WEAPONS, AND THEN PICKING UP WEAPONS

Your weapon selection on a given map is limited, naturally, by what weapons are available on that map. However, there is more to it than simply what weapons you *can* acquire. You also have to prioritize what weapons you *should* acquire.

Depending on the map, the Rocket Launcher might be only marginally effective, but relatively difficult to reach. It might be out of the way, or in a location that leaves you vulnerable and is highly dangerous. Either way, if there are better alternatives that are more easily reached, that should weight your decision making in the field.

Determining what weapons to go after (and use regularly, for that matter), should be a decision influenced by several factors.

The first is your personal skill with all the weapons. If you know you are simply better with three of the weapons available on a map, those three weapons should carry a greater weight for you.

Next is the utility of a given weapon on the map you are playing on. If the map has lots of tight corners, restricted sight lines, and narrow hallways, the Flak Cannon and Rocket Launcher become more useful than the Sniper Rifle or Stinger.

The game mode also has a substantial impact. VCTF and Warfare both place a larger emphasis on vehicle and anti-vehicle combat, which gives more weight to weapons that can be used against vehicles in a pinch. They also tend to feature outdoor, long-range combat areas, which weakens the feasibility of close-range weapons somewhat.

Because both VCTF and Warfare feature Weapon Lockers near most spawn points, your weapon loadout is often provided without much effort, but quite often, a few key weapons are located out of the way on a map, and must be sought out intentionally.

Duels are the most rigorous test in terms of choosing weapons. The simple act of going after a weapon means not going after a respawning piece of armor, Health Vials, a power-up, or even a respawning opponent. Seconds count, and position and item timing matter even more. Learning to control (and use!) weapons in a dueling environment serves you well when it comes to choosing and pursuing weapons in all other game types.

On the smaller maps suited to duels, going after a weapon that is effective on that map is often a substantial risk, either because of the weapon's position (highly exposed, or located in a dead end), or because your opponent knows exactly where you are going. Expect to come under fire with your opponent having the edge by knowing *exactly* where you have to step, if only for a split-second.

Team Deathmatch actually shares more in common with Dueling when it comes to going after weapons than it does with FFA DM. Team positioning and weapon control is a key part of any successful team's overall strategy, and shutting off the opposing team from a handful of critical weapons can sway the match in your favor.

Vanilla DM, fought free-for-all, with the winner being the player with the most frags, has slightly different prioritization. Generally, you want to be scoring the highest number of kills in the shortest amount of time possible. That often means seeking out the most populated and frequently traveled weapons on the map, even if it means exposing yourself to risk that would be unacceptable in a TDM or Duel situation.

CTF mixes up weapon selection a bit by reprioritizing the weapons. Depending on if you are playing offense or defense, you may be patrolling only a portion of the map, and often, the defensive positions favor weapons that are less useful on offense, where you must maintain almost constant motion (and frequently be firing on the run against angry chasers).

As a general rule of thumb, the weapon selection available on a map tends to reflect the nature of the map (barring rare exceptions, you don't run into the AVRiL on a map without something for it to lock onto!), and most maps usually have a few extras available to round out the choices.

Ammunition can be a consideration in both your selection and your usage of weapons as well. If you tend to use certain weapons more heavily than others (particularly weapons that burn up ammo quickly), you need to memorize the specific locations of all ammunition for that weapon on the map.

On many maps, weapons have two ammo packs placed in close proximity to the weapon itself, but extra ammo may be located elsewhere on the map. It's crucial when you have other objectives to attend to, like defending the flag, picking up the Damage Amp, or patrolling armor locations.

Larger maps often have multiple locations where you can acquire the same weapon from, and in the case of team maps with symmetrical layouts, you can often acquire a key weapon while traveling through the opponents area of the map, saving precious time by skipping the detour on your side of the map after respawning.

The flow on a map (that is, where players tend to travel, even if there are many other routes they *could* travel) has a heavy impact on the utility of weapons as well. If a map has some outdoor areas, and some tight indoor areas, but players rarely travel inside (which can be for any number of reasons), the mid- and long-range weapons are generally better targets than close-range tools.

Now, obviously, the ideal situation is to pick up every weapon a map has to offer, and use the best weapon you have available as the situation dictates. Practically however, this is difficult or impossible.

Unless you're playing in a match with vastly disparate skill levels, you're going to faceplant from time to time, losing your gear. Similarly, you're going to run out of ammo for your favored weapons, and you must make do with other weapons, weapons that may not suit the situation (or your personal skills and preferences).

While improving your skills with all weapons is part of the answer, it is equally important to understand the position of all weapons on a map, as well as all ammo on a map, and the utility of each weapon as it relates to player behavior on that map.

STINGER SPRAY

The Stinger's primary fire is ideal for shooting down the Redeemer, and for knocking down Hoverboarders.

Knowing that the Rocket Launcher and Flak Cannon are the two most effective weapons on a map for you, and the Stinger and Sniper Rifle are nearly useless can heavily influence the routes you take, and the routes your opponents take.

This is an important point. You need to be thinking about all the considerations above, and making decisions consciously, rather than simply wandering around the map looking for the closest weapon and target.

Such behavior, while a fine way to learn the maps initially, is a also a fine way to wind up so much paste in a duel against a skilled player, or for your team to get nearly shut out in a TDM match, or your defenders to fold to the offense in a CTF match because they're wielding Bio Rifles against targets at a great distance blasting them with Shock Rifles.

Because *UT3* is such a fast paced game, there is danger in assuming that you can simply react to situations as they arise with raw reflexes and instinct, and always come out on top (which to be fair, with enough talent and training, you often can).

But the truly lethal player is always thinking, always one step ahead, and when you eat a Shock Combo around a corner when your opponent can't even see you, you know he's thinking carefully about where you are moving from, and what you are moving to.

TRAINING

In terms of acquiring a competent level of weapon proficiency it is certainly enough to simply play *UT3* a lot, experiment with the different game modes and Mutators, play online and off, and gradually acquire familiarity with each weapon.

However, if you truly wish to excel with *UT3*'s arsenal, a more rigorous and directed approach can pay off with sharper accuracy, faster weapon switching, and better overall usage of every weapon in the game.

Deliberately training your weapon skills is a step that is *not* necessary for simply enjoying the game (though training in and of itself is often both challenging and enjoyable), but if you seek a higher level of play, doing so is highly advisable.

TRAINING TECHNIQUES

While simply playing games online (or, to begin with, offline against bots) is the best way to become familiar and comfortable with the game, training your weapon skills requires more intense and deliberate focus on improving your skills.

WEAPON TRAINING

The first, and simplest method is to focus on one weapon, and one weapon only. Fans of Instagib are probably already well aware of how playing tons of Instagib improved their Shock Rifle and Sniper Rifle aim, as well as their ability to evade shots from those weapons.

The principle here is identical. Pick a weapon, any weapon (even the Impact Hammer!), and deliberately use nothing but that weapon while you play. Ideally, do this online, against other live players. You probably don't want to do this sort of training in a Team Deathmatch game, unless you really want to annoy your teammates.

Constant training with a single weapon exercises a whole host of skills simultaneously. You learn where that weapon is located on a level. You learn where the ammunition is located. You learn how to fight with the weapon, and how to fight against every other weapon. You learn what terrain is favorable or unfavorable for that weapon.

Training with single weapons improves your overall skill substantially, as it teaches you how to fight effectively with every weapon in any situation. It also teaches you when a given weapon is *not* the best for a specific situation! Knowing when you're outmatched and should retreat is just as important as knowing when you have a favorable or superior match up against your opponent.

There are several subsets of weapon training you can focus on while working your way through the various weapons. Once you've spent a fair amount of time training each weapon, move on to working with specific sets of weaponry.

PROJECTILE WEAPONS

Very simply, train with all the weapons that fire projectiles, rather than the weapons that instantly hit their targets. This means using the Bio Rifle, Flak Cannon, Rocket Launcher, Link Gun primary fire, Stinger secondary fire, and Shock Rifle secondary fire.

Projectiles require different aiming techniques compared with instant hit weapons, and to utilize them effectively, specifically training with only projectile weapons is effective.

The various projectile weapons break down into different groups, depending on their behavior.

The Bio Rifle, Shock Rifle secondary, and Flak Cannon primary fire require close-range to hit effectively, and usually need to be shot directly at your target, or barely ahead of their movement.

The Rocket Launcher and the Flak Cannon secondary are usually used by aiming *near* an opponent on the ground, or where an opponent is moving, rather than directly at the opponent. Because the projectiles they fire travel relatively slow (and they are fairly small), they can be easily evaded if fired directly at an alert opponent.

Using the splash damage makes rockets nearly unavoidable at close-range. The arc of the Flak Cannon's secondary fire makes it a trickier weapon to use as a close-range explosive, but it has similar properties that must be practiced.

The Link Gun primary and Stinger secondary fire are rapid fire projectile weapons (especially in the case of the Link Gun). Both should be used by leading your opponents' movement. Done properly with the Link Gun at close or mid-range, and you can keep a constant stream of damaging bolts impacting your target.

The Stinger secondary shots are slower, which makes saturating an area with projectiles more difficult. In exchange, the bolts have significant knockback when they do hit, which can help you to "pin" an opponent in close quarters or rough terrain (and can help to disrupt their aim slightly).

All projectiles suffer from the weakness of being avoidable by an actively dodging opponent. No matter how good your aim is, a mobile opponent can often avoid some or all of your fire (or lessen the damage, in the case of explosive weapons).

Learning to use the various projectiles on all types of terrain against all other weapons effectively is important, as you can gradually improve your targeting and weapon choices to best suit the situation.

While you can't prevent opponents from dodging your shots, you *can* make it significantly more difficult for them to do so, in some situations guaranteeing that your opponent is going to take *some* damage, no matter how well they dodge (especially true with the explosive weapons).

Projectiles have the benefit of suppression, something that is generally harder for instant hit weapons to do. A constant stream of plasma from the Link Gun primary fired down a narrow hall is not something that a smart player is going to walk into. Similarly, firing a stream of rockets at a doorway makes it a difficult threshold for an opponent to cross.

Projectiles are also capable of indirect fire, a technique that is impossible for instant hit weaponry. Several of the projectile weapons can hit opponents around corners, behind cover, or on sharply differing elevation levels. Tossing grenades, flak shards, rockets, or bio sludge around corners can allow you to hurt, kill, or herd an opponent towards a different location—all useful tactics.

Don't hesitate to "waste" ammo when using projectile weapons. If you know where an opponent is, even if you can't see them, use your projectile weapons to threaten your opponent. Keeping pressure on a target at all times is simply good play.

SURVIVING THE SHOCK COMBO

Because the Shock Combo is so lethal, and because skilled UT players know this and use it often, it is just as important to learn to fight *against* the Combo as it is to learn to use it effectively.

While there are some situations where you are going to get nailed with a Combo and croak almost instantly, regardless of any slight Armor or extra Health you might have picked up, in such cases, you usually would be just as dead if you were blindsided by several other dangerous weapons.

Don't worry about it when that happens. If you get surprised or hit from an odd angle, the delivery weapon doesn't really matter; a face full of Flak or a triple spiral Rocket barrage is just as lethal.

Instead, you should concentrate on avoiding Shock Combos by being alert and aware for players who have the Shock Rifle out and are aware of your presence (or likely to become aware before you can get into close-range).

First, the Shock Combo is weaker at long-range, and difficult or impossible to use at close-range.

Because of the reload time on the secondary fire (a bit more than half a second), there is a minimum distance for the Shock Combo. Inside that minimum range, you can't be hit by the Shock Combo.

Don't let that lull you into thinking the Shock Rifle is toothless up close. Eating Shock Cores on the way to close-range might nullify a Shock Combo, but it also hurts quite a bit, and you can lose a lot of health to an accurate player even if you manage to avoid the Combo.

Still, if you are armed with a close-range weapon, and you can either get the drop on a Shock Rifle user, or quickly get into close-range, you can all but eliminate the danger of the Shock Combo, and usually inflict greater damage with your close-range weapon of choice.

At long-ranges, the Shock Combo can still be used, but it is *much* easier to see coming, and thus avoid completely. Of course, at long-ranges, the Shock Rifle primary fire is still a threat, so if you aren't armed with long-range weapons yourself, your best option is simply getting out of line of sight completely.

When it comes to mid-range fighting, you have to be alert and aware of the Shock Rifle user's position relative to yours. The absolute worst move you can make in such a situation is moving towards the Shock Rifle from medium-long-range to medium range, while they are aware of your position.

Doing so sets you up for a perfect Shock Combo, *especially* if the terrain favors Shock Combo usage. In such situations, it is often best to simply back off completely and come at the Shock Rifle from a completely different direction.

Another alternative is using the Shock Cores against the opposing Shock Rifle armed target. If you are using a Shock Rifle of your own, you can detonate *any* Shock Cores, not just your own. They also nullify in midair on contact with one another, so if you are both attempting to score a Shock Combo, some of the Cores may be destroyed prematurely.

Fighting against the Shock Combo when used by a skilled player is difficult, but the main point is awareness. As long as you are alert to the threat, you can active to minimize the danger, or avoid it completely, and that's the best you can do against any weapon, no matter how dangerous.

INSTANT HIT WEAPONS

Training with instant hit weaponry means using the Enforcers, Shock Rifle primary, Link Gun secondary, Stinger primary, and Sniper Rifle.

There are fewer divisions in behavior with the instant hit weapons than there are with the projectile weaponry.

The Shock Rifle and Sniper Rifle are single shot, instant hit weapons with relatively high damage. Comparatively, the Stinger primary and Link Gun secondary fire streams of damaging fire that requires constantly tracking your target to inflict damage.

Enforcers lie somewhere in between the two, as they are more rapid-fire than the Shock Rifle or Sniper Rifle, but considerably slower than the Link or Stinger shots. Dual-wielded enforcers behave more closely to the Stinger in terms of battlefield usage, while a single starting Enforcer usually must be used with more accurate single shots to be effective.

The single shot weapons require serious accuracy training to be effective. Even more than any other weapons, they stress having a good frame rate, a good ping, a comfortable mouse, and a comfortable sensitivity. Because your single shots must be spot on (and usually against a mobile, evasive target), your ability to instantly track a target and "pull the trigger" at just the right moment is critically important.

Your damage potential with these weapons is limited by your accuracy, but it is also limited by how quickly you can track your target and take the shots. Every extra millisecond you spend tracking your target is time lost that could be spent firing another damaging shot.

Obviously, with perfect accuracy, the best possible Shock Rifle attack would be multiple hits in a row, while holding the trigger down for no delay between shots.

In practice, achieving such accuracy is all but impossible. Instead, you should generally be tapping the fire button after you line up each shot. With practice, you can get the delay down to almost nothing. Use the reload time between each shot to line up the next, losing as little time following your target as possible.

Conversely, the two rapid fire weapons require that you track a target constantly with the weapons fire to deal damage.

Because of this, both the Stinger and the Link secondary suffer when there is a lot of cover. Both are best used against a target when there is little or no terrain for them to dodge behind. While you can manage to deal serious damage with single hits from the Shock or Sniper rifles, a split second of fire from the Stinger or Link inflicts little damage.

Note also that the Stinger primary fire has a spin-up time, it does not fire at full speed initially, making it a poor weapon to be using against an opponent who has a weapon that is more "front loaded" in terms of damage (like someone firing flak shards in your face repeatedly at close-range).

Unlike the Link, the Stinger's shots are not 100% accurate. There is a slight variance around the center point of your crosshair, enough that at medium or long-range, you may not hit with every shot, even if you track your target perfectly.

The Link secondary is perfectly accurate, but it has a limited range. This puts you at risk against opponents using dedicated close-range weaponry that deals their damage all at once. You might be doing excellent damage over time, but a single rocket to the face or a load of flak can end your Link stream quickly. Similarly, opponents can often get out of range of the Link beam if you are hitting near its maximum range.

SNIPING

The Sniper Rifle does deserve special mention as far as training goes. Because you can zoom in with the sniper rifle, it is the only true ultra-long-range weapon in the game.

While this is usually not a significant boon during most types of DM, there are several large CTF maps, and almost all VCTF and Warfare maps have vast outdoor expanses—perfect for long-range sniping.

Learning to effectively snipe is a unique skill, almost disconnected from other types of weapon training. Because you are engaging at such long distances, you may be targeting opponents who are entirely unaware of you.

Even the most skilled players tend to relax slightly when they believe they are in safe terrain, easing up on constant evasive dodging and movement. Disabuse them of this notion with a bullet to the head.

While long-range sniping is a unique skill that requires plenty of practice to become effective, even with middling accuracy, you can still be effective at disrupting enemies at great distances.

Unless they have Sniper Rifles of their own handy, or vehicles with long-range weaponry, they can't do much to retaliate, giving you plenty of time to take multiple shots!

AARGH, I CAN'T HIT ANYTHING!

You may find after training intensely with either weapon grouping that you have a bit of trouble readjusting to the other weapon type.

Because projectile weapons and instant hit weapons use such different methods of targeting, and different methods of effectively dealing damage, you may find that your accuracy with the other group has taken a dip after training hard with one set of weapons.

This is generally unavoidable, but the effects are rarely lasting. Take a break for awhile and come back to reap the benefits, once your reflexes have had a chance to absorb the training.

The last cluster of weapons to train with is pretty simple. After you've gone through each of the weapons individually, then all the projectile weapons, and then all the instant hit weapons, you should have a *great* feel for what weapons you prefer, and which weapons you aren't quite so hot with.

Training with the weapons you are weakest can be a little unpleasant once you've become more familiar with the game, but it is an important part of your growth. It's easy to settle into using the subset of weapons that you are "best" with, but this weakens you in situations where you *must* fight with weapons that you are uncomfortable with (and genuinely less effective with).

This is especially critical in Duels, TDM, and organized CTF games, and somewhat less important in free-for-all DM, VCTF, or Warfare.

ACCURACY TRAINING

Unsurprisingly, your accuracy with the weapons is a key component in your overall lethality. High accuracy, especially with instant hit weapons, makes you *significantly* more dangerous. Consider how dangerous a skilled sniper is on defense when playing CTF, or how lethal the Shock Rifle becomes at medium range when used by a brutally accurate player.

Generally, training your accuracy is an automatic side effect of any play, and any training. However, when you are specifically focusing on accuracy, you should be playing "tight", rather than loose and sloppy. It's easy to get on a server and fool around. If you're trying to train your accuracy specifically, you should be focused and intent, aiming to make every shot count, with every weapon.

A large part of improving your accuracy is playing against opponents who are extremely proficient at movement and dodging. New players, or unskilled players that make easy targets are the worst possible subjects for improving your accuracy skills. Hitting a player who only walks in straight lines down a hallway is considerably easier than a player who constantly strafes from side to side, dodging and jumping off walls while they move, even with no enemies in sight.

You need to find skilled players, and that means either tracking down a server online that is frequented by good players, or making friends with skilled players who are willing to spar with you.

Naturally, participating in clan matches is (usually) a good way to battle proficient players, but it isn't the best way to train, as you may not play that clan frequently. If they're amiable, track down some of their more dangerous players after a match and ask to practice with them. Few competitive players are likely to turn down a chance to improve their abilities (especially if you employ gratuitous flattery—butter them up, *then* put holes in them).

One last piece of advice for training: *Turn off your crosshairs!*

Disabling the crosshairs causes your vision and focus to shift during combat. Rather than focusing almost entirely on a point at the center of the screen, you should find that your focus relaxes and you start soaking in the entire screen.

This has a curious effect on your aim, particularly with close-range projectile weapons. It also causes you to take snapshots with instant hit weapons, rather than deliberately trying to "line up" a shot under the crosshairs—you can't! Instead, you simply try to center a target quickly and pull the trigger.

The intent here is to make your targeting automatic, rather than deliberate. If you're thinking about a shot, you're taking too long, especially given how deadly the combat is in *UT3*.

FIGHTING OUTNUMBERED

The last type of specific training you can focus on is fighting against multiple opponents simultaneously.

As a general rule, going up against even two roughly evenly skilled opponents is pure suicide. The weapons are too lethal, and usually the best you can manage is taking one down before you go down as well.

However, just because it is extremely difficult does not mean you should not practice dealing with the situation.

Different weapons can handle multiple targets with varying levels of effectiveness. There's nothing quite as satisfying as gibbing two players at the same time with a triple rocket shot.

Beyond simple satisfaction (or rampant egotism), training against multiple opponents is important. In just about any game mode, you're going to encounter situations where you must fight more than one enemy target at the same time, and the more practice you have dealing with the situation, the better.

In a free-for-all Deathmatch, it is often possible to go into a room with four players blasting away and come out standing (possibly even up by four frags). In any sort of team environment, managing the same feat is vastly, vastly more difficult. Four players gunning for you is not the same thing as four players all shooting at each other.

Ideally, this sort of practice should be done against clan mates, or friends online who are willing to team up against you. Failing that, hop on servers running any sort of team mode, and deliberately get yourself into situations where you are up against multiple enemies at the same time.

Really, if you can take down even one opponent in a situation where you are outnumbered, you are doing well. Even better is taking down one opponent and getting away alive from the rest!

You shouldn't go into the situation expecting to kill all of your opponents simultaneously, as doing so is extremely difficult unless the skill levels involved are vastly disproportionate. Instead, try to come out standing, regardless of how many opponents you take down. Even damaging one or more of your foes and retreating to recover health can be helpful for your team (more helpful than dying without dealing any damage!).

Fighting outnumbered stresses all your skills to the limit, and teaches you how to use your weapons to their best effect against multiple targets, as well as how to use terrain and dodging skills to avoid incoming fire.

COMBINING WEAPONS

Weapon switching is a critical part of fighting effectively on any level. If you're running into a wide open area, the Shock Rifle or Sniper Rifle should be in your hands. Entering a close-quarters series of narrow hallways? Get out the Rocket Launcher, Flak Cannon, or in a pinch, the Bio Rifle and charge up it secondary shot. Are you at medium range with mixed terrain? The Stinger or Link Gun work well, and the Rocket Launcher isn't bad. Of course, if you know you're heading into a traffic jam, bring along an AVRiL to clear the way.

There is more however. In a general engagement, the weapon your opponent is using, the terrain you're fighting on, your personal skill, and even your available ammo supplies can all dictate what weapon you use.

Running away with the flag? You don't have time to keep the Stinger or Link Gun trained on an opponent, though you could spray plasma fire backwards, you're usually better off tossing flak shells, sludge, or rockets backwards. Moving forward, you can use the Shock Rifle or Sniper Rifle if you've got a clear line of sight to engage targets before they close the distance to you.

Just switching to the most appropriate weapon is important, because it is important that you have the right tool for the job ready at hand *before* you get into an engagement. At long-range, and sometimes at medium range with cover, you can usually switch fairly safely, but the closer your opponent is, the more dangerous it is to switch weapons in mid-battle.

All weapons have a putdown time and an equip time. When you switch from one to another, the times are added. Putdown from your current weapon, plus the equip time of the weapon you're switching to. In addition, some weapons have a cool down time that must expire before you can switch or fire again, be aware of these quirks before you go switching from one weapon to another.

Because the weapons have varying damage payloads in terms of alpha strikes, you need to figure out what the best tool for the job at hand is. A solid rocket, flak, or secondary Bio Rifle hit are almost always fatal, as are sniper headshots, and close-range Shock Combos. The more rapid-fire weapons tend to deal less damage per hit, but can be easier to score *some* hits with. In a team situation, this is quite helpful, but on your own, dying while your opponent is *almost* dead is not at all helpful.

If you know you're engaging a weakened opponent, or you're getting into a firefight, using a weapon that is easy to hit with can be useful for aiding your team (or stealing some frags in free-for-all Deathmatch). If you're not certain you're going to be coming up against weak targets, use the best weapon you have for dealing lethal damage quickly, on the terrain you're moving into.

AWARDS (OR, YOU ARE AWESOME)

In addition to the various weapon Awards you can get for scoring many kills with the various weapons, there are also the usual Unreal Award for killing rapidly, and killing many targets without dying.

KILLING SPREES

SPREE	KILLS
Killing Spree	5
Rampage	10
Dominating	15
Unstoppable	20
Godlike	25
Massacre	30

MULTI KILLS

AWARD	# KILLS WITHIN SECONDS
Double Kill	2
Multi Kill	3
Megakill	4
Ultrakill	5
Monsterkill	6

SPECIAL AWARDS

There are a few other Awards you can get for certain events.

AWARD	EVENT
Hat Trick	3 Flag Captures in the same game
Denied	Have your Redeemer shot down, a power-up snatched in front of you, die about to cap a Flag or an Orb
Last Second Save	Kill an enemy Flag Carrier or Orb runner near their node (essentially the "positive" version of Denied)
Nodebuster	Cap 10 enemy Nodes with your Orb
Flawless Victory	Win a CTF or Warfare match giving up no captures or any Power Core damage
Eagle Eye	Kill an air vehicle with the Goliath or Paladin primary fire, or kill the Scorpion or Viper while they are in self destruct mode
Pancake	Crush a player with the Manta from above
Bullseye	Kill a player with the self destruct of the Viper or Scorpion
Road Rampage	Kill 10 players by running them over in a vehicle
Vehicular Manslaughter, Road Rage, Hit & Run	Randomly awarded for killing a player by ramming them with any vehicle

These are the stars of the show. You must become intimately familiar with each and every weapon present in UT3 if you are to become a masterful player.

Each weapon begins with a data block describing the unique characteristics of the weapon. Following is commentary on the usage of the weapon in a variety of situations, and a breakdown of a weapons match-up against each other weapon in the game.

WEAPON RANGES

A quick note, we're not saying that certain weapons are *only* effective at a specific range, merely than they tend to be more effective in that rough range bracket.

Just about every weapon (in either fire mode) can transition up or down one range category without too much trouble. Rockets work well at close range, and they're ok at medium distances on the right terrain.

The only real 'hard' exceptions are the Link Gun secondary, which has an actual maximum range, and the Impact Hammer, which isn't really going to impress a sniper. It goes without saying that the Impact Hammer is a close range weapon *only*.

■ Primary Fire   □ Secondary Fire

Bio Rifle
Stinger
Enforcer
Sniper Rifle
Flak Cannon
Shock Rifle
Link Gun
Rocket Launcher

IMPACT HAMMER

EQUIP TIME 0.45 SECONDS
PUTDOWN TIME 0.33 SECONDS

AMMUNITION
N/A

WEAPON NOTES

For both primary and secondary fire, the Impact Hammer auto-discharges on contact with a player or vehicle once it has been charged for one second.

Jackhammer Award is given for 15 Impact Hammer kills.

PRIMARY FIRE

CLASSIFICATION	INSTANT HIT

Can be held to charge and increase damage. Releases on contact with another player. Can also be manually released against the ground to "jump".

DAMAGE	20 minimum, 140 maximum
VEHICLE DAMAGE	20%
NODE DAMAGE	100%
RATE OF FIRE	Varies, 2.5 second to fully charge
SHOTS TO KILL (BASE)	Varies, one fully charged
SHOTS TO KILL (100/50)	Varies, two minimum

SECONDARY FIRE

CLASSIFICATION	INSTANT HIT

Can be held to charge and increase damage. Releases an EMP burst on contact.

DAMAGE	20 minimum, 150 maximum, does not damage players
RATE OF FIRE	Varies, 2.5 second to fully charge
SHOTS TO KILL (BASE)	No damage vs. players
SHOTS TO KILL (100/50)	No damage vs. players

Essentially a hydraulic ram, the Impact Hammer can be charged up to inflict devastating damage at point blank range, but that is its weak point. It is the only melee weapon in the game, and with most opponents packing heavy duty ranged firepower, using the Impact Hammer effectively is difficult, to say the least.

One significant advantage that the Impact Hammer has is that it does not actually require a "shot" to hit with it. Instead, anytime you have the Impact Hammer charged, simply touching a target head-on is enough to release the stored power, releasing all the damage in a single massive blow.

A fully charged Impact Hammer tends to be lethal to all but heavily armored opponents, and makes for a humiliating and demoralizing kill.

The best situation to use the Impact Hammer in (if there is such a thing) is in close quarters and narrow passageways, where your opponents have a tough time maneuvering. Ideally, you can get an angry foe chasing you, charge the hammer fully, then slam into them when they come barreling around a corner.

Similarly, if you lack a better weapon, and the map favors the Impact Hammer, rather than running around with your Enforcer out, charge up the

Impact Hammer fully and make your way through the tightest halls you can find, preferably on your way to finding a better weapon. Don't get carried away with the Impact Hammer hunting, but running into an opponent usually results in a mess, and the acquisition of a new weapon at the same time!

It is possible to use the Impact Hammer on slightly more open ground, but you must be absolutely comfortable dodging and wall jumping if you're going to have the faintest prayer of closing with an aware opponent who is actively evading you and firing at you with any number of heavy weapons.

An *unaware* opponent on the other hand, can sometimes be unpleasantly jolted from the side or rear if you move quickly. Unfortunately, an unaware target usually means you're in the middle of a firefight running around with a charged Impact Hammer; you really don't want to be that guy.

Curiously, the Impact Hammer can also be used as a mobility tool. You can "Impact Hammer jump', by releasing a charged hammer directly into the ground. This *does* inflict damage on yourself (around 50 for a fully charged blast), but it can be used to shortcut around parts of some maps (generally in DM, if you're Impact Hamming jumping in CTF, you have other problems).

The Impact Hammer suffers from an audible noise while it is charging, making it a foolish choice if you know your opponents are alert to auditory cues (even more in a Duel, where a single noise can give away your position).

Secondary fire on the Impact Hammer is a special-purpose attack. It charges up an EMP burst. This burst deals no damage to players, however, it has the unique ability to dislodge power-ups from a player. UDamage, Jump Boots, even the Shield Belt, all can be knocked out of a player by the slightest tap of the secondary fire.

This is *not* a safe attack to be performing on another player, and in general, confined to either humiliation or desperation. The only truly necessary use of this attack is on the map Fearless, where the invincibility power-up leaves no other options besides straight avoidance.

The secondary attack *does* deal damage to vehicles, though if you're in a situation where you're attacking a vehicle with a melee weapon, odds are, you're going to be road kill shortly.

ENFORCER

EQUIP TIME | 0.2 SECONDS
PUTDOWN TIME | 0.2 SECONDS
EQUIP TIME (DUAL-WIELDING) | 1.0 SECONDS

PRIMARY FIRE

CLASSIFICATION	INSTANT HIT

Fires a single bullet, semi-auto or automatic. Each shot past the first has slightly increasing inaccuracy, up to a maximum variance.

DAMAGE	20
VEHICLE DAMAGE	33%
NODE DAMAGE	50%
RATE OF FIRE	0.36
SHOTS TO KILL (BASE)	5
SHOTS TO KILL (100/50)	8

SECONDARY FIRE

CLASSIFICATION	INSTANT HIT

Fires three bullets rapidly, more inaccurate than primary fire by default, lengthy cool down after firing.

DAMAGE	20
VEHICLE DAMAGE	33%
NODE DAMAGE	50%
RATE OF FIRE	3 shots, 0.12 seconds apart
COOL DOWN	0.97
SHOTS TO KILL (BASE)	2
SHOTS TO KILL (100/50)	3

AMMUNITION

STARTING AMMO	50
MAXIMUM AMMO	100
ENFORCER CLIP	16
AMMO FROM WEAPON LOCKER	50

ENFORCER NOTES

0.6 seconds after shooting the Enforcer primary returns to perfect accuracy, useful for knocking down escaping Hoverboarders.

Get the Gunslinger Award with 15 Enforcer kills (dual-wielded or not).

The Enforcer is your default sidearm, and usually only used until you can find something better. An automatic pistol, it is reasonably accurate, has a decent rate of fire, and inflicts low damage per hit.

While it is generally no match for weapons acquired on the battlefield, the Enforcer has one unique property—it can be dual-wielded. If you kill another player who has an Enforcer equipped, you can pick up the Enforcer in your offhand, and from then on, use both Enforcers twin-fisted.

Having two Enforcers firing simultaneously raises the damage output (and accuracy) to a point that is actually fairly dangerous, and rather useful in a mid-range firefight on uneven terrain with cover available.

The primary fire on the Enforcer is single-shot, either semi or automatic. Generally, firing semi-automatic is more accurate, as you can aim each shot individually, rather than having automatic shots go astray due to your movement, or the movement of your target.

Secondary fire sprays a quick triple shot, with a longer reload time than the primary fire. The secondary fire is decent for inflicting finishing damage on a wounded target, or up close, but it is not extremely useful at mid or long-range, as it is less accurate than the primary fire.

Speaking of accuracy, other than the Stringer, the Enforcer is the only weapon that is not 100% accurate in terms of its hit locations. All other instant hit weapons in the game land shots exactly where you have your crosshair pointed. Plant your crosshairs on a distant target with the Shock Rifle primary fire and pull the trigger to score a hit every time; that isn't the case with the Enforcer.

The first shot with the Enforcer is right on target, but if you continue to fire shots, each shot after the first becomes increasingly inaccurate, up to a maximum spread around your target point.

The inaccuracy isn't enormous; you can still use the Enforcer at close-medium range without worrying about your rate of fire, but as targets get farther away, don't be surprised if you miss shots that you were sure were on target.

Unless you pick up a second Enforcer quickly, on its own, it is not a weapon you want to be using for any great length of time. Its only real advantage is that you always have it as a fallback weapon should you run completely out of ammo for other, nastier firepower.

The Enforcer is mildly effective against opponents at medium range when you have no other good mid-range weapons, but the number of hits you need to take down a healthy target is prohibitive in terms of time taken. Unless you know you're shooting at a damaged target, spend your time finding another weapon, rather than drawing attention to yourself.

In situations where you simply must have an instant hit weapon, even an inaccurate one, the Enforcer can do in a pinch. Absolutely have to nail that fleeing flag carrier and the only other weapons you have are the Flak Cannon and the Bio Rifle? Rather than spraying shots that aren't even likely to reach your target, switch to the Enforcer and pepper your target with some bullets. You aren't likely to kill an armored target without a serious string of hits, but a weakened foe just might kick the bucket from a handful of Enforcer shots.

Likewise, against foes on elevated terrain, the Enforcer may be one of the few weapons you have that has a chance of dealing any damage at all. If you can shoot while on the move to better fighting ground, don't hesitate to pull it out and take a few shots.

Up close and at long-range, the Enforcer is a poor weapon. If you have no better options, even the Impact Hammer is often superior at close-range, and at long-range, the Enforcer is unlikely to land any significant number of hits.

You do have the advantage of triple-shot secondary fire at close-range, but in most situations where an opponent is deliberately closing with you, *they* have a better close-range weapon, and intentionally closing to utilize the secondary fire is a good way to get a face full of flak.

You can use the secondary fire as a finisher, after tapping them with three or four shots, you can get the last shot or two needed by using the secondary fire. An ice-cold execution on a spawned player is two taps with the primary and a point blank burst from the secondary, but getting such a combination on skilled players is difficult, and even one Health Vial messes up that combination.

Dual-wielded, the Enforcer becomes a considerably nastier weapon at close-range. The problem at that point becomes ammunition. While it can put out respectable damage at even medium range, there are very few ammo packs for the Enforcer present on any maps, so frequently the only way to get more ammo is taking down freshly spawned players who happen to be wielding it.

For all gametypes and weapon match ups, we're assuming you have a single Enforcer present. If you have two, it is a much more effective weapon choice, easily worth using if you lack a better instant hit alternative alternative.

DUELS

If you're using the Enforcer in a duel, the match just started, you just got fragged, or you're losing *really* badly. Find a better weapon, fast.

If you just died and you know for certain your opponent is weak, quickly close with their last known location to finish them with a few Enforcer shots, but be careful. Skilled opponents will make a beeline for the nearest health, and landing two hits on someone you were sure was at 30 health who promptly picked up two health packs is just going to increase their lead.

Also, be careful about taking potshots at your opponent if they aren't certain of your location. Firing the Enforcer gives it away instantly, and also puts up a giant "HUNT ME" sign.

TEAM DEATHMATCH

Weak, but not quite as bad as in duels. Firing at an opponent engaged with a teammate can finish them off, or weaken them enough for your teammate to seal the kill.

Similarly, multiple players firing Enforcers at a single target can take down a full health player rapidly, and even a small amount of armor or health vials on top won't last much longer.

Just don't get in the habit of using it more than you have to; as scary as roving packs of Enforcer wielding players might be, roving packs of players armed with real weaponry are a lot scarier.

DEATHMATCH

Not good. If you're using it in Deathmatch, you're telling every nearby player to kill you. You can sometimes pick off players involved in sprawling firefights, but you should usually be thankful they aren't shooting at *you*, and go find yourself a real gun.

CTF

Bad. Just like Deathmatch, it alerts the enemy team that you're a weak target. Worse, it alerts the *enemy team*, not just random players in a free-for-all Deathmatch. You have the Translocator for a reason, use it!

VCTF AND WARFARE

Awful! Get on your Hoverboard and go find a Weapon Locker.

OK, NOT COMPLETELY AWFUL

There is one handy use for the Enforcer in both VCTF and Warfare, and that is knocking down a player on a Hoverboard.

This is especially useful in VCTF for stopping a flag carrier, if you just don't have another weapon handy that can do the job.

Remember, the Enforcer's first shot is always accurate, so as long as you're lined up, you can easily knock down even a distant Hoverboarder.

VS. BIO RIFLE
Not bad if you can stay out of range of the sludge. The Bio Rifle isn't a great weapon at a distance, and you can exploit that, particularly if you have an elevation advantage.

VS. FLAK CANNON
Awful at close or mid-range, and at long-range you aren't likely to deal much damage at all. If you have a substantial height advantage, however, you can usually score hits fairly safely. Substantial because the Flak Cannon secondary is still a threat if you aren't out of range.

VS. LINK GUN
Poor, unless you are out of range of the secondary fire. If you can, you might actually be able to avoid the primary fire plasma bolts long enough to deal some damage.

VS. ROCKET LAUNCHER
Basically identical to the Flak Cannon match up, that is, really bad up close, and not great at medium range. The Rocket Launcher is worse at dealing with a height advantage however, barring lobbing the odd grenade up at you.

VS. SHOCK RIFLE
Generally quite bad. If your dodging skills are fantastic and your opponent is having a bad day, you might score a few more hits than you deserve, but you're generally not going to come out on top.

VS. SNIPER RIFLE
Poor up close, though not *completely* awful. The Sniper Rifle does have a slow rate of fire, but banking on your opponent's lack of skill is rarely a great strategy.

Downright suicidal at a distance of course.

VS. STINGER
This is a horrible situation. A pistol versus a minigun, what were you expecting?

VS. VEHICLES
Seriously, do we have to spell this one out? Find a better weapon!

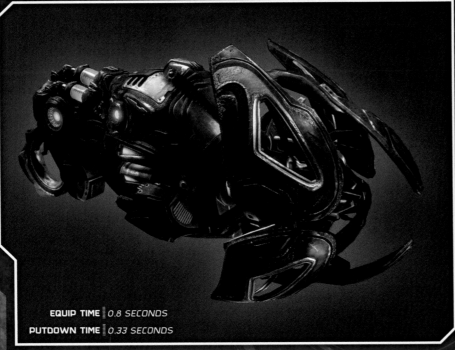

EQUIP TIME | 0.8 SECONDS
PUTDOWN TIME | 0.33 SECONDS

PRIMARY FIRE

CLASSIFICATION	PROJECTILE

Primary fire launches an explosive ball of goo that sticks to any surface for 3 seconds. Contact with a player causes it to explode.

DAMAGE	21
VEHICLE DAMAGE	80%
NODE DAMAGE	100%
RATE OF FIRE	0.35
PROJECTILE SPEED	20m/sec
SHOTS TO KILL (BASE)	5
SHOTS TO KILL (100/50)	8

SECONDARY FIRE

CLASSIFICATION	PROJECTILE

Secondary fire charges up a ball of Tarydium sludge. When fired, it can stick to any player it strikes. If it hits a surface, it sticks for up to 9 seconds, and can be detonated prematurely by any weapon fire. After firing a charged secondary shot, there is a brief cool down before it can be fired again.

DAMAGE	Varies, 210 max
VEHICLE DAMAGE	80%
NODE DAMAGE	100%
RATE OF FIRE	Varies, 3.5 seconds maximum charge time
PROJECTILE SPEED	40m/sec
BLAST RADIUS	2.4m
COOL DOWN	0.33
SHOTS TO KILL (BASE)	Varies, one fully charged
SHOTS TO KILL (100/50)	Varies, one fully charged

AMMUNITION

STARTING AMMO	25
MAXIMUM AMMO	50
BIO-RIFLE AMMO	20
AMMO FROM WEAPON LOCKER	50

BIO RIFLE NOTES

The Bio Hazard Award can be acquired after 15 kills with the goo.

The Bio Rifle is a peculiar weapon. Firing globs of processed Tarydium sludge, it is recycling at its finest! The gleaming green goo sticks to any surface it lands on, allowing you to create miniature minefields of damaging slime.

Primary fire launches individual sludge balls, dealing fairly low damage per hit, but they fire quickly, and you can saturate an area with them to create a slime field. They also work well for covering a corner, or a specific target (a flag, a power-up, or a weapon for example).

The balls of slime explode on contact with another player, or if any player touches the slime while it is attached to a surface. Note that tossing an extra ball of slime onto a spot on the ground (or wall, or even ceiling) that already has slime causes both balls to explode on contact—and this does *not* deal damage to nearby targets.

If you're trying to saturate an area with slime, spread it around. In any case, the balls dissipate after 3 seconds, so you must constantly replenish a slime field.

Holding secondary fire allows you to charge up a larger, charged ball of slime. This ball not only inflicts far more damage if it hits a target, it sticks to the target if the glob touches a player anywhere. Get the shot in the air close to your target to guarantee that it sticks tight.

Even better, a fully charged secondary shot deals *massive* damage, *and* it sprays out four extra globs of primary fire slime around the main ball. Even if you miss your target, planting a charged ball of slime can be useful, as it creates an instant slime field, with an extra special surprise package of Tarydium goo in the center.

There's more: the primary ball is so volatile, it explodes with enough force to damage a nearby target even if it isn't touched, and you can trigger the explosion yourself by shooting the ball with any weapon to create a sort of triggered slime mine.

Left untouched, a charged shot lasts up to 9 seconds. Oh, and be careful. Someone *else* can detonate the charged ball with a shot (or an explosion) just as easily as you can, which is bad news if you're near it.

Both shot types fire in an arc, and while they travel fairly quickly, it is possible for an opponent to dodge almost all of your shots fairly easily, which is never a pleasant experience.

Dodging the slime field created from such a barrage can be more difficult. Figure out where your opponent is trying to move (or dodge), and plant Bio Rifle shots ahead of your target. You don't need to hit your opponent directly with this weapon to get kills.

Unsurprisingly, the Bio Rifle is not an effective weapon at longer ranges, as you simply can't fire the slime a great distance with any accuracy at a moving target. You *can* create a slime field at a reasonable distance, which can work in a pinch if you just don't have any other tools at your disposal.

The Bio Rifle is best used on terrain that is restrictive, preventing your targets from easily evading the fire. The weapon has a solid rate of fire, so it is difficult to dodge all the incoming slime if you pin a target in a narrow hallway, the corner of a room, or between obstacles in rough terrain.

It is also a solid weapon for fighting on differing elevation levels. If your foe is above you, the arcing slime can still land hits, and if they are below you, it is easy to lob shots down while staying completely out of sight, or to charge up a ball of goo and peek out to fire it.

The secondary fire is best used as a single charged shot, hopefully sticking to your foe for a quick kill, but whether you land the shot or not, you are usually best served by following up with a different weapon. It takes too long to recharge a secondary shot, and the primary fire is often not the best finisher.

Because the secondary charged shot takes a second for the slime to explode once it sticks to a player (or gets hit by a follow-up shot), it is not at all uncommon to land a fully charged shot, die to your close-range opponent, and then have them die from the slime. Pyrrhic victories aren't productive in Duels or Team Deathmatch, though mutual annihilation is perfectly acceptable on a flag runner in CTF if you just don't have any other options.

Ammunition is a real problem with the Bio Rifle. Secondary fire eats up 10 ammo per shot when fully charged, and the primary fire shoots quick enough that your remaining ammo stores are easily consumed, given the number of hits it takes to down a target (and the usual miss-rate while firing a barrage).

Because the Bio Rifle is a good weapon for very specific situations, it is usually best to use it only for those situations, rather than as a primary, all-around weapon.

Running around with the secondary charged to paste the first target you find on a close quarters map is reasonably effective, running around expecting to take opponents armed with more lethal mid-range or long-range weaponry is dangerous.

One last point: be careful with the Bio Rifle in close-range situations. Killing yourself on your own slime field is rather humiliating.

For all weapon match ups, you can safely assume the Bio Rifle is inferior at long-range; it isn't meant for that type of combat!

DUELS

Primary fire isn't fantastic against many other weapons that are likely to be readied by your opponent, but a fully charged secondary is a real threat. It can kill even an armored opponent, or severely damage a really heavily stacked opponent.

However, don't rely on it more than the opening salvo. Launch the charged secondary, then switch to something better suited for the engagement.

Primary fire can be used to create a slime field in an area ahead of an opponent, but savvy foes aren't going to walk through the slime (or they'll just jump over it), so don't expect it to take down a skilled opponent alone.

You can use it as a suppressive indirect weapon choice if you simply don't have any other options available. Inflicting even a little damage risk-free is never bad.

TEAM DEATHMATCH

Generally not a weapon you're likely to be concerned with defending (or reaching). In cases where you've been taken out and you need to get back into the fight, a fully charged secondary shot can often do the trick. Killing an opponent guarding a weapon, armor, or power-up spawn point is quite helpful for regaining momentum.

If you have the upper hand and you're hunting downed opponents, be aware of the Bio Rifle's spawn point (or spawn points). Any players patrolling near them should be alert for the danger of an opponent firing a charged secondary shot. If possible, fresh targets should be engaged from a great enough distance to render the threat ineffectual.

DEATHMATCH

Heavily varying effectiveness, depending on the map layout. In some cases, you can saturate a common contested area with slime and score a few free kills from a safe distance, or a safe height.

As far as traveling through a map on your way to other weapons or important pick-ups, having a charged secondary shot ready presents a respectable threat.

CTF

The Bio Rifle can be helpful for defending the flag. Charged secondary, or even sprayed primary fire can inflict incidental damage at the very least. The Bio Rifle is not the best weapon in the arsenal for defending the flag, but if you don't have any other options available, it can do in a pinch.

On offense, pasting a flag defender with a charged secondary shot is always a satisfying way to clear a path to the flag. However, its effectiveness in this regard is dependant on the specific CTF map. If you need to use the Translocator to reach the flag from a favorable angle, the time it takes to charge up a secondary shot can be detrimental to your flag running efforts.

VCTF AND WARFARE

In VCTF, just like CTF, it can be helpful for defending the flag, but in both VCTF and Warfare, it is not especially helpful against most vehicles, and the usually wide open terrain is not friendly to the Bio Rifle at all.

VS. ENFORCER

Decent at close-range, completely superior in terms of potential alpha strike damage with the secondary fire. Also decent from an elevated position.

Due to projectile travel, your damage output with primary fire is actually *lower* over time than that of the Enforcer, so much depends on the accuracy of your opponent, and your own evasive skills.

VS. FLAK CANNON

Up close, quite bad. The Flak cannon excels at close-range, and its potential damage output is far higher than yours. Pretty much your only chance of coming out of this engagement alive is having a secondary shot fully charged—and even then, you're likely to go down with your opponent.

From roughly medium range, you can throw slime at your opponent with somewhat more safety, and from elevated ground, you can threaten the Flak user (watch out for Flak Shells lobbed up at you). Just don't be surprised if you still take a beating at mid-range. Even at short distance, Flak shards can deal a surprising amount of damage.

VS. LINK GUN

On open ground at close-range, not a good match up. The Link's average damage seriously exceeds your damage output potential. However, on terrain with enough cover, or in situations where you have elevation advantage, you can exploit the Link's weakness to shift the advantage in your favor.

Because the Link needs a clean line of sight to deal damage, you may even have time to charge up a secondary shot in mid-fight.

VS. ROCKET LAUNCHER

Not a safe fight to have at short range. Unlike the Flak cannon, the Rocket Launcher lacks the ability to fight back easily against an elevated foe, so if you're going to engage a rocket armed opponent, either come in with a charged secondary shot, or attack from above.

As with the Flak Cannon battle, you can engage with more safety at medium range, even though doing so usually lowers your damage output. Be aware that medium range also allows the Rocket Launcher to achieve a lock, which can make avoiding the rockets difficult if there is insufficient cover, or you're slow in dodging the incoming shots.

VS. SHOCK RIFLE

Tricky. At close-range, where you can best deal damage, the Shock Rifle can still deal a lot of harm, and navigating your own slime field while dodging is challenging.

Be careful about maneuvering too far from your opponent and into Shock Combo distance, your odds are usually better if you can prevent your opponent from using the combo at all.

VS. SNIPER RIFLE

Decent up close, terrible at a distance—no surprises here!

VS. STINGER

Similar to the Link match up, the outcome of the fight is usually determined by the terrain during the engagement. This is *not* a battle you want to have on open ground. With enough cover, or an elevation advantage, you can put up a respectable fight, though you're still likely to take a lot of collateral damage.

SHOCK RIFLE

EQUIP TIME 0.45 SECONDS
PUTDOWN TIME 0.33 SECONDS

PRIMARY FIRE

CLASSIFICATION	INSTANT HIT

Shock primary fire is an instant hit beam of energy that causes a considerable amount of knockback.

DAMAGE	45
VEHICLE DAMAGE	70%
NODE DAMAGE	80%
RATE OF FIRE	0.77
SHOTS TO KILL (BASE)	3
SHOTS TO KILL (100/50)	4

SECONDARY FIRE

CLASSIFICATION	PROJECTILE

Secondary fire launches a floating Shock Core. The Core deals more damage than primary fire, and has a faster rate of fire, but it travels slowly through the air. Hitting *any* Shock Core with the Shock Rifle primary fire triggers a devastating explosion.

DAMAGE	55
VEHICLE DAMAGE	80%
NODE DAMAGE	100%
RATE OF FIRE	0.6
SPLASH RADIUS	2.4m
PROJECTILE SPEED	23m/sec
SHOTS TO KILL (BASE)	2
SHOTS TO KILL (100/50)	3

AMMUNITION

STARTING AMMO	20
MAXIMUM AMMO	50
SHOCK CORE	10
AMMO FROM WEAPON LOCKER	30

SHOCK RIFLE NOTES

The Shock Combo deals 215 maximum damage at the center point, diminishing in a linear manner out to 5.5 meters from the blast point (i.e., at 2.25 meters, it deals half damage, at 90% from the center, it only deals 10% damage, etc.).

Earn the Combo King Award for 15 kills with the Shock Combo (and the eternal enmity of your foes).

The Shock Rifle is a powerful mid-range weapon, and with its Shock Combo, it is a lethal weapon against even heavily armored opponents.

While its rate of fire (and need for accuracy) make it relatively ineffective at close-range, at mid-range, the Shock Rifle is one of the most dangerous weapons in the game.

First off, the primary fire is an instant hit beam of energy, and its rate of fire, while slow in comparison to the real rapid-fire weapons, is still quicker than the Sniper Rifle. This allows you to take quick, repeated shots at even those enemies at long-range. In a pinch, the Shock Rifle can serve as a long-range weapon if you have nothing better to use.

At mid-range however, the primary fire can be used more accurately, and the Shock Combo can be utilized to devastate careless opponents. Approaching an alert player armed with the Shock Rifle from a distance or down narrow hallways or constrained terrain typically results in a quick (and explosive) death.

The secondary fire on the Shock Rifle actually inflicts more damage, fires faster, *and* has slight splash damage on impact, but it is still generally not a terribly effective weapon even at close-range. The single projectile tends to be rather easy to avoid.

The key to the secondary fire is the Shock Combo. Hitting a floating Shock Core with the primary fire causes a devastating explosion, dealing critical damage to any target close to the blast, and heavy damage even at a slight distance from the Shock Core center.

As an added benefit, firing Shock Cores repeatedly at a targets location tends to result in the occasional accidental direct hit with a Shock Core. While this can disrupt a Combo, it's still 55 damage to the face, which is never a bad thing. One follow-up primary fire shot can kill an unarmored target.

Performing a Shock Combo on the move is one of the most difficult shots you can attempt to make in *UT3*, particularly if you are dodging and moving heavily while firing Shock Cores. However, while training yourself with the Shock Combo is a constant and ongoing process, even new players can perform a stationary Shock Combo. Fire a Shock Core, don't move, wait until the Core reaches your desired target area, then trigger the Shock Combo.

While standing still is just about the worst possible bit of advice we can give you, there *are* situations where you are reasonably safe. For example, in a Duel, you

know precisely where your opponent is, and they are out of line of sight. Firing a Shock Core at their next probable location and triggering a Shock Combo is a safe and effective tactic.

Standing still in the middle of a more frantic Deathmatch or CTF game is usually a lot more dangerous, but it only takes a few seconds to trigger the Combo and move on.

While hitting a moving Shock Core, *especially* one fired at an angle while you are moving is an extremely difficult shot, you can make some moving shots easier by controlling your movement. Strafing away from the Core without adjusting your aim, and then strafing back to line up the shot is considerably easier than making a shot where you have changed both your position, and the position of your crosshair.

These sort of intermediate mobile Shock Combo shots are good practice for the most difficult shots. Firing Shock Cores up or down at an angle, all while moving, dodging, wall jumping, and changing your aim on the fly. Such shots are difficult even for the best of players, so don't worry too much about landing such shots without a great deal of practice.

Even without the ability to land moving Shock Combos, the Combo is still a powerful part of the Shock Rifles overall effectiveness, and learning to utilize it is *extremely* important, as it is one of the single most damaging weapon attacks you can make in the entire game.

DUELS

Very powerful. Because many favored Duel maps tend to be relatively small, the Shock Combo can often be used to devastating effect. It can cover any type of important item spawn point (or for that matter, player spawns, although initial invincibility renders that nasty tactic slightly more difficult).

The Shock Combo is ideal in situations where you can predict your opponent's movement. Have a Shock Core floating in the air waiting for them to arrive while you have the primary fire shot lined up, and you can kill or cripple your foe with a single blast. And if they happen to bump into the Shock Core accidentally? Still 55 damage to the face.

Even ignoring the Shock Combo, the Shock Rifle primary fire is still a respectable weapon. In any situations where you are fighting at a good distance, you can use it as a long-range weapon quite effectively.

TEAM DEATHMATCH

Again, quite powerful. Here however, you have to be careful with Shock Combos when your teammates are in close proximity to enemy players. Taking down your friends with a Shock Combo is embarrassing and rather detrimental to your chances for victory.

Multiple players armed with Shock Rifles covering enemy approaches is extremely difficult to get around, and the sheer damage dealt by the Shock Combo makes it an effective weapon for taking down heavily armored players.

The Shock Combo is powerful enough on several maps that the Shock Rifle should be guarded, both to arm your team, and to prevent the enemy team from gaining access to a weapon that can strip armor so quickly.

Players armed with the Shock Rifle should seek out positions that offer perfect views for using the Shock Combo to cover ground, or abusing the Shock Rifles long-range primary fire. In cramped quarters, there are better close-range alternatives.

DEATHMATCH

The Shock Rifle is a bit weaker in free-for-all DM, as it lacks the offensive punch needed to quickly take down a player. Since winning in DM is all about racking up frags quickly, there are better weapons for scoring kills with great speed.

The Shock Combo is still quite effective for taking out players, but scoring a Shock Combo in the middle of a group of fighting players is harder than it sounds. For one, you tend to attract the ire of every player nearby once you detonate a single Combo, and for another, rapidly moving players often accidentally intercept your Shock Core before you can trigger the Combo.

Still a decent choice at long-range, but you should usually be tracking down weapons with a better alpha strike potential, the better to down players rapidly and rack up frags. Hurting a player with a single primary or secondary shot and then having someone else cherry pick the kill is never a good feeling.

CTF

A fantastic defensive weapon, the Shock Rifle primary can be used to deal damage to approaching players from a distance, and when they get closer, you can use the Shock Combo to devastating effect.

Unlike most other game modes, you *know* where an offensive player is going to move. Either they go for the flag while you are covering it with the threat of a Combo blast, or they have to fight you directly, both desirable outcomes.

The Shock Rifle is still solid for long-range combat while moving through the map, but because you are generally Translocating through the center to reach the enemy base, you may not be using it often, unless you are playing forward defense just outside your own base.

The Shock Combo can be useful both for taking out flag defenders, and for clearing out chasers while you are running with the flag. If you know the position of a flag defender, you can often land a lethal Combo before they can move.

Similarly, while running, you can be assured that every nearby enemy player is going to aggressively pursue you, and this myopia can be deadly. If you know two players are coming up behind you down a narrow hallway, you couldn't ask for a more ideal situation to land a Shock Combo.

VCTF AND WARFARE

The Shock Rifle is a solid weapon in both modes. In VCTF, it is just as handy for guarding the flag as it is in regular CTF, and in both modes, the Shock Rifle primary fire is great for dealing steady damage to vehicles at a distance. It also has considerable knockback, which can be useful for knocking aircraft or light vehicles around.

Since the Shock Rifle is the only long distance weapon besides the Sniper rifle that is completely accurate, it can also be used to score a few long distance shots on infantry while running around on larger maps.

In Warfare, the Shock Combo can also sometimes be used effectively against Node defenders (or to score a killshot on an inattentive Orb carrier), or to deal some extra damage to an exposed Power Core in the absence of a more damaging alternative.

If you happen to be shooting a Node or Power Core with the Shock Rifle, use the secondary shots. The Shock Cores fire more quickly and deal full damage.

 VS. ENFORCER
Solid at any range. Up close, you can use Shock Cores effectively, and at mid or long-range, accurate primary fire is deadly to an Enforcer user who cannot fire accurately at a distance with any rapidity.

 VS. FLAK CANNON
Very bad up close, solid from a distance. The Flak Cannon can't do much at long-range, while you can still pick away with primary fire. At mid-range, you can get off Shock Combos or use primary fire, but be careful, the Flak Cannon can still deal decent damage if you don't avoid incoming shards and shells well.

 VS. BIO RIFLE
Great at a distance, somewhat dangerous up close, as the Bio Rifle can score easier primary fire hits, or far more deadly, land a charged secondary shot.

 VS. ROCKET LAUNCHER
Terrible up close, good from a distance. Medium range is a bit more dangerous than the flak battle, as the splash is usually slightly trickier to avoid than flak shells, though this depends considerably on the terrain. The Flak Cannon is better at firing up onto ledges with flak shells, where grenades from the Rocket Launcher take time to load.

 VS. LINK GUN
Good at a distance, but not great up close. Both of the Link Gun's firing modes are more dangerous up close, where a hail of plasma bolts or a stream of energy can be seriously damaging.

VS. SNIPER RIFLE
The Shock Rifle is the only other instant hit weapon in the game that is perfectly accurate, so you're better off against a Sniper Rifle at a distance than other weapons.

However, while the damage over time between your primary fire and the Sniper Rifle is actually comparable (assuming similar accuracy, a dangerous assumption), you have to watch out for headshots, and the sniper usually only needs two hits to your three for the kill.

Up close, your greater fire rate, access to Shock Cores, and the Shock Combo all make this a favorable match up.

 VS. STINGER
Ok up close, and good at a distance if you have some cover. However, fighting the Stinger on open ground is never a good idea, and similarly, trying to score Shock Combos on flat terrain isn't wise either. You can strafe in and out of cover, firing a Shock Core or two and then going for a Shock Combo hit on the move, but that makes for a more difficult shot, and any competent Stinger user at a distance will quickly evade the incoming Cores.

If the terrain is more constricted, you can frequently get off Shock Combos safely from an angle, and since the Stinger is poor at handling targets at steep angles on ledges, you can pick away at a Stinger user from an elevated position.

 VS. VEHICLES
Primary fire is great for knocking light vehicles and aircraft around, but it isn't an ideal anti-vehicle weapon in general, dealing reduced damage to both vehicles and Nodes. If you have a teammate nearby, you can use it to paralyze a light vehicle while they take care of it with heavier weaponry.

EQUIP TIME 0.45 SECONDS
PUTDOWN TIME 0.33 SECONDS

PRIMARY FIRE

CLASSIFICATION	INSTANT HIT

The Link's rapid fire plasma is ideal for saturating narrow areas with suppressive fire, and it is utterly lethal in combination with the Berserk power-up.

PRIMARY FIRE NOTES	
DAMAGE	26
VEHICLE DAMAGE	60%
NODE DAMAGE	80%
RATE OF FIRE	0.16
PROJECTILE SPEED	28m/sec accelerating to 100m/sec by 60m/sec
SHOTS TO KILL (BASE)	4
SHOTS TO KILL (100/50)	6

SECONDARY FIRE

CLASSIFICATION	INSTANT HIT

Secondary fire projects a solid beam of energy, dealing continuous damage to an enemy target. The Link beam can also be used to heal friendly vehicles, and repair Nodes in Warfare. Firing the Link beam drains 8.5 ammunition per second. Secondary heals vehicles at 35 armor/sec. and Nodes at 100 armor/sec.

DAMAGE	100 per second
VEHICLE DAMAGE	80%
NODE DAMAGE	100%
MAXIMUM RANGE	18m
TIME TO KILL (BASE)	1 second
TIME TO KILL (100/50)	1.5 seconds

AMMUNITION

STARTING AMMO	50
MAXIMUM AMMO	220
LINK GUN AMMO	50
AMMO FROM WEAPON LOCKER	100

LINK GUN NOTES

Shaftmaster Award for 15 kills with the secondary fire.

The Link Gun is an interesting weapon, notable for its variety of special uses, rather than its raw power. While its primary fire is actually one of the most *potentially* damaging attacks in the game against other players, actually landing the hits is considerably more difficult.

The Link Gun's primary fire launches a continuous stream of plasma bolts that rapidly accelerate to a high top speed. The difficulty arises from actually scoring the four hits needed to kill a healthy target, or the six needed to kill an even slightly tanked up opponent.

Because they are individual projectiles, they are easily evaded at a distance, because rapid enemy movement is impossible to compensate for. While you can absolutely devastate someone running a straight line (say, running down a narrow hallway and unaware of you), such situations are rare at best.

In an open fight, with an alert opponent who is dodging your attacks, scoring plasma hits at anything beyond fairly short range is extremely difficult.

On the bright side, the Link Gun has plentiful ammo supplies, so unleashing a continuous stream of plasma at a target area as suppressive fire is reasonably effective, especially in narrow hallways. Only a fool is likely to run out into a barrage of plasma bolts. Just don't expect to drop dodging opponents or distant opponents easily.

Secondary fire on the Link Gun has numerous unique characteristics. First, it projects a beam of energy 18 meters in distance. The beam deals solid damage, but to achieve its full damage potential, you must hold it on your target perfectly until they are dead. This is actually easier than landing primary fire hits on skilled opponents, if your own aim is good, it is nearly impossible for even adroit targets to avoid your beam for more than the time it takes you to readjust to a sudden dodge.

However, because the beam's length is limited, and its burst damage potential is nonexistent, using the beam places you at great risk against other close-range weapons that have superior alpha strike potential. It is always a dreadful feeling to lance a target perfectly with the beam, then die to a single well placed rocket, a face full of flak, or even a Shock Combo.

Secondary fire is ideal for finishing off weakened targets, as it is so difficult to avoid. If you are working in tandem with teammates, or if you know your opponent is weak, it is a great choice for dealing the last few points of damage needed to score a kill.

LINK GUN SPECIAL ABILITIES

While the secondary fire on the Link Gun deals only moderate damage and has a fairly short maximum range, it has several special traits that make it an important tool in several game modes.

First, let's discuss the Link itself. As the name suggests, the Link Gun can actually link up with other nearby players who are also firing the Link beam. When more than one player on the same team firing the Link secondary stand close enough together, an actual visible "link" beam forms between the players. Any number of players on the same team can form this link. While linked, the damage from the beam increases. There is a maximum bonus reached when at least three players link together, but there is no upper limit to the number who can be linked to one another. That is, you could have your whole team of six in a VCTF match linking one another, and every single player would be receiving the full damage bonus of three players.

Needless to say, three Link beams trained on the same target, each with a damage bonus can quickly reduce even a heavily armored target to ash. Of course, three players concentrating on one opponent is usually fatal for the poor target with any weapon, and standing close enough to enable the link renders you and your teammates rather vulnerable to weapons with considerable splash damage, or even rapid firing weapons; so many targets in one area make for easy hits. There is more however. In addition to the "linking" possible with the Link Gun for the damage bonus, the Link is also a critical tool in Warfare, and a useful one in VCTF.

The Link beam has a healing property when used on a friendly vehicle, or on a friendly Node (in Warfare), though Power Cores in Warfare cannot be healed.

You can heal any vehicle, even friendly vehicles being driven by other players (handy when you're following along behind a Goliath, Darkwalker, or even the mighty Leviathan). You can also help Nodes to build more quickly, and to repair Nodes taking damage in battle.

Vehicle repairs can suck up a good bit of your time, but they are often quite worthwhile for critical heavy vehicles, or air vehicles, which tend to be rather rare. Note that linking together with other Link Gun secondary users on your team does heal Nodes or vehicles more quickly, and can be useful to quickly get a critical Node online, or to make a tough vehicle even nastier.

Finally, there is one last special property of the Link Gun's secondary beam that is important to know. Hitting any player with the beam causes a state known as "Lockdown". In essence, what happens is that the continuous pulses of damage push the target slightly, and frequently shove the player you are striking with the beam ever so slightly into the air. A player in the air *cannot jump, and cannot dodge*. This has important implications when it comes to tackling a highly skilled evasive player. Without the ability to jump, dodge, or wall dodge, your unfortunate beam target becomes that much easier to track with the solid stream of energy, increasing your damage output.

In addition, Lockdown is highly useful when you have a teammate around, *especially* if the player with the Link Gun strikes the target from the side or rear while he is engaged from the front by a player using another weapon. Any weapon in the game becomes that much more deadly against a target that has weakened mobility, and while the relatively short range of the Link beam prevents this tactic from being useful in all situations, it is still effective enough that it is worth using, particularly when you do not have a more lethal weapon handy, or a weapon appropriate to the current combat situation.

LINKING

The Link range is short; you must be within 3.2m of another player using the Link beam to charge your weapon.

The damage bonus is 1.5x for two players, and 2x for three (or more) players.

DUELS

Not a great weapon, except for the primary fire's ability to cover an entrance, or the secondary's to finish off a weakened target. In a general engagement, you're going to be at a significant disadvantage against a lot of other more specialized weapons, either due to range, or instant damage potential.

CTF

Not bad, as many of the same principles of Team DM apply here as well. However, because your team is frequently split into offense defense in CTF (rather than hunting in packs in TDM), you are less likely to have friendly targets nearby for linking.

Additionally, Lockdown is basically useless against targets who are actively translocating, though it can be helpful against a flag runner, who can no longer use his Translocator.

VCTF AND WARFARE

Very important in Warfare, and occasionally quite helpful in VCTF as well. The healing effect of the Link beam is important for quickly building Nodes, and repairing key vehicles (especially aircraft, and potent heavy vehicles).

As a general combat tool, rather poor, there are other weapons better suited to fighting against vehicles, and the frequently open terrain in both game modes usually renders the Link Gun ineffective against other players.

TEAM DEATHMATCH

Potentially lethal, if your team is well organized, and you have practiced using the Link effectively with them, you can inflict serious damage by having multiple team members firing secondary Link beams.

The Lockdown effect of the beam also makes it useful for pinning a target while a teammate takes them apart with another weapon.

DEATHMATCH

Poor, as its damage output lacks the punch needed to quickly rack up frags. Primary fire can be used to spray down a multi-player battle, but other weapons can perform the same task, and usually deal more damage while doing so.

VS. ENFORCER
A good match up at any close-range, though only middling at any significant distance. Either of you are likely to waste a lot of ammo before either you, or your target, goes down. The Enforcer's inaccuracy makes it difficult to land hits at a distance, and the Link's plasma is easily dodged.

VS. FLAK CANNON
Awful at close-range, not bad at medium or longer, but watch out for secondary flak balls. One annoyance is that the Flak user can duck in and out of cover to take shots at you, while you generally need open line of sight to have a chance of dealing damage. Evaluate the terrain and the distance before engaging.

VS. BIO RIFLE
Good in situations where the Bio Rifle user does not have a fully charged secondary shot. You can generally out damage the Bio Rifle in most other situations, as its goo is even more easily avoided than your plasma bolts, and at close-range, even the Link beam can frequently take down a fully healthy Bio Rifle user before they can return the favor.

VS. ROCKET LAUNCHER
Again, quite dreadful at close-range. However, at medium range, the Rocket Launcher is still quite dangerous, and on open ground, where you can track your target with primary fire more easily, you are at some risk from the Rocket Launcher gaining a lock on you. Not an ideal match up, but doable at range. Closer in, if you have a height advantage, you can sometimes use the Link beam to score some easy damage, though watch out for the occasional lobbed grenade from below.

VS. SHOCK RIFLE
A tricky fight. Up close, your primary fire can tear up a Shock Rifle wielder, but at medium range, the fight becomes rather difficult. If they are dodging your fire heavily, it makes it more difficult for them to get off a Shock Combo, but more difficult isn't impossible, and in any case, if they are dodging well, their primary fire can still hurt you badly.

VS. SNIPER RIFLE
Good at close-range, and decent at mid-range, depending heavily on your opponents accuracy. Curiously, the Link is one of the few weapons that is *OK* against the Sniper Rifle at a great distance. Not great by any stretch of the imagination, or even good, but ok.

Sniper Rifle users often act literally like a sniper. They find a perch, set up shop, and look for targets. If you can spot the sniper before they spot you, you can unleash a hail of primary fire bolts at their position. By the time they notice, they're eating plasma in the face, spoiling their shot, and possibly even dying. This is hardly the sort of fight you want to be provoking, but if you know certain locations that are likely sniper haunts, it's worth burning some ammo to saturate the area.

VS. STINGER
A difficult match up. At a distance, the Stinger's slight inaccuracy can give you a fighting chance with primary fire, but this cuts both ways, as your plasma bolts can be more easily evaded. At closer ranges, the Stinger's primary fire is more accurate, and its secondary becomes much more dangerous. Similarly, you gain the use of the Link's secondary, and your primary fire can usually score hits more rapidly.

Often a pyrrhic encounter, be wary of engaging an alert opponent armed with the Stinger, you might win the fight only to fall to the nearest vulture swooping in for an easy kill.

VS. VEHICLES
Not great. Primary fire can be used to spray down a large vehicle if you lack anything better to use. It's usually pretty easy to land hits on the slower vehicles. Secondary fire is usually suicide, as it is highly noticeable, without being highly damaging. On friendly vehicles, the healing property of the Link beam make it highly useful for backing up a friendly teammate, or ducking into cover and repairing your ride.

STINGER

EQUIP TIME | 0.6 SECONDS
PUTDOWN TIME | 0.33 SECONDS

PRIMARY FIRE

CLASSIFICATION	INSTANT HIT

Primary fire requires a short spin-up time; until 5 shots are fired, the minigun does not fire at full speed. It takes about .75 seconds to fire the first five shots, and the spin-up is "front loaded", so the first shot is almost twice as slow as normal, and each shot speeds up gradually until the full speed of 10 shots a second is reached.

DAMAGE	14
VEHICLE DAMAGE	60%
NODE DAMAGE	60%
RATE OF FIRE	0.1, roughly 0.75 seconds to spin up
COOLDOWN	0.27
SHOTS TO KILL (BASE)	8
SHOTS TO KILL (100/50)	11

SECONDARY FIRE

CLASSIFICATION	PROJECTILE

Secondary fire's Tarydium shards cause heavy knockback, while consuming 2 ammo per shot.

DAMAGE	38
VEHICLE DAMAGE	60%
NODE DAMAGE	60%
RATE OF FIRE	0.28
COOL DOWN	0.33
PROJECTILE SPEED	50m/sec accelerating to 80m/sec by 90m/sec
SHOTS TO KILL (BASE)	3
SHOTS TO KILL (100/50)	4

AMMUNITION

STARTING AMMO	100
MAXIMUM AMMO	300
STINGER AMMO	50
AMMO FROM WEAPON LOCKER	150

STINGER NOTES

15 kills with the Stinger nets the Bluestreak Award.

The Stinger is a powerful minigun, with a secondary fire mode that shoots Tarydium spike projectiles.

With an excellent primary fire rate and a high sustained damage potential, the Stinger is a lethal weapon on open ground at medium range. It is slightly inaccurate however, so it becomes less useful at great distances.

The Stinger's secondary fire is an interesting change from *2K4's* minigun, as it fires rapidly moving projectiles that inflict high damage per hit, and have significant knockback. Should you score a killshot with one of the Tarydium spikes, it actually impales the body, sticking it to the nearest surface.

The Stinger is a superb suppression weapon for open terrain, as your targets essentially have no recourse against the damage. If they're in range and in line of sight, you're going to hurt or kill them.

While the Stinger is powerful on open ground, its utility weakens if there is a lot of cover, where targets armed with single shot weapons can pop in and out of cover, avoiding much of your damage output.

In addition, the Stinger's spin-up time and rapid ammo consumption once firing at full speed mean that targets have time to get behind cover immediately after you open fire, and you cannot maintain full firing speed for an extended period of time, even with a full ammo load.

The Stinger makes an awesome finisher for damaged targets, as all you need is a steady hand to deal the last few hits on a weak foe.

Because the weapon switch time from another weapon in combination with the spin-up time is quite lengthy, damaging a target with another weapon and switching to the Stinger in mid-fight is inadvisable, but you can certainly pull it out if you or your target duck behind cover, and if you are coming up on a target you know is damaged from another firefight, have the Stinger ready to finish the fight.

At long-range, the Stinger's primary fire loses much of its potency due to the spread of the bullets. You might score the odd hit, but don't expect to take down healthy targets with any regularity.

Up close, the Stinger can deal out excellent sustained damage, but you are at great risk from other weapons that have better front-loaded damage potential. Even a fully spun up Stinger isn't much help if you eat a flak blast at point blank range.

To aid with that weakness, the Stinger's secondary fire is excellent at close and close-medium range. It deals heavier damage per hit, and more importantly, knocks your target around, potentially disrupting their aim. Of course, it can disrupt *your* aim as well, but since you're the one spamming away with the shards, hopefully you can deal the few hits necessary to kill your target.

The projectiles from the secondary fire are difficult to hit with at longer ranges, but you can use them somewhat effectively to needle a narrow hallway or doorway entrance, and if you spot a target near a ledge over dangerous terrain, you can occasionally knock them off with a well placed shot or two.

The Stinger's secondary Tarydium shards also have heavy knockback against vehicles, on par with the Shock Rifle. You can use this to seriously disrupt a light vehicle's movement.

Be careful trying to switch between secondary and primary fire, the secondary shots have a cool down time associated with them, and in combination with the spin-up on the primary fire, it takes a long time to get back up to full speed with the minigun.

The Stinger is a simple and straightforward weapon, but effective in the right situations. Generally, if the terrain favors Stinger usage whatsoever, it's worthwhile to burn up your ammo in pursuit of kills, and use it as a finisher if you have time to switch weapons.

DUELS

Very good on any map with open terrain, just beware of savvy opponents who quickly retreat when they hear the Stinger spinning up. You may do little more than alert them to your location and then be peppered from a distance with Shock or Sniper shots.

If you are running around with the Stinger out, you can use the secondary fire in a pinch should your opponent get up close to you unexpectedly. It's not a great option against serious close-range weapons, but better than trying to spin up the primary fire while you're eating rockets or flak.

If you seriously damaged your opponent in a fight and they retreat, use the Stinger to finish them off if you know you can intercept them before they reach any health pick-ups.

TEAM DEATHMATCH

Solid, especially with extra teammates using the Stinger as well. Two players with good aim targeting an opponent with the Stinger primary fire is completely lethal, and nigh-impossible to avoid even with cover, as you can attack from two angles.

Generally, ammo becomes the limiting factor here, as it is hard to keep even one Stinger fully supplied.

DEATHMATCH

Decent. The sustained damage and ease of hitting targets is great, but again, ammo is a concern, and more critically, the lack of burst damage may result in the frustrating experience of damaging many targets heavily, but killing none. In free-for-all, only killshots count, not damage dealt.

CTF

Great for mowing down a flag runner who cannot translocate. Rather awful for midfield battles against translocating targets.

Flag defenders should stock up on ammo, and have the weapon ready should an enemy manage to pick up the flag. The terrain around the flag room may weaken the Stinger's effectiveness, so you may need to use other weapons to cover and chase from the flag room, then switch to the Stinger when the terrain opens up to finish off a flag runner.

VCTF AND WARFARE

No good for damaging vehicles or Nodes, but the secondary fire is useful for disrupting the movement of lighter vehicles. On the upshot, *hitting* vehicles is extremely easy in the open, so even though you're dealing less damage, you can still empty a full Stinger into almost any vehicle with ease.

VS. BIO RIFLE

Great at pretty much any range, and at your favored medium range, the Bio Rifle is in serious trouble, as it cannot be used effectively at a distance where the Stinger is extremely lethal. Mind the charged sludge shots!

VS. ENFORCER

Massively superior, at any range. Only dual Enforcers at close-range really have a chance of taking you out.

VS. FLAK CANNON

Ugly up close, great at a distance. This is a pretty simple match up, if you've got the range, you're in decent shape. Up close, you can only hope they have poor accuracy while you spam Shards and pray you can dodge out of range quickly.

VS. LINK GUN

Good at medium or even long-range, where the Link isn't much of a threat. Up close, you come into the danger zone, where the Link Gun's primary fire exceeds even your fully spun up damage output. Try to keep your distance, you can usually win this engagement fairly safely.

VS. ROCKET LAUNCHER

Awful up close, good at medium range. On open ground, the rocket launcher still presents a threat, as skilled users can deal splash damage fairly easily, but you should usually be able to come out of the fight standing, if not a bit battered.

At a greater distance, you can deal damage safely, but at the cost of a lot of wasted ammunition.

VS. SHOCK RIFLE

Poor at long-range, and medium range is tricky. While you can deal heavy damage, it is also right around the distance that Shock Combos are a serious threat. Much of this comes down to the skill of the Shock Rifle user, and the terrain on which the engagement takes place.

Close-range is usually good, though you may take some painful hits in the process of downing your opponent.

VS. SNIPER RIFLE

No surprises here, horrible at long-range, better the closer you get. Indeed, the closer you engage the Sniper Rifle at, the better off you are, as headshots are hard to land while moving, and harder still up close.

VS. VEHICLES

Good for constant damage, at the cost of sinking your ammo supply into a single target. If you do have this out for an infantry fight, consider using the secondary fire instead, to knock the offending vehicle away while you either seek cover, or let a teammate finish it off. Just don't go trying to knock around the Goliath or Darkwalker, they aren't impressed.

FLAK CANNON

EQUIP TIME 0.75 SECONDS
PUTDOWN TIME 0.33 SECONDS

PRIMARY FIRE

CLASSIFICATION	PROJECTILE

Fires 9 flak shards in a slightly randomized cluster. Each shard can bounce off two surfaces. The center shard has a special damage bonus if it impacts a player at point blank range. 80% to vehicles.

DAMAGE	18 per shard, 162 maximum, 244 point blank
VEHICLE DAMAGE	80%
NODE DAMAGE	100%
RATE OF FIRE	1.1
PROJECTILE SPEED	70m/sec
SHOTS TO KILL (BASE)	1
SHOTS TO KILL (100/50)	1

SECONDARY FIRE

CLASSIFICATION	PROJECTILE

Fires a single flak shell in an arc that detonates on impact, inflicting damage and spraying 5 flak shards randomly around the shell. The Flak Shell does not generate shards if it impacts a vehicle.

DAMAGE	100
VEHICLE DAMAGE	80%
NODE DAMAGE	100%
RATE OF FIRE	1.1
PROJECTILE SPEED	24m/sec
BLAST RADIUS	4m
SHOTS TO KILL (BASE)	1
SHOTS TO KILL (100/50)	2

AMMUNITION

STARTING AMMO	10
MAXIMUM AMMO	30
BIO-RIFLE AMMO	10
AMMO FROM WEAPON LOCKER	20

FLAK CANNON NOTES

Flak Master Award for 15 kills.

A staggering monster at close-range, the Flak Cannon is premiere Unreal short-range slaughtering tool.

The Flak Cannon primary fire shoots out a cloud of flak shards, each dealing heavy damage. In addition, the central shard deals *massive* damage when fired at point blank range.

FLAK HEART

The central shard damage bonus is time dependant, and location dependant. If the shard hits a player within .2 seconds of being fired (very short range), it gets the damage bonus.

How much of the damage bonus is determined by the hit location, the closer to the center of your target you hit, the higher the damage is, while a glancing hit at the edge of the player deals less.

Calculations aside, you can safely assume that any sort of point blank shot is going to be lethal to all but the most absolutely tanked up of targets.

While the Flak Cannon's primary fire launches a spray of shards in a shotgun-like manner, it is *not* a shotgun, as the shards are projectiles, and the travel time means that at any range beyond ultra-close in battles, you must predict the movement of your target slightly.

Note that the flak shards can also bounce twice when they impact a surface, so with some practice, you can bank shots off walls, floors, or even ceilings to hit targets at odd angles. Because so many Unreal levels have widely varying terrain, performing such shots consistently is tricky, but on maps or in areas with more "normal" halls and rooms, you can often make bank shots with some degree of accuracy.

While the Flak Cannon primary fire is ultra-lethal at close-range, it is very much designed for close-range combat *only*. To that end, the flak shards lose damage as they travel, eventually decreasing all the way down to a mere 5 damage per shard. When combined with their natural spread as they travel, you aren't going to be threatening any snipers.

Fortunately, while the Flak primary is meant for short or short-medium range engagements in tight terrain, its secondary fire adds some versatility to the weapon.

COVER ME

At medium range, the Flak Cannon isn't the best weapon, but you can still deal solid damage with the primary fire, and if they are close enough, using secondary fire can be quite effective as well.

Because you have a relatively long reload between shots (at least compared to many other weapons), try to duck behind any available cover between shots, leaping out to fire, and then move back out of sight.

At extremely close-range, you should be aggressively sticking to your target to land a lethal primary fire shot, but at medium range, your flak loses effectiveness, and you may need to rely more on your secondary fire, which usually means you need more time to kill your target. More time in the open is bad against several weapons, so use any cover you can find.

The Flak Cannon secondary fire launches the entire flak canister as a tumbling arcing projectile, which detonates on impact, spraying a few shards around.

The flak shell is quite damaging, and nearly as effective as a rocket from the Rocket launcher. In addition, the unusual arcing flight of the shell makes it a great weapon for lobbing up onto higher terrain.

Don't expect the extra shards from the flak shell detonation to greatly assist in adding bonus damage, they're a nice extra perk if they happen to ricochet and deal some extra damage, but they're too random to be a predictable source of damage.

Because the primary and secondary fire share identical reload times, you should feel free to mix up your shots as you move and dodge in combat with an opponent. As they move farther away, or behind cover, lob a flak shell. If they're moving towards you, at close-range, or moving into a tight space, use the primary fire.

Landing hits with both the primary and secondary fire modes of the Flak Cannon requires some practice. Both are essentially slow firing targeted projectile attacks, and if your prediction abilities are poor, against an agile opponent, you can deal precisely zero damage over several shots—a frustrating experience, to say the least.

A related concern—be careful about getting lured into charging opponents just because you have the Flak Cannon in your possession. Savvy foes will backpedal nearly as quickly as you can charge, and if you're walking into a Shock Combo, you are not long for this world.

Instead, you should seek out terrain that favors the Flak Cannon to begin with, rather than aggressively chasing alert opponents and trying to close the distance while they're firing at you with long or mid-range weaponry.

Only a perfectly targeted triple rocket barrage can eclipse the potential damage dealt by the Flak Cannon at close-range. Learn to use this weapon well, and you become a serious danger in all close-range engagements. As the Sniper Rifle is to long-range engagement, the Flak Cannon is to close-range brawls.

DUELS

A superb weapon to ambush with, a dangerous weapon to approach with. Only a foolish opponent is going to willingly engage you at close-range if you're firing flak shots, instead, they'll try to lure you into a Shock Combo, a rocket barrage, or some other sort of nasty mid or long-range threat. However, if you do manage to get up close and personal, if your aim is good, you can take down even a heavily armored foe with just one or two shots.

The Flak Cannon is overwhelmingly powerful on small maps, and still quite strong on even larger maps that have many interior areas or cramped spaces. It is considerably less effective in wide open terrain, where its comparatively slow shots can be dodged, and the damage fading of the primary fire becomes a detriment to its effectiveness.

TEAM DEATHMATCH

A great weapon to cover any cramped interior space. Set up shop guarding a key power-up or armor location, and lay waste to any opposing players who approach you. With early warning from your teammates, you can be ready for any approach to your area.

In terms of chasing and general combat, the Flak Cannon isn't always the weapon of choice, as it is only middling at medium range, even with its secondary fire helping its effectiveness. It is also dangerous to be using in a close-range fight around teammates if team damage is enabled.

DEATHMATCH

Very strong. You can hunt down players in any tight corridors or rooms and lay down a beating with the primary fire, and the secondary fire gives you a heavily damaging weapon for short-medium range engagements. It's also great to lob into the middle of a multi-player firefight.

Because the Flak Cannon has heavily front-loaded damage, it is ideal for rapidly taking down freshly spawned players, as long as you can get into range.

CTF

Not bad for defending chokepoints, if you can catch players in narrow spaces before they can translocate, it can be lethal. Solid for defending the area immediately around the flag, since enemy flag runners have to pick up the flag and then leave while you're engaging them.

Also not a bad weapon for flag running while in narrow halls, as the secondary fire can be used to leave presents behind you as you run, as long as you're skilled in both wall dodging and spinning to fire shots behind you.

VCTF AND WARFARE

Generally not a great weapon to be using as you move around the maps. Secondary fire does have a substantial knockback effect against vehicles, but its lack of range often puts you at risk of being run down or blasted with heavy vehicle weaponry.

Primary fire is great against Nodes up close, as it can tear them down rapidly at point blank range.

In Warfare, some Nodes have interior terrain that is restrictive for vehicles to access, the Flak Cannon can often be used quite effectively against players on foot in these locations.

VS. BIO RIFLE

Almost completely dominant, with the only exception being the chance of running into a fully charged secondary shot. Otherwise, barring a huge skill disparity, you should always come out on top in this battle.

At medium range, you may eat some damage from sludge spray, but your flak shells are much more individually lethal.

VS. ENFORCER

Great at close-range, ok at medium range. Neither of you are great at long-range, switch weapons or get closer.

VS. LINK GUN

Great at close-range, and solid at medium range. Just outside your lethal flak range, the Link Gun has enough range to unleash a hail of lethal plasma. You generally don't have to worry too much about the secondary beam unless you have no extra health or armor at all, and their aim is incredibly good. One flak shell to the face is often enough to stop an annoying shaft user.

VS. ROCKET LAUNCHER

A hard battle, the Rocket Launcher is nearly as lethal at close-range as the Flak Cannon, and at medium range, it is slightly superior, with direct fire shots that reload ever so slightly faster.

Frequently an entertaining battle if you enjoy fast paced dodging, but also a dangerous fight to engage in if you're looking for a clean victory. Even if you do manage to paste the rocket user, odds are, you're going to eat a good bit of splash damage doing so.

VS. SHOCK RIFLE

Good up close, not at all good at medium range. At just about the range where using the Flak Cannon becomes less effective, the Shock Rifle becomes incredibly dangerous.

Most skilled Shock Rifle users are also extremely familiar with Flak users trying to close the distance with them, so be extremely careful about rushing a Shock Rifle user who is aware of your presence. If they *aren't* aware, you may be able to close the distance quickly and engage from close-range, but be careful if the terrain doesn't favor an ambush.

At long-range, take cover or use a different weapon, rather than getting picked apart while you ineffectually launch shards.

VS. SNIPER RIFLE

You know this one. Long-range is bad, close-range is good. Medium range isn't great here either, even with its longer reload time, the Sniper Rifle is pinpoint accurate at medium range even while dodging, and your shots are not.

VS. STINGER

Great up close, tricky at medium range. On open ground, this is generally a suicidal engagement, but if there is enough cover, you may be able to come out standing.

If your opponent is impatient, let them burn down their ammo while you pop out occasionally to fire at them and keep their interest. When they run out, you can rush in during the brief delay as they switch weapons. Even if they stop firing, you can rush them, as it takes time for the Stinger to fully spin up to lethal speed.

VS. VEHICLES

Not good, though you can use secondary flak shells to give light vehicles a serious concussion; the knockback is quite substantial.

ROCKET LAUNCHER

EQUIP TIME 0.6 SECONDS
PUTDOWN TIME 0.33 SECONDS

PRIMARY FIRE

Shots to Kill in parenthesis denote close-range detonations dealing 50% damage (you planted a rocket right at the foot of your target, hitting them for 50 points of splash damage).

CLASSIFICATION	PROJECTILE
DAMAGE	100
VEHICLE DAMAGE	80%
NODE DAMAGE	110%
RATE OF FIRE	1.0
SPLASH RADIUS	4.4m
PROJECTILE SPEED	27m/sec
SHOTS TO KILL (BASE)	1 (2)
SHOTS TO KILL (100/50)	2 (3)

SECONDARY FIRE

Both secondary fire modes can be held for nearly a second after being fully loaded, giving you a moment to line up your shot.

CLASSIFICATION	PROJECTILE
DAMAGE	100-300
VEHICLE DAMAGE	80%
NODE DAMAGE	110%
RATE OF FIRE	Varies, around 2.5 seconds to fully load
COOL DOWN	0.44 seconds
SPLASH RADIUS	4.4m (per individual rocket)
PROJECTILE SPEED	27m/sec
SHOTS TO KILL (BASE)	Varies, one if loaded
SHOTS TO KILL (100/50)	Varies, one if loaded

AMMUNITION

STARTING AMMO	9
MAXIMUM AMMO	30
ROCKET PACK	9
AMMO FROM WEAPON LOCKER	18

ROCKET LAUNCHER NOTES

Lock on can be acquired after tracking a target for 1.1 seconds, at a maximum range of 180m.

Rocket Scientist Award for 15 kills with the Rocket Launcher.

GRENADES

CLASSIFICATION	PROJECTILE
DAMAGE	100-300
VEHICLE DAMAGE	80%
NODE DAMAGE	110%
RATE OF FIRE	Varies, around 2.5 seconds to fully load
COOL DOWN	0.44 seconds
SPLASH RADIUS	4m
PROJECTILE SPEED	14m/sec
SHOTS TO KILL (BASE)	Varies, one if loaded
SHOTS TO KILL (100/50)	Varies, one if loaded

The Rocket Launcher is a highly versatile close and mid-range weapon, dealing high damage per shot, with a large splash radius that can be used to deal damage even if your opponent is adept at dodging. It is also extremely flexible, with multiple secondary fire modes, and a lock-on capability that is useful against vehicles and helpful against targets at mid-range on open ground.

Primary fire launches a single rocket, which moves at a decent speed. It's fast enough to hit targets at close-range nearly instantly, and farther out at medium range fast enough to be a threat if you can predict your targets movement well.

Prediction is a key component of fighting well with the Rocket Launcher in any situation—because of the projectile travel time, and splash damage, you need to be planting rockets right at the feet of your opponent to deal damage efficiently.

While rockets deal heavy damage on a direct hit, landing such a hit isn't easy anywhere beyond extremely short range. Instead, most of your damage is going to come from splash, by detonating rockets at the feet of your target.

Landing hits *near* your target is considerably easier than hitting your target directly. Even if your opponent jumps or dodges, if your shot is well aimed, they're going to take some damage.

Secondary fire is highly versatile. Holding secondary fire loads up to three rockets, which can then be fired in a horizontal spread pattern. The blast from a triple rocket barrage is enough to take down all but the most heavily armored of foes.

If you tap primary fire while loading up rockets, you change the firing pattern from a spread to a tight spiral. It's useful for dealing maximum damage on a single

point, such as an opponent chasing you around a corner, or ducking out from behind cover to launch a barrage at a slow vehicle.

Pressing primary fire twice while loading rockets disables the rocket's propellant, and instead launches the rocket casings as grenades. The bouncing of these explosives is highly unpredictable, but they are useful for lobbing down narrow hallways, and are also the only effective use of the Rocket Launcher against a target concealed on an elevated ledge or cliff of any sort.

As if that wasn't enough, while firing rockets with secondary fire (either spread or spiral), you can lock on to any player or vehicle by holding your crosshair on them for just over a second. Once you have achieved a lock, you can release secondary fire to instantly launch the rockets with a slight homing capability active.

This homing is rarely enough to impact on an alert player who knows you are firing at them, but they are quite handy for shooting at distant players involved in firefights, or at large or slow moving vehicles.

Loading secondary fire gives you a terribly nasty close-range damage payload, but unlike the Bio Rifle secondary, you cannot hold the shots indefinitely. Once fully loaded, you only have about a second to release the rockets before they fire automatically.

However, because the time from the first rocket loaded (which takes less than a second) to the time you are fully loaded is several seconds, you can begin loading rockets when you *know* you are going into an engagement, or if you know you are being pursued by another player. At worst, you release a single rocket, and more likely, two or three.

Do *not* use secondary fire while engaged in an active battle with another player unless they are using a poor close-range weapon or you are confident you can avoid or absorb their fire while loading up shots. Almost always, you're better off firing primary shots to bounce your opponent around and deal constant damage to kill them as quickly as possible. Secondary fire is *always* slower than primary for launching single rockets.

Ammo is often an issue with the Rocket Launcher. Lobbing rockets towards targets at medium range involves a lot of weak hits and misses, causing you to deplete your ammo supply quickly. Remember the locations of rocket ammo on the map you're playing on if you plan to be using it heavily.

Don't be stingy with your shots with the Rocket Launcher. Ideally you should be using the delay between each shot to perfectly line up your next, so there is never a pause in your fire. In addition, firing rockets continuously at a key entrance is a potent suppressive technique, as it is difficult to get past the blast radius without taking damage. Enemies tend to be reluctant to go through it, much like a spray of Link plasma.

The Rocket Launcher is a strong and flexible weapon, learn to use it well and it can become a powerful part of your arsenal.

DUELS

A solid weapon, the front-loaded damage makes it a threat, and you can use its various fire modes to good effect. Knowing where your opponent is and loading up rockets in advance of engaging is a common and strong tactic. Grenades also give you a bit of flexibility for dealing with odd terrain.

TEAM DEATHMATCH

Again, an amazingly useful weapon, just be extremely careful if you're playing with team damage enabled. Rocket splash is easy to harm teammates with.

Ideally, in a TDM match, you should be covering a location that has favorable terrain for the Rocket Launcher. Cover for you to use between shots is helpful, as is elevation. Landing splash hits on targets below you is easy, and if you're set up guarding a location with just such a setup, you can cause serious problems for enemy players entering the area.

DEATHMATCH

A strong weapon, as it can take out most players in just a few shots, and its splash damage makes it powerful against packs of players as well. The fact that you can load up more rockets before coming around a corner into a mixed firefight is yet another bonus, as a triple rocket barrage is usually fatal for whoever you aim at, and the collateral damage makes for easy finishing of anyone who was too close to the blast.

CTF

Solid on offense, and not bad for flag running, since you can periodically turn and sling rockets or grenades behind you. On defense, there are generally better weapons for punishing flag carriers, though you can wait for an enemy to enter the vicinity of the flag and start loading rockets. Unless they engage you immediately, if they go for the flag, you can have a triple rocket barrage waiting for them.

Chasing flag carriers or firing at translocating players is not especially effective with the Rocket Launcher however, so you're usually going to be using it either on flag defenders, or while running with the flag.

VCTF AND WARFARE

Decent against vehicles, and good against Nodes.

Primary fire deals nice steady damage against Nodes, which is handy if you're firing from a good distance away.

Against vehicles, charge up secondary fire and unload a barrage with a lock. On open ground, only amazingly agile vehicles can avoid the tracking, and slower vehicles are basically guaranteed to be hit. Fully loaded secondary fire is basically a substitute AVRiL.

VS. BIO RIFLE

Good in all situations except those involving a fully loaded secondary Bio Rifle shot and your face.

VS. ENFORCER

Good at close or medium range. Long-range usually isn't worth the trouble of engaging, either get closer while loading up some shots, or use a different weapon.

VS. FLAK CANNON

A messy fight. At extreme close-range, the Flak Cannon has the advantage, but at greater distances, the fight is much more even. Both weapons tend to deal partial damage every shot, though it is *generally* easier to land rocket splash hits than flak shard hits.

Be ready for flak shell shots, they are nearly as fast and have almost as much splash as your rockets, making medium range a tricky engagement as well.

Generally, maintaining some distance makes this a safer battle.

VS. LINK GUN

Comfortable at medium range, and good up close if you get the drop on them. If they're aware of your approach, be careful— walking into plasma streams is not healthy.

VS. SHOCK RIFLE

Good at close-range, dicey at medium range. At the range where the Shock Combo comes into play, fighting with the Shock Rifle user is dangerous. In addition, accurate primary Shock Rifle shots can hurt you badly while you're trying to score lightly damaging medium range splash. Bad at long-range, the Shock Rifle primary fire can tear you up and you can't retaliate effectively.

VS. SNIPER RIFLE

Dreadful at a distance, and not amazing at medium range, largely because a Sniper Rifle user is usually going to be seeking to gain distance from you, or they'll make use of cover and take potshots at you while ducking out of sight to reload.

You do have the advantage of indirect fire and splash though, so if you can make use of cover of your own, you can usually manage to deal damage more safely.

VS. STINGER

Awful on open ground, otherwise, quite good at medium or close-range. Up close, you may take some pain from the Stinger, but you can usually down your opponent faster than they can manage to take you out.

At medium range, make use of cover to fight, otherwise, disengage. You don't want a fully spun up Stinger firing at you while you lob rockets in return.

VS. VEHICLES

Solid, decent damage with lock-ons, but because you usually need to load up shots, and then get a lock on to fire, this is a time consuming process. In other words, don't try this against a Manta or Viper bearing down on you.

SNIPER RIFLE

EQUIP TIME 0.6 SECONDS
PUTDOWN TIME 0.45 SECONDS

PRIMARY FIRE

CLASSIFICATION	INSTANT HIT
DAMAGE	70
VEHICLE DAMAGE	40%
NODE DAMAGE	40%
RATE OF FIRE	1.33
SHOTS TO KILL (BASE)	2
SHOTS TO KILL (100/50)	3

AMMUNITION

STARTING AMMO	10
MAXIMUM AMMO	40
BIO-RIFLE AMMO	10
AMMO FROM WEAPON LOCKER	10

SNIPER RIFLE NOTES

Headshots (zoomed or not) deal 150 damage. 15 headshot kills gives the Headhunter Award.

SECONDARY FIRE

CLASSIFICATION	SPECIAL

Secondary fire allows the Sniper Rifle to zoom in.

The Sniper Rifle is the pre-eminent long-range weapon in the game, so effective in fact, that a skilled player with a Sniper Rifle in a VCTF or Warfare match can suppress an entire enemy infantry advance if not dealt with.

The Sniper Rifle deals heavy damage on any hit, but headshots are nearly always lethal, as they deal 150 damage. Only well armored targets can survive such a hit, and even if they do, they're going to be crippled, and easy prey for you or any teammates nearby.

Appropriately, the Helmet armor provides protection against headshots, though there isn't any way for you to know this while you're shooting at a target. Any hit on a target wearing a Helmet strips the Helmet armor completely, but deals no other damage to the target.

To score a headshot, you normally must hit a sphere around the head of your target, a bit larger than the head itself. However, if you are moving, headshots can ONLY be scored directly against the head.

HEADSHOT!

Remember, when you are stationary, headshots are *easier* to land, as the target zone for a headshot is ever so slightly larger than the players head.

If you are moving at all, the target zone becomes literally the head only, which is an extremely difficult target to hit, at any range.

In practice, this means that scoring headshots at a distance while zoomed is a bit easier, and trying to score a headshot while dodging rockets at close-range is considerably more difficult.

The bonus hit zone around a players head while stationary encourages use of the Sniper Rifle at long-range, while comfortable ensconced in a nice sniper perch, preferably an area where you have clean sight lines, and difficult terrain for an enemy to flank you or get behind you while you're comfortably camping.

The Sniper Rifle has both a steep and a rewarding learning curve. As an instant hit weapon with perfect accuracy, it can become an *incredibly* lethal weapon in the hands of a skilled player. Your opponents have no recourse against superb aim with this weapon. If you can target them accurately in mid-dodge, the only way to avoid being shot is to not be seen in the first place.

Up close, the Sniper Rifle's lengthy reload time makes it a poor weapon to use, but even at medium range, if you can dodge well, it is still a dangerous weapon. 70 damage is a lot and, if you score a headshot, you're usually the one walking away from the fight.

Curiously, the Sniper Rifle has a damage bonus against light vehicles, specifically the Manta, Viper, and Scorpion. This additional 50% damage bonus, applied after the penalty against vehicles, results in the Sniper round dealing 42 damage to light vehicles. It still takes 5 shots to down a Manta or Viper, but as you can score headshots against players in those vehicles, at least you get a bit of added damage if you miss the headshot.

The Sniper Rifle is a powerful weapon in the right hands, but it can be frustratingly difficult for a new player. It requires steady aim, and there is no reward for a near miss. In addition, real long-range sniping plays differently than any other on-foot combat with the other weapons.

Becoming a skillful sniper requires steady aim, concentration, and a lot of practice, but the rewards are substantial. Good snipers are a powerful asset on most VCTF and Warfare maps, and they can be deadly on some CTF and DM maps as well.

FIGHTING SNIPERS

Being on the receiving end of a headshot from long-range (or more frustratingly, up close) is rarely a pleasant experience. One moment you're running to your next destination, the next, you're headless.

It is important that you recognize when a sniper is active in the area you're fighting in, and learn how to avoid or deal with the sniper.

Much like the Shock Combo, which is incredibly dangerous in certain situations at medium range, the Sniper Rifle is so powerful at long-range that it is important to know how you can deal with the weapon.

Flatly, at long-range, you *can't* deal with the Sniper Rifle. You have three options; one, get out of sight and avoid the sniper's line of fire entirely. Two, bring a vehicle. The Sniper Rifle does poor damage to vehicles. Three, you can counter-snipe. Sometimes the best answer for one headshot is another.

Closer in, your options open up. The Shock Rifle is just as accurate as the Sniper Rifle, and fires more quickly, so you have a roughly even chance of coming out on top, pitting your accuracy against your opponent's, barring headshots.

Most medium range weapons also work fairly well against the Sniper Rifle, its lengthy reload gives you time to get in a lot of shots with rapid fire weapons, or a chance to maneuver—either closer to your target, or out of sight completely.

In some cases, you may simply have to accept a death from the Sniper Rifle at range and then use the knowledge of their position to retaliate. Watch for the tracer from the sniper bullets. If they miss a shot, the lengthy tracer points a finger back at your erstwhile assassin. Get behind cover and find a safe route to the sniper.

Several weapons aren't bad for forcing a sniper to move. Remember, if the person using the Sniper Rifle is moving, headshots are harder to land. Spray Link Gun primary fire, rockets, Shock Rifle fire, even Stinger secondary shards.

Anything to force a stationary sniper at a distance to move is worth the ammo. Better down a few shots than dead, all you need to do is buy a bit of time to get closer to the sniper (or to bypass them completely on the way to another goal).

DUELS

The effectiveness of the Sniper Rifle in duels varies hugely based on your personal skill with the weapon. While most duels are fought on close to mid-range style maps, the Sniper Rifle can still be used to deadly effect even at medium range, or at short range with the proper terrain (by taking a quick shot, then backing off rapidly).

Headshots are a huge momentum shifter, as only the Flak Cannon at close-range can deal out as much damage as quickly. The Bio Rifle secondary, Shock Combo, and Rocket Launcher secondary all require more time to approach the damage of a headshot.

Remember that standing still even for a split-second increases the area you can score a headshot, so if you're going for upper body hits naturally, try to incorporate a quick stop-shoot-move sequence into your normal dodging and evasive movement patterns.

TEAM DEATHMATCH

The best weapon for covering open spaces, backed up by a good close-range fighter nearby, you can provide serious coverage for your team, and act as area denial, potentially protecting key resources for your team.

DEATHMATCH

Generally not an amazing weapon for racking up frags quickly, unless your accuracy is superb. Also, finding a peaceful place to perform long-range stationary sniping from is usually quite difficult, and at shorter ranges, the reload time on the Sniper Rifle makes it unimpressive for large brawls.

CTF

Fantastic for defense on many maps. Sniping can often be used for aggressive forward defense, damaging or killing incoming players even if they are translocating rapidly (the Sniper Rifle is one of the few weapons that can take advantage of the momentary Translocator delay).

Also a great weapon for last second saves on flag runners, as it is the only weapon besides the Shock Rifle that can potentially stop a distant flag carrier.

VCTF AND WARFARE

Fantastic for defense, and often good for offense as well. Because both game types have large open spaces, and often have many great sniper perches, the Sniper Rifle is frequently quite powerful.

It is also extremely helpful in VCTF for killing escaping flag runners, and in Warfare, you can use it to "start the assault" on a Node by hitting the Node from a distance to stop respawns, then focus on the players immediately around the Node. Hit the Node every third or fourth shot to keep respawns shutdown while your teammates move in, and you can be a great help in clearing a Node completely.

The Sniper Rifle is assumed to be superior at long-range to all other weapons, and inferior at close-range. Commentary focuses on medium range engagements.

VS. BIO RIFLE

Messy most of the time, with goop flying all over the place and the odd explosion jostling your aim, you may frequently come out of this battle more heavily damaged than you might like.

VS. ENFORCER

Much of this comes down to the discipline of the Enforcer user and the terrain—if they fire shots rapidly, the inaccuracy should give you the edge you need to win the fight, but if they stagger their shots and use cover, you can take a surprising amount of damage in this fight. A pretty serious accuracy duel, but you have the advantage of much heavier frontloaded damage. Score a single shot and switch weapons to finish the fight.

VS. FLAK CANNON

Usually a pretty good match up, just watch out for well aimed flak shells, the Flak Cannon still has a fair amount of bite at medium range.

VS. LINK GUN

Rather good with cover, as you can duck out of sight and leap out to take shots. In constrained hallways or narrow spaces, usually not a good battle to get into. On more open ground, you have more room to dodge around, but avoiding all the incoming spray is hard, and if you're just close enough for the shaft to reach you, you're going to take a lot of damage if you do come out alive.

VS. ROCKET LAUNCHER

Usually good, but much of this comes down to the terrain. Some medium range engagements are easy for rocket users to nail splash damage hits in, and without cover, you can take a lot of damage or go down before you score the hits needed to kill your target.

VS. SHOCK RIFLE

For the instant hit weapons, this is much like the flak/rocket dual. It's close to even, much of the battle coming down to the accuracy of each player. Watch out for Shock Combos though, they can end the battle very quickly indeed.

VS. STINGER

Horrible on open ground, but solid if you have cover to dodge behind while reloading. Also quite good if you can get an elevation advantage and duck in and out of sight.

VS. VEHICLES

Generally rather bad, outside the special ability to snipe Viper or Manta pilots.

You *can* hit vehicles easily at any range, you just aren't going to do much damage in the process. If anything, save your sniping for airborne vehicles, which are hard for most other weapons to hit.

LONGBOW AVRIL

EQUIP TIME | 0.75 SECONDS
PUTDOWN TIME | 0.45 SECONDS

PRIMARY FIRE

CLASSIFICATION	PROJECTILE

Primary fire is a "light" lock on any enemy vehicle.

DAMAGE	200 (125 against players and Nodes, 200 vs. vehicles)
RATE OF FIRE	1 second to fire, 3 seconds to reload
SPLASH RADIUS	3m
PROJECTILE SPEED	11m/sec, accelerating to 56m/sec by 15m/sec
KNOCKBACK	150k

AMMUNITION

STARTING AMMO	5
MAXIMUM AMMO	15
LONGBOW AVRIL AMMO	5
AMMO FROM WEAPON LOCKER	5

AVRIL NOTES

AVRiL rockets CAN be shot down. Raptors have a slight hitbox bonus against them with primary fire.

Scoring 15 vehicle kills with the AVRiL nets the Big Game Hunter Award.

SECONDARY FIRE

CLASSIFICATION	SPECIAL

Projects a targeting laser that results in a "hard" lock on enemy vehicles, guiding the missile unerringly to its target. Can also be used to "herd" Spider Mines, up to 8 at a time.

The AVRiL (Anti Vehicle Rocket Launcher) does exactly what it says. It hits vehicles hard, and hits them easily. When a light vehicle is barreling down on you at high speed, the AVRiL is your weapon of choice for blasting the threat into a smoldering wreck.

The AVRiL Longbow is a critical weapon in both game modes that include vehicles, as it deals high damage, automatically locks on to vehicles, and can be manually guided with secondary fire.

The Longbow has a lengthy reload time, so it is best used from behind cover at a distance, where you can duck in and out between shots. Light vehicles can be vaporized instantly with a single hit, and even heavier vehicles can't take many shots.

Two players on defense with AVRiLs ready can shut down nearly any vehicle, and on offense, bringing AVRiL's along can help you break down vehicle defenses near the flag or a Node.

Always be sure to locate the Longbow spawn points, if you spawn even somewhat near it, you should usually take the time to pick it up, unless you have a time critical mission to take complete. In Warfare, you can take teleports to pick up an AVRiL if your spawn location doesn't have one nearby.

The AVRiL is, unsurprisingly, an awful weapon against other players. It is (at best) an extremely slow Rocket Launcher—not what you want to be using in any serious fight (though good for humiliating a target, if you're feeling particularly nasty).

If you're targeted by an AVRiL lock-on, you receive an audible warning, and you have a split second to decide if you can attempt to shoot down the missile, take the hit, evade, or bail out. If you're in a light vehicle (notably the Manta, Scavenger, or Viper), you're usually best served by getting out immediately, you can't take even a single shot).

REDEEMER

EQUIP TIME ┊ 2 SECONDS
PUTDOWN TIME ┊ 1.6 SECONDS

PRIMARY FIRE

CLASSIFICATION	PROJECTILE

The Redeemer blast deals its damage in multiple repeating "waves", each projecting out to a greater distance until the maximum distance is reached. It deals damage a total six times, at ranges of 12.5% of maximum, then 30%, 47%, 65%, 82.5%, and finally 100% (40m). The waves go out first at 500ms after impact, then 200ms for each additional wave. 0.9 seconds after detonation it causes knockdown. The Redeemer instantly destroys Nodes, but only deals about 1000 damage to a Power Core.

DAMAGE	250
SPLASH RADIUS	40m
PROJECTILE SPEED	20m/sec
SHOTS TO KILL (BASE)	1
SHOTS TO KILL (100/50)	1

AMMUNITION

STARTING AMMO	1
MAXIMUM AMMO	1
AMMO FROM PICK-UP	N/A
AMMO FROM WEAPON LOCKER	N/A

REDEEMER NOTES

150% against vehicles

SECONDARY FIRE

CLASSIFICATION	SPECIAL

Secondary fire allows the Redeemer to be remotely controlled.

The Redeemer is a massively powerful weapon, capable of vaporizing infantry, destroying nearly any vehicle in a single shot, and crushing Nodes in one hit.

As a powerful super weapon, it only has a single shot, and a lengthy respawn time, so when you get your hands on this hardware, make good use of it. On the few Deathmatch and CTF maps it is present in, it is massive overkill (though great for clearing out flag defenders in CTF). In VCTF and Warfare however, it is an important tactical weapon, as it can punch a hole in solid defenses, or break a Node more safely than even an active Orb.

Secondary fire with the Redeemer allows you to enter guided mode, which lets you manually steer the Redeemer while it is in flight. This is handy for hitting a distant target without exposing yourself to risk, and on larger maps, you can plant yourself somewhere quite safe and still devastate a distant target, even behind tricky terrain.

Note that the Redeemer *can* be destroyed in mid-air, much like the AVRiL rockets. An alert defender may be able to take it out, so try to either take your shot from short range with primary fire, or come in from an odd angle with secondary fire.

Other than the Shaped Charge, the Redeemer is the only other weapon capable of destroying Barricades on certain maps.

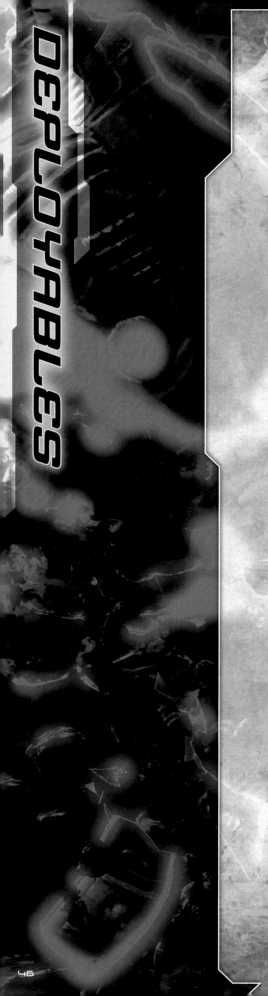
Deployable items are a special class of weaponry, either picked up as a sort of power-up and dropped to activate, or deployed by the Necris Nightshade. Most are fairly straightforward in their behavior, all are quite helpful when used well.

MOBILE TRAPS!

One absurdly cool trick you can pull off with some of the deployable items is attaching them to vehicles. Get a Spider Mine stuck to a flying vehicle and you've got a flying bomber.

Stick an EMP on a ground vehicle, and you can do a drive-by EMP blast on enemy vehicles!

Drop an Energy Shield onto a friendly vehicle, and you have a mobile barrier that can be used to screen friendlies from enemy fire, or protect you as you move towards a key location.

SHAPED CHARGE

The Shaped Charge is a powerful explosive, usually used for either destroying Barricades, or blasting Nodes with a massive explosion.

The Shaped Charge has a lengthy delay before it detonates once placed, so it is difficult to use against mobile targets. You might be able to surprise an advancing push of players on foot, or nail a slow moving vehicle, but generally, it is best used against its primary targets.

The Shaped Charge takes 10 seconds to detonate once planted, has a 60 second respawn timer, and deals 1200 damage to any target. The blast radius is 10m.

SPIDER MINE

The Spider Mine Trap is a powerful anti-vehicle defense weapon, and also helpful against players. Once the trap is placed, any enemy presence within a short distance triggers the walking mines within the trap, which emerge and scuttle toward their prey rapidly.

Fast moving vehicles that graze the detection zone may escape unharmed, but unaware marks that drive over the trap are likely to end up as bits of fiery wreckage. Slow vehicles anywhere near a trap are as good as dead.

Spider Mine Traps have 15 Spiders within, and usually around 8 to 10 emerge to chase a nearby target. The Spider Mine Trap itself lasts for two and a half minutes, has a 30m detection range, and anadditional 15m as the Spiders can chase a target.

Spider Mines deal 95 damage on contact, with a 5m blast radius.

HERDING!

The AVRiL's secondary fire allows you to maintain a lock on vehicles; it also allows you to herd Spider Mines!

Direct the AVRiL's laser targeter to a friendly Spider Mine Trap, and watch the Spiders scuttle out to follow your team. You can then direct them freely, as soon as they get within range of a target, their automatic tracking takes over and they'll go on the attack.

EMP MINE

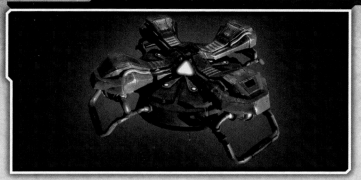

The EMP Mine is a helpful deployable against enemy vehicles. When a vehicle gets too close to the planted mine, it emits a devastating blast of energy that shuts down any vehicle in the vicinity.

The EMP Mine lasts for a decent amount of time once planted (60 seconds), and has no limit on the number of detonations, so once it is in place, you can be certain that no vehicles will be threatening you from whatever path you block off with it.

The EMP blast radius is 10m, and it disables vehicles for 20 seconds, plenty of time to destroy them, or kill their passenger.

The EMP does *not* trigger against cloaked vehicles.

STASIS FIELD

The Stasis Field is a unique deployable that creates a large rectangular area of "slow time', greatly slowing any vehicles, players, or projectiles that enter its area, and stopping instant hit weapons. This makes it ideal for blocking off an access route to a Node or flag area, as any players or vehicles that attempt to get through the field are so much fresh meat for defenders in the area.

Stasis Fields can be deployed by the Nightshade, or occasionally found as a pick-up on some levels.

Be aware that the Stasis Field has no friends once deployed. It can just as easily hamper your team, so be sure that you choose its deployment location carefully, and notify your team where it is positioned. Because most vehicles are considerably larger than players on foot, it is possible to deploy the field in such a way that a player can slip by one edge of the field that is blocked by terrain, something that can be quite handy for a flag runner returning to base.

Normally, the stasis field lasts for 3 minutes once deployed (180 seconds), however, any time a player or vehicle enters its area, it begins to "drain" at a rate of 3 extra seconds countdown per player or vehicle inside it. In other words, with three players inside, the 180 seconds would be draining at 10 seconds per second of real time (3 per player plus 1 for its normal decay).

There is one final extremely quirky use for the Stasis Field. Not only does it slow down players, vehicles, and projectiles, it actually slows down any item respawners located within it! Any respawn points the field covers causes the points to slow down by a factor of 8, meaning an item that respawns in 30 seconds would take 240 seconds! In practice, this means that items taken from inside the field won't respawn until the field itself is gone.

The Stasis Field can be set on flags or Nodes, but doing so causes it to drain by an extra 4.5 seconds (5.5 seconds per real second total), assuming no players or vehicles within it. This still allows the Stasis Field to be a significant obstacle for the offensive team, but it won't last for the full three minutes.

ENERGY SHIELD

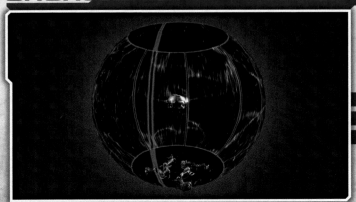

The Energy Shield is a defensive deployable, primarily useful from screening Nodes or flags from distant enemy fire. Once deployed, the Energy Shield creates a large, semi-spherical barrier that can soak up damage from enemy.

Duration	30s
Respawn Time	90s
Notes	1000 health per face, 6 faces

UT3 has a wide variety of items and power-ups scattered about the various levels. Most are fairly simple (health, ammo, and armor for example), but the respawn times on power-ups are particularly important, and some extra information on key pick-ups is included here as well.

AMMUNITION

ENFORCER

Ammo Amount	16
Respawn Time	30s

BIO-RIFLE

Ammo Amount	10
Respawn Time	30s

SHOCK RIFLE

Ammo Amount	10
Respawn Time	30s

LINK GUN

Ammo Amount	50
Respawn Time	30s

STINGER

Ammo Amount	50
Respawn Time	30s

FLAK CANNON

Ammo Amount	10
Respawn Time	30s

ROCKET LAUNCHER

Ammo Amount	9
Respawn Time	30s

SNIPER RIFLE

Ammo Amount	10
Respawn Time	30s

AVRIL

Ammo Amount	5
Respawn Time	30s

HEALTH ITEMS

HEALTH VIAL

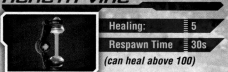

Healing:	5
Respawn Time	30s

(can heal above 100)

HEALTH

Healing:	25
Respawn Time	30s

BIG KEG'O'HEALTH

Healing:	100
Respawn Time	60s

(can heal above 100)

ARMOR

Armor absorbs damage from the strongest item to the weakest. In other words, the Shield Belt takes damage first, then if you have them, the Body Armor, Thighpads, and last the Helmet.

The Helmet is a special exception if you take a headshot from the Sniper Rifle (even with a Shield Belt active), as it destroys the Helmet completely and nullifies the headshot.

HELMET

Armor	20
Damage Absorption	20%
Respawn Time	30s

The Helmet offers special protection against Helmet headshots, if you have even 1 armor from a Helmet left, it completely absorbs a single headshot, removing any remaining Helmet armor.

THIGHPADS

Armor	30
Damage Absorption	30%
Respawn Time	30s

BODY ARMOR

Armor	50
Damage Absorption	50%
Respawn Time	30s

SHIELD BELT

Armor	100
Damage Absorption	100%
Respawn Time	60s

The Shield Belt can be knocked off of you if you are hit by the Impact Hammer secondary fire.

POWER-UPS

All power-ups can be knocked off of you if you are hit with the Impact Hammer secondary fire. They also drop if you are killed before their duration has expired.

Berserk and UDamage both apply to vehicles!

JUMP BOOTS

Duration	3 super jumps
Respawn Time	60s

Effect: Grants a 15m jump height. Activates upon double jumping. Also grants a 15m additional "grace" height before you take falling damage, added atop the normal distance you can fall without being injured.

UDAMAGE

Duration	30s
Respawn Time	90s

Effect: Double Damage. UDamage makes instant hit weaponry exceptionally dangerous, and splash weapons become easy to score kills with as well.

BERSERK

Duration	30s
Respawn Time	90s

Effect: Double Firing Speed. For "beam" type weapons (like the Link Gun secondary fire), it doubles their rate of damage. Berserk also grants FULL ammunition for all weapons you are holding when you pick it up.

Berserk turns rapid-fire weapons into lethal killing machines, as the huge stream of shots becomes harder to avoid.

INVISIBILITY

Duration	30s
Respawn Time	90s

Effect: Cloaks you while active, making it difficult for other players to spot you.

INVINCIBILITY

Duration	30s
Respawn Time	120s

Effect: Complete immunity to damage. Either hit the player using this with the Impact Hammer secondary, or avoid them entirely!

ROAD RAGE

Vehicles are a relatively new addition to the Unreal series, and they have enabled new types of vehicle-focused combat. In *UT3*, Vehicle CTF has been formally added to the list of gametypes, with six custom maps supporting vehicle combat and flag running action. Warfare is a new gametype, though it echoes strongly of Onslaught from *UT2K4*, with some aspects of Assault present. In Warfare, you struggle to capture and control nodes that open access to the enemy team's Power Core. Destroying the enemy Power Core earns victory for your team.

With the advent of the conflict between Axon and Necris forces, new Necris vehicles join the battle. In general, they tend to use energy powered weapons, and have unique forms of mobility in comparison to the more traditional (but still powerful) Axon vehicles.

Vehicles (and the vehicle gametypes) provide an entirely different layer of gameplay atop that present in Deathmatch or CTF. While all the weapons are present, and on-foot combat is still very important, learning to both use and fight against all the vehicles is critical for success in both VCTF and Warfare.

VEHICLE TYPES

The Axon and Necris vehicles are sharply differentiated in their physical appearance, weapon loadouts, and mobility. The various Axon vehicles tend to be recognizable (albeit futuristic) variations or extrapolations on "normal" human vehicle types. The Goliath is a massive tank, the Scorpion is a quick buggy, the Hellbender is a sturdy truck, and so on. Most (though not all) of the Axon vehicles are relatively straightforward, often tracked or wheeled.

The Necris vehicles on the other hand, are rather less recognizable. The Scavenger's passenger seat is the inside a transparent sphere, and it moves by dragging itself with sinuous tentacles, leaping, or retracting its "arms" and rolling rapidly across terrain. The monstrous Darkwalker is a three-legged battle tripod, with amazing vertical mobility, as it can freely stride across terrain that other ground vehicles could not hope to cover.

Learning to use *all* the vehicles is important, as different maps in VCTF and Warfare have different vehicle types present, and frequently, all must be used effectively to defeat your opposition.

Fortunately, doing so is not difficult. While the different Axon and Necris vehicles may have wildly differing mobility and appearances, the basic controls remain the same, and all you need to learn to use them effectively is their individual unique abilities.

THE HOVERBOARD

RESPAWN TIME N/A

HEALTH	N/A									
TOP SPEED	18m/sec									
MANEUVERABILITY	N/A									

PRIMARY FIRE		SECONDARY FIRE	
None		None	
TURRETS		SPECIAL ABILITIES	
None		None	

While any Hoverboard user can grapple onto a friendly vehicle, there is a limit to the number of players that can grapple onto a vehicle. Most smaller vehicles only allow a single player to attach, while larger vehicles provide two "hook" points for the Hoverboards.

SINGLE HOVERBOARD VEHICLES

Manta	Nightshade
Raptor	Scavenger
Scorpion	SPMA
Viper	

DOUBLE HOVERBOARD VEHICLES

Cicada	Fury
Goliath	Hellbender
Leviathan	Nemesis
Paladin	

The Hoverboard is a simple transport device used to zip around the battlefield in VCTF and Warfare games. You can even pull off stunts... Hold the crouch button and "prewind" a twist to either side to spin in midair, or tap secondary fire in midair to kick the board out. Of course, mess that up and you go sprawling.

And speaking of being sent flying, if you suffer *any* damage while on the Hoverboard, you are knocked flat on your face, stunned and unable to retaliate to any unfriendly presence in the area.

Use the Hoverboard to quickly get from place to place, but get off immediately if an enemy comes into view, or if you come under fire, unless you absolutely *must* keep moving (you're carrying the flag and praying fervently).

The Hoverboard gives you great forward momentum, use this even when you dismount. Instead of simply tapping the Hoverboard button again to get off, jump first, *then* dismount. Done properly, you get a nice surge of forward momentum, and you can even use this on ramps to send yourself flying through the air.

This is quite handy on plenty of the maps to quickly dismount and hit the ground running towards an interior area, or to get a bit of extra speed when you're being pursued, and you must dismount to avoid being knocked off your board.

Grappling onto vehicles generally requires a bit of teamwork, otherwise you may end up attached to someone in a Scorpion who isn't going anywhere near where you need to be.

In VCTF in particular, grappling onto a vehicle for flag transport is important. The Hoverboard is the only "vehicle" that the flag can be carried in, so grappling onto a faster (or flying!) vehicle can speed your return trip.

THE AXON RESEARCH CORPORATION [ARC]

A specialist in the development of military weapon systems, the Axon corporation has long been the biggest supplier of weaponry and vehicle systems for the New Earth Government's military forces. Their advanced technology was vital in the wars against the Skaarj, and it is just as important now during the conflict against the Necris forces.

CICADA

RESPAWN TIME 45 SECONDS

HEALTH	500	
TOP SPEED	40m/sec	
MANEUVERABILITY	High	
PRIMARY FIRE		SECONDARY FIRE
Drunken Missiles		Missile Barrage
TURRETS		SPECIAL ABILITIES
One, Underbelly		Lock-on

PRIMARY FIRE

CLASSIFICATION	PROJECTILE

Fires single drunken missiles that spiral down to impact and detonate on contact. These rockets only deal 80% damage to Nodes.

DAMAGE	50
RATE OF FIRE	0.25
SPLASH RADIUS	4.4m
PROJECTILE SPEED	20m/sec accelerating to 80m/sec by 15m/sec

SECONDARY FIRE

CLASSIFICATION	PROJECTILE

Loads up to 16 missiles, unleashing them to home in on a single target. These rockets only deal 80% damage to Nodes. The missiles' target location is set the instant you press and hold the secondary fire button.

DAMAGE	50
RATE OF FIRE	0.5
SPLASH RADIUS	4.4
PROJECTILE SPEED	20m/sec accelerating to 80m/sec by 15m/sec

CICADA NOTES

The Cicada is the only aerial vehicle that seats two.

TURRET PROFILE

UNDERBELLY

PRIMARY FIRE

CLASSIFICATION	INSTANT HIT

The underbelly Turret's primary fire is a rapidly firing, low damage energy Turret.

DAMAGE	25
RATE OF FIRE	0.2

SECONDARY FIRE

CLASSIFICATION	SPECIAL

The Cicada's Turret can launch flares capable of breaking an AVRiL lock.

RATE OF FIRE	1.5

The Cicada is a heavy air-support gunship. It is *not* an effective air-to-air fighter, but it is excellent for hovering over a ground target and saturating the area with explosive rockets.

The Cicada is armed with primary fire drunken rockets, and secondary fire homing rockets that can be loaded into a 16-rocket barrage, all of which unerringly seek out your chosen target.

The Cicada also seats a secondary Turret gunner, who can provide rapid anti-infantry fire, and launch flares to knock AVRiL shots off course (important, as the Cicada tends to quickly come under enemy fire from a great distance if it hovers in an area for any length of time).

Because the Cicada's flares reload faster than a single AVRiL, it is possible to completely nullify a single AVRiL-armed player trying to take you down. Multiple AVRiLs are considerably more difficult to distract, usually requiring some maneuvering behind cover to safely avoid.

A greater threat tends to be players using Instant Hit weapons. Like all air vehicles, the Cicada is relatively fragile, and concentrated Shock, Sniper, or vehicle fire can take it down quickly.

GOLIATH

RESPAWN TIME: 45 SECONDS

HEALTH	800	
TOP SPEED	12m/sec	
MANEUVERABILITY	Low	

PRIMARY FIRE	SECONDARY FIRE
Cannon	Zoom
TURRETS	**SPECIAL ABILITIES**
One, Minigun	None

PRIMARY FIRE

CLASSIFICATION ⦙ PROJECTILE

The Goliath's main Turret fires a shell that, while it is a projectile, travels so fast as to be nearly instant hit. The heavy tank round also deals 25% *more* damage to Nodes, and 30% more to the light vehicles (Manta, Scorpion, and Viper). The bonus against light vehicles is useful only for the extra splash damage, as it can kill each of those vehicles in one shot.

DAMAGE	300
RATE OF FIRE	2.5
SPLASH RADIUS	13.2m
PROJECTILE SPEED	300m/sec

SECONDARY FIRE

CLASSIFICATION ⦙ SPECIAL

Secondary fire allows you to zoom in on distant targets.

TURRET PROFILE

MINIGUN

PRIMARY FIRE

CLASSIFICATION ⦙ INSTANT HIT

The rapid-fire Minigun is ideal for killing nearby infantry and damaging light vehicles. The Minigun only deals 50% damage to Vehicles and Nodes.

DAMAGE	16
RATE OF FIRE	0.1
SPREAD	0.05

SECONDARY FIRE

CLASSIFICATION ⦙ SECONDARY

Secondary fire allows you to zoom in on distant targets.

The Goliath is a massive armored tank, a superb anti-vehicle and long-range combatant. The Goliath's main cannon inflicts devastating damage even at great distances, though it reloads slowly.

In addition, the Goliath has a Minigun Turret that can be manned to provide close-range anti-infantry cover. It's useful if the Goliath must get into close quarters with infantry, as the main cannon is ill-suited to blasting fast-moving infantry or light vehicles up close.

The Goliath's main cannon, in combination with its healthy armor make it an ideal support vehicle for covering a push against an enemy held Node, or the enemy Flag. It must be supported, however, as it quickly becomes a high priority target, and it is not nimble enough to evade incoming fire or highly maneuverable vehicles or infantry up close.

HELLBENDER

RESPAWN TIME 30 SECONDS

HEALTH	600	
TOP SPEED	19m/sec	
MANEUVERABILITY	Medium	
PRIMARY FIRE		SECONDARY FIRE
Shock Coer		Shock Beam
TURRETS		SPECIAL ABILITIES
One, rear		Shock Combo

PRIMARY FIRE

CLASSIFICATION	PROJECTILE

The Hellbender's primary fire launches Shock Cores.

DAMAGE	25
RATE OF FIRE	0.4
SPLASH RADIUS	2.4m
PROJECTILE SPEED	22m/sec

SECONDARY FIRE

CLASSIFICATION	INSTANT HIT

The Hellbender's secondary fire is a Shock Beam.

DAMAGE	25
RATE OF FIRE	0.75

HELLBENDER NOTES

The Hellbender's Shock Combo deals 200 damage with a 10.5m radius.

TURRET PROFILE

REAR TURRET

PRIMARY FIRE

CLASSIFICATION	INSTANT HIT

The Hellbender's Shock Turret fires a highly damaging Shock Beam. This beam only deals 85% damage to vehicles.

DAMAGE	120
RATE OF FIRE	0.5

SECONDARY FIRE

CLASSIFICATION	SPECIAL

Secondary fire allows you to zoom in on distant targets.

The Hellbender is a medium speed, armored vehicle that can provide excellent cover fire against enemy infantry, and it is reasonably effective against other light vehicles as well. It's well-armored, so it can provide close-range support with it's primary chain-Shock Cannon, or from a distance with its secondary Shock Beam Turret.

The Hellbender is not quick enough to keep up with the extremely agile vehicles, nor is it tough enough to stand up to the heavy vehicles, so it is best used at close or medium range against infantry or Nodes, and at medium or long-range with its Turret against more dangerous vehicle threats.

The Hellbender's chain Shock Combo can be used to devastating effect against massed infantry, or stationary vehicles. Each explosion deals up to 200 damage, with a large damage radius. Since you can chain a large number of Shock Cores together into one massive blast, it is possible to inflict heavy damage across a large swathe of terrain. Larger and slower vehicles can also be hit with multiple explosions.

LEVIATHAN

RESPAWN TIME SPECIAL

HEALTH	6500	
TOP SPEED	17m/sec	
MANEUVERABILITY	Very Low	

PRIMARY FIRE	SECONDARY FIRE
Bolt Cannon	Zoom
TURRETS	**SPECIAL ABILITIES**
Four, Front Left and Right, Rear Left and Right	Singularity Cannon; must deploy to fire

PRIMARY FIRE

CLASSIFICATION	PROJECTILE

Primary fire launches rapid-fire particle bolts that detonate on impact. These bolts only deal 50% damage to vehicles and Nodes.

DAMAGE	100
RATE OF FIRE	0.3
SPLASH RADIUS	6m
PROJECTILE SPEED	24m/sec accelerating to 70m/sec by 400m/sec

SECONDARY FIRE

CLASSIFICATION	SPECIAL

Secondary fire allows you to zoom in on distant targets.

LEVIATHAN NOTES

All the Leviathan's Turrets have the same secondary fire: an energy shield that absorbs all damage for four seconds, before recharging for five seconds.

TURRET PROFILE

BEAM TURRET
PRIMARY FIRE

CLASSIFICATION	INSTANT HIT

The Leviathan's Beam Turret fires rapidly and deals moderate damage. These beams deal 200% damage to vehicles.

DAMAGE	35
RATE OF FIRE	0.3

SHOCK TURRET
PRIMARY FIRE

CLASSIFICATION	PROJECTILE

The Leviathan's Shock Turret rapidly launches Shock Cores. If detonated by a Shock Beam, the resulting Shock Combo has deals 120 damage in a 5.5 meter radius. The Leviathan Shock Cores also auto-detonate if they approach any target, vehicle, player, or Node. These Shock Cores only deal 25% damage to vehicles.

DAMAGE	45
RATE OF FIRE	0.5
SPLASH RADIUS	2.56m
PROJECTILE SPEED	30m/sec

ROCKET TURRET
PRIMARY FIRE

CLASSIFICATION	PROJECTILE

The rocket Turret fires four rockets per shot at 0.15 seconds apart, with a two second reload time between volleys. These rockets deal 50% bonus damage to vehicles.

DAMAGE	80
RATE OF FIRE	2
SPLASH RADIUS	3.6m
PROJECTILE SPEED	100m/sec

STINGER TURRET
PRIMARY FIRE

CLASSIFICATION	INSTANT HIT

The Leviathan's Stinger Turret is essentially a heavy Turret mounted version of the infantry based Stinger, capable of firing the Tarydium shards extremely rapidly. These shards only deal 25% damage to vehicles.

DAMAGE	30
RATE OF FIRE	0.1
PROJECTILE SPEED	90m/sec, accelerating to 120m/sec by 60m/sec

The Leviathan is a monstrous armored behemoth, bristling with an assortment of heavy weaponry, and armed with a devastating main cannon that is so powerful, it can only be fired once the Leviathan has anchored itself in place with stabilizing supports.

The Leviathan seats up to *five* players, one driver armed with the primary cannon controls, and up to four Turrets, one mounted on each corner of the Leviathan. In addition to the four separate weapons provided by the four Turrets, each Turret can also deploy an energy shield, to block incoming fire.

The Leviathan is easily the toughest vehicle in the game, but it is also one of the slowest and least maneuverable. This is quite literally its only weak point. It tends to become the target of the entire enemy team when it is brought onto the field, it is important that a Leviathan push is supported by other vehicles and infantry. The Leviathan usually cannot stand up to massed enemy fire, even when fully loaded.

The Leviathan's main cannon should usually only be deployed to devastate enemy Nodes, heavy enemy vehicles, or to directly attack the enemy's Power Core—if it can reach it. The main cannon takes too long to deploy, charge up, and fire to deal with rapidly moving targets.

The Leviathan's main cannon explodes with the force of a Redeemer, and deals 50% bonus damage to vehicles. However, it does not knock down like a Redeemer shot (although, just like the Redeemer, not much is going to live through the blast in any case). The Leviathan's main cannon deals 1500 damage to Nodes, and about 1000 to a Power Core.

MANTA

RESPAWN TIME *30 SECONDS*

HEALTH	200		
TOP SPEED	36m/sec	24m/sec while "crouching"	
MANEUVERABILITY	Very High		

PRIMARY FIRE		SECONDARY FIRE	
Plasma bolts		Lowers Manta to crush infantry	
TURRETS		SPECIAL ABILITIES	
None		The Manta can jump and "crouch"	

PRIMARY FIRE

CLASSIFICATION ▦ PROJECTILE

The Manta's primary fire is a rapid-fire twin plasma cannon.

DAMAGE	40
RATE OF FIRE	0.2
PROJECTILE SPEED	40m/sec accelerating to 140m/sec by 320m/sec

SECONDARY FIRE

CLASSIFICATION ▦ SPECIAL

Pressing and holding secondary fire allows you to temporarily lower the Manta's hover level to crush infantry.

MANTA NOTES

The Manta can jump, high enough to clear low obstacles and other vehicles.

The Manta is an ultra-rapid hover transport vehicle. Extremely nimble, it can fly across the battlefield to quickly reach a target, and its rapid fire primary plasma cannons can deal impressive damage to slower vehicles or Nodes.

Against infantry, the Manta is a threat due to sheer speed and agility. The secondary fire causes the Manta to come crashing down close to the ground, shredding any infantry unfortunate enough to come into contact with it.

The Manta can also jump a good distance, useful for reaching high terrain, evading incoming fire, and setting yourself up for flattening an unfortunate enemy player on foot nearby.

RESPAWN TIME 45 SECONDS

HEALTH	800	
TOP SPEED	20m/sec	
MANEUVERABILITY	Low	

PRIMARY FIRE	SECONDARY FIRE
Shock Cannon	Shield
TURRETS	**SPECIAL ABILITIES**
None	Energy Blast

PRIMARY FIRE

CLASSIFICATION : PROJECTILE

While it fires awfully slowly, the Paladin's Shock Cannon packs a punch.

DAMAGE	200
RATE OF FIRE	2.35
SPLASH RADIUS	9m
PROJECTILE SPEED	180m/sec

SECONDARY FIRE

CLASSIFICATION : SPECIAL

Holding the secondary fire projects a shield after 1.8 seconds. The shield is capable of absorbing 1200 damage, and while it is inactive (either due to being destroyed, or if you release the shield, after 2.5 seconds, it begins to heal at a rate of 350/sec.

PALADIN NOTES

Firing the primary cannon while the shield is active causes a proximity explosion around the Paladin, useful for clearing out infantry that are difficult to hit with the Paladin's slow firing main cannon. Triggering the explosion causes 200 damage in an 18m radius centered around the Paladin.

The Paladin is a heavy support vehicle and the only primarily defensive vehicle in the game. It has a powerful primary fire energy bolt, but with a slow refire rate, it is not intended as a primary assault vehicle.

The Paladin's secondary fire provides its more common battlefield role: defending other players and vehicles. The Paladin can project a powerful energy shield, easily capable of absorbing light fire, and it is large enough to protect several players or smaller vehicles moving in its wake.

The Paladin is often a difficult vehicle to use effectively, as it is not speedy, and quick vehicles often flank it, forcing you to decide between screening incoming fire from a distance, or protecting yourself from threats to the sides or back. Because of this weakness, it is important that a Paladin push is supported by other players who can deal with light vehicles (or players) seeking to get around the energy shield.

In addition, covering an approach with the energy shield is tricky, as players are frequently going to ignore the Paladin entirely and focus on squishier targets.

Using the shield combo explosion is useful for dissuading enemy infantry from closing on the exposed flanks or rear of the Paladin, as it can easily damage and knock infantry away. The primary fire cannon, while slow, is deadly enough to kill a Manta in a single hit, and seriously damaging to even heavier vehicles, as well as lethal to infantry.

RAPTOR

RESPAWN TIME *30 SECONDS*

HEALTH	300	
TOP SPEED	50m/sec	
MANEUVERABILITY	High	
PRIMARY FIRE		SECONDARY FIRE
Plasma Cannon		Homing Missile
TURRETS		SPECIAL ABILITIES
None		None

PRIMARY FIRE

CLASSIFICATION ▌ PROJECTILE

The Raptor's primary fire is a rapid-fire Plasma Cannon. The Raptor's cannon deals considerably more damage at close-range. 20 damage is reached after its shots have been in the air for about a second. At extremely close-range, the Raptor can deal upwards of 50 damage a shot, though of course, flying this close usually makes the Raptor a prime target.

DAMAGE	20
RATE OF FIRE	0.2
SPLASH RADIUS	4m
PROJECTILE SPEED	40m/sec accelerating to 250m/sec by 400m/sec

SECONDARY FIRE

CLASSIFICATION ▌ PROJECTILE

The Raptor's homing missile can lock on and track enemy aircraft, the Manta, and the Viper. It also deals 50% more damage to all vehicles.

DAMAGE	100
RATE OF FIRE	1.2
SPLASH RADIUS	3m
PROJECTILE SPEED	40m/sec accelerating to 80m/sec by 320m/sec

RAPTOR NOTES

The Raptor's primary fire shots receive a slight advantage against incoming AVRiL shots, their collision detection is slightly more lenient, as they are treated as being "larger" projectiles for purposes of shooting down the AVRiL. This makes it slightly easier to destroy incoming missiles, though you shouldn't expect to survive in the open against a lot of anti-air fire.

The Raptor is an air-to-air fighter than can also provide solid ground support if it is unopposed in the skies. It is lightly armored, rendering it vulnerable to concentrated fire from infantry on the ground, and it makes a wonderfully juicy AVRiL target, given the usual lack of cover while flying.

However, utilized carefully, the Raptor can provide either ultra-fast transport for a single player, or covering fire for a ground advance, either against enemy ground forces, or clearing the skies of enemy aircraft.

The Raptor's primary fire is a rapid-fire plasma cannon, and while it deals low damage per hit, it does deal slight splash damage, meaning it can harry infantry, and deal good constant damage to any slower vehicles.

The Raptor's secondary fire is a slower firing missile, but it has strong homing capabilities against other aircraft, the Manta, and the Viper, making it ideal for taking down enemy aerial vehicles or Mantas. For normal vehicles and infantry, the Raptor's primary fire is generally more effective.

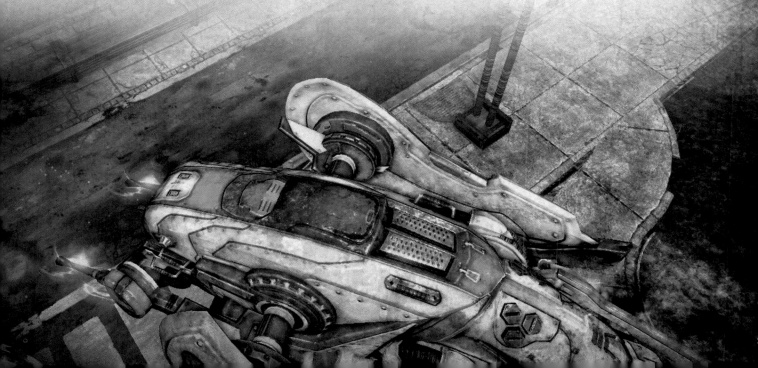

SCORPION

RESPAWN TIME ⦙ *30 SECONDS*

HEALTH	300									
TOP SPEED	22m/sec			40m/sec while "boosting"						
MANEUVERABILITY	Medium									

PRIMARY FIRE	SECONDARY FIRE
Anti-Matter Turret	Blades

TURRETS	SPECIAL ABILITIES
None	Boost, Self Destruct

PRIMARY FIRE

CLASSIFICATION ⦙ **PROJECTILE**

The Scorpion's anti-matter Turret launches an explosive energy ball in a high arc. This weapon deals 25% less damage to vehicles and Nodes.

DAMAGE	100
RATE OF FIRE	0.65
SPLASH RADIUS	4.4m
PROJECTILE SPEED	80m

SECONDARY FIRE

CLASSIFICATION ⦙ **SPECIAL**

Holding secondary fire activates the Scorpion's front mounted blades, capable of instantly decapitating other players on foot.

DAMAGE	Always lethal

BOOST EXPLOSION

CLASSIFICATION ⦙ **SPECIAL**

Ejecting from the Scorpion while boosting sends the Scorpion into a lethal self-destruct sequence, detonating on impact.

Boosting lasts for 2 seconds, and has a recharge time of 5 seconds.

DAMAGE	600
SPLASH RADIUS	12m

SCORPION NOTES

Max speed while boosting 40m/sec

The Scorpion is a rapid transport vehicle, though it is not quite as fast or maneuverable as the Manta, it is slightly sturdier, and with its Boost capabilities, it can achieve extremely high speeds on straight stretches of terrain. Its Self Destruct special ability to inflict some damage once you have arrived at your destination. The Scorpion is armed with primarily anti-infantry weaponry, as its primary fire Turret shots are explosive and fairly short range, and its scything blades are useful for cutting down players on foot as you make your way to (or arrive) at a target area.

HIGH FLYING STUNTS

Ejecting from the Scorpion or the Viper to trigger a detonation launches you high into the air. As an added bonus, you do *not* take falling damage after coming down from this launch. Use the height to drop yourself on elevated terrain, or to quickly reach a nearby location while making yourself a difficult target.

SPMA — SELF PROPELLED MOBILE ARTILLERY

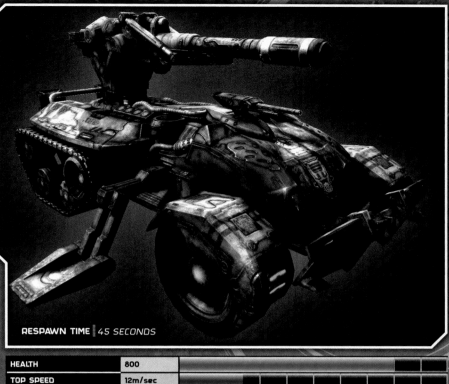

RESPAWN TIME | 45 SECONDS

HEALTH	800	
TOP SPEED	12m/sec	
MANEUVERABILITY	Very Low	

PRIMARY FIRE	SECONDARY FIRE
Shock Turret	Deploy
TURRETS	SPECIAL ABILITIES
None	Long-range bombardment

PRIMARY FIRE

CLASSIFICATION	PROJECTILE

Primary fire launches Shock Cores.

DAMAGE	25
RATE OF FIRE	0.4
SPLASH RADIUS	2.4m
PROJECTILE SPEED	22m/sec

SECONDARY FIRE

CLASSIFICATION	INSTANT HIT

Secondary fire shoots a weak Shock Beam which can detonate the Shock Cores.

DAMAGE	25
RATE OF FIRE	0.75

SPMA NOTES

The SPMA can perform the chain Shock Combo just like the Hellbender, dealing 200 damage in a 10.5m radius.

ARTILLERY CANNON

PRIMARY FIRE

CLASSIFICATION	PROJECTILE

The main artillery piece can only be fired once the SPMA is deployed.

DAMAGE	250x9
RATE OF FIRE	4
SPLASH RADIUS	13.2m
PROJECTILE SPEED	80m/sec

Once deployed, the SPMA can launch its remote viewing camera (1.5 second reload time) to set up its long-range bombardment. Once in place, the artillery has a 4 second reload time, launching a mirving shell that splits and drops 9 bomblets, each exploding with full force.

SECONDARY FIRE

CLASSIFICATION	PROJECTILE

Secondary fire while deployed fires the targeting camera. Tapping secondary fire again while the camera is in mid-air freezes it in place, allowing you to target artillery strikes from long-range. Curiously, the falling camera is actually dangerous—watch out from above!

RATE OF FIRE	1.5

The SPMA is an indirect fire artillery piece, the main cannon can only be fired while deployed and locked in place. The SPMA has a very unique delivery system for its projectiles, as it can first launch a camera into the air, "deploy" the camera in mid-air, and then use the floating camera to perfectly target artillery strikes.

Because most vehicles and players simply move too quickly to hit with artillery barrages, the SPMA is best used for suppressive fire on stationary targets. Flag areas, Nodes, spawn points, and occasionally, on heavy enemy vehicles that aren't moving around much.

The SPMA camera can be taken down a single shot.

THE PHAYDER CORPORATION

A secretive and comparatively unknown corporation (at least in comparison to the Axon, Liandri, and Izanagi), the Phayder company makes its home on Omicron 6, and specializes in the development of nano-technology and genetic modification. Their most significant breakthrough has been the development of a sentient nanomachine substance known as Nanoblack.

Their development of Nanoblack has given rise to the physically and mentally enhanced Necris, a class of warriors infused with Nanoblack in place of their blood. In addition, the Nanoblack has been used in the construction of highly advanced military machinery.

DARKWALKER

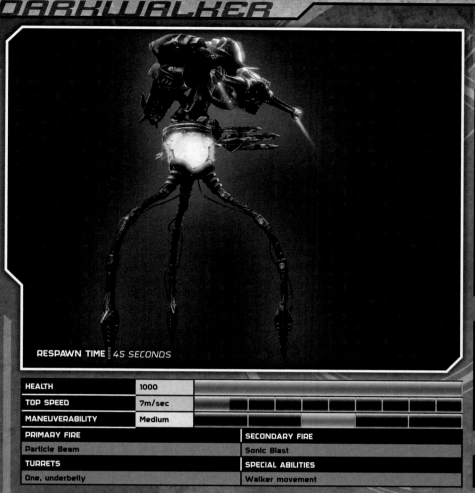

RESPAWN TIME 45 SECONDS

HEALTH	1000
TOP SPEED	7m/sec
MANEUVERABILITY	Medium

PRIMARY FIRE	SECONDARY FIRE
Particle Beam	Sonic Blast
TURRETS	**SPECIAL ABILITIES**
One, underbelly	Walker movement

PRIMARY FIRE

CLASSIFICATION	INSTANT HIT
DAMAGE	120 per "pulse", every 0.4 seconds of contact, 360 vs. vehicles
RATE OF FIRE	1.5s fire time, 1.5s reload time
	Vs. Vehicles: 0.4 seconds before dealing 120 damage every 0.4 seconds
	Vs. Players: Instant, then 0.4 seconds for the same player.

The Darkwalker's energy emitters fire a continuous stream of devastating power, lethal to infantry and highly damaging to vehicles and Nodes.

SECONDARY FIRE

CLASSIFICATION	SPECIAL

Secondary fire causes the Darkwalker to project a concussive wave of sound, knocking nearby infantry off their feet, and pushing light vehicles away. Knocks Viper and Manta pilots out of their vehicles.

RATE OF FIRE	7s
RANGE	15m

DARKWALKER NOTES

The Darkwalker's three legs allow it to climb atop almost any obstacle or elevated platform.

TURRET PROFILE

UNDERBELLY

PRIMARY FIRE

CLASSIFICATION	PROJECTILE

Primary fire for the underbelly Turret is a rapid-fire energy cannon.

DAMAGE	30
RATE OF FIRE	0.15
PROJECTILE SPEED	80m/sec accelerating to 200m/sec by 400m/sec

SECONDARY FIRE

CLASSIFICATION	SPECIAL

Secondary fire allows you to zoom in on distant targets.

The Darkwalker is an awe-inspiring three-legged combat walker. Armed with a powerful twin energy beam as its primary weapon, it can cut swaths of destruction across the battlefield, vaporizing infantry instantly, and inflicting heavy damage to vehicles.

In addition, infantry that get in close to exploit its blind spot can fall prey to its secondary fire, a monstrous howl that knocks infantry away from the Darkwalker, and temporarily stuns them.

Not only that, the Darkwalker supports a Turret gunner, who is armed with a rapid fire energy cannon that can assist in handling nimble targets.

The Darkwalker's three sinuous legs give it amazing vertical mobility in comparison to conventional vehicles, as it can stride over enormous boulders, and climb atop structures that other ground vehicles and players simply cannot reach.

While powerful, the Darkwalker is not without its weak points. As mentioned, the Darkwalker cannot use its primary fire energy beam up close, and while it can knock infantry away with its sonic scream, it cannot do so continuously, meaning at least some infantry can stay out of line of sight beneath it. In addition, quick vehicles can easily outpace the Darkwalker's Turret, as it slowly rotates from side to side.

At medium and long-range, the Darkwalker is lethal, as its Turret traversal rate is not a disadvantage, and it can zoom in with enough precision to decimate distant targets, but it is weak up close, especially against agile targets. At long-range, the only defense against its devastating arc of destruction is hiding behind very hard cover.

RESPAWN TIME 30 SECONDS

HEALTH	400
TOP SPEED	30m/sec
MANEUVERABILITY	High

100m/sec while "boosting"

PRIMARY FIRE	SECONDARY FIRE
Particle Beam	Speed Boost
TURRETS	SPECIAL ABILITIES
None	None

PRIMARY FIRE

CLASSIFICATION | INSTANT HIT

The Fury's tentacles project a blazing energy beam that "sticks" to any target it contacts.

DAMAGE	120 per second
RATE OF FIRE	0.5
RANGE	80m

SECONDARY FIRE

CLASSIFICATION | SPECIAL

Pressing secondary fire activates the Fury's thrusters, giving it a sudden boost of forward momentum. 1 second forward thrust, 0.7 seconds sideways, 100m/sec for the duration of the boost.

RATE OF FIRE	1.5

FURY NOTES

Can "dodge" from side to side.

The Necris aircraft, the Fury is armed with an energy beam similar to that used by the Darkwalker. The Fury is highly agile in mid-air, and it is a strong ground support vehicle, falling somewhere between the Cicada and the Raptor in terms of air-to-air and air-to-ground effectiveness.

The energy beam used by the Fury requires that you stay locked onto a single target to deal lethal damage, at least against vehicles or Nodes. Players on foot are vaporized nearly instantly by the energy stream.

The Fury's energy beam is "sticky", and can be used to shove lighter targets on the ground. This usually isn't noticeable against infantry, as they die quickly to the stream of pain, but light vehicles can be moved around a bit, hampering their mobility.

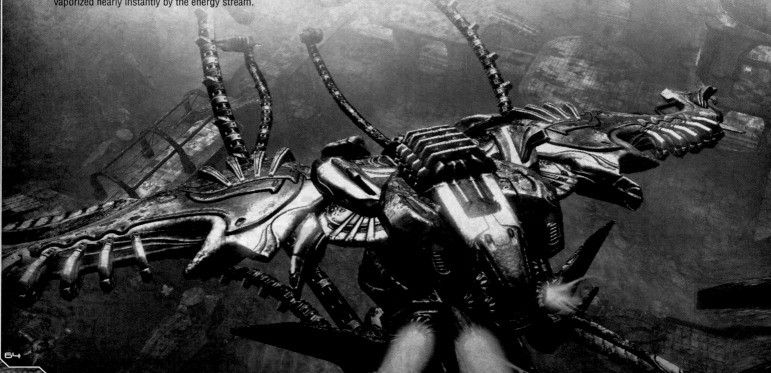

NEMESIS

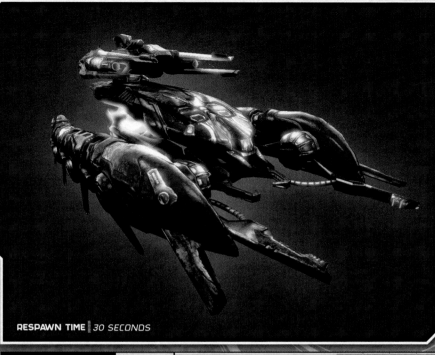

RESPAWN TIME *30 SECONDS*

PRIMARY FIRE

CLASSIFICATION INSTANT HIT

The Nemesis's main cannon is a rapid-fire plasmid cannon.

DAMAGE	50
RATE OF FIRE	0.36

SECONDARY FIRE

CLASSIFICATION SPECIAL

Secondary fire allows you to zoom in on distant targets.

NEMESIS NOTES

Tapping the jump key causes the Nemesis to raise its Turret. This greatly slows the Nemesis, but speeds up its firing rate considerably, allowing you to deal heavy damage to infantry or vehicles from a distance.

Tapping the crouch key causes the Nemesis to lower its Turret, fixing it in place, while granting the Nemesis faster movement and a greatly lowered profile in exchange for the loss of Turret mobility.

HEALTH	600		
TOP SPEED	10m/sec	4m/sec raised / 22m/sec Lowered	
MANEUVERABILITY	Med., Low, Very Low		
PRIMARY FIRE		SECONDARY FIRE	
Plasmid Cannon		Zoom	
TURRETS		SPECIAL ABILITIES	
None		Turret Elevation	

The Nemesis is a heavy weapons platform, capable of laying down a lethal field of fire from its twin energy cannons. Primary fire shoots its rapid-fire cannons, and secondary fire is a simple zoom function, allowing you to target distant foes with ease.

However, the Nemesis has another special ability; it can raise its turret, slowing its movement massively, but greatly increasing its rate of fire. The fire speed increase is so great, it can deal devastating damage to enemy vehicles and kill infantry immediately as well.

If the Nemesis "crouches", it lowers its Turret, restricting it to forward fire only, but gains a speed boost while moving.

The Nemesis is decently armored, but it is normally not an especially fast moving vehicle, and its mobility is greatly hampered while its Turret is extended. Finding cover at a distance and using the height gained by extending the Turret can provide you with a dangerous long-range support weapon, clearing the way for other players to reach a key Node, or to get to the Flag unimpeded.

NIGHTSHADE

RESPAWN TIME 45 SECONDS

HEALTH	600					
TOP SPEED	9.2m/sec cloaked		20m/sec uncloaked			
MANEUVERABILITY	Medium					

PRIMARY FIRE	SECONDARY FIRE
Energy Beam	Cloak
TURRETS	SPECIAL ABILITIES
None	Can deploy mines and other special weapons

PRIMARY FIRE

CLASSIFICATION ┊ INSTANT HIT

A short-ranged beam of energy, it has similar properties to the Link Gun secondary fire, and can be used to repair friendly vehicles or Nodes. The beam deals 20% less damage to vehicles, and it causes lockdown like the Link secondary.

DAMAGE ┊	120/sec
RANGE ┊	18m

SECONDARY FIRE

CLASSIFICATION ┊ SPECIAL

Secondary fire activates or deactivates the Nightshade's cloaking device.

NIGHTSHADE NOTES

While uncloaked, the Nightshade can move more quickly. The Nightshade can deploy Spider and EMP Mines, as well as Stasis Fields and Energy Shields.

The Necris Nightshade is a powerful support vehicle, capable of deploying any of four different useful anti-vehicle weapons. The EMP Mine, Spider Mine Trap, Stasis Field, and Energy Shield can all be deployed on the battlefield to protect critical locations, such as the flag room in VCTF, or specific Nodes in Warfare.

The Nightshade is cloaked, allowing it to freely move about the battlefield, but the cloak can be dropped by using secondary fire. While uncloaked, the Nightshade moves more quickly, but only use this ability while on friendly ground, the Nightshade is not a heavy combat vehicle.

The Nightshade's primary fire energy beam is useful for repairing friendly vehicles and Nodes, and can be used against nearby enemy infantry or vehicles in a pinch, though be aware that attacking causes your cloak to weaken.

DEPLOYABLE SWAP

Using the weapon switch function allows you to change the selected deployable while using the Nightshade.

SCAVENGER

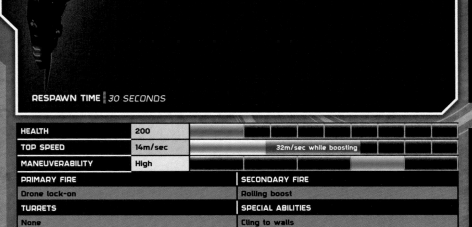

RESPAWN TIME 30 SECONDS

HEALTH	200	
TOP SPEED	14m/sec	32m/sec while boosting
MANEUVERABILITY	High	

PRIMARY FIRE	SECONDARY FIRE
Drone lock-on	Rolling boost
TURRETS	**SPECIAL ABILITIES**
None	Cling to walls

PRIMARY FIRE

CLASSIFICATION SPECIAL

Primary fire causes the Scavenger's orbiting Nanoblack drone to lock on to a target.

DAMAGE	30
RATE OF FIRE	0.2

SECONDARY FIRE

CLASSIFICATION SPECIAL

Secondary fire causes the Scavenger to retract its tentacles and begin a sudden roll forwards. If done in the air while moving quickly, the Scavenger gains more forward speed. Can deal up to 190 damage, down to a minimum of 50. If the ball isn't moving fast enough, no damage is dealt.

Triggering the roll gives a 2 second speed boost, and has a recharge time of 2 seconds.

DAMAGE	50 minimum, 190 maximum.

SCAVENGER NOTES

Pressing primary fire while rolling deploys the tentacles as makeshift spikes on the sides of the rolling ball.

The Scavenger can "cling" to surfaces by holding jump while near them, allowing it to reach some difficult locations.

Scavenger can heal Nodes.

The Scavenger is one of the strangest vehicles in the game. A transparent Nanoblack sphere at the center of three individually articulating legs similar to those on the Darkwalker, the Scavenger drags itself across the ground at a moderate pace using its Nanoblack legs. In addition, it can jump a good distance in the air, and even use its legs to latch onto walls and climb to higher elevations.

The Scavenger's primary weapon is no cannon or energy beam, but rather, a floating orb of energy that can be locked onto any target, vehicle, infantry, or even Node. Once locked, the orb floats around its target, constantly damaging it as long as you maintain a lock.

However, slowly killing your target with the orb is only one way of taking down a target. The secondary fire on the Scavenger causes the arms to retract, and launches the odd vehicle forward as a rolling ball of a death. While rolling, you can tap the primary fire to extend the arms as spikes, spinning and eviscerating nearby infantry.

The Scavenger is lightly armored, but due to its vertical mobility, it can be a very useful transport vehicle, and its anti-infantry capability is solid. Just be careful to attack from an odd angle, coming straight at a target is a good way to get blasted out of the fragile shell.

VIPER

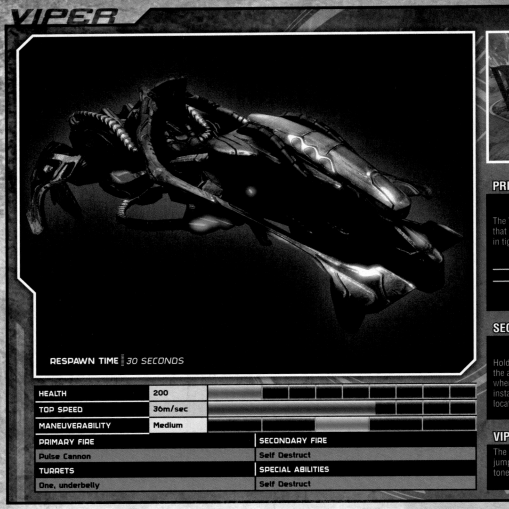

RESPAWN TIME ▌*30 SECONDS*

PRIMARY FIRE

CLASSIFICATION ▌ PROJECTILE

The Viper's rapid-fire cannon shoots balls of energy that can bounce off terrain to create lethal ricochets in tight areas.

DAMAGE	40
RATE OF FIRE	0.2
PROJECTILE SPEED	40m/sec accelerating to 140m/sec by 320m/sec

SECONDARY FIRE

CLASSIFICATION ▌ SPECIAL

Holding secondary fire causes the Viper to leap into the air, however, unlike holding the jump button, when secondary fire is released, it causes the Viper to instantly eject you and launch itself towards the last location of your crosshairs.

VIPER NOTES

The Viper Self Destruct can also be activated while jumping, if you press eject while you can hear the tone indicating enough height for a vehicle launch.

HEALTH	200	
TOP SPEED	36m/sec	
MANEUVERABILITY	Medium	
PRIMARY FIRE		SECONDARY FIRE
Pulse Cannon		Self Destruct
TURRETS		SPECIAL ABILITIES
One, underbelly		Self Destruct

The Viper is the Necris' fastest transport vehicle, capable of achieving amazing speeds on open ground. In addition, it is able to make huge vertical leaps, easily carrying it over rough terrain.

The Viper is armed with a rapid-fire energy cannon for its primary weapon, the shots from which ricochet and bounce off terrain, making it a powerful weapon in cramped quarters. Combined with its mobility, it is also excellent for taking down the heavier, but slower, vehicles.

The Viper also has a Self Destruct ability similar to that of the Scorpions, while leaping into the air, it can lock onto a target and fired as an immense vehicular missile, ejecting you in the process. Not only is the explosion devastating, you are also protected from any falling damage due to the ejection, and you can even use the height and momentum to carry you to a specific target.

TURRETS

While not precisely a vehicle in the traditional sense, Turrets do share vehicle damage reduction traits, and generally come in anti-infantry and anti-vehicle varieties, just as vehicles tend to be better at dealing with certain types of threats.

Some Turrets are track mounted, allowing you a limited amount of mobility while manning the Turret.

Other than the Hoverboard, turrets are the only vehicle that you can enter while holding the flag or carrying the Orb. This can be useful for giving you some extra sturdiness, and note that the Orb does work as a defensive shield on a friendly Node while you are in a turret, if the turret is close enough to the Node (such as the Center Node on Avalanche).

BEAM TURRET

TURRET PROFILE

HEALTH	400
PRIMARY FIRE	Beam
SECONDARY FIRE	Zoom
RESPAWN TIME	45s

PRIMARY FIRE

CLASSIFICATION   **INSTANT HIT**

The Beam Turret has a rapid-fire energy lance, excellent for knocking light vehicles around, and dealing damage at a distance. The beam is also decent against players at mid- or close-range. Note that the Beam Turret's damage is reduced against vehicles, only dealing 70% of its normal damage.

DAMAGE	34
RATE OF FIRE	0.22

SECONDARY FIRE

CLASSIFICATION   **SPECIAL**

Secondary fire allows you to zoom in on distant targets.

ROCKET TURRET

TURRET PROFILE

HEALTH	400
PRIMARY FIRE	Quad rocket barrage
SECONDARY FIRE	Zoom
RESPAWN TIME	45s

PRIMARY FIRE

CLASSIFICATION   **PROJECTILE**

Primary fire launches four rockets in quick succession (0.15 seconds between shots). These rockets deal 150% damage against vehicles, making this the best anti-vehicle Turret for large and slow-moving vehicles.

DAMAGE	80
RATE OF FIRE	2s
SPLASH RADIUS	3.6m
PROJECTILE SPEED	100m/sec

SECONDARY FIRE

CLASSIFICATION   **SPECIAL**

Secondary fire allows you to zoom in on distant targets.

Each of the vehicles, in addition to its basic (or not so basic) stats has a series of comments comparing that vehicle against others in combat. Note that the combat charts do not include the Nightshade, SPMA, or Leviathan, as the first two are support vehicles, and the Leviathan is a rather special case. Plus, you can safely assume that you're going to get well and truly pasted going up against a fully manned Leviathan in pretty much any vehicle—sage advice!

The Nemesis may come out sounding exceedingly lethal, and it is, but it is also an easy target, and far more fragile than the Darkwalker or the Goliath.

The chart is useful simply for getting a quick reference of the effectiveness of one vehicle against another. It is not an absolute, and for vehicles with turrets, whether the turret(s) is(are) manned or not has a significant impact on the outcome of a battle.

The Hellbender's turret for example, is very lethal against aircraft. Similarly, the Darkwalker's turret gives it the ability to fight off more agile targets that its beam turret simply cannot track.

As another example, the Cicada is nearly untouchable by some ground vehicles, but it has a difficult time doing effective damage against agile targets, making it a safe but slow engagement, and therefore not always an optimal use of your time when you could be popping up and down behind terrain while unloading fully charged rocket barrages onto a key Node.

See the more detailed notes to get a better idea of how the actual engagement may work out. It is worth keeping in mind the general power of one vehicle against another, as vehicle match-ups are somewhat more static than on-foot combat, but you can and will run into bizarre cases of a Manta destroying a Raptor, so don't take the comparisons as concrete rules—they're guidelines, not certainties.

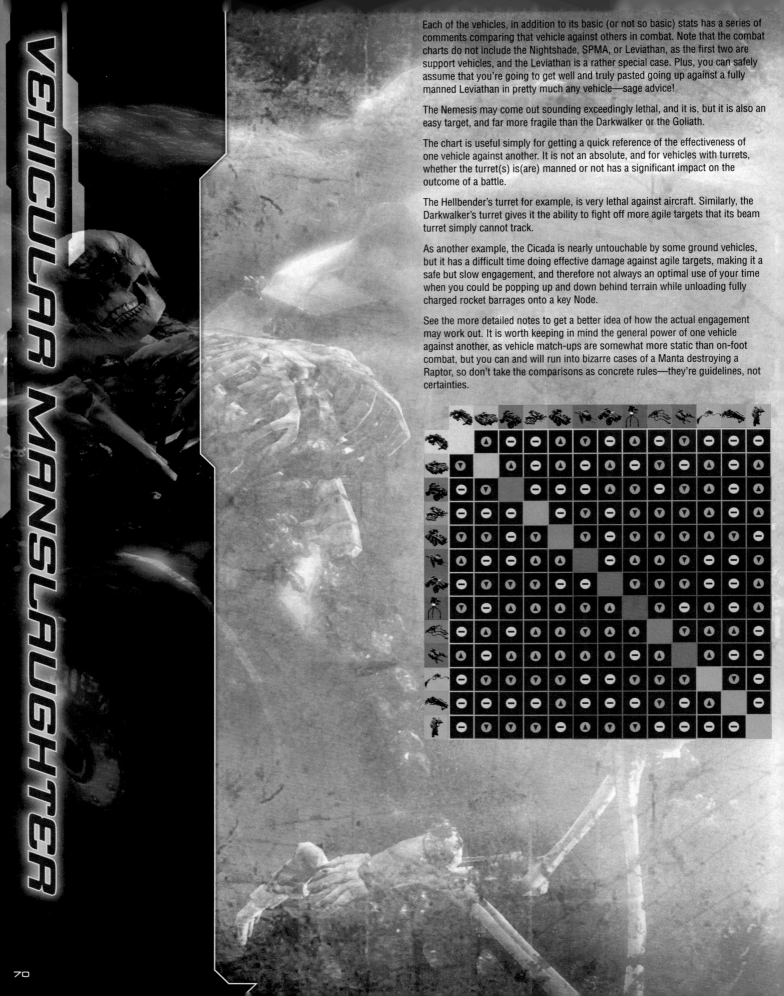

CICADA VS.:

VS. GOLIATH

Like the other air vehicles, the Cicada is well-suited for dealing with this armored behemoth. While it takes a *lot* of pounding to take down a fully healthy Goliath (or worse, one being actively healed), you can easily fire at it from a great distance and deal constant damage.

The Goliath is slow enough that it has a hard time evading your fire unless it is concentrating solely on doing so.

You aren't at *too* much risk from the Goliath's main cannon, just be sure to keep ahead of its Turret traversal, you don't want to be an embarrassing aerial fireworks display.

If the Goliath's Minigun is manned, it is more of a threat, as you cannot avoid the rapid-fire shots easily. Keep maximum distance to cause the natural spread of the Minigun to lower its damage output if you must engage.

VS. HELLBENDER

Not fantastic, the Hellbender is reasonably quick. If you happen to catch one unawares, you may be able to score some damage from a solid stream of rockets, but if it becomes aware of you, it can easily outrun your rockets, and worse, its rear Turret is a serious threat. Avoid fighting if the Turret is manned and the gunner is aware of you.

VS. MANTA

Pretty terrible chances here. Hitting the Manta while it is in motion is all but impossible, and the Manta rarely stays still long enough to be a good barrage target. Don't waste your time with this one.

VS. PALADIN

Good, similar to the Goliath match up, with two notable exceptions. The first is that the Paladin can screen your fire fairly easily, and the second is that the Paladin's cannon, while slow, packs a whallop—and it is quicker than the Goliath's main cannon. Be careful

VS. RAPTOR

The Raptor is a born aerial fighter, and its air-to-air missiles can take you apart with incredible ease. If there's a Raptor in the air with you, get out of the skies!

VS. SCORPION

Not good, worse than the Hellbender, ever so slightly better than the Manta. Generally a Scorpion is used to quickly jet from one location to another, then either used for light anti-infantry combat, or immediately boost detonated. In either case, you're not likely to have enough time to destroy it.

VS. DARKWALKER

Decent if you can get behind it. The Darkwalker's Turret traversal is quite slow, so as long as you stay out of its line of fire, you can pepper it with long-range explosives.

VS. FURY

Also quite bad. The Fury isn't quite the anti-air machine that the Raptor is, but its energy beam is still a far more effective air to air weapon than your drunk missiles are. If you have a Turret gunner, you might be able to come out of this fight in one piece, but otherwise, avoid.

VS. NEMESIS

Awful. The Nemesis has extremely rapid fire instant hit weaponry, it can track you quickly, and if elevated, tear you apart in seconds. Avoid at all costs!

VS. SCAVENGER

Decent. The Scavenger is toothless against you, but it is annoyingly mobile, and it has a small target profile, making it difficult to attack from a distance.

VS. VIPER

Very bad. The Viper is just as hard to hit as the Manta, though it lacks some horizontal maneuverability, it still moves so fast as to render it impossible to hit while in motion.

VS. INFANTRY

Decent, but not fantastic. However, you can play cover games, and with a Turret gunner, down incoming AVRiL shots fairly safely.

GOLIATH VS.:

VS. HELLBENDER

Great. It's reasonably easy to hit, and only takes a few shots to destroy. Its Turret can deal some heavy damage to you at a distance, but its primary fire usually can't harm you enough before your main cannon blasts it out of existence.

VS. MANTA

Excellent at a distance, awful up close. Up close, your only real chance is if the terrain is tremendously restricted, otherwise, you're going to have problems. The Manta *can* dodge your shots at long-range, but even a glancing blow can be fatal to the light craft.

VS. PALADIN

A bit of a brutal brawl, but you're usually going to come out on top—*if* you're dealing with primary fire. If the Paladin is shielding itself, you may have a harder time taking it down before other enemy players engage in the fray.

VS. RAPTOR

Awful, you don't want to be going up against the Raptor in the Goliath unless you have the Minigun Turret manned. You *can* blast the Raptor out of the sky if it is unaware of you at a distance, but if it is alert, you're not going to be able to track it fast enough to get a shot off.

VS. SCORPION

Great at any range. The Scorpion simply doesn't have the weaponry to fight against you. However, the Scorpion *can* boost detonate into you, so watch out for this. Thankfully, the boost detonation requires that the Scorpion propel itself towards you at great speed in a straight line, making it an easy target for the time it needs to reach terminal velocity.

VS. DARKWALKER

A tough and ugly fight. If the Darkwalker has you in its sights (and worse, has a Turret gunner), you're going to drive away from the fight bloody, if you drive away at all.

Ideally, you want to use the Goliath's slightly superior maneuverability to evade *some* of the incoming fire, but this is difficult at best.

If you don't have a choice, go into the fight with guns blazing. Worst case scenario: you go down, but the Darkwalker is critically injured and can be taken down by your teammates.

VS. FURY

Bad match up, just like the other aircraft, you simply cannot track the Fury quickly enough to bring your cannon to bear unless you are at a great distance. You can man the Minigun to fire at it, and given the Fury's need to get within moderate range, this can be an effective tactic to damage or possibly destroy it.

VS. NEMESIS

A painful battle. Usually one you can come out from alive, especially if you get the first shot in, but a raised Nemesis has a brutal rate of fire. If possible, try to engage this battle from a distance with cover. Poke out, take a shot, then back up again. The Nemesis requires continuous line of sight to deal its heavy damage, you do not.

VS. SCAVENGER

Great! Pop that rolling ball and cackle with malicious glee.

VS. VIPER

Good at a distance, not so hot as it gets closer. Similar to the Manta, this thing is a *pain* to hit at full speed, and more critically, its suicide detonation is a bit harder to hit than the Scorpions.

The Viper *does* slow down when it leaps into the air to prep for a suicide dive, so if you have your Turret lined up, you have a chance to quickly take a shot—you're only going to get one!

VS. INFANTRY

Awesome at any range. Up close, a manned Minigun is an asset, but you can switch to it quickly if necessary to gun down a player on your flanks or rear.

At a distance, glorious gibs galore!

HELLBENDER VS.:

VS. MANTA
Solid with your Turret, rather awful with your primary fire. If you have to, switch to the Turret even if it means staying still. The Manta can hit you moving nearly as easily, and you can knock the Manta around with your Turret, and destroy its lighter armor more quickly than it can yours.

VS. PALADIN
Not great. The Paladin is seriously armored, and its primary fire hurts, even though it shoots slowly. If you must engage, engage either on the move, or from cover, where you can dodge its shots while your Turret peppers it.

At closer range, you may be able to deal some heavy damage with your Shock combo chains.

VS. RAPTOR
Good with your Turret, awful with your primary fire. If the Turret isn't manned, man it yourself! The Raptor may have a hard time hitting you on the move at great distances, so if you're on the way to an important target, avoid the fight altogether if you don't have a Turret gunner.

VS. SCORPION
Decent, your main threat is a boost detonation. The Scorpion's weaponry is somewhat dangerous against you at mid-range, but your Turret is far superior at great distances. At close-range, you're pitting Shock chains against the Scorpion's energy bombs, but you have the armor advantage.

VS. DARKWALKER
Bad, bad match up. The best you can hope for is plinking away a bit at a distance with your Turret, but at a distance, the Darkwalker does a lot more than 'plink' with its main gun.

At close-range, you may be able to outmaneuver it, enough to deal damage with Shock chains, but even this is a risky maneuver if it has a manned Underbelly Turret.

VS. FURY
Similar to the Raptor fight, your Turret is quite useful. The Fury's shorter range means that you can *possibly* outrun it in the open, though its boost guarantees its going to catch up if the pilot really wants you dead.

VS. NEMESIS
An awful fight, the Nemesis can tear you apart in the open, and both of your weapons require being in the open to fight effectively. Your best chance is backing out of sight and firing Shock chains in the general direction of the Nemesis, but this usually isn't enormously effective.

VS. SCAVENGER
A decent match up, the Scavenger is rather frail, and a very easy target for your Turret. Your primary fire is rather less useful against it though, as it can maneuver quickly enough to avoid the bulk of incoming shots.

VS. VIPER
Not a great fight, the Viper can usually evade your Shock chains, and hit you with a constant stream of fire while doing so. Your Turret is very helpful, just watch out for suicide dive-bombing should the Viper pilot decide he doesn't like the odds.

VS. INFANTRY
Good at short and medium range, your Turret is *very* helpful at a distance. Otherwise, you must get closer to effectively utilize the Shock Combo explosions.

MANTA VS.:

VS. PALADIN
Very dangerous to approach at range, the Paladin's primary fire can execute you in a single shot. At extreme close-range, you need to watch out for the Paladin's energy blast, which can damage you if you're hugging its sides.

Otherwise, up close, you can generally evade the Paladin's Turret, and pepper it with constant fire, as it is simply too slow to evade you.

VS. RAPTOR
Very bad, not only can you not fight back against it, the Raptor's missiles lock onto Mantas! Use your mobility to get under cover and avoid this 'fight' entirely.

VS. SCORPION
Decent, you can outmaneuver the Scorpion—just keep your distance, the Scorpion doesn't need to face you to fire its primary weapon at you.

VS. DARKWALKER
Very risky—while you can outmaneuver the Darkwalker just like the Goliath, you're playing a *very* dangerous game of cat and mouse. Get too far, it can track you with its Turret, and you're toast.

Get too close, and its howl can knock you right out of your Manta, paralyzing you long enough to be incinerated. If the Darkwalker's Turret is manned, you're in for an even worse match up, as it can easily track you.

VS. FURY
Bad, though not quite as dreadful as the Raptor. You don't want to be fighting it, but you can at least avoid it somewhat more safely while it tries to close the distance to hit you with its laser.

VS. NEMESIS
Awful, the Nemesis' Turret tracks quickly, and its rapid-fire shots are a death sentence for your lightly armored craft. Avoid this beast in the open.

VS. SCAVENGER
Decent, though the Scavengers jumping makes it something of a pain to hit. In addition, while its Nanoblack orb isn't usually a huge threat, against your light armor, it can strip away your defenses fairly quickly.

VS. VIPER
A rather strange fight—generally, both the Manta and the Viper are used for fast transport. Finding a Viper rider who *wants* to fight you is an oddity to begin with.

In any case, this is a dangerous match up, your weapons are similar, and your maneuverability is matched by the Viper's speed. You do have better horizontal mobility, but the Viper's shots bounce, meaning that in any sort of enclosed terrain, you're likely to eat a fair number of ricochets.

Avoid this battle unless you have a good reason for pursuing it.

VS. INFANTRY
Varies enormously. Essentially the Manta is great against infantry—but infantry with the right weapons are great against the Manta. A single AVRiL shot can send you sky-high, and even repeated Shock Rifle blasts can knock you silly, unable to move around at all.

On the flip side, catching an unaware player on foot is a free kill, squash them, smirk, move on to the next target.

PALADIN VS.:

VS. RAPTOR

If you can manage to land a shot, you're doing pretty well. Otherwise, use your shield to screen the incoming fire and move on to other targets, let your teammates handle the aerial threat.

VS. SCORPION

Reasonable, the Scorpion has paper-thin armor compared to your hull, giving you the time you need to land a few primary fire shots, which is all it takes to blast the Scorpion.

Watch out for boost detonations though, you make a very tempting target, you can try to screen some of the damage, depending on what angle the Scorpion comes in towards you.

VS. DARKWALKER

Not a good battle. You can fire at it from a great distance, but the Darkwalker can do the same. You can shield its incoming fire, but that prevents you from retaliating effectively. If you must engage, simply accept that you're going to take a beating, and try to deal as much damage as possible.

VS. FURY

Much like the Raptor, this isn't really a target you want to be going after. If you can land hits on it, you can down the Fury, but getting those hits is the tough part, if the Fury is alert and engaged with you.

VS. NEMESIS

Not great, the Nemesis is, variably, faster, more maneuverable, or has greater firepower, depending on its form. You are more heavily armored, but if you engage in a fight, you're going to take heavy damage if you come out alive at all.

VS. SCAVENGER

Solid. The Scavenger can dodge a lot, but it doesn't take many hits to pop its glistening shell.

VS. VIPER

Good at a distance, where you can line up a shot and it can't really retaliate. Landing that shot is difficult however, and closer in, you are at risk from a dive bombing detonation attack from the Viper. Shield the blast if you do get targeted.

VS. INFANTRY

Decent. Your primary fire is *lethal* to infantry, but it shoots very slowly, and you can't track infantry up close easily. Your blast combination at point blank range can ward off infantry that get very close, but this isn't a frequent occurrence.

RAPTOR VS.:

VS. SCORPION

Quite good, you can easily pepper the Scorpion from the air with your primary fire, the only way it can avoid you is by getting under hard cover.

VS. DARKWALKER

Dangerous—usually safe, but if the Darkwalker gets a bead on you, you are in serious trouble. Try to come up on the Darkwalker from behind, and make sure its Turret never gets a chance to face you.

VS. FURY

Great—keep your distance and use your air to air missiles to down the Fury before it can bring its arcing energy beam to bear.

VS. NEMESIS

Dreadful, the Nemesis is essentially a mobile Beam Turret, exactly the sort of weaponry you do *not* want to be exposed to. Avoid!

VS. SCAVENGER

Only ok, largely because the Scavenger is such a small target, landing shots on it can be difficult if the "driver" (roller?) is alert and actively evading incoming fire. You can usually take it down, it just takes a bit of focused attention.

VS. VIPER

Quite good, just like the Manta, your missiles can acquire a lock on this light vehicle, and it doesn't take much to down it. As long as the terrain doesn't provide cover for the Viper, you can take it down with ease.

VS. INFANTRY

Solid—remember that your primary fire pulse cannons DO have splash damage, so you don't need to hit infantry players directly. Saturate the area around a target and you can eventually take it down. Also, shooting a continuous stream of shots at a target is a good idea anyway, as it gives an increased chance of your shots intercepting an AVRiL fired at you from the ground near (or from) your target.

SCORPION VS.:

VS. DARKWALKER

Not good. If you somehow manage to get off a boost detonation on the Darkwalker's core, you can deal some solid damage, but doing so is difficult at best.

Otherwise, you're likely to get completely incinerated or blasted apart by its Turret before you can even get into range to use your energy bombs.

VS. FURY

Awful, you have no means of retaliating, and it can easily scorch your hull from the sky. Stay away!

VS. NEMESIS

Very bad, the Nemesis can tear you apart at a distance with ease. A boost detonation on the Nemesis is very worthwhile however, try to come up on the Nemesis while it is unaware of your presence, and get the boost lined up before it can bring its cannons to bear.

VS. SCAVENGER

Decent; neither of you have stunning primary weaponry, and you're both lightly armored, so you can come out of this battle on top with a little luck and solid aim.

VS. VIPER

Not a good fight, the Viper is too difficult to hit if the pilot is even remotely intelligent, and it can easily spray fire at you from a distance.

VS. INFANTRY

Similar to the Manta, the Scorpion is quite good against infantry, but also very vulnerable to infantry armed with anti-vehicle weaponry.

Your extendable blades, your hull, and your primary fire energy bombs are all useful against infantry, just don't expect to come out of an engagement against multiple alert infantry targets in one piece.

DARKWALKER VS.:

VS. FURY
If you can manage to get it into your sights at long-range, you can blast it out of the sky, but otherwise, the Fury can outmaneuver your Turret, and harass you from behind.

VS. NEMESIS
Usually results in a victory, though a costly one. If you have a Turret gunner, your firepower greatly outclasses the Nemesis, and so does your armor, making for a stronger match up.

VS. SCAVENGER
Good, you can vaporize the Scavenger from a distance, and up close, your Turret can easily take it apart.

VS. VIPER
Generally excellent. At a distance, you can fry it with your primary Turret, and if it gets too close, not only is the Viper vulnerable to your Turret, you can also howl to knock the Viper away and send the pilot crashing to the turf, to be expunged.

VS. INFANTRY
Fantastic, one swipe of your massive energy beam is enough to powder freshly spawned infantry, and even armored troops aren't going to take a second blast.

At close-range, your Turret works well, and your devastating howl knocks infantry off their feet, leaving them stunned long enough to easily finish off.

FURY VS.:

VS. NEMESIS
Not good, like the other aircraft, the Fury is highly vulnerable to the Nemesis' rapid fire and pinpoint accurate Turret. Avoid this vehicle!

VS. SCAVENGER
Great, you can fry the Scavenger from above, and it can do little to retaliate, plus you can boost to catch up to it fairly easily.

VS. VIPER
Not great, as the Viper is extremely fast, so your chances of cooking the Viper depend entirely on catching it at a location it is trying to assault—generally either a Node or near the flag.

VS. INFANTRY
Decent, you are vulnerable to the usual anti-air weaponry, and your primary weapons comparatively short range necessitates hovering over infantry—usually not a safe place to be.

Still, you can deal solid damage, and definitely provide heavy distraction while engaged.

NEMESIS VS.:

VS. SCAVENGER
Excellent, you can easily vaporize the Scavenger with only a few moments of concentrated fire.

VS. VIPER
Good at any range, just watch out for suicide dive bomb attacks, the Viper's explosion can deal devastating damage, and you lack the single shot damage needed to stop it from impacting.

VS. INFANTRY
Great against infantry in the open, not so good against infantry with cover. They can easily duck in and out of line of sight while peppering you with fire. Seek out cover of your own if you're going to fight back.

SCAVENGER VS.:

VS. VIPER
Not so hot, the Viper is far faster than you, and can maintain distance to shoot at you, then back off if you do manage to get your Nanoblack orb locked on target.

VS. INFANTRY
Solid, you can lock on with your orb from a distance or, preferably, use your maneuverability, jumping, rolling, and spike spinning to crush or impale infantry.

Just be wary, the Scavenger is usually best for negotiating tricky terrain, not engaging in open battle, you are lightly armored.

VIPER VS.:

VS. INFANTRY
Ok at a distance, and at full speed, you can easily run down unsuspecting players.

Your dive bomb suicide attack is great for clustered defenders near a flag or Node, but it can be dodged fairly easily in the open.

Just be careful about getting in a protected shooting battle—you make a prime target for AVRiL big game hunters.

BEFORE YOU CAN RUN...

To begin with, the most basic movement is simply walking forwards or backwards, and strafing from side to side. The very newest players tend to run in straight, curving lines, moving only forwards, turning slightly as they spot a new area or item of interest, and occasionally backpedaling from a threat, without heed to the terrain behind them.

A veteran player tends to move in constant left and right angled lines, sweeping their view constantly in an arc to locate threats, while strafing from side to side to vary their movement pattern.

Amusingly, very skilled players who spend a lot of time in highly competitive games often have a hard time hitting very new players with projectile weapons, as their movement patterns are so radically different from those of a more experienced player.

It is important to understand how your movement changes your target profile for someone attempting to hit you with any of the weapons.

For projectile weapons, constant dodges, wall jumps, double jumps, and sudden shifts in direction can throw off tracking, ensuring that even a skilled player is going to fire Link plasma in the wrong direction, score glancing hits with rockets, miss completely with close range flak shots, and generally having to work a lot harder to take you down.

With instant hit weaponry, erratic motion is the hardest to hit, with jittering movement perpendicular to your target. Moving forwards or backwards relative

to your opponent when they have an instant hit weapon does little to affect their chances of hitting you (unless you're nearly vertical relative to their position, where your forward or backwards movement is again perpendicular to their aim).

By constantly moving in one direction, you make yourself extremely easy to track, but if you break up your movement lines in a highly random manner, by mixing up your left and right movements utterly inconsistently, and even occasionally stopping for a split-second, you can throw off smooth tracking by even the best players.

In close and midrange combat, your movement relative to your target is also important, and it must factor in your weapon, your opponents weapon, and the terrain around you. Sometimes, you must choose whether to focus on evading fire, or landing shots—it is considerably more difficult to concentrate on a difficult shot while you are in the midst of an erratic movement and dodging pattern.

Strafing is a critical component of your movement, and if you do not naturally blend strafing in with your forward and backwards movement, all while turning and tracking your targets, you should constantly practice it, even while simply walking from one place to another. Strafing allows you to continue moving to a destination, even while aiming 90 degrees to the left or right, and still allows you to compensate for changing terrain, unlike running backwards.

Running backwards through levels is a fairly advanced skill, and it is useful in DM, and very useful in CTF, where you must frequently fight off pursuing enemies while moving towards your base as quickly as possible.

JUMPING

Jumping is a very basic movement skill, and should be incorporated into your normal movement and strafing.

Jumping in *Unreal* has several applications, the most basic of which being simply to get over rough terrain without a pause in your movement, but with double jumps, you can also jump a considerable distance, and adjust your trajectory in midair, useful while engaged in combat.

Double jumping is simply tapping jump again while midair—this does *not* give you a huge boost of height, but it does add considerable distance to long jumps, increasing your airtime enough to cross considerable gaps.

Experiment with double jumps on all levels, you may find many areas where you can just barely scale a rise, or clear a gap.

In addition to jumping, it is also possible to perform one unique *Unreal Tournament* move, that being 'lift jumping', which is simply using the momentum gained while traveling up a lift to boost your vertical leap by a huge amount.

While taking any lift in the game upwards, jump just as the lift approaches its midpoint, where its movement speed is the greatest. Done properly, this should shoot you up into the air. While in the air, you can perform a double jump,

allowing you to gain another slight height boost, and give you more control over your landing site.

When we speak about control while jumping, we're talking about *air control*, and that is the ability to adjust your movement with your normal ground movement keys, even while in midair. Realistic, this is not, highly useful, it is.

Air control allows you to drop off a cliff and pull backwards in midair, just enough to hit a recessed ledge below you. You can use it to change your landing spot from any high fall, and you can even use it to adjust your position while double jumping.

This is particularly useful with the double jump, as the second jump can be partially redirected—try jumping to the right, then strafe to the left in midair while performing the second jump. You can nearly stop your motion, important in combat, where varying your motion is so incredibly crucial in throwing off a skilled players aim.

Jumping is also very important in combination with dodging, as it gives you two forms of rapid position shifting, and it allows you to perform walldodges, a vital movement technique.

DODGING

Dodging is unique to *Unreal Tournament*, and it is an additional movement ability that gives you more options for navigating difficult terrain, avoiding incoming shots, and moving more quickly through levels.

Because dodging is not a specific single button, but rather, a double tap in a movement direction, this has implications for your movement due to simple physical limitations. As an example, if you are strafing right, and you want to dodge right, you must release the right strafe button, if only for a split-second, creating a slight hitch in your movement.

To compensate for this, the best way to keep yourself moving and dodge at the same time is to mix a second direction with your dodge. If you want to dodge left or right, be moving forwards or backwards. Similarly, if you want to dodge forwards or backwards, strafe to the right or left.

Another benefit of this is that it is simply more comfortable to do this—double tapping forward while trying to run forward is somewhat awkward, but if you shift your aim so that your right or left strafe is moving you at an angle close to your original direction, you can dodge forward and quickly re-center your aim to propel yourself towards your destination.

This principle works identically for strafing to the side—you can run forwards, angle yourself, dodge to the right or left roughly in line with your original forward movement, then re-center yourself and continue moving forwards.

Both movement and dodge combinations have other advantages—quickly moving through levels with a combination of dodges is only one. Because the various mixes of movement and dodging allow you to shift your aim while still moving in a different direction, you can track targets to attack or evade as needed, a vital skill in both DM and CTF.

Basic dodging is only the beginning of the potential however, walldodging in combination with double jumps add even more mobility to your arsenal.

If you are just beginning to learn dodging, we strongly recommend you begin with basic left and right dodges—they are typically the most useful, as you are usually oriented facing your opponent, so side dodges shift your position rapidly in relation to your opponent (again, perpendicular movement), and in addition, they are simply easier to perform while moving forwards, the most common direction you move while playing.

MOVEMENT ODDITIES

First, it is possible to 'perma crouch' by double tapping crouch. Handy if you're hiding out somewhere or sniping tucked away in a corner and you don't feel like holding the button the entire time.

Second, and more oddly, you can dodge moving right, by double tapping *left*. The same applies while moving forward (double tap back), though that's usually a finger contortion of epic proportions with most movement setups.

WALL DODGING

Walldodges are performed simply by jumping or double jumping until you are touching a wall, then dodging in any direction that takes you *away* from that wall. In other words, if you jump into a wall on your right, dodging to the left will cause you to walldodge off of the wall.

An important point to note about this is that your position relative to the wall is determined by which direction you are facing. This is critical, because it means you can double jump towards a wall straight ahead of you, turn your view to the right, and then dodge to the right, because you are now dodging off of a wall to your left.

The angle required is not especially sharp either, there's quite a bit of flex allowed, as a consequence, with practice, you can constantly jump towards walls ahead of you and dodge off of them in a zigzag pattern, moving through levels extremely rapidly. Even if you're angled only slightly away from a wall, you should be able to dodge away from it.

With enough practice, every outcropping, rock, pillar, doorway, and pole on a level starts to look like a potential walldodge target, and this skill is *incredibly* important for flag runners to master in CTF, and for DM players both for mobility and for evasion purposes.

Forwards and backwards walldodges are considerably more difficult. Backwards walldodges tend to have little utility, simply because you never want to be facing a wall instead of an opponent, but forwards wall dodges can be used if you are jumping directly back from an opponent for any reason.

Most frequently however, sideways walldodges are the easiest to utilize, both in combat, and for moving about a level. They have the considerable benefit of allowing you to keep your target in your sights, due to the lenient nature of the required angle on a sideways walldodge.

One other point about walldodging—the act of dodging actually provides a slight vertical lift, and this can be combined with a double jump to reach a ledge that would otherwise be too high to reach.

Crisscrossing wall dodges are possible in *many* maps, and are exceedingly useful while flag running in normal CTF (nearly essential against skilled opponents, you need the extra speed).

MOBILITY

Double jumping gives you a height boost, but walldodging also gives you a slight height boost. In combination, it is possible to reach platforms you might not think are within reach.

Similarly, dodges give a *lot* of lateral movement, so a well aimed walldodge can send you flying across even fairly sizable gaps.

Another important point—dodges move you more while you are holding the dodge direction. As a random example, if you're at the bottom of Vertebrae moving along the center walkways, you can dodge to the Shield Belt or Redeemer while holding the dodge or moving forward. Simply tap dodge while standing still and you'll drop to the water below.

Dodging on sloped ground is one of the few situations in which you can't simply dodge in combat for evasive purposes. While dodging down a slope is useful, dodging up a slope (or stairs) doesn't move you at all, and in fact stops your motion for a moment—potentially lethal in a firefight.

The situations in which these moves are useful are literally too numerous to list, but experiment with dodging over gaps and walldodging to reach distant targets—there are many, many areas in which these moves are useful.

DUEL

Duels are a unique subset of Deathmatch, where it is only you and one opponent. Duels have weapons stay disabled by default, which is critically important—it means that weapons become just as much of a resource as armor.

Power-ups are often disabled in this mode as well, so check what settings you're playing with before you plan your routes and decide what area of the map to control.

Smaller maps tend to be better suited to duels, and this can de-emphasize mid or long range combat, important if you prefer fighting at a distance.

Duels tend to reward a mix of highly conservative and highly aggressive play, where you go back and forth with your opponent, never over-committing to a fight if you can back off to heal. This continues until one player scores a kill, then the

winner of the battle must quickly capitalize on the advantage to track down the spawned player and rack up several frags to pull ahead.

This usually ends when the player with the upper hand goes down in a fight, then there's a scramble to reassert control of the level (generally by getting a strong weapon or two, and the armor on the map). Then the see-saw battle for a kill resumes.

Duels are highly intense, challenging matchups of personal skill. There are no teammates to fall back on, no vehicles to minimize the importance of weapons or movement skills on foot.

Learning to fight well in Duels trains a host of skills that carry over extremely well to TDM, DM, and CTF.

TEAM DEATHMATCH

Team Deathmatch is similar to Duels in many respects, in that two teams vie for control of the level. Individual skills are critical important here as well, as the level of your team must be roughly equivalent to your opponents to have a chance of an even battle, but teamwork is paramount.

Rather than focusing on single items (though you must still control armor, power-ups, and health), TDM tends to focus on areas of control, where dominant map positions are the key to victory, and pinning your opponents in undesirable locations on the map allows you to gain a lead.

Most mid-and large sized maps are suitable to larger TDM games, though it is possible to play enjoyable 2v2 matches on some of the small maps, which are a nice mix of the Duel and TDM styles.

Unlike Deathmatch, your kill/death ratio is paramount in TDM, so learning to disengage from unfavorable situations or 2on1 fights quickly is very important. Most matches tend to be played with a time limit, not a frag limit, so maintaining a positive ratio is critical for your team to have a chance at victory.

This means that playing excessively aggressively can hurt your team badly, and the scoreboard can be a bit misleading because of this. You might have the most frags on your team, but if you also have the most deaths, and more deaths than frags, you're doing worse than the guy with five kills and no deaths.

When you do go hunting for kills, travel in packs, ambush lone players whenever possible, the point isn't to engage in fair fights, its to crush the opposing team with teamwork whenever possible.

CAPTURE THE FLAG

Capture the flag is a classic game mode, with a very simple premise—two teams, Red and Blue, each with a flag, must pick up the enemy flag and return it to their own flag to score. If your flag is missing, your offense must recover it while your defense protects your flag carrier.

CTF has a lot in common with the team play emphasis of TDM, but in many ways, it is even more demanding of specific focus from your teammates. While in TDM you may be responsible for a specific area of the map, the situations in TDM are very fluid, and change constantly from players dying and respawning in other areas of the map, necessitating constant repositioning.

In CTF, players spawn in or near their own base, and a division in roles between offense and defense is paramount—you *must* have your flag defended, and you *must* have dedicated flag runners.

Unlike DM, **kills count for nothing**, and this is a critical point—you win CTF by capturing the flag, either over a timed match, or to a certain capture limit. In either case, your personal frag count is meaningless.

On offense, it does not matter how many times you die trying to run the flag. Having defenders fragging the enemy offense is obviously important, but as a general rule **engaging in midfield battles does not help your team**. Indeed, it can make it more difficult for your offense, as the killed players respawn back in their base, often in front of or behind your flag runners.

Defense is usually split into two roles, that of an actual flag room defender, and a midfield defender who warns the inner defense of where attackers are coming (while trying to damage them a bit on the way in, to hurt their chances of getting out of the flag room alive).

Because dying does not matter, and with the presence of the Translocator as a movement device, your offense can zip across the map to push on the enemy base very quickly. Generally, the offensive players need to acquire some armor on the way in, because the flag run *out* of the enemy base is the hard part, not getting in with the assistance of translocation.

Once your flag runner is carrying the flag, he can no longer use the Translocator without dropping the flag, and so he must get back to base on foot. As a result, your most evasive and nimble players, as well as your best on foot fighters, should be your flag runners. Keep your quick-thinking and highly alert players on defense to intercept and down enemy offense as it moves in and out of the base.

Escorting the flag carrier is vital, because once they're running the flag, the enemy team can easily catch up via translocation, and only by killing their nearby players to spawn them far enough back in their base can you hope to return home safely. Be sure to never pick up Health or armor in front of your flag runner!

TRANSLOCATOR

The Translocator is a unique transportation tool, only usable in Capture the Flag. The translocator is a small projectile device that launches a translocation disc in a shallow arc, a good distance ahead of you. By tapping alt-fire, you instantly teleport to the location of the disc.

A few notable points. First, the Translocator has 7 'charges' or shots, with a slight (.25 second) delay between shots, and it recharges one shot every 1.25 seconds or so. In practice, this means that as long as you're translocating a good distance each throw (rather than rapidly spamming teleports), you can cross any midfield of any CTF map in the game without running out of charges.

The Translocator is a vital tool for moving about on CTF maps, as it allows you to quickly reach any area on the map with great speed, and with considerable safety as well.

There are only two ways to hurt a translocating player—the first is destroying the disc. If you damage the translocation disc before a player teleports, and they *do* teleport (rather than throwing a fresh disc), they're instantly fragged.

The other is hitting the 'ghost' left behind by the translocation. For a split second (literally, a tiny fraction of a second), the ghostly image left behind by a translocation can be injured. The timeframe involved is so short that only the instant hit weapons really have a chance of dealing damage, making the Shock Rifle and Sniper Rifle useful for taking shots at players translocating towards your base—as long as your aim is on target, even if they teleport right as you fire, you're still going to hit them.

It is possible to damage players with projectile weapons, if you happen to be up close firing at them between translocations, even if they teleport, if a rocket is already in flight, they may get hit.

Still, as a general rule, combating a rapidly translocating player in the field on offense is a waste of time, because they'll be out of your range in seconds, and time spent firing at them means you're not translocating towards armor, power-ups, or the enemy flag.

TELEPORTATION

One handy trick with the Translocator on defense—drop the disc on an armor or power-up spawn, and resume your defensive duties.

After a few battles (or if you manage to back off in a fight and pull out your Translocator), you can teleport to your pre-placed disc, often instantly grabbing health, armor, a power-up, or popping up in a different area of your base completely.

Why chase a flag runner out when you can teleport ahead of them on a ledge overlooking their exit route?

MIDFIELD RUGBY

You may find that some of the commentary on the CTF maps doesn't match your experiences on public servers. This isn't surprising—very frequently, in non 'serious' matches, players in CTF will spend a fair amount of time just fighting in the midfield (or in the bases), rather than explicitly defending the flag or focusing on running the flag.

Everything written here is written with the assumption that you're aiming to win CTF matches—and you win CTF matches by capturing the flag, not by fragging players. Indeed, killing players in the midfield while you're trying to run the flag can actually be counterproductive. You lose health and ammo, they respawn back in their base, either ahead of you, or close to your teammate who is running the flag!

This is sort of an odd, unintuitive bit of logic, but avoiding combat and focusing on reaching the flag quickly via translocation is usually a more certain path to victory than engaging in combat with every enemy player you encounter in the midfield.

Essentially, the real brawl begins when a player picks up the flag—at that point they can no longer translocate, so they become a real target, and chasing players have to stop translocating to actually try to *kill* the flag carrier.

Playing aggressive defense on many CTF maps is quite helpful, and several CTF maps rely on forward defenders alerting flag room defenders on incoming enemies. The role of the forward defense is to warn the flag room defenders of *where* they are coming in, and if possible, to weaken them.

This has a huge benefit for your whole team effort, as a weakened enemy flag runner heading for your flag room is no problem for an organized defense, *and* they are essentially wasting time—walking dead men. Meanwhile, the enemy team is down a player on defense, so your own flag runners have a better chance of success.

Conversely, if you spend much of a CTF match in the midfield battling every target you see (and killing a fair number of them), they're constantly respawning *back in their base*, which, needless to say, does not help a flag carrier's odds of getting out in one piece with the flag.

Don't let any of this dissuade you from fragging every player you run across in a random pub game, there's nothing *wrong* with doing that, just be aware of the consequences.

A lot of this oddity stems from the combination of the Translocator (which allows for extremely rapid movement, and is very difficult to effectively fight), and the spawn locations (spawning in or near the base at all times). The result is that the surest path to victory in a CTF match isn't quite as simple as shooting everyone that moves.

Because a skilled translocator can get across a map while only being visible for mere seconds, actually engaging such a target in combat is difficult or impossible. If you *do* want to engage a dedicated offensive translocator, instant hit weapons are your best weapon. There is a split second of vulnerability after a translocation, where the 'ghost' left behind from the teleport can still be hit—if you had a shot lined up, and your target teleports just as you fire, you're still going to land the hit. The same is not true if you fire a projectile, even the quicker moving ones usually can't hit the ghost (barring situations where you're shooting a rocket at a player point blank just as they teleport).

VEHICLE CAPTURE THE FLAG

Vehicle Capture the Flag is exactly what it sounds like. Capture the Flag, with vehicles! There are a few simple points about this mode in the ways that it differs from regular CTF. Much like vanilla CTF, VCTF is won with flag captures, not kills. Again, dividing your team up into flag area defense, midfield defense, and offense works well. There are a few wrinkles added due to the presence of vehicles however—for one, denying and destroying your opponents vehicles improves the odds of your offense getting out alive with the flag, so your midfield 'defense' is really an offense focused on destroying as many of the other teams vehicles as possible, either with your own vehicles, or with the AVRiL. For another, getting out with the flag safely is *hard*. There's no Translocator in this mode, instead, you can only carry the flag while on your Hoverboard, *not* in a vehicle. You *can* however, grapple onto a vehicle—even an air vehicle. If the map has a Raptor or a Fury, that's your fastest ticket home as a flag runner. Otherwise, the quicker vehicles (Manta, Viper) work best for flag transport. If you don't have a friendly vehicle to grapple on to, flag running is a tricky business. You must take the route back to your base that impedes enemy vehicle movement the most, and move in such a manner as to make distant sniper or Shock Rifle fire as inaccurate as possible, to avoid being knocked off your Hoverboard at long range. If you *are* knocked down while boarding, the flag drops nearby, allowing it to be instantly returned, though if you're still a good distance from whatever hit you, you may be able to pick it up again.

VCTF and Warfare both have a considerable emphasis on vehicle combat. Vehicular combat is considerably simpler than on foot battle.

For the most part, certain vehicles are simply superior to other vehicles, barring very strange engagement scenarios.

As a result, using your vehicles as effectively as possible against unfavorable matchups for your target is important, to get the most mileage out of all of the armor available to you.

Learn the various special quirks of the vehicles—the Viper and Scorpion self destructs are quite useful for example, as is the Darkwalker's ability to crouch (you can even squeeze into the Floodgate Node on Floodgate!).

Fighting *against* vehicles on foot in the open is generally suicide, but with rough terrain, or buildings or structures offering concealment, you can present a considerable threat to any vehicle, even the heaviest ones.

While most weapons deal reduced damage to vehicles, don't let that stop you from shooting at them. Concentrated fire from multiple players can take down even a Goliath, even without an AVRiL.

The AVRiL is a key anti-vehicle weapon, and learning to use it well means *not* standing out in the open in the path of a Goliath. Instead, use your smaller size and greater agility to avoid vehicles entirely, popping out only briefly to fire off a shot, then ducking back to reload.

WARFARE

Warfare is the most complex game mode in *Unreal Tournament 3*, an update to the Onslaught mode in UT2k4. In Warfare, the Red and Blue teams each have a Power Core—destroying the enemy team's Core secures victory. All other considerations are secondary—frags don't count, only destroying the Core. To do so, you must first 'link' to the enemy Power Core, by connecting a series of Nodes to the enemy base. Each map in Warfare has a Prime Node (sometimes one for each team) that connects to the Power Core. Capturing this Node allows you to damage the enemy Power Core.

A Warfare map can be as simple as a Power Core for each team, and a single Prime Node in the center of the map. Whoever controls the Prime Node can attack the enemy Power Core, while the other team struggles to recapture the Prime Node to protect their core.

Some Warfare maps are considerably more complex—there may be an intermediate Center Node between a Prime Node for each base, and there can also be 'unlinked' secondary Nodes. These secondary Nodes are *not* necessary to link to the enemy Core and destroy it, but they always offer some bonus to the team that controls them—it may be a powerful vehicle, another Orb spawner location, or a special effect unique to the map.

Be sure to check the Node descriptions for each Warfare map in this chapter, you can find out the specifics of the unique effects of any of the Nodes, as well as see the Node linkages at a glance.

NODES

Capturing Nodes in Warfare is quite simple. If a Node is uncaptured (neutral), simply touch it on foot (not in a vehicle) to claim it for your team. Any captured Node automatically builds itself fully after about 30 seconds have passed. A fully built Node is then 'active', and links to any connected Nodes, allowing you to move on and attack the next Node in line.

You can speed up the construction process by repairing the Node as it builds with the Link Gun secondary fire. Nearly every weapon locker at every Node on every Warfare map has the Link Gun, so this is almost always an option.

Keep in mind that Nodes are healed more slowly by the Link Gun as they approach full health, so if you're on offense, you may want to dump about 50 ammo into it, then move on, since it takes nearly another 50 to get it to full health. By the time you arrive at a new Node, the one behind you is frequently built if you assisted it slightly, saving you time on the move.

If a Node is in enemy hands, shoot it! Destroying an enemy Node is simply a matter of blasting it until it reverts to a neutral, unclaimed Node. At that point, either team can claim it again, but usually, if you're in the process of blasting a Node to bits, enemy team players are dead, or respawning too far away to reclaim it.

You can damage a Node by shooting either its base *or* the floating Node sphere itself. From a distance, attack the sphere, and up close, you can pound away on the base if you prefer.

Nodes are pretty sturdy—not many infantry weapons are great against them, the Flak at point blank, and Rockets from a distance are about your best options, vehicle weapons, the Viper and Scorpion detonation, the Redeemer, or the Shaped Charge are all great options for destroying a Node quickly.

The ultimate option for capturing (or protecting) a Node is the Orb.

A critically important point: *a Node that is under attack prevents players from spawning or teleporting to the Node.* A Node is considered under attack if it takes *any* damage, even an Enforcer shot from half way across the map. Not only that, a Node remains contested for about 5 seconds after being damaged.

This is *very* important for attacking enemy Nodes, as you can lock down the Node *before* you get close to it. While you are fighting near the Node, try to hit it every couple of shots to prevent any freshly killed enemy players from respawning while you battle anyone nearby.

NODE BUSTING

Nodes have 1500 armor, Power Cores 5000, though both take reduced damage from most infantry and vehicle weapons.

THE ORB

The Nodebuster Orb is a vital tool in Warfare, and one of the new additions to UT3's Warfare mode over 2k4's Onslaught. In essence, the Orb is a Node 'superweapon'. While carrying the Orb, if you touch a Neutral or enemy Node (no matter if it is fully healthy or not!), you instantly capture the Node for your team with a fully built Node sphere!

You still can't capture unlinked Nodes, they must be connected to a friendly Node, but this is still an incredibly powerful offensive resource, and must be used constantly. To balance out the power a bit, there are numerous warnings to alert you of an enemy Orb approaching one of your Nodes. First, you get an audio warning, second, it shows up on your minimap, and third, both Red and Blue Orbs have giant pillars of light that project from them up into the sky, making them very easy to spot from a distance.

Oh, and you can't carry the Orb inside a vehicle, or take it through a teleporter…

There is more however, not only is the Orb a powerful offensive weapon, it is also a powerful *defensive* weapon. If you are carrying your Orb, and you are standing in line of sight of one of your Nodes (within a reasonable distance), a beam of energy projects from the Orb to the Node, shielding it from all enemy damage and capture attempts. To destroy a Node protected by an Orb carrier, you must first kill the Orb carrier, then you can tackle the Node.

Because the Orb must be carried on foot, this makes protecting Nodes that are on open ground difficult, as enemy vehicles can easily run you down or blast you from a distance. However, many Node locations are within terrain that restricts direct vehicle access, so you can often dodge enemy fire, while fighting back with an AVRiL.

One last note about the Orb—if it is dropped on the ground, a teammate can pick it up, but if it an enemy Orb is dropped nearby, approach it and tap use to destroy the Orb. This hurts you badly (to the tune of 100 health or so), but it is almost *always* worth doing, as it forces the Orb to respawn back at their closest Orb Spawner.

ORB SPAWNERS

While the Orb always spawns at your Power Core, on some Warfare maps, you can also acquire additional Orb Spawner platforms. Doing so is very useful, as it allows you to bring the Orb forward more quickly. This is especially important on the larger maps, where it can be excessively time consuming to Hoverboard from your base carrying the Orb.

SPAWNING

While respawning in DM (anywhere on the map away from enemies, or near your teammates in TDM), CTF, or VCTF (in or near your base) is quite simple, spawning in Warfare is considerably more complicated.

In Warfare, you always spawn at your base, or at one of your Nodes. The Nodes you control can change from moment to moment, so your spawning locations change constantly.

This is very important for a lot of reasons—for one, securing secondary Nodes can provide another place to spawn.

Another is that you don't directly control your spawn point, it is chosen based on your 'role selection', a slightly obscure but very important mechanic.

Essentially, if you bring up the large map screen in Warfare, you can see a selection option for different 'roles' that you can play in Warfare. These don't give you special abilities, but they *do* influence where you spawn, and they also affect what voiceovers you receive.

As an example, if you choose the Orb Runner role, you will *always* spawn at a Node that has your Orb. Similarly, the Special Ops role gives you voiceovers to notify you of a Shaped Charge spawn, the Redeemer spawn, or a support vehicle like the Nightshade.

Choosing 'Disabled' shuts off the guides and the the voiceovers, while No Preference gives you a range of voiceovers, and usually a preference for offensive spawns.

TELEPORTS

Every controlled Node (and your home base) has a teleport located somewhere near the Node.

Touch a teleport and tap the use button and you can then instantly teleport to any other friendly Node that is *not* under attack.

This is incredibly handy for popping to a Node to grab an AVRiL, or to get to a Node to check on a key vehicle spawn. Use and abuse them!

ROLE	EFFECT
Attack	Voiceovers alert you to what Node to attack, tries to spawn you at forward-most Node
Defend	Voiceovers alert you of what Node to defend, tries to spawn you near the Orb, or at the Power Core if it is under attack
Orb Runner	Always spawns you at the Orb, voiceovers alert you to the Orb respawning, and its location
Special Ops	Voiceovers alert you of deployable items, the Redeemer, and support vehicles (SPMA, Nightshade, Leviathan)

OFFENSE AND DEFENSE

Unlike the DM modes, where you're simply trying to score frags, Warfare's focus on territory control via the Nodes results in a constantly shifting offensive and defensive battle.

Secondary Nodes further complicate the situation, as they are not necessarily strictly critical to winning the map, but they can provide an offensive or defensive edge in some cases.

As a general rule, you still want to have an offensive and defensive assignment for your teammates, but defense has to be *much* more pro-active in Warfare than in CTF or VCTF. They must constantly shift from Node to Node, using the Orb to protect the enemy Prime Node once it is secured, and fighting off enemy offensive pushes against your Nodes and key secondary Nodes as well.

Meanwhile, your offense needs to push hard to reach the enemy Prime Node, possibly focusing on a key secondary Node if it is one of the special Nodes that can win the battle on its own (notably on Floodgate or Power Surge).

Vehicles play an enormous role in Warfare combat, so fighting in them and against them is an important skill to master. The Hoverboard lets you quickly get from place to place if you must, but usually, it is a better idea to use a teleport to reach a vehicle, or at the very least, make sure you have an AVRiL handy if you set out on foot.

Sniping is highly effective on defense, due to the distances involved on most Warfare maps, and by sniping, we mean not just with the Sniper Rifle, but also finding a nicely elevated and protected position and using the AVRiL against incoming enemy vehicles as well.

BARRICADES

One last random tidbit about Warfare: some maps have vehicle barricades, these can all be destroyed with either the Shaped Charge, or with the Redeemer.

In one very special case (Avalanche) destroying the barricade isn't used for removing a vehicle obstacle, it triggers a massive avalanche, devastating multiple Nodes and any enemy in the path of the unleashed torrent!

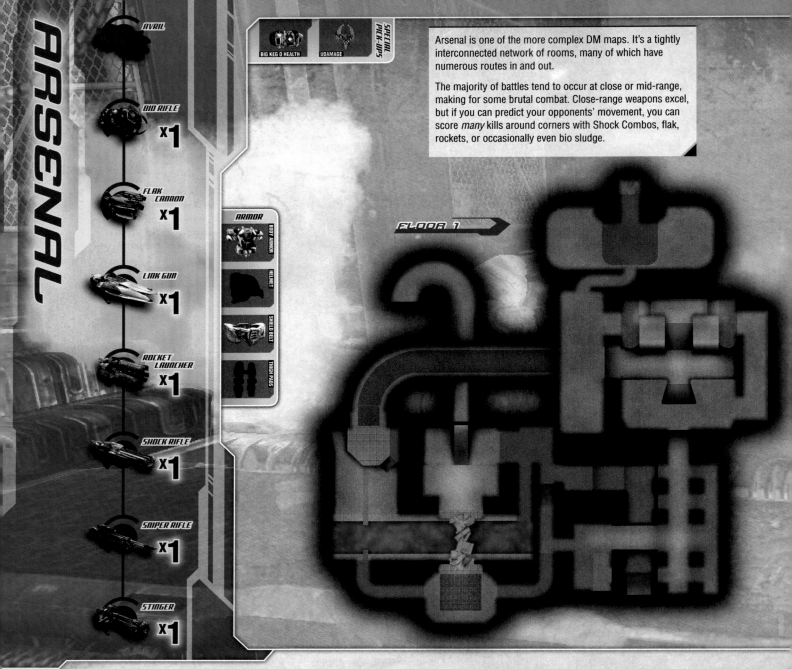

ARSENAL

AVRIL

BIO RIFLE x1

FLAK CANNON x1

LINK GUN x1

ROCKET LAUNCHER x1

SHOCK RIFLE x1

SNIPER RIFLE x1

STINGER x1

SPECIAL PICK-UPS

BIG KEG O HEALTH | UDAMAGE

ARMOR

BODY ARMOR | HELMET | SHIELD BELT | THIGH PADS

FLOOR 1 →

Arsenal is one of the more complex DM maps. It's a tightly interconnected network of rooms, many of which have numerous routes in and out.

The majority of battles tend to occur at close or mid-range, making for some brutal combat. Close-range weapons excel, but if you can predict your opponents' movement, you can score *many* kills around corners with Shock Combos, flak, rockets, or occasionally even bio sludge.

DUEL

It's a large map for duels, and with so many high-powered pick-ups, you are frequently going to get into inconclusive battles if you engage cautiously. There

aren't any strict dead-ends on the map, so unless you can pin your opponent in one area, they can usually slip away to another part of the map.

Timing the UDamage, Shield Belt, and Health Keg should be your major priorities. The UDamage in particular can break a lock. Trying to hold down the weapons is basically impossible, they are scattered everywhere on the level, and your opponent is going to be close to *something* no matter where they spawn.

Stalking your opponent through the halls is tricky; make full use of sound to locate your target. If you can surprise your opponent, the advantage can be enough to tilt the battle in your favor.

Don't hesitate to throw projectiles down the halls if you have a rough idea where your target is. Unless you're trying to be stealthy, it's worth going for some cheap damage when you can.

Because there are only a few locations for regular Health pick-ups, if your opponent disengages after you dealt serious damage, try to intercept on their most likely route to recover from the battle.

DEATHMATCH

A constant battle, the more players present, the more vicious the combat becomes. You're going to want to go after the Flak Cannon and Rocket Launcher regularly, as both can score quick kills, and that's just what you need on this map. Trying to take down opponents with the Stinger or Link Gun may leave you frustrated when someone else swoops in and steals your kills.

Again, time the power-ups, but prioritize the UDamage. Don't necessarily focus on obtaining it, but try to be in position to kill anyone else who does. A pre-loaded triple spiral rocket barrage to the face is a nice present for someone leaping up to the UDamage.

Arsenal is what it says; all the weapons are present, and indeed, the majority of them have a room built entirely around them. Each of these rooms connects to several nearby areas, creating constantly shifting engagements, though you can usually expect to run into players using the weapons around their spawn points, especially in vanilla DM.

The map is arranged roughly in a north/south line, if you treat the UDamage as the north end and the Shield Belt and Body Armor as the south end. The Big Keg o' Health is located relatively near the UDamage, though reaching it requires the Jump Boots (just below it).

There are only a few locations to pick up regular Health, by the Sniper Rifle, by the Shield Belt, and by the UDamage. Each location has two Health pick-ups. Otherwise, the Health Keg and Shield Belt are your only other options for quick revitalization.

FLOOR 2

You're probably going to find it impossible to lock down all the power-ups completely. If you favor one section of the map over the others, fight near the closest power-up and hope you can at least manage to control that one.

TEAM DEATHMATCH

Generally, your team needs to decide which side of the map you're going to try to control. Of the two power-up sides, the UDamage and Keg side have more offensive power, but the Shield Belt and Body Armor offer more defense, and the Body Armor respawns more quickly than the Keg and UDamage combo.

If you end up on the armor side of the map, you're going to have to either make a timed push to seize the UDamage before it spawns, or expect to deal with a push from the other team when they acquire the UDamage. Long distance Sniper or Shock Rifle fire damage amped is not pleasant.

If you're holding the UDamage side of the map, your lack of armor can be a problem, you may want to try to hold the area between the Health Keg and the Body Armor, using your players around the Sniper Rifle and Shock Rifle rooms to protect the UDamage area.

Because the UDamage takes awhile to spawn, you should freely engage, and press any advantage you get between spawns, then return to guard it as its spawn time nears. Expect a rush for the UDamage as the spawn time approaches, you must either be the ones going for it, or be ready to paste anyone the instant they get near it. Jump Boots can help avoid a slip-up jumping up to reach it.

WEAPONRY	Flak Cannon
HEALTH & ARMOR	Health x2, Vials
POWER-UPS	None

The Shield Belt area holds the Flak Cannon, two of the four Health pick-ups on the entire level, and access to the Body Armor, Shock Rifle, and Bio Rifle areas.

There are *three* distinct levels to fight on in the Shield Belt area. The first is the walled area around the Shield Belt itself, giving plenty of cover to dodge around.

The second is the lower level, where the Flak Cannon is located. This area actually has a bridge crossing over it—walldodge to this bridge from behind the Shield Belt area to avoid dropping down to the Flak Cannon.

The last is up near the Health pick-ups, and a ramp leads up into the hall towards the Bio Rifle.

With the considerable cover in this area, close range weaponry is quite powerful, as are indirect fire weapons. If you're going to use instant hit weaponry, you may want to keep your distance from the Shield Belt itself.

2: BODY ARMOR

WEAPONRY	Rocket Launcher, Stinger
HEALTH & ARMOR	Body Armor
POWER-UPS	None

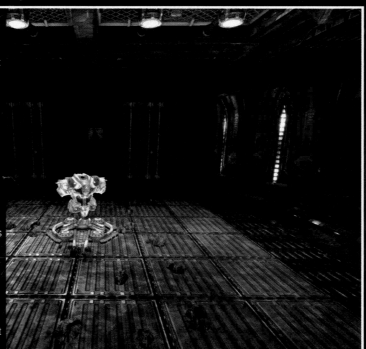

Just to the west of the Shield Belt, the Body Armor area has several important items, with the Rocket Launcher just under a bridge in front of the armor, and a Stinger in the open room to the west of the armor.

The long ramp across the bridge from the armor leads up to the Sniper Rifle area, and the hallway below takes you into the network of tunnels leading to the Jump Boots. Below the ramp is a passage that leads below the Bio Rifle.

There is a smooth curving ramp that leads down from the Body Armor to the Stinger area, and the halls towards the Shield belt are also quite tight. Otherwise, this area is more open.

If you prefer fighting with less cover, you may wish to haunt this area, as you can put the Shock Rifle or even Sniper Rifle to decent use, with fairly clear lines of sight compared to most other sections of the map.

The 40 maps that make up the *Unreal Tournament* world cover a massive variety of game types, sizes, and unique environments.

Becoming intimately familiar with each and every one of the maps is a slow process, but an important one. Next to your own personal movement, weapon, and vehicle abilities, knowledge of the maps is the next most vital skill you can have.

Exactly how much you need to know (right down to the most fiddly of possible wall jumps or just where a given vehicle can squeeze) really depends on the game mode (and the quality of your opponents of course).

Generally, the more intimate game types (Duels, Team Deathmatch, and CTF) are more demanding in terms of knowing the precise ins and outs of each map, while in VCTF and Warfare, you can get by with a more general knowledge of the layouts—but even on the largest Warfare maps, there are often useful power-ups off the beaten path, or bits of terrain effectively on offense or defense.

DEATHMATCH

Deathmatch is the simplest mode, and the vast majority of what you need to know to excel is covered in the weapons chapter.

For basic free for all Deathmatch, it is important to remember that the goal is the highest frag count—not the least deaths. There are no points for second place.

As a result, your tactics in DM should be considerably different than in a Duel or TDM match. Dying does not matter nearly as much, where it hurts you seriously in Duels, and hurts your team in TDM. In DM, you want to be at the center of the action, all of the time.

Find the areas on the levels where the largest concentration of players are hanging out, and go after them with the heaviest one shot kill weaponry you can find. Finesse, avoidance, and survival are less important than aggression, speed, and scoring kills.

There is one other important consideration for DM, and this is shared with all DM types, and CTF, though it is de-emphasized somewhat in VCTF or Warfare—that consideration is movement.

MOVEMENT

WALK WITHOUT RHYTHM

In *Unreal*, movement is life.

Your movement skills are just as, if not more important than your aim. The ability to avoid projectiles, and make yourself a *very* difficult target for instant hit weapons is a vital skill, and one that must be trained continuously.

The very best players have incredible agility, using every available surface for walldodging, dodging incoming projectiles instinctively, and moving in a stutter-step manner that is extremely difficult to track with instant hit weaponry.

If you are new to *Unreal Tournament*, mastering the advanced movement abilities available to you is an involved process, and it is easy to feel overwhelmed with managing 20 different weapon firing modes on top of moving, jumping, and dodging in three dimensions, all while tracking and evading your opponents.

Training your movement should be a gradual process, starting with the basics, and slowly progressing through the various maneuvers that are possible.

THIS IS WAR

In the vehicle gameplay modes, movement skills are *slightly* deemphasized—it is far easier to be effective in some of the more powerful vehicles than it is to fight on foot against a highly skilled opponent up close.

However, even Warfare, which features some of the most vehicle heavy fighting in the game still requires that you defend certain Nodes on foot, and most VCTF maps have certain areas that only players on foot can access or use effectively.

Not only that, with the AVRiL, and certain other weapons in specific situations, an agile player on foot who uses cover effectively is a serious threat to even the heaviest vehicles, and a lethal one to the lighter ones.

The skills you learn from becoming a more mobile and evasive player on foot also apply to the more maneuverable vehicles, and teach you the value of using your movement capabilities to their fullest extent—one of the reasons a Manta or Viper can be so dangerous against a Goliath.

3:

WEAPONRY	Sniper Rifle
HEALTH & ARMOR	Health x2
POWER-UPS	Big Keg O Health

The Sniper Rifle room is important, as it contains the Health Keg, located on a rafter above the Sniper Rifle, and the pair of Health pick-ups, on the spiral ramp beside the rifle.

The only way to get up to the Health Keg is impact jump, or (preferably) to take the Jump Boots just below the rifle and jump back up.

The Sniper Rifle area is connected to several parts of the map. To the south, you can reach the bridge to the Body Armor. Below, by the Jump Boots, you can go down the tunnel to the Stinger, east to below the Bio Rifle, or north to the UDamage room.

It is also possible to go east from the Sniper Rifle directly to reach the Bio Rifle itself.

The area around the Sniper Rifle is fairly constricted, not ideal for use of the rifle itself. You may have better luck with it in the Body Armor area to the south.

4: SHOCK RIFLE

WEAPONRY	Shock Rifle
HEALTH & ARMOR	Vials in side hall
POWER-UPS	None

The Shock Rifle room has interesting terrain, with significant height variance and a lot of cover. Exploit Shock Combos in this room, if you choose to hunt in here.

The east side has a hallway that connects the upper and lower levels with a few Health Vials in it. The south side has a tunnel leading down to the Shield Belt.

North up the ramp takes you to the UDamage, and west, either to the upper Bio Rifle hall, or the lower area below the Bio Rifle.

There isn't any health aside from the Vials here, or any armor, so you aren't likely to survive long if you try to hold out in this room for an extended period of time.

If you need to restock, make your way over to the Sniper Rifle or UDamage rooms.

WEAPONRY	Bio Rifle
HEALTH & ARMOR	None
POWER-UPS	None

The Bio Rifle hall is quite narrow and constrained, running north to the UDamage, south to the Shield Belt room. You can also quickly drop down to the Shock Rifle to the east, or the lower area below the Bio Rifle to the west.

The lower area is fairly extensive, but it has no useful pick-ups, so you aren't likely to see a lot of traffic in that area.

The Bio Rifle hall itself is actually ideal for charged secondary shots with the Bio Rifle, so be careful if you're running through this area, or you may die a gooey death to a freshly spawned player who just picked it up.

Generally this area is used purely for transit through the center of the map from one place to another, there aren't any items in the area worth fighting over, and you're dreadfully exposed to attack from any number of directions while in this location.

UDAMAGE

WEAPONRY	Bio Rifle
HEALTH & ARMOR	Health x2
POWER-UPS	None

The UDamage is the other "end" of the map from the Shield Belt. The room itself is quite simple; a ledge runs around the edge of the room, and a lift at the back goes between the ground floor and the ledge.

Down on the ground floor, you can grab the Link Gun, and take a tunnel out to the Jump Boots.

The ledge exits to the Shock Rifle

The UDamage itself is located up in a small niche, only accessible via Jump Boots, or lift jumping up from the lift behind it (the usual way to access it).

The room itself is quite defensible, and with speedy access to the Sniper Rifle area, you can resupply on health, possibly grabbing the Keg as well.

The lack of armor on this side the map makes getting tanked up rather

AVRIL

BIO RIFLE x2

FLAK CANNON

LINK GUN

ROCKET LAUNCHER x1

SHOCK RIFLE x1

SNIPER RIFLE x1

STINGER

SPECIAL PICK-UPS

BERSERK

ARMOR

BODY ARMOR

HELMET

SHIELD BELT

THIGH PADS

Biohazard is a *very* small Deathmatch map, suitable for Duels, or (at most) 2v2 TDM. Larger DM matches are going to be frantic and messy at best.

The map is a simple two level affair, with a Shield Belt on the lower level, and the Berserk power-up tucked away in an upper corner.

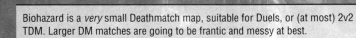

FLOOR 1

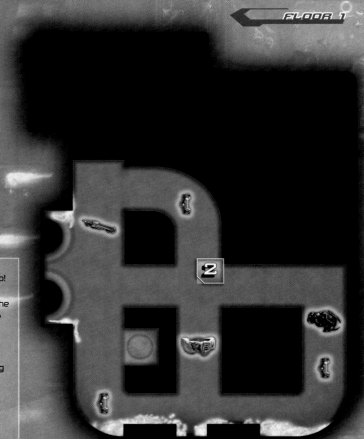

BIOHAZARD

The Berserk is protected by a trap! Fire at the small glowing panel beside the stairs leading up to the power-up, and you can seal the Berserk chamber off, flooding it with toxic Tarydium gas. This is lethal to any players trapped inside, so be careful about going for the Berserk if an enemy is aware of your position.

You may want to Impact jump up to the Berserk and drop out, to minimize the time spent on the stairs up to the power-up spawn point.

DUEL

An intense map for duels, controlling the upper level, the Shield Belt, and the Berserk is critical. The lower level is where you want to pin your opponent, and run them down like a trapped rat.

From the upper level, you can see to the lower level easily, and toss rockets, grenades, sludge, and Shock Combos at your foe.

If *you* get trapped below, be careful about using the jump pads. They make a distinctive noise, and the loss of control makes you a very easy target. This does limit your options to the stairs, or a desperation impact hammer jump, but you can fight back from below with the Shock or Bio Rifles, if not truly effectively.

Be careful about picking up the Vials while below, they instantly give away your location to an alert opponent.

The upper floor has a large open center area, and plenty of health to recharge after a battle. Time the Shield Belt relentlessly, grabbing it constantly can put you in control of the match.

The upper level holds all of the health (four pick-ups), the Rocket Launcher, Sniper Rifle, and Bio Rifle.

The lower level has the Shock Rifle, another Bio Rifle, and three sets of triple Health Vials.

Ammunition is *very* limited on this map, with only one Sniper Rifle and Shock Rifle packs, and two Bio Rifle packs.

Generally, most of your ammunition is going to come from slain opponents, so expect to use the Sniper Rifle and Shock Rifle rather frequently, as rockets and even bio sludge are easy to run low on.

 FLOOR 2 ➡

RELOAD

The Berserk's special ability of loading you to maximum ammo for your carried weapons is especially important on this map, given the limited ammunition available. It's the only way to totally load up on rockets, not to mention the devastating offensive boost it gives you.

SNIPER CAMPING

The Sniper Rifle platform has a great line of sight to both jump pads up from the lower floor; the only way an enemy can get up without you spotting them is from the steps near the Bio Rifle.

If you don't see or hear your opponent for a moment, you can safely assume they're heading up from that direction (or waiting stationary downstairs)

DEATHMATCH ➡

It's pure pandemonium with more than four players. Use the Rocket Launcher and Shock Combos relentlessly, patrol the Health on the upper floor, and time the Berserk and the Shield Belt.

TEAM DEATHMATCH ➡

This map makes for a tight 2v2, but any more than that and you're looking at a spawn-die-spawn-die sort of match.

With doubles, have one player camping out on the upper floor guarding the Health, while the other sweeps the lower floor, falling back to recover when he gets damaged.

1: UPPER FLOOR

WEAPONRY	Bio Rifle, Rocket Launcher
HEALTH & ARMOR	Health x4, Vials
POWER-UPS	Berserk

The open floor around the Rocket Launcher is perfect for mid-range fighting, though there is no cover to speak of.

Around the Bio Rifle, the sloped stairs provide easy targets for rocket splash damage, but since rocket ammo is so limited, you can't keep this up for long.

As far as the Bio Rifle goes, charged secondary shots on players using the jump pads work well, spraying primary fire can't be done with great frequency without running dry on ammunition.

The Berserk platform is easily targeted by any weapon, but the Berserk is so critical on this map that it's always worth going for.

If you can't reach it in time, have a charged secondary Rocket or Bio ready for the person going for it, or a Shock Combo.

The plentiful Health on this floor is vital to controlling the map. Pick it up any time you take the slightest damage to deny your opponent the ability to recover.

The Sniper Rifle is an oddity, as this map has no long range space whatsoever, but you can use it to good effect against players using the jump pads, or in the narrow hallways on the bottom level. It does have the advantage of using ammunition slowly, relevant if you run dry with your other weapons.

2: LOWER FLOOR

WEAPONRY	Bio Rifle, Shock Rifle
HEALTH & ARMOR	Shield Belt
POWER-UPS	None

The lower floor is a series of constrained hallways, each with a few Health Vials in them (just enough to alert your opponent to your location).

The Shield Belt down here is a critical map resource, and the only way to get beefed up, other than harvesting Vials, which isn't exactly the path to power.

The two jump pads leading to the upper level are very easy for your opponent to hear, and just as easy for them to hit you while you're in the air. Unfortunately, you don't have much choice if you want to get to the upper level. The stairs near the Shock Rifle are the only other way up.

The Shock Rifle and the Bio Rifle down here can both be used to fire at your opponent above, though this is a difficult proposition at best.

Getting back up to the upper level if you're pinned down here is very difficult in a Duel. In other game modes, combat tends to flow up and down constantly, though most of the focus is on the upper floor near the Rocket Launcher spawn point.

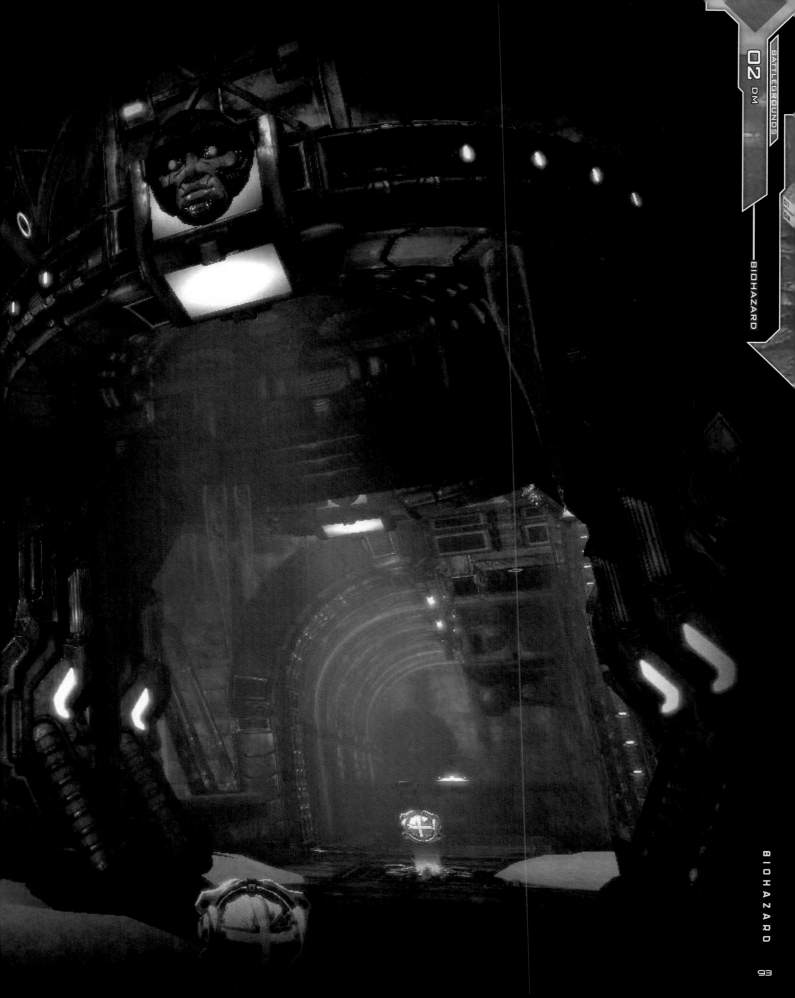

CARBON FIRE

AVRIL

BIO RIFLE x1

FLAK CANNON x1

LINK GUN x1

ROCKET LAUNCHER x1

SHOCK RIFLE x1

SNIPER RIFLE x1

STINGER x1

SPECIAL PICK-UPS

UDAMAGE | BERSERK

ARMOR

BODY ARMOR

HELMET

SHIELD BELT

THIGH PADS

FLOOR 1

A medium sized DM map, Carbon Fire takes place high above the streets of Hyperion, the Liandri capital city. Set inside a robot factory, a bot-construction conveyor belt runs through the map, and a disposal pit holds *both* power-ups, allowing for instant Juggernaut status.

DUEL

Carbon Fire is a bit big for a duel, and with the split nature of the level (and the general lack of Vials as sound cues) it is possible to spend a bit of time hunting the other player.

You should generally work on controlling the Body Armor and Thighpads, and hang out on the upper floor near the Health. This gives you a height advantage, and allows you to easily restore yourself if you do engage in battle. You can roam quickly between the two sides, only dropping down occasionally to pick up the Body Armor.

If you do happen to have power-ups enabled, going for them is incredibly dangerous, the only even remotely safe way out is Impact Jumping.

94

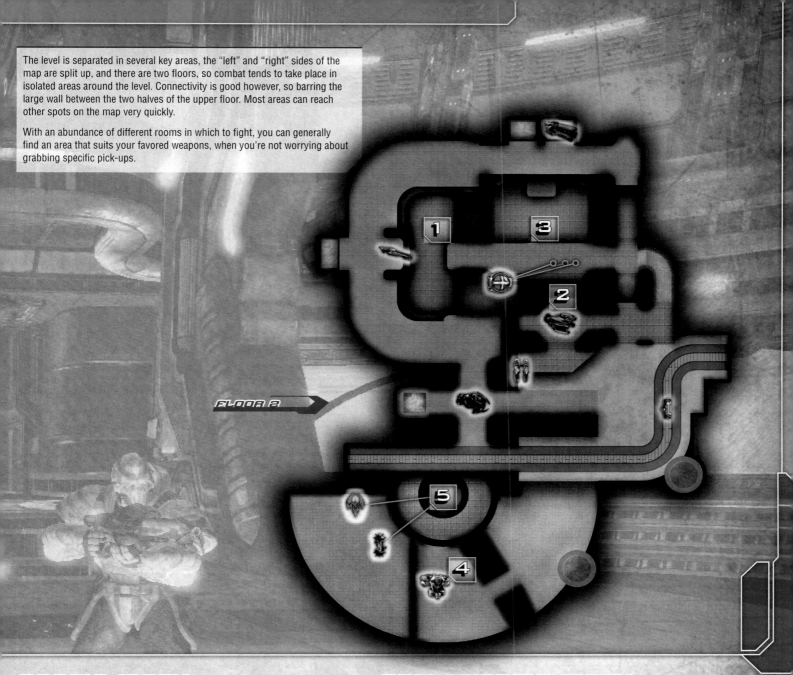

The level is separated in several key areas, the "left" and "right" sides of the map are split up, and there are two floors, so combat tends to take place in isolated areas around the level. Connectivity is good however, so barring the large wall between the two halves of the upper floor. Most areas can reach other spots on the map very quickly.

With an abundance of different rooms in which to fight, you can generally find an area that suits your favored weapons, when you're not worrying about grabbing specific pick-ups.

FLOOR 2

DEATHMATCH

There isn't one single area on the map that tends to draw more attention than others, so rather than lurking near a specific location, concentrate on staying near Health and armor, preferably on the second floor.

The second floor gives you a good vantage point on most areas below, but if you hear combat occurring on the ground level anywhere near the Stinger hallway, you're likely going to have to drop down if you want to get in on the action.

Going after the Berserk and UDamage is nearly always suicide, unless you're heavily armored and you don't mind taking the damage to Impact jump out, you can expect someone to push the button on the disposal pit and whack you. If you *do* manage to get out with both power-ups intact and quickly sweep the Body Armor and Health nearby to recover, you can rack up a devastating string of frags.

TEAM DEATHMATCH

Map control on Carbon Fire is tricky, the important locations are split up just enough that holding all of them spreads out your team, and there are so many weapons scattered about the map, it is difficult to lock down the opposing team's access. The Thighpads and upper triple Health hallway are both important, as is the Body Armor and the double Health pick-ups down below near the Sniper Rifle. The Berserk and UDamage are very important, if your team can guard the switches in the disposal pit room, you should be able to get one member of your team (preferably the most armored) to acquire both power-ups.

18 SHOCK RIFLE ROOM

WEAPONRY	Shock Rifle
HEALTH & ARMOR	None
POWER-UPS	None

The Shock Rifle room is two floors, consisting of the Shock Rifle up on a ledge, and a lower ground level.

Facing out towards the Stinger, both floors wrap around to the left and right to connect to the room adjacent to the Rocket Launcher (on the left) or to the power-up pit (on the right).

You can also go straight ahead, either on the upper floor (to reach the triple Health gallery), or through the bottom floor to reach the Stinger).

There is little in the way of other resources in this room, and the terrain is nearly perfect for Shock Combos, so be careful about hanging around this area for any reason other than grabbing your own Shock Rifle.

WEAPONRY	Rocket Launcher, Flak Cannon
HEALTH & ARMOR	Health x3, Thighpads, Vials
POWER-UPS	None

The upper level has superb connectivity to all parts of the map, as well as several important pick-ups.

On the upper floor, you can find the Rocket Launcher, the Flak Cannon, the Thighpads, and *three* Health pick-ups, as well as a few scattered Vials.

On the Rocket Launcher side of the map, a room with lifts connecting the ground floor and upper ledge provides access to the Rocket Launcher itself, and an easy jump across to the triple Health pick-ups in the middle of the map.

Note that the Rocket Launcher itself is located up on a ledge that you *can't* jump back to if you jump down. You can get back up to it easily enough via either the lifts in the room next to it, or from the triple Health hall, but not from right in front of it.

On the opposite side of the wall from the three Health pick-ups is a small raised ledge holding the Flak Cannon and the Thighpads. It's easy to zip

around the corner to grab both, so you can easily recover and armor up in this area.

The hall beside the Thighpads has a conveyor belt running along it, transporting robots slowly throughout the complex—watch out, these bots can interfere with your movement.

Near the conveyor belt is an area with transparent windows looking down on the ground floor outside. From here, you can ride a lift that deposits you right by the Link Gun below, near both the Body Armor and the Sniper Rifle, a quick way to get between the two floors, and the inner and outer areas.

Down at the end of the conveyor belt, you can find the Bio Rifle on the upper hall, overlooking the power-up pit below.

The upper floor is an important area, as the abundance of Health and the easy access to any part of the level, plus the height advantage, make it a solid place to engage in battle.

3: LOWER LEVEL

WEAPONRY	Stinger
HEALTH & ARMOR	None
POWER-UPS	None

The lower level runs beneath the upper floor in the center of the map, where you can find the Stinger. The Stinger is centrally located, from there, you can set out in any of four directions, straight towards the Shock Rifle, the Rocket Launcher room, a spiral up to the Thighpad area, or down a lengthy hallway to the Sniper Rifle.

There isn't much in the way of goodies to be found below however, so unless you're simply trying to transition from one part of the map to another without being spotted by players above (or grabbing the Stinger), don't spend a lot of time here.

4: OUTSIDE

WEAPONRY	Link Gun, Sniper Rifle
HEALTH & ARMOR	Health x2, Body Armor
POWER-UPS	None

The outer area has several yummy pick-ups, including the Body Armor, and a helpful pair of Health kits. The Body Armor is located immediately adjacent to the power-up pit, while the Health Packs are beside the Sniper Rifle, the Link Gun, and the lift up to the second floor.

This area is largely a transitional space, generally not the best place to be hanging out and fighting. Fortunately, you can quickly get back

up to the upper floor from here. The two quickest ways are using the lift that goes from the Link Gun up to the second floor near the Thighpads, or taking the lift up from the power-up pit area to the second floor by the Bio Rifle.

You can also head to the center of the map on the bottom floor if you go down the hall near the Sniper Rifle, though there isn't much of interest besides the Stinger.

5: POWER-UP PIT

WEAPONRY	Bio Rifle
HEALTH & ARMOR	Health, Vials
POWER-UPS	UDamage

The robot disposal pit has both UDamage *and* Berserk present, both waiting temptingly on a platform down inside the pit. If you hop down to the platform, it begins to rise slowly to the ground level again. Wait until it gets near the top to grab the power-ups, to maximize their usage.

However, the room *also* has three buttons, two on the ground floor, and one on the upper level overlooking the room, any of which can be touched by another player. Doing so fries anyone down in the pit. Since stepping on the platform triggers level-wide alarms, don't expect to get out in one piece on a busy map. You can Impact jump out to get out more quickly, but if you do so with the UDamage, you better be armored-up.

Otherwise, this room serves as a transitional area, you can take a lift up beside the pit to reach the Bio Rifle on the upper level, or travel to the Shock Rifle, Sniper Rifle, or Body Armor from here.

AVRIL

BIO RIFLE
x2

FLAK CANNON
x2

LINK GUN
x1

ROCKET LAUNCHER
x2

SHOCK RIFLE
x2

SNIPER RIFLE
x2

STINGER
x1

SPECIAL PICK-UPS

UDAMAGE | JUMP BOOTS | REDEEMER

ARMOR

BODY ARMOR

HELMET

SHIELD BELT

THIGH PADS

Deck is a straightforward DM level, fundamentally divided into three levels. The bottom level is located around an immense pool of Tarydium sludge, the center level is focused around a series of three ramps in the middle of the map, and the top floor can only be reached from two of the ramps in the center room.

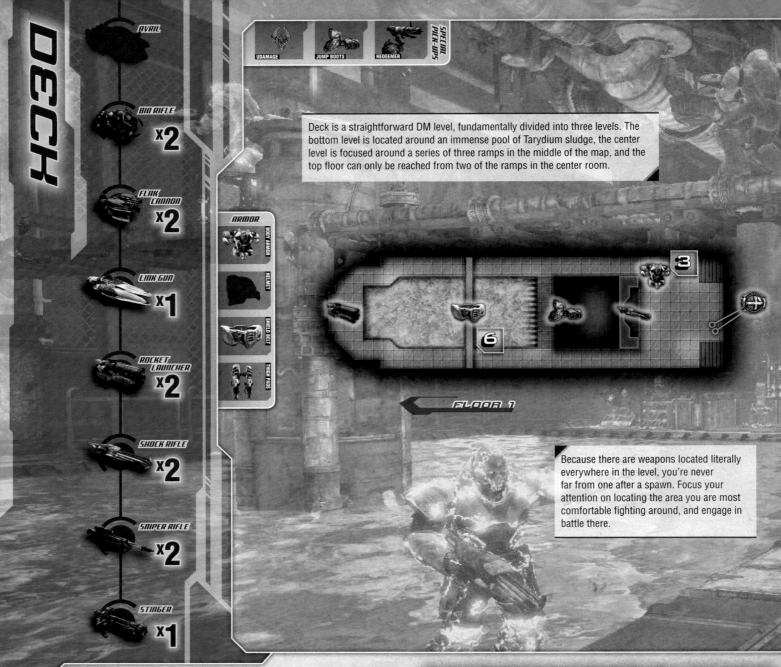

3

6

FLOOR 1

Because there are weapons located literally everywhere in the level, you're never far from one after a spawn. Focus your attention on locating the area you are most comfortable fighting around, and engage in battle there.

DUEL

Deck is slightly large for duels, so you usually have time immediately after spawning to find your closest favored weapon, and possibly acquire some armor, depending on how aggressively your opponent is controlling the three armor spawns.

The upper sniper perch is a key location if you're skilled with the Sniper Rifle or Shock Rifle, as it is difficult to assault, easy to escape from, and can rapidly reach any location on the level.

It is very important that you time the Power-Ups on the level, as well as the armor. You need to be in position to get your chosen item *before* it appears, ideally arriving just as it spawns, then vacating the area before a savvy opponent attacks you in an exposed position.

Depending on your combat preferences, you can try to lure your opponent into one of the more narrow spaces for close range fighting, or attempt to keep the fight in the center room, where you have distance and an open line of sight.

Health is located in only two places on the level, so unless you're willing to alert your opponent to your location by picking up Vials—be careful.

DEATHMATCH

Time the Shield Belt relentlessly, and make sure you're either picking up every Redeemer and UDamage spawn, or punishing anyone going for them.

Combat tends to flow through the center room constantly, and the Body Armor area is also hot. Patrol these areas from the sides or above, and ambush anyone already involved in a fight. Try to avoid getting into needless medium or long range fights with single targets in the hallways.

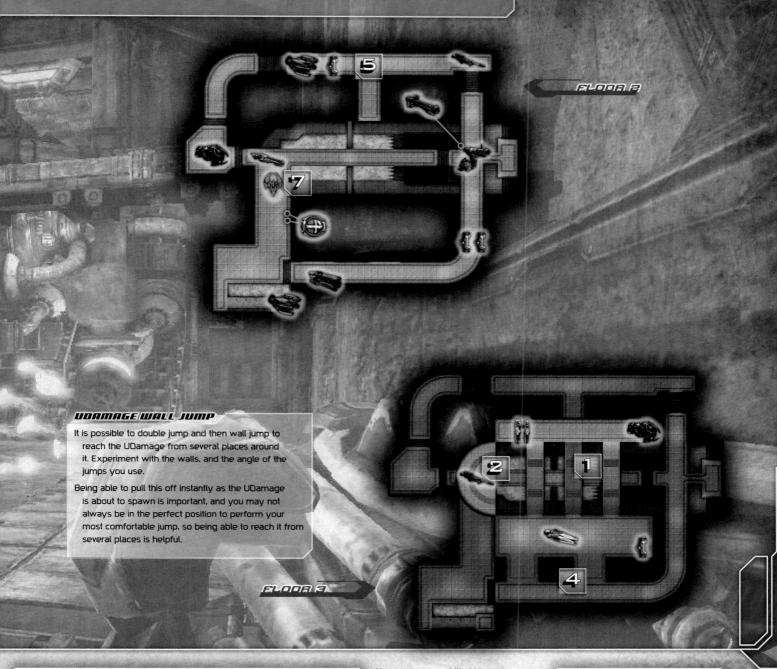

UDAMAGE WALL JUMP

It is possible to double jump and then wall jump to reach the UDamage from several places around it. Experiment with the walls, and the angle of the jumps you use.

Being able to pull this off instantly as the UDamage is about to spawn is important, and you may not always be in the perfect position to perform your most comfortable jump, so being able to reach it from several places is helpful.

FLOOR 3

If you can't kill them quickly, or you're inappropriately armed for the engagement, disengage and go hunting elsewhere, rather than wasting time with an alert opponent when there are distracted targets elsewhere.

TEAM DEATHMATCH

Controlling Power-Up and armor spawns is critical here, as is control of the central room.

Have your most skilled long range fighter in position on the upper level, while your close range fighters patrol the halls and the Body Armor area.

Because of the abundance of weaponry present on this map, even freshly spawned players are likely to quickly acquire at least one weapon. For this reason, try to have players fighting near the weapons they are most comfortable *against*.

Keeping your entire team armored is difficult, don't hesitate to grab all of the Health Vials to supplement your survival chances, but don't abandon critical locations to gain a tiny bit of extra health.

Because skilled teams are likely to be timing the Power-Ups as well as you are, be ready for combined assaults on the UDamage. The Shield Belt and Redeemer are difficult to protect, as players can reach them very quickly, but be sure to have teammates in locations that can cover the approaches as their spawn time nears.

If you're on the losing side, be careful about exposing yourself in the central room, and try to avoid the enemy UDamage as long as possible should you miss its spawn. Leading the UDamage holder on a chase that ends up with you dead is still better than fighting, dying more quickly, and exposing more of your teammates to the danger as well.

CENTER ROOM

WEAPONRY	Link Gun, Stinger
HEALTH & ARMOR	Vials
POWER-UPS	None

The central room connects to all parts of the map, and as such, it is both an important control point, and a dangerous area to fight in.

Unless you're setting out to control the room yourself, limit your movement through this area, moving through it quickly to reach the Shield Belt, UDamage, Body Armor, or the upper level.

The Jump Boots make getting around in this room slightly safer, though accurate players are still a serious threat while you are in midair.

Remember that you can walk along the narrow edge from the Stinger over to the large platform with the Link Gun, allowing you to quickly move between the Rocket Launcher hall and the Body Armor area.

UPPER LEVEL

WEAPONRY	Sniper Rifle, Bio Rifle
HEALTH & ARMOR	Thighpads
POWER-UPS	None

The upper deck of Deck is an important location for controlling the map, though it is usually hotly contested.

You can quickly drop down from the upper level to reach any point on the map, making escape quite easy. Because long range instant hit weapons are the most suitable for fighting from up here, this isn't a good place to hang out if you are unskilled with those weapons.

The Thighpads usually aren't worth the time it takes to reach them from other areas of the map, and the danger of exposing yourself, they're more of a nice perk if you are hanging around in this area anyway.

The Bio Rifle can be used to rain sludge down on targets below, but the Sniper Rifle or Shock Rifle are generally far more effective if your aim is solid.

3: BODY ARMOR

WEAPONRY	Shock Rifle, Redeemer
HEALTH & ARMOR	Body Armor, Health
POWER-UPS	None

One of only two locations on the map with Health, and with armor and a strong weapon present as well, this location tends to see a lot of traffic.

It is usually only safe to quickly hit this room for your needed items, then get out fast. If you come in from the Tarydium pool with Jump Boots, escaping is usually quite safe. Otherwise, you're forced to either take the long run down to the teleport, or use one of the two lifts to reach the center level.

Because the room is frequently patrolled or guarded, those lifts can be death traps, as they are usually the only viable exit.

The Redeemer is located on a small platform above the Body Armor room, but you can only reach it with Jump Boots, from the teleport at the end of the Tarydium pool, or by lift jumping.

4: ROCKET HALL

WEAPONRY	Rocket Launcher, Flak Cannon
HEALTH & ARMOR	Vials
POWER-UPS	None

This is one of the two lengthy hallways flanking the center room. This one has a small alcove containing the Rocket Launcher, and a small pool of Tarydium sludge at one end that houses one of the two Flak Cannons on the level.

Neither the rocket nor the flak areas are especially safe to fight in, as the rocket area is enclosed by walls, and the flak area is even worse, with an open (and lethal) pit of sludge around it.

Fighting in the hallway itself, or the small open room above the Flak Cannon is safer, just be aware of the lack of cover.

Fighting at either end of the hall, only long range weapons are effective.

Because multiple close and mid-range weapons are located around this hall, lots of fighting with the rocket, flak, and Link guns frequently occurs here. If you aren't comfortable fighting those weapons on this terrain, avoid this area!

From this hall, you can quickly reach the UDamage area, the Link Gun side of the center room, or the area just above the Body Armor room's lifts, beside the Stinger.

5: SNIPER HALL

WEAPONRY	Sniper Rifle, Flak Cannon
HEALTH & ARMOR	Vials
POWER-UPS	None

The Sniper Rifle located on the Body Armor end of the hall makes this a dangerous hallway to run down from the Flak Cannon end. Depending on where you enter it, you may wish to quickly grab the Flak Cannon and back out to the UDamage, or duck through the side exit to the central area.

There is a bit of cover around the Flak Cannon side of the hall, but unless you have a different weapon handy, firing flak down the hall at a sniper usually ends in a quick trip to the grave.

6: TARYDIUM POOL

WEAPONRY	Rocket Launcher
HEALTH & ARMOR	Shield Belt, Vials
POWER-UPS	Jump Boots

The Tarydium waste pool on the bottom floor of Deck is *not* a safe place to fight. With narrow walkways on either side of the pool, the only semi-safe area to battle is the ground around the Rocket Launcher. Because that is located immediately next to the teleporter that deposits you at the Redeemer (just above the Body Armor area), you can duck through it quickly to escape.

Even so, you are dreadfully exposed to potshots from anyone on the center or upper levels, and few targets are likely to present themselves. You can use the area immediately around the teleport to wait for someone going for the Shield Belt, but that's not a great reason to pin yourself in this area.

The Shield Belt itself is located on a very narrow pipe that stretches across the Tarydium pool. You can get to it from below by using Jump Boots, but it is typically safer to drop down from above when it is spawning, grab it, and then either hit the teleport out, zip over to the Body Armor room, or use Jump Boots to get up to the central area quickly.

The Jump Boots are important for getting out of this area without going through the teleport, or taking the lifts—both of which deposit you around the Body Armor area, and an astute opponent will be waiting for you when you come out. Glance down to see if they are up before dropping down, grabbing them increases your chance of getting back out from the bottom floor alive.

'7: UDAMAGE

WEAPONRY	Shock Rifle, Bio Rifle
HEALTH & ARMOR	Health
POWER-UPS	UDamage

This is a critical location, as it is one of only two areas with Health pick-ups, has the Shock Rifle present, and has decent cover for close range fighting, courtesy of the crates around the UDamage.

The UDamage itself is located atop one long set of crates, exposed to fire from the central room. It is possible to wall jump to reach it, or you can drop down to it from the upper level, use the ramps in the central room, or reach it with the Jump Boots.

You can Impact Hammer jump to it of course, though doing so is usually not a good idea unless you simply can't reach it any other way. Taking a solid chunk of damage before you reach an area that is likely to be targeted by every other player on the map is risky, to say the least.

Expect an explosion of violence in this area when the UDamage spawns, and it tends to see a fair amount of traffic from people looking for Health or checking on the spawn as well.

The Bio Rifle is located in a small room just behind the UDamage crate area, connected to the Sniper Rifle hallway. You can duck back into this area to lure opponents into a slightly more open combat space, or to retreat into the hallway as necessary.

The narrow channels created by the crates around the UDamage are actually ideal for lobbing charged secondary goo globs, but they're *also* ideal for the Flak Cannon, and with one located on each side of this area, as well as a nearby Rocket Launcher, this is not a safe place to be charging up multiple shots!

DEFIANCE

AVRIL

BIO RIFLE x1

FLAK CANNON x1

LINK GUN x1

ROCKET LAUNCHER x1

SHOCK RIFLE x1

SNIPER RIFLE x1

STINGER x1

SPECIAL PICKUPS
UDAMAGE

ARMOR
BODY ARMOR
HELMET
SHIELD BELT
THIGH PADS

Taking place in the buildings and alleys of Oxida Nova, Defiance is a fairly small deathmatch arena. It feels a bit larger than it is due to the highly discrete combat areas. The level is broken up into chunks, each with varied terrain, so it is easy to haunt one specific part of the map that best suits your combat preferences.

There is plenty of armor scattered about the map, making it possible to get seriously buff. Most of the armor is concentrated on one "side" of the level, which is also conveniently close to the UDamage. The damage amp is a lethal power-up due to Defiance's connectivity and small combat areas.

DUEL

Defiance is small enough for dueling, but the abundance of armor and the highly segregated nature of the level complicates control significantly. It is easy to escape an engagement and difficult to control all the armor on the map—not to mention the UDamage.

In general, the upper level provides the fastest way to reach any point on the level, so if you can frag your target and then return to the center of the map, you can usually quickly locate their spawn point with the first few items they pick up.

Pay attention to the Health spawns, since four of them are located near the Sniper Rifle room, only two remain on the upper floor, meaning a damaged player trying to control the top must frequently come down to recover from a messy fight.

If you're on the losing end of an engagement, be careful about what items you go for, you can be certain your opponent is sweeping the level as quickly as possible, you need to consider your destination carefully in relation to the last position of your opponent.

FLOOR 2

FLOOR 3

DEATHMATCH

The Shield Belt and the UDamage should be your priorities, grabbing the Thighpads and the Helmet is worthwhile if you happen to be the in area, but not worth focusing on.

As with dueling, the upper floor is key to quickly finding engagements, important for keeping up with the frag leaders in general free for all. The Sniper side of the map is reasonably easy to camp out on, as you have clear line of sight to any threats, and plenty of health to recover from battle.

TEAM DEATHMATCH

A difficult map to control, but the Shield Belt through the UDamage is usually the right general area to dominate. This gives you control of the Shield Belt, Helmet, Body Armor, UDamage, four Health pick-ups, and several weapons to fight with.

Don't bother poking out into the Shield Belt room with any regularity (other than perhaps picking up the Flak Cannon), you can head over to grab it close to its spawn time, focusing your attentions more on the Sniper Rifle and Shock Rifle rooms, and their attendant Health and Armor pick-ups.

The Rocket Launcher side of the map has considerably less goodies, with only the Stinger, Bio Rifle, and Link Gun nearby, and only two Health pick-ups on the upper floor.

1: RIVERSIDE, OUTER AREA

WEAPONRY	Sniper Rifle
HEALTH & ARMOR	Vials, Health x2, Body Armor, Helmet
POWER-UPS	None

The "outside" area of Defiance has three levels: 1) a wide open ground area with the Helmet and two Health pick-ups tucked away, 2) an upper rooftop and walkway holding the Sniper Rifle, and 3) a lower tunnel containing several Vials and the Body Armor.

The lower Body Armor tunnel is actually accessible from several areas on the map, from this room at one end, from a manhole entrance by the Flak Cannon (which can be seen through a grate by the Helmet), and from the Shock Rifle room, at the other end of the tunnel.

The roof of the building that has the Sniper Rifle on top can be reached from a lift inside the building. On the bottom floor of that building is the two Health Pick-ups, which can't be reached from near the lift. You must come in from another direction

The walkway from the Sniper Rifle has several Vials on it, and leads on way to the UDamage spawn point, and the other to a ledge overlooking the Shield belt room.

There are ground level exits from the room to the Shield Belt on one side (to a hallway containing yet more Vials), and on the other side, to the Shock Rifle room.

The upper walkway is the safest place to engage in combat in this room, you really don't want to be fighting from the ground level against a sniper who can duck in and out of sight, or someone lobbing flak or rockets down on you.

The open spaces are well-suited to midrange weaponry, and there is ample room to dodge on the ground level, though this is more difficult on the narrow walkway above.

2: SHOCK RIFLE AND STINGER AREA

WEAPONRY	Shock Rifle, Link Gun, Stinger
HEALTH & ARMOR	Vials, Health x2
POWER-UPS	UDamage

The Shock Rifle room is quite small, with the Shock Rifle resting in the center of the room behind an open crate, and a small staircase leading up to a ledge that overlooks the room.

The ledge has a pair of important Health pick-ups on it, and you can jump from there to the top of the crate in the middle of the room, and then one more time over to the Link Gun ledge on the opposite side of the room.

Other than the Link Gun, there are three routes out of the room, down into the Body Armor tunnel, to the right of that into the Sniper Rifle area, or off to the left into the Stinger room, up a short ramp with a few Vials on it.

you *can* reach it from here via an Impact jump. Given the proximity of Health pick-ups, this isn't a bad plan, just watch out for an angry sniper if you stole his prize when you land on the walkway.

The Stinger is located on a raised ledge that can just see into the Shock Rifle room, and from it, you can either take a lower path that crosses into the Flak Cannon or the bottom entrance to the rocket room. The upper paths from the Stinger lead to the Health near the Rocket Launcher, or to the ledges overlooking the Shield Belt Room (right near the Link Gun ledge).

Because the Stinger is connected to so much of the rocket side of the

3: SHIELD BELT AREA

WEAPONRY	Bio Rifle, Flak Cannon
HEALTH & ARMOR	Vials, Shield Belt
POWER-UPS	None

The Shield Belt room is important, but other than the Shield Belt itself, the room is lacking in useful assets, and it is dangerous to fight in the area, as most of the entrances have an elevated view of the ground level.

The Shield Belt itself is located at the end of a ruined street and the Bio Rifle is in the room adjacent and above it.

The Flak Cannon is down below the Bio Rifle. From there, drop down a manhole to reach the Body Armor tunnel.

If you're looking for the Flak Cannon or timing the Shield Belt, sweep this room briefly, but don't hang around camping the Shield Belt in the open. It's exposed, and there is no health around to recover from a fight.

4: ROCKET ROOM

WEAPONRY	Rocket Launcher
HEALTH & ARMOR	Vials, Health x2, Thighpads
POWER-UPS	None

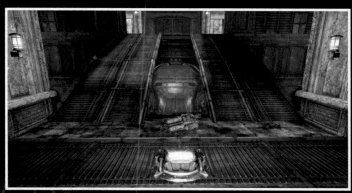

The Rocket Launcher room is separate from the rest of the level by a single hallway, though it is possible to reach the room from below or above.

The room itself holds a Rocket Launcher at the base of a pair of ramps, above the hallway from below, and behind the Rocket Launcher up on a ledge, the single pair of Thighpads provide some armor.

You can reach the Thighpads via ramps on the side of the room, and the raised platform is also a superior area to fight from if you are going to be engaging in this room.

The two Health pick-ups nearby are just outside the room, and other than the few Vials leading to the Thighpads, that's the extent of the useful goodies in the area.

Generally, you should stop by here if you really want to get the Rocket Launcher, then return to the other side of the map, or to sweeping the upper levels.

DEIMOS

WEAPONS

- **AVRIL**
- **BIO RIFLE** x1
- **FLAK CANNON** x1
- **LINK GUN** x1
- **ROCKET LAUNCHER** x1
- **SHOCK RIFLE** x1
- **SNIPER RIFLE** x1
- **STINGER** x1

SPECIAL PICKUPS
UDAMAGE | REDEEMER | BIG KEG O HEALTH | JUMP BOOTS

ARMOR
BODY ARMOR | HELMET | SHIELD BELT | THIGH PADS

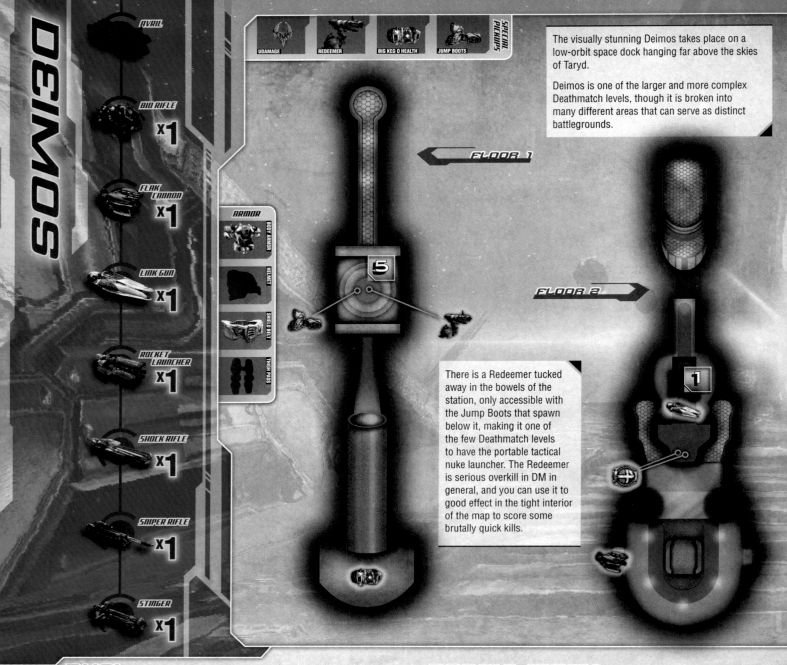

FLOOR 1

FLOOR 2

The visually stunning Deimos takes place on a low-orbit space dock hanging far above the skies of Taryd.

Deimos is one of the larger and more complex Deathmatch levels, though it is broken into many different areas that can serve as distinct battlegrounds.

There is a Redeemer tucked away in the bowels of the station, only accessible with the Jump Boots that spawn below it, making it one of the few Deathmatch levels to have the portable tactical nuke launcher. The Redeemer is serious overkill in DM in general, and you can use it to good effect in the tight interior of the map to score some brutally quick kills.

DUEL

Deimos is a too large for a really focused duel, but if you do choose to play on here, expect to spend plenty of time hunting for your opponent.

Hang out in areas with good sightlines to the bulk of the station, and you can engage your opponent when you do spot them. The Shield Belt, Body Armor, and UDamage are all fairly easy to cover from the top level, though you give up on the Health Keg and the Redeemer by doing so.

The turret is unlikely to be useful, since your opponent probably won't walk into its line of sight, so you're going to have to track down your opponent to get in a fight at all. Expect a slow paced match.

DEATHMATCH

Most of the fighting in Deimos tends to occur in and on the station, and in and on the shuttle, with players more rarely heading down to the lower levels of the station, or heading to the upper reaches to procure the Sniper Rifle.

Since the greatest concentration of players is usually inside, that's where you need to be to rack up the frags.

Keep a very careful watch on the UDamage spawn, it is accessible from several parts of the station, you either want to be there first, or killing anyone going for it.

112

Most frequently, combat occurs inside the walls of the orbital station, but occasionally it spills out onto the roof of the facility, forcing combatants to contend with lowered gravity.

A docked shuttle provides a second discrete arena, a location where you can fight in, on, and under the shuttle itself.

Finally, an orbiting defense platform provides a Beam Turret that can be reached via a teleport, and the turret has line of sight to most of the shuttle side of the space station. This is rather unusual, only one other level has anything of this nature (Heatray's Darkwalker), though its impact on the flow of the map is not quite as massive as that particular unwelcome Necris guest.

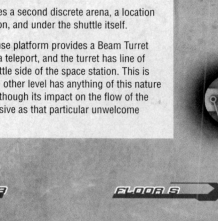

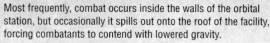

FLOOR 3

FLOOR 5

FLOOR 4

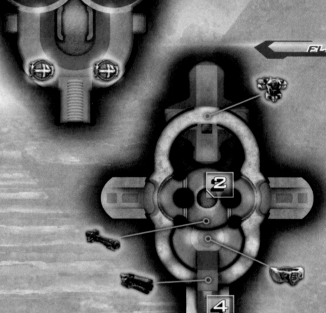

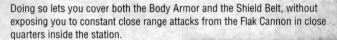

SPACE FIGHTING

One of the few levels in the game to feature low-gravity combat, the outer areas of Deimos are all low-grav regions.

You can tell when you're going into or out of a low-gravity area, as the transparent atmosphere shields are green (if you're going into normal gravity) or red (if you're going outside).

Most of the areas that are low-grav are fairly obvious; they're on the outside of the station below it, and on the outside atop it.

The low-grav is useful in a few places, as you can double jump out to the UDamage or Body Armor from the top of the ship, or double jump back up from all the way below the shuttle if you have the Jump Boots on.

Combat in low-gravity greatly favors instant hit weapons and knockback, the Sniper Rifle and Shock Rifle are both very dangerous on the top or bottom of the ship, as dodging is slowed down considerably, and has a very long predictable drift.

The Body Armor and Shield Belt are on opposite ends of the station, so checking on one or the other occasionally is worthwhile, but don't expose yourself to fire going for them, you can often score more kills targeting other players who get in a fight over them.

Of the two, the Body Armor is safer to grab and get out quickly, while the Shield Belt is exposed to fire from many directions (including above, through the energy field that can be fired through).

TEAM DEATHMATCH

Control on Deimos is a nebulous concept, the level is so broken up that it is difficult to lock the opposing team into an unfavorable area.

Generally, if you're confident at range, you can hang out on the outskirts of the station, and force the players within to come out to fight you, taking advantage of the Health pick-ups on either side of the station outside, and the double Health pick-ups in the shuttle.

Doing so lets you cover both the Body Armor and the Shield Belt, without exposing you to constant close range attacks from the Flak Cannon in close quarters inside the station.

It is worth having someone who is monitoring the Shield Belt also periodically drop down into the grav-tunnel to reach the Health Keg, and someone watching the Body Armor and Shock Rifle on the shuttle to descend for the Redeemer occasionally.

The UDamage is crucial for pulling ahead in the frag count, and should you manage to secure it while still healthy and armored, you can use it to perform a sweep of the station interior, quickly clearing out spawned players. Don't go inside if you pick it up half dead though, you're just handing it over to the other team.

OUTSIDE, UPPER DECK

WEAPONRY	Bio Rifle, Sniper Rifle
HEALTH & ARMOR	Health x2, Vials
POWER-UPS	None

The outer area of Deimos is the most extensive, and also the most exposed, both to players who have picked up the Sniper Rifle and are camping out up here, and to the Beam Turret in the distance.

The Sniper Rifle is reachable via a pair of gravity lifts, and the Bio Rifle is out on the deck just below it.

From the upper deck, you can also quickly reach several important nearby areas. One end holds the UDamage spawn and Body Armor, and on other has the Shield Belt and Rocket Launcher area.

Not only that, there are several types of ammo available on the upper floor, Vials around the edges, and a Health pick-up on each side of the station, next to portals leading in to the interior.

The upper deck is very useful for traveling from one part of the station to another quickly, and more safely than the interior, where a face full of flak is a common occurrence.

2: OUTER RING AND UPPER FLOORS

WEAPONRY	Stinger
HEALTH & ARMOR	Vials, Health x2, Body Armor
POWER-UPS	UDamage

The upper area inside the station holds the Stinger, two Health Pick-ups, and, out in the half circle gallery, Health Vials and the Body Armor.

You can travel between the mid and upper levels of the station via a large circular lift platform, and get in and out of the station easily through several nearby atmospheric shields.

The hallways inside are fairly constricted, though it is possible to get a fair amount of distance from your target. That's great for mid-range weapons, though only middling for the Stinger, since they can usually dodge

out of sight swiftly. Take the Stinger up onto the station's topside to wreck a player with no cover and low gravity.

You can get out to the shuttle from here easily, or through passages into the grav-chute leading to the Health Keg, or the upper floor around the Rocket Launcher and Shield Belt.

3: LOWER FLOOR AND DOCKED SHUTTLE

WEAPONRY	Shock Rifle, Link Gun, Flak Cannon
HEALTH & ARMOR	Health x2
POWER-UPS	None

The lower floor of the station holds the Flak Cannon, a very useful weapon inside the station. You can also pass into the grav-chute leading to the Health Keg (or below to the Redeemer), though taking either path from this particular area is fairly slow. You can reach the Redeemer more quickly from the Shuttle and the Health Keg is more accessible from the Rocket Launcher.

If you travel out from the station to the shuttle, you can find two Health pick-ups inside by the ship controls, right next to the Link Gun.

The top of the shuttle is the home to the Shock Rifle (and good terrain to use it on, so be careful if there are players nearby). The area outside the shuttle is all low gravity, so be ready for it.

There's a teleport out to the satellite platform with the Beam Turret inside, at the back of the shuttle. You can usually make the teleport to get behind the turret user even if it is manned unless he's actively saturating the hall behind the teleporter with fire.

The back of the shuttle also has an atmospheric shield that you can drop through to get to the bottommost level of the station, down where the Redeemer is located.

Fighting on the lower level of the station or inside the shuttle itself is purely close range combat, while the deck around the Shock Rifle is completely open—bring appropriate weaponry.

4: ROCKET AREA

WEAPONRY	Rocket Launcher
HEALTH & ARMOR	Vials, Shield Belt, Health Keg
POWER-UPS	None

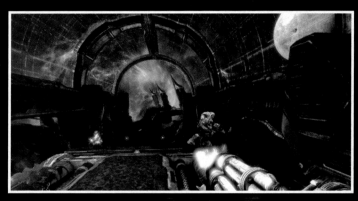

At the other end of the station from the docked shuttle, you can find a covered hallway containing the Rocket Launcher, and down below it in an open room, the Shield Belt.

This entire area is low gravity, so be prepared when you come out here. The Stinger from the middle level works well, as do the Shock Rifle or Sniper Rifle.

The entire transparent "ceiling" above the Shield Belt and Rocket Launcher can be walked on, but also fired through, which makes it easy to attack anyone going for either item.

This area is connected to the upper floor of the station from the Shield Belt room, or under the stairs below the Rocket Launcher. You can also get down into the grav-chute tunnel to the Health Keg by dropping off the very end of the station past the Rocket Launcher (watch your step).

There are a few jump pads around the Rocket Launcher platform, and one to get back up if you do drop down to the Health Keg area.

5: BOTTOM FLOOR AND SATELLITE

WEAPONRY	None
HEALTH & ARMOR	Vials
POWER-UPS	Jump Boots, Redeemer

The very bottom of the station is not a good area to fight in; rather, it's useful for acquiring the Redeemer.

There is a pair of Jump Boots located just below the Redeemer itself. To reach it, you must jump up (with the boots) to a tiny ledge on either side of the room, then jump up again to get the Redeemer.

The ceiling above the Redeemer is transparent, so it is possible to see if it is up from the bottom level of the station before you come down here to grab it.

As long as you don't slip while jumping up to the Redeemer, you can use the last remaining charge on your Jump Boots to get back up into the shuttle, just get right below it and double jump up. This is *vastly* preferable to the other route up to the station, which is a slow slog up through the grav-chute leading to the Flak Cannon or the Health Keg.

The Vials in the chute serve as more of a warning to players above you than any helpful health boost, but if you must, you can get back up that way.

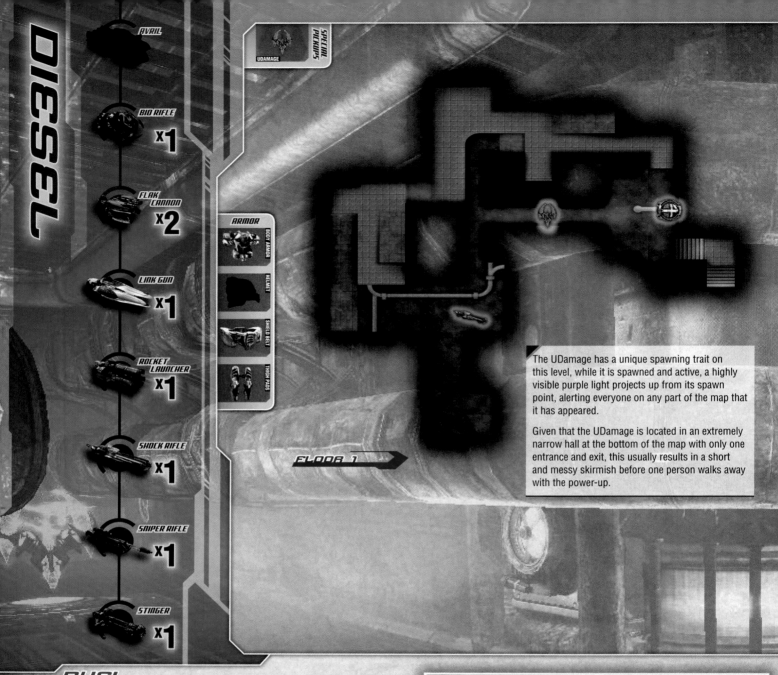

DIESEL

- AVRIL
- BIO RIFLE x1
- FLAK CANNON x2
- LINK GUN x1
- ROCKET LAUNCHER x1
- SHOCK RIFLE x1
- SNIPER RIFLE x1
- STINGER x1

ARMOR
- BODY ARMOR
- HELMET
- SHIELD BELT
- THIGH PADS

SPECIAL PICKUPS
- UDAMAGE

FLOOR 1

The UDamage has a unique spawning trait on this level, while it is spawned and active, a highly visible purple light projects up from its spawn point, alerting everyone on any part of the map that it has appeared.

Given that the UDamage is located in an extremely narrow hall at the bottom of the map with only one entrance and exit, this usually results in a short and messy skirmish before one person walks away with the power-up.

DUEL

Diesel is well-suited to duels. Reaching any part of the map can be done in seconds, and controlling the level is a constant struggle over the various resources.

The triple Health and Body Armor on the upper floor are attractive, as is the ability to spot a target nearly anywhere else on the level, though it is exposed to sniper or Shock Rifle fire from a distance.

The side hallways have some Health, the Shield Belt, and Thighpads, so if you are pushed out of the center (or if you simply prefer fighting in the side halls), a decent stand won't be an impossibility.

The lower area around the UDamage is unsafe, the only real reason to drop down is to grab the Shock Rifle, or if you're playing with power-ups enabled, to go for the UDamage.

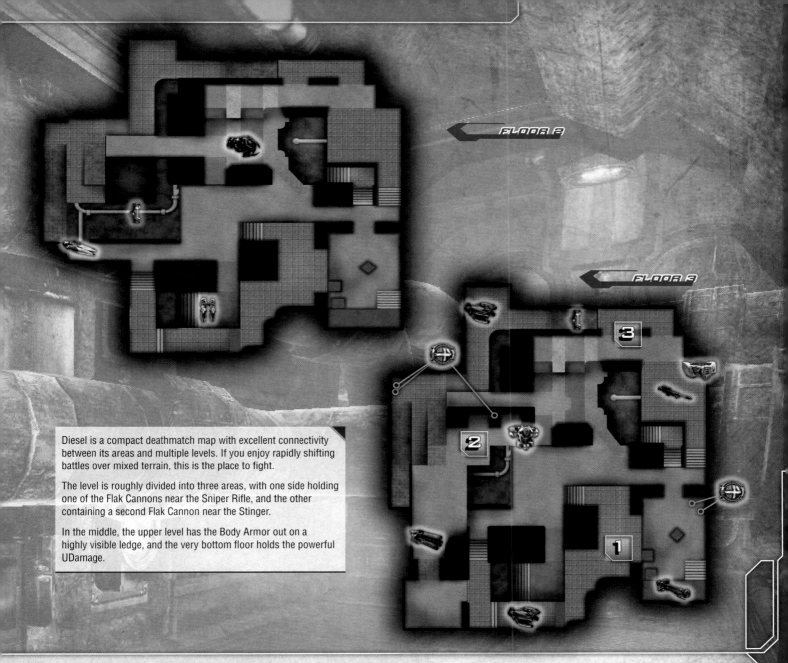

FLOOR 2

FLOOR 3

Diesel is a compact deathmatch map with excellent connectivity between its areas and multiple levels. If you enjoy rapidly shifting battles over mixed terrain, this is the place to fight.

The level is roughly divided into three areas, with one side holding one of the Flak Cannons near the Sniper Rifle, and the other containing a second Flak Cannon near the Stinger.

In the middle, the upper level has the Body Armor out on a highly visible ledge, and the very bottom floor holds the powerful UDamage.

DEATHMATCH

This map gets awfully messy with any large number of players. You may have more luck patrolling the side hallways and tackling freshly spawned players than trying to deal with the pandemonium in the center of the map.

If the player count isn't excessive, you can try to battle the middle, but you are exposed to attack from numerous directions. Doing more than trying to grab the Body Armor and recover with the health nearby is usually difficult.

Hunt the largest pack of players fighting each other, pick them off, and then run off to recover (possibly while cackling in an evil manner).

TEAM DEATHMATCH

This map is too small for sizable TDM games, but it makes a very suitable level for 2v2 matches if you enjoy small scale teamplay. The Body Armor and Thighpads are generally a bit safer to try to control than the Shield Belt, as you must venture out of position to acquire it and it spawns less frequently.

The UDamage is critical, if you can have your teammate guard you while you go for it, you have a good chance of mopping up the enemy team for a short time.

18: STINGER AND FLAK CANNON SIDE

WEAPONRY	Stinger, Flak Cannon
HEALTH & ARMOR	Health x2, Thighpads
POWER-UPS	None

The Stinger is located up on a ledge in a corner of the map in a room littered with several storage boxes. On the other side of the room from the Stinger, you can hop on some of the boxes to reach a pair of Health pick-ups.

From the Stinger, you can travel quickly to the center of the map, down the hall towards the Sniper Rifle, or left of the Stinger to reach the Flak Cannon.

The Flak Cannon rests just above the Thighpads, and is another quick transit point to the map center or bottom.

This area is well-suited to mid and close range combat, convenient, given the weapons present here.

2: BODY ARMOR AND UPPER FLOOR

WEAPONRY	Bio Rifle, Link Gun, Rocket Launcher
HEALTH & ARMOR	Health x3, Vials, Body Armor
POWER-UPS	None

The upper level and center of the map hold plenty of goodies, but it is a major point of conflict, as most players are going to regularly pass through here looking for healing or armor.

The Bio Rifle is out on an open floor in the mid level, just below the Sniper Rifle room, and above the UDamage hall. From the open floor, you can walk over to the middle level below the Body Armor by walking across a pipe littered with Vials.

The Link Gun is tucked away in a narrow hall just above the Shock Rifle on the bottom floor, and you can travel from the Link Gun to the upper level. The Link Gun hall has a few small circular windows that you can shoot out from, though their viewing angles aren't great for targeting most areas.

The Rocket Launcher is located up on the upper platform, right near the Body Armor and the single Health pick-up on the upper floor.

Down a short ramp from the Rocket Launcher, you can find the other two Health pick-ups, making this area great for recovering from a tough fight.

The upper level can easily drop down to the Shock Rifle below, or reach either Flak Cannon with some concealment. Traveling to the Sniper Rifle or the Stinger rooms requires dropping down and a short run across the middle floor.

Because the Body Armor is out on an exposed ledge, don't linger around it, or you're guaranteed to draw fire from nearby players.

3: SNIPER RIFLE AND FLAK CANNON SIDE

WEAPONRY	Flak Cannon, Sniper Rifle
HEALTH & ARMOR	Vials, Shield Belt
POWER-UPS	None

The Sniper side of the map has considerably less in the way of useful goodies, other than the Shield Belt and a few Vials; this area is mostly useful if you want to grab either weapon located here. Because you can get the Flak Cannon on the other side of the map near the Thighpads, it's only really beneficial if you want the Sniper Rifle or you happened to spawn nearby.

The Shield Belt is located up on a few crates behind the Sniper Rifle, and requires some jumping to reach, so it isn't safe to go for if there are enemies who have a bead on you.

There is just enough distance along the outsides of the map for the Sniper Rifle to be useful, and it is also handy for taking shots at players running around on the upper level. Otherwise, be careful about walking around with it out, most of the map requires weapons more suitable for close combat.

4: LOWER FLOOR

WEAPONRY	Shock Rifle
HEALTH & ARMOR	Health
POWER-UPS	UDamage

The bottom floor *would* have good connectivity to most of the level—if it weren't for the incredibly unsafe and narrow UDamage hall and an inconveniently placed pipe beneath which you must crouch to pass.

Generally, you should only be dropping down here if you want the Shock Rifle, you're going for the UDamage, or you happen to be slightly damaged near the Bio Rifle or the Sniper Rifle. You can easily run back up from the Health to reach the Stinger or Sniper Rifle.

The lower floor has a single Health pick-up (below the Sniper Rifle), the Shock Rifle (just below the Thighpads), and of course, the UDamage (inside the aforementioned narrow hall).

It is also possible to get over to the second Flak Cannon, the UDamage hall exits to the Shock Rifle under the low pipe, or a straight walk out to the Flak Cannon.

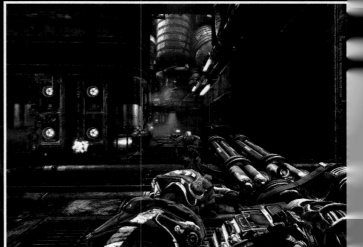

FEARLESS

AVRIL

BIO RIFLE x1

FLAK CANNON x1

LINK GUN x1

ROCKET LAUNCHER x1

SHOCK RIFLE

SNIPER RIFLE

STINGER x1

SPECIAL PICKUPS

INVULNERABILITY

ARMOR

BODY ARMOR

HELMET

SHIELD BELT

THIGH PADS

FLOOR 1

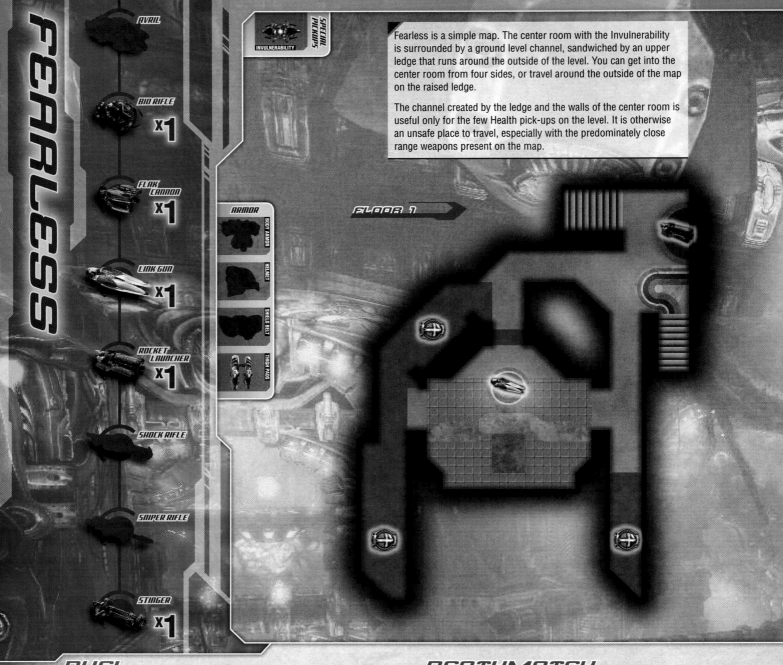

Fearless is a simple map. The center room with the Invulnerability is surrounded by a ground level channel, sandwiched by an upper ledge that runs around the outside of the level. You can get into the center room from four sides, or travel around the outside of the map on the raised ledge.

The channel created by the ledge and the walls of the center room is useful only for the few Health pick-ups on the level. It is otherwise an unsafe place to travel, especially with the predominately close range weapons present on the map.

DUEL

The tight quarters of Fearless make for a solid duel map, especially if you're a fan of close combat. Neither the Shock Rifle nor the Sniper Rifle are present, so you can get all up close and personal with the Flak Cannon or Rocket Launcher.

You can't get especially buff on this map, only a lonely pair of Thighpads provides any protection, so your only other recourse is gathering Vials, which is likely to alert your opponent to your location instantly. If you don't *care* that they know (or you want to them to know), pick them up anyway, the extra health helps when there isn't much armor around.

Naturally, unless you have power-ups turned off, the Invulnerability is the focus of the battle. In this mode, more than the others, you may be forced to use the Impact Hammer secondary to jar the power-up lose, since avoidance may not be possible if your opponent is skilled.

DEATHMATCH

This is a messy, brutal map for free-for-all. With more than a few players on a map with so many close range weapons, this battle often turns into a race for the frag limit with gibs flying every which way.

The center room tends to see a good amount of traffic, even when the Invulnerability isn't spawned, and since all the health and the (single) bit of armor is on the outer ring, you're usually better off patrolling the outer area, only swooping into the center if you see a few players duking it out on the ground floor

Fearless has the honor of being the only map in the entire game with the Invulnerability power-up. Given it's obscene power, this isn't surprising—invincibility is hard to fight against.

It is rather easy to know when the Invulnerability spawns—the entire level begins whispering, and your screen is covered in a suffuse glow. The Invulnerability itself is located on top of an ornate statue at the center of the (small!) level, so expect a mad dash for it once it appears.

This is the one situation in just about all of *UT3* where the Impact Hammer's secondary fire ability to knock power-ups off players is truly useful. There isn't any other way to deal with an invincible player, and while tackling them with an Impact Hammer isn't the safest maneuver, if you get forced into battle, it certainly can't hurt.

Plus, if you *do* knock it off and pick it up immediately, you're rather safe. And it makes for a wonderfully humiliating kill.

Still, don't go running around trying to knock it off if you can help it, avoidance is the best policy. Run away, stay away, and wait for it to wear off.

Make it a priority to capture the Invulnerability, even at the cost of dying. You can't lose much armor, but losing the Invulnerability is a bad thing. You can't simply frag the carrier and take it for yourself. Whoever gets the most runs while invincible tends to emerge the victor, unless every player on the map is enormously skilled at avoidance.

TEAM DEATHMATCH

Far too small for bigger TDM games, Fearless can be played as a decent 2v2 map. Aim for controlling the Flak Cannon and the Rocket Launcher as much as possible. There are only a few Health pick-ups on the map, along with the Thighpads, so most of the match is going to come down to the weapons, rather than the armor.

The Invulnerability is once again the centerpiece of this battle, and as with Duels, you *may* be able to knock the power-up off with the Impact Hammer if you can lure the bearer of the invincibility into one of the narrow side passages. Don't count on it though; try to go after their teammate while they're hunting you, to at least equalize the frags lost.

1: CENTER ROOM

WEAPONRY	Link Gun
HEALTH & ARMOR	Vials
POWER-UPS	Invulnerability

Impact jump up to the Invulnerability if you happen to be nearby and you can't reach the lifts in time. Best case, you get there just ahead of someone else, and since you're going to be invincible anyway, who cares if you take some damage.

Worst case, you land near someone who is invincible—but you can at least quickly attempt to zap them with a secondary EMP blast to dislodge the Invulnerability.

The center room is very simple, a Link Gun rests on the ground level, and two lifts provide access to the platform atop the statue in the middle of the room where the Invulnerability spawns.

Exits from the ground floor of the room allow you to reach the lower "ring" around the outside of the level, where the Health pick-ups spawn, though you can get to the upper level by the Bio Rifle by going up one of the lifts.

2: BIO RIFLE AREA

WEAPONRY	Flak Cannon, Bio Rifle
HEALTH & ARMOR	Health x2, Vials
POWER-UPS	None

The area "behind" the statue in the center area has the Bio Rifle on the upper level and the Flak Cannon nearby in a corner.

There are three vials near the Bio Rifle, and the lower channel that runs around the center room holds a pair of Health pick-ups. One is directly below the Bio Rifle, the other just below the Flak Cannon.

The Flak Cannon leads over to the Stinger area, while the Bio Rifle drops down to the Rocket Launcher.

There isn't much to this area, the outer ledge wraps around most of the edge of the level, while the inner channel is exposed to attack from above, and unsafe to travel unless you're quickly picking up health and returning to the upper level.

3: STINGER AREA

WEAPONRY	Stinger, Rocket Launcher
HEALTH & ARMOR	Health, Thighpads
POWER-UPS	None

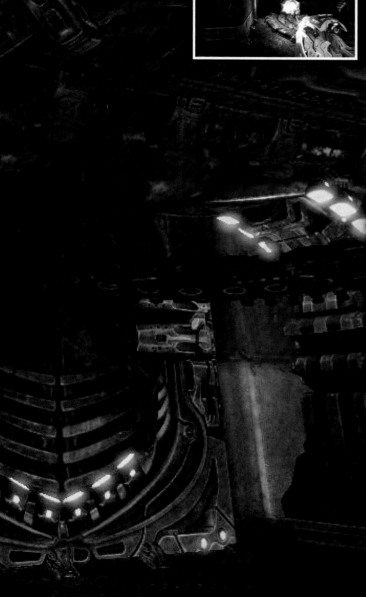

The Stinger is located directly in "front" of the statue at the middle of the map, and it is directly adjacent to the Thighpads, and down in the lower area, a single Health pick-up.

The Rocket Launcher is down some stairs near the Stinger in the opposite corner of the level from the Flak Cannon.

Between the two sides of the map, this side is slightly better for healing, as you can pick up the Thighpads, the Health below them, and the Health just up the channel below the Falk Cannon.

As with the Bio Rifle side of the map, the outer area is uncomplicated, with a raised ledge marching around the outside of the level, while a lower inner channel holds the health pick-ups and the lower entrances to the center room.

You can hop over from the Stinger platform to a small ledge overlooking the center room, atop which rest four Vials, useful for a quick health boost.

AVRIL

BIO RIFLE
x1

FLAK CANNON
x1

LINK GUN
x2

ROCKET LAUNCHER
x1

SHOCK RIFLE
x2

SNIPER RIFLE
x1

STINGER
x1

SPECIAL PICKUPS

JUMP BOOTS

REDEEMER

ARMOR

BODY ARMOR

HELMET

SHIELD BELT

THIGH PADS

FLOOR 1

FLOOR 2

3

Gateway is an unusual map, as it consists of three completely distinct areas: one in the Izanagi wilderness, another in an abandoned base on the Onyx Coast, and another high above the streets of Hyperion.

Portals connect each of the three areas, allowing you to quickly move between them. Because each area has its own unique geography and weapons, it is possible to spend most of your time in one area for the duration of a match.

The Izanagi area is a large cavernous area, with two distinct levels and two pairs of Jump Boots for quick transport. The Jump Boots are also handy in the other map sections.

DUEL

Duels are exceedingly strange on this map, as the completely separate nature of the areas means it is entirely possible to be in different areas, and move between them missing each other continuously.

Another issue is that if you greatly prefer fighting in one area, and your opponent another (say, you hate low-grav and your opponent loves it), there's not a lot of incentive to expose yourself by going through a portal while your opponent lies in wait with an appropriate weapon armed.

You *can* get nicely buffed up on here, with three pieces containing armor, and there is plenty of health in each area to recover. Engaging in frequent battle isn't necessarily a problem. Just be careful heading through portals if you're uncertain of your opponents location.

On the bright side, the portals are all located at opposite ends of the areas, only the ones in the snowy region can really be covered effectively from one lookout, though instant hit weapons can be a threat in the wilderness from a camper perched on the upper levels of the area.

If it is active, the Redeemer is a ready made answer to a camper in any area, such as up at the Shield Belt with a Sniper rifle.

WILDERNESS

1

2

The wintry base is small and compact, perfect terrain for the Flak Cannon present there, while the Hyperion area is low-gravity, ideal for sniping or using the Shock Rifle which you can pick up in the area.

Every area has some armor and some health, so it possible to stay in one region for an extended period of time if you aren't being excessively pressured, though the discrete splits make for an unusual experience in Duels or TDM.

DEATHMATCH

Deathmatch is tricky on Gateway, as the focal point of conflict tends to move from one area to another, as the spawns of players shift them about the map. There isn't a good way to predict this, so you generally need to constantly move from one area to another, constantly hunting down new targets.

Since you can get through the areas so quickly, consider checking for armor, if it isn't up, zip over to one of the other regions, one place is as good as another to fight in, and you may as well be going after armor to improve your survival chances.

TEAM DEATHMATCH

Team Deathmatch is nearly as strange as Dueling on this map, as you can usually lock down two areas, but that leaves at least one for your opponents. Depending on what weapons your team prefers, you may want to pick the areas you attempt to control based on that fact.

The other is terrain. If you have accurate players, the Hyperion area is best, up close combat works well in the snowy base, and mid-range battles and elevation are frequent in the Izanagi wilderness area.

The Redeemer is important, and it requires the Jump Boots from the wilderness area, which are also quite useful for getting to the Shield Belt more quickly in the Hyperion section.

Be ready for a fight any time you go through a portal, odds are, most entrenched teams are going to have players camping out watching the doorways while they wait for health or armor to spawn.

GATEWAY

129

1: SNOW BASE

WEAPONRY	Link Gun, Flak Cannon, Sniper Rifle
HEALTH & ARMOR	Health x3, Vials
POWER-UPS	Redeemer

The snowy region is the smallest of the three, with a small snowed over warehouse holding the Flak Cannon, while the Link Gun rests between a few shipping crates outside.

You can find a Sniper Rifle on the top of the building, and the Thighpads rest atop one of the crates. You can get over to the Thighpads by dodging over from the small staircase beside the warehouse, or from the rooftop by the Sniper Rifle.

There are three Health pick-ups in this area, one by the Link Gun, the other two up in a small bunker by the portal to the wilderness. You must crouch to reach them, so don't go for the health if you know there are enemies in the area.

The Hyperion side portal is right by the Link Gun, while the Izanagi portal (which deposits you on the Stinger side of that area) is near the double Health pick-ups.

GOODIES

There are several Flak Cannon ammo packs located on top of a few crates in the corner of the base interior, but you can only get to them by lift jumping up from the Flak Cannon (unless you want to needlessly burn health on an Impact Jump).

Of greater interest is the Redeemer located up on the cliff wall at the back of the base, just above the double Health bunker.

To reach it, you must jump up into the air with the Jump Boots equipped, allowing the strong wind to push you back into the Redeemer.

2: WILDERNESS CAVERN

WEAPONRY	Bio Rifle, Stinger, Rocket Launcher
HEALTH & ARMOR	Health, Vials
POWER-UPS	Jump Boots x2

The wilderness area takes place on a small stream near a massive cavern. The cave has two levels, the upper floor holding the Rocket Launcher, and the lower level a pair of Health pick-ups, along with one of the Jump Boots in the area.

The other pair of Jump Boots are located down in the street, just below a moderate sized spire of rock, atop which rests the Body Armor.

Both Jump Boots are immediately useful. Use them near the Body Armor to leap up and grab it. From there, jump up again to get to the Rocket Launcher. Similarly, the pair inside the cavern can be used to jump up to the Rocket Launcher immediately.

The Stinger is located on one side of the Health packs in the lower cavern hallway, while the Bio Rifle is on the other side.

Both teleports emerge facing each other. The teleport to the snow base is on the Stinger side, while the Hyperion portal is on the Bio Rifle side.

The teleports emerge on small rocky ledges that stretch right up to the Rocket Launcher, or you can head straight forward to get to the lower stream level, going into the cave, or out to the Jump Boots.

If you're going to be fighting in this area, the upper Rocket Launcher area is the dominant fighting position, especially if you have Jump Boot charges and you can quickly get away from danger.

Speaking of the Jump Boots, remember that their charges are highly useful in the other areas. While they are dangerous to use in the low gravity of the Hyperion section, they allow you to get up to the Shield Belt more easily, and in the snow base, they allow you to reach the Redeemer.

3: HYPERION SKYLINE

WEAPONRY	Shock Rifle, Link Gun
HEALTH & ARMOR	Health, Vials
POWER-UPS	None

GRAVITY SHAFT

The grav-chute area of the Hyperion platform is a special field that nullifies gravity, allowing you to move freely in any direction (albeit slowly) while you are within the field.

This is a rare effect. The only other time you run into the field is on DM-Deimos, where the grav-shafts on the upper and lower parts of the space station allow for vertical travel.

Be very careful about using the one here if there are active players in the area, you make a very easy target for instant hit weapons while inside the field.

The Hyperion area is a large platform located high in the sky, and the entire area has lowered gravity. This area is paradise for snipers, and with twin Shock Rifles on either side of the central tower, accurate players can have a field day with the slowly moving jumping players.

A grav-chute at one end of the map allows you to get from the ground level up to the portal that leads to the snow base, while on the opposite end of the platform. A teleport to the Bio Rifle side of the wilderness area is just above the twin Health packs at the end of the platform.

The large tower at the center of the platform has the Shield Belt atop it which is only reachable either with Jump Boots, or by jumping into the giant turbine at the end of the platform (by the double Health pick-up). Just be careful! You're dangerously exposed to accurate Shock Rifle or Sniper Rifle fire while you make the long leap up to the Shield Belt.

Near the grav-chute is a string of Vials, behind which rests several packs of Sniper Rifle ammo. It's handy if you're planning on sniping extensively in this part of the level.

Inside the tower on the ground level, you can find a Link Gun, and on the raised sections of the platform on either side of the tower, a pair of Shock Rifles.

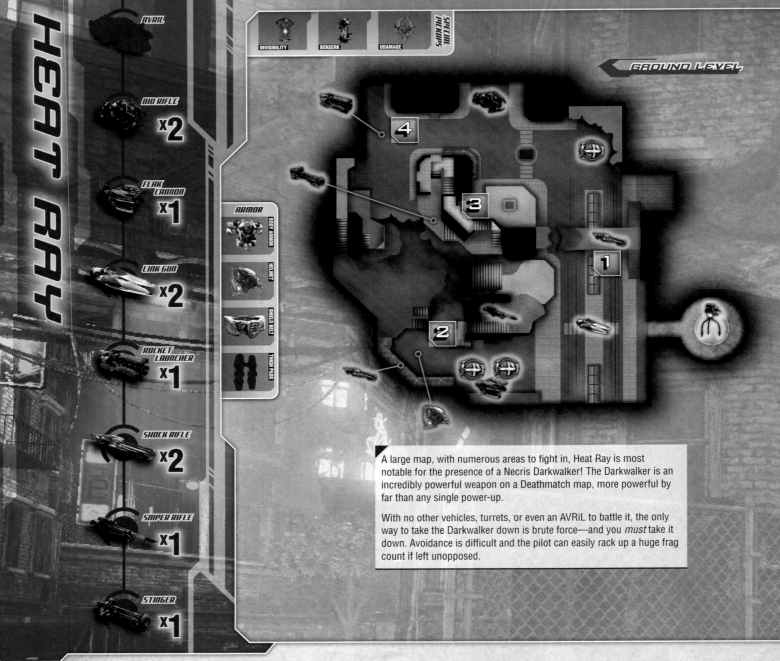

HEAT RAY

AVRIL

BIO RIFLE **x2**

FLAK CANNON **x1**

LINK GUN **x2**

ROCKET LAUNCHER **x1**

SHOCK RIFLE **x2**

SNIPER RIFLE **x1**

STINGER **x1**

SPECIAL PICKUPS

INVISIBILITY | BERSERK | UDAMAGE

ARMOR

BODY ARMOR

HELMET

SHIELD BELT

THIGH PADS

GROUND LEVEL

A large map, with numerous areas to fight in, Heat Ray is most notable for the presence of a Necris Darkwalker! The Darkwalker is an incredibly powerful weapon on a Deathmatch map, more powerful by far than any single power-up.

With no other vehicles, turrets, or even an AVRiL to battle it, the only way to take the Darkwalker down is brute force—and you *must* take it down. Avoidance is difficult and the pilot can easily rack up a huge frag count if left unopposed.

DUEL

This map is ill-suited for duels, moreso than even the largest maps in the game, as the presence of the Darkwalker is massively imbalancing for one-on-one fights.

It is possible to hide out in the buildings and take shots at the Darkwalker from a distance, since you don't have to worry about other players dying (as in TDM) or someone else racking up more kills (in DM), you can take your time fighting against it.

If you do manage to down the Darkwalker, you can use the Juggernaut to exact vengeance against your opponent, but you have to track them down to do so, which is tricky, given the plentiful cover and distances involved.

Tracking the Invisibility is also highly useful, as it gives you a massive advantage in a one on one battle, nearly guaranteeing surprise, and hampering your opponents aim to boot.

Other than the Darkwalker and the invis, focus your efforts on controlling (at least) the Body Armor, and if possible, the Shield Belt as well.

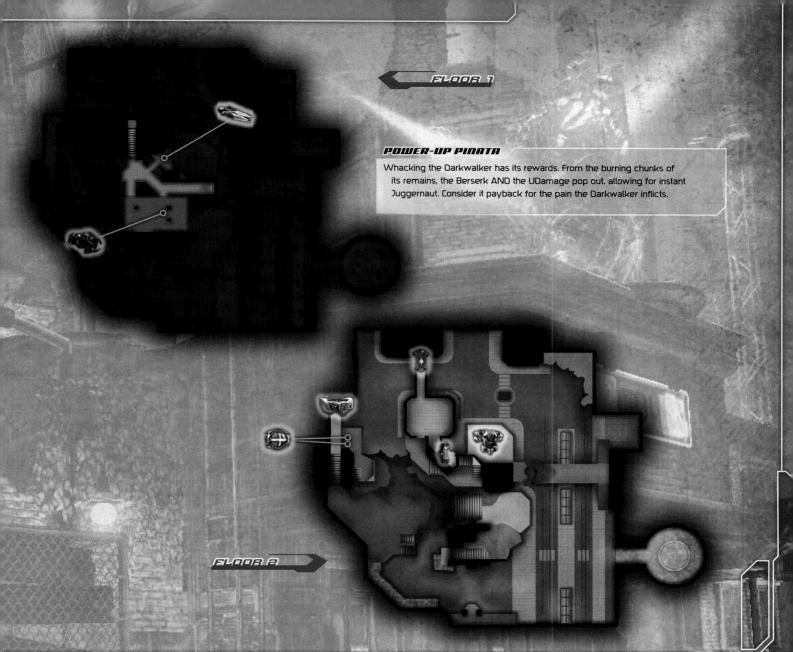

FLOOR 1

POWER-UP PINATA

POWER-UP PINATA

Whacking the Darkwalker has its rewards. From the burning chunks of its remains, the Berserk AND the UDamage pop out, allowing for instant Juggernaut. Consider it payback for the pain the Darkwalker inflicts.

FLOOR 2

DEATHMATCH

Again, the Darkwalker plays a huge role in the combat here. The player who can abuse the Darkwalker the most, bail out when it is nearly destroyed, and then reap the power-ups as well, can reach a dominating lead.

Even if a few players are skilled and alert enough to avoid the Darkwalker, there are nearly always targets in the open somewhere, and since the Darkwalker can (with a bit of crouching) reach all parts of the map; only the interior areas are safe from it.

Other then the Darkwalker, running the Shield Belt and Body Armor frequently is important, the Helmet is usually less of a consideration, since headshots are less dangerous than having multiple players firing at you, and the 20 armor doesn't help much.

TEAM DEATHMATCH

Once more, the Darkwalker dominates the tactical considerations on this map. Ensuring that your team gets ahold of the Darkwalker is vital, and then once you do, flushing out enemies in cover to be vaporized by it can build up a massive lead.

When the Darkwalker is not in the scene, concentrate on the Invisibility, Shield Belt, and Body Armor, just as you do in duels. Again, the Helmet is only of middling concern, if you happen to be in the area, pick it up, but don't go out of position to do so.

The Body Armor and Shield Belt side of the map provide most of the weapons, and four Health pick-ups, leaving only two by the Flak Cannon near the Helmet room.

The only weapon you may want to go out of position to get is the Sniper Rifle, which is just up the stairs inside a building by the Helmet area, but if you're focusing on the other side of the map, you can expect this area to have unfriendlies roaming nearby.

WEAPONRY	Shock Rifle, Link Gun
HEALTH & ARMOR	Health, Vials, Body Armor
POWER-UPS	None

The large street in front of the shuttle dock that provides the Darkwalker is lengthy and narrow, constrained by buildings on either side, with trees and signs breaking up line of sight across the center of the street.

The Shock Rifle is located on a raised section of road, reachable from a crumbled section of the same street that provides a ramp up to it. Nearby, just in front of the Darkwalker's spawn point is the Link Gun.

Down at the end of the street beyond the Shock Rifle is a blasted out crater containing a single Health pick-up, with five Vials at the edge of the crater.

A jump pad in the crater leads up to the top of a nearby building where you can find the Body Armor. Note that you can hop through a ruined hole in the wall of the Stinger building if you jump and walldodge to get inside. This is useful for transitioning from the Body Armor right into the hall that leads to the Invisibility or the Stinger.

There is a second jump pad beside the building near the Link Gun, and you can use it to quickly hop up to the center of the map, useful for grabbing the nearby Sniper Rifle, or transitioning to another part of the map.

The long open spaces of this street are well-suited for mid- or long-range combat. With the weapons here, battles are easy to participate in even if you are freshly spawned here.

2: HELMET AREA

WEAPONRY	Shock Rifle, Flak Cannon, Sniper Rifle
HEALTH & ARMOR	Health x2, Vials, Helmet
POWER-UPS	None

A small room holding the Shock Rifle and Helmet is tucked away in one corner of the map—roughly straight out from the Darkwalker spawn point. Perhaps more importantly, there are two Health pick-ups in the alley leading to the Helmet area, and via a jump pad nearby, the Flak Cannon on an upper ledge.

The area beside the Helmet connects to several spots at the center of the map. You can go through a lower tunnel to reach the tunnels beneath the buildings, up some short ramps to the middle of the map, or into a ruined building opposite the Shock Rifle that contains the Sniper Rifle.

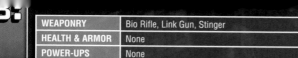

WEAPONRY	Bio Rifle, Link Gun, Stinger
HEALTH & ARMOR	None
POWER-UPS	None

The largest building on the map is the ruined building that holds the Stinger. You can get into the building from numerous areas. There is a jump pad by the Rocket Launcher, you can jump in through an upper window from the Body Armor, you can walk into it from the middle of the map, or you can get in from the bottom level where the Bio Rifle is located.

Because this building offers concealed movement from place to place, this is the safest part of the map to be when the Darkwalker is roaming, but because it is almost entirely enclosed spaces and narrow hallways, bring some close-range weaponry, and expect short and bloody fights.

The bottom floor of the building is a short series of tunnels that connects a staircase leading from the bottom level up to the Stinger and the upper floor, a doorway leading to a Link Gun (in the narrow alley created by the Stinger building and the Body Armor building), and another short hall that leads out to the Helmet area.

The middle level is ruined, and partly exposed to fire from either the center of the map, or the Rocket Launcher and Shield Belt corner. You can grab the Stinger from there, and quickly reach either area, or continue to the upper floor.

The highest level of the building has a hole in the wall that allows you to jump out to (or back in from) the Body Armor, and following it a bit farther leads to a hole that drops you right down on the Invisibility power-up ledge.

ROCKET LAUNCHER CORNER

WEAPONRY	Bio Rifle, Rocket Launcher
HEALTH & ARMOR	Health x3, Shield Belt
POWER-UPS	Invisibility

The Rocket Launcher corner of the map has the important Shield Belt nearby, as well as a fair amount of Health.

You can find two Health pick-ups on the ledge just below the Shield Belt, and a second on a small wooden ramp attached to the side of the Stinger building.

You can get into the Stinger building from the Rocket Launcher easily, as there is a jump pad nearby that deposits you right at the Stinger.

The Invisibility is visible from the Rocket Launcher, up on a ledge. Normally you need to get to it from the top floor of the Stinger building, but there are a few shortcuts you can

jump onto a narrow pipe on the outside of the building. With a little work, you can then double jump and control your path to get into a window on the side of the building. This deposits you inside the Stinger Building looking right out at the Invisibility platform, a double jump away.

The Shield Belt is up on a very high ledge at the back of the level, reachable via a short flight of stairs.

Of greater interest to snipers in the audience, if you hop up onto the ruined railing by the Shield Belt, you can then double jump up again to get to the upper reaches of a blasted out building.

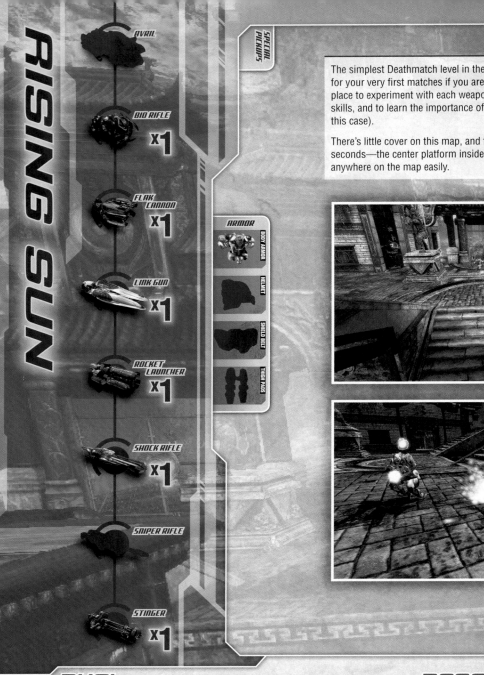

SPECIAL PICKUPS

AVRIL	
BIO RIFLE	x1
FLAK CANNON	x1
LINK GUN	x1
ROCKET LAUNCHER	x1
SHOCK RIFLE	x1
SNIPER RIFLE	
STINGER	x1

ARMOR

BODY ARMOR	
HELMET	
SHIELD BELT	
THIGH PADS	

The simplest Deathmatch level in the game, Rising Sun is a training arena, suitable for your very first matches if you are new to *Unreal Tournament*. This is a great place to experiment with each weapon, practice lift jumping and basic movement skills, and to learn the importance of controlling a certain item (the Body Armor, in this case).

There's little cover on this map, and finding your opponent is the work of a few seconds—the center platform inside the pagoda structure can spot a target anywhere on the map easily.

DUEL

This map is well-suited to simple duels, though with so little cover, there is a considerable emphasis on your aiming and dodging skills. You can play standoff with the Shock Rifle, Stinger, or Link Gun, or try to hide out around the pagoda to force a close-range engagement.

Use the Body Armor as bait if you already have it, you can take out your opponent with a well placed triple rocket barrage, a Shock Combo, or even a fully charged Bio Rifle secondary glob if you know where they're going to move.

DEATHMATCH

With more than a few players, this map turns into a complete mess; you can try to hang out on the center platform to engage spawning players on the edges.

The Vials and Body Armor may give you a little extra survivability, but don't stress their acquisition. This map is more about racking up kills as quickly as possible.

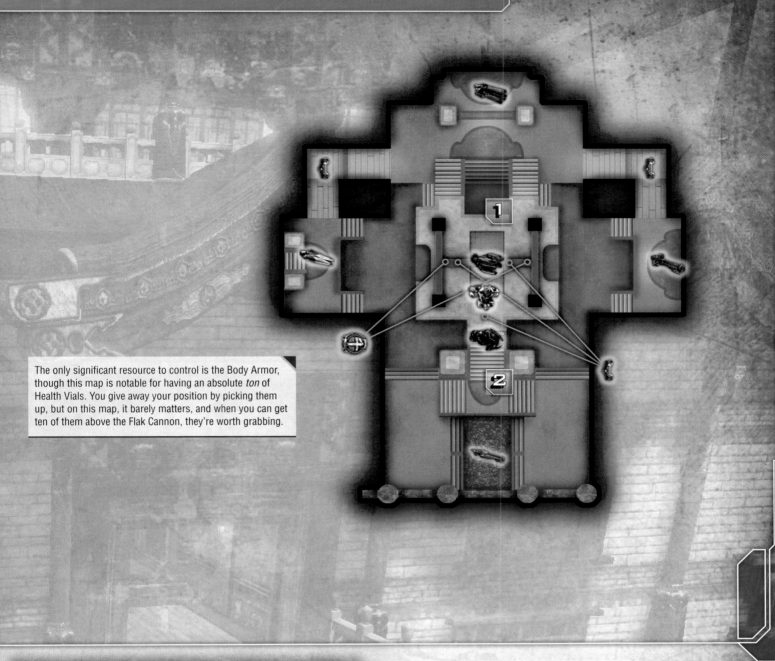

The only significant resource to control is the Body Armor, though this map is notable for having an absolute *ton* of Health Vials. You give away your position by picking them up, but on this map, it barely matters, and when you can get ten of them above the Flak Cannon, they're worth grabbing.

TEAM DEATHMATCH

Rising Sun can't support more than a 2v2 with any degree of sanity, and even that is more of a Deathmatch where you avoid shooting your teammate. You can make a stronger effort to control the Body Armor and center platform than in general free for all, but a lot comes down to your individual skills, rather than your teamwork.

1: CENTRAL PAGODA

WEAPONRY	Flak Cannon, Bio Rifle
HEALTH & ARMOR	Health x2, Vials, Body Armor
POWER-UPS	None

The pagoda holds the Flak Cannon on the upper level, and below, the Bio Rifle and the Body Armor inside a small hallway beneath the flak platform.

By lift jumping up from either of the side lifts, you can reach a wooden beam hanging over the Flak Cannon, a beam *covered* in Health Vials, ten in all.

One point about the Body Armor: there is a grating in front of the Body Armor facing the Rocket Launcher. This grating is *not* a completely transparent "window", it can block incoming fire.

There are still more Vials near the Body Armor, four on the Rocket Launcher side, two more by the Bio Rifle.

2: OUTER CROSS

WEAPONRY	Shock Rifle, Stinger, Rocket Launcher, Link Gun
HEALTH & ARMOR	Vials
POWER-UPS	None

The area around the pagoda is organized in a cross, if you treat the Rocket Launcher as the "top" of the cross; the Shock Rifle is at the bottom, with the Link Gun on the left and the Stinger on the right.

The Link gun and Stinger have short L shaped hallways that connect to the Rocket Launcher, inside which you can find another four Health Vials each.

The outer weapons are all on slightly raised platforms, with short stairs ascending to their level. This can give you a very mild height advantage if you're fighting around them, with the exception of the Shock Rifle, which is down below the single staircase leading up to the pagoda.

The left and right sides have lifts to get to the Flak Cannon in the pagoda, while the top and bottom have ramps and staircases respectively.

AVRIL

BIO RIFLE
x1

FLAK CANNON
x1

LINK GUN
x1

ROCKET LAUNCHER
x1

SHOCK RIFLE
x1

SNIPER RIFLE
x1

STINGER
x1

SPECIAL PICKUPS
REDEEMER

ARMOR
BODY ARMOR
HELMET
SHIELD BELT
THIGH PADS

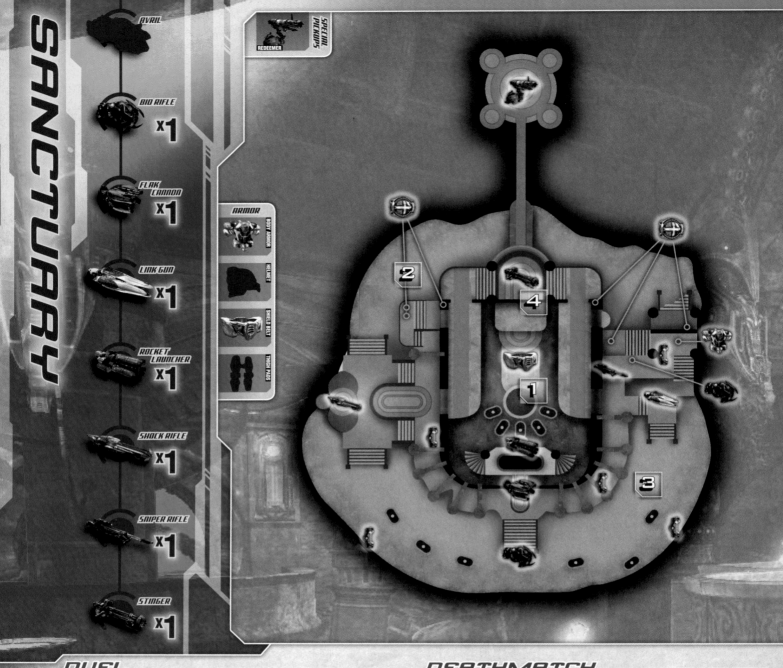

DUEL

Sanctuary is generally much too large for Dueling. The open area in the middle of the temple does make for an easy space to locate your foe, but if you happen to be wandering around on the outside of the temple, locating each other can be difficult.

The roof of the temple provides the best means of finding your opponent. Get up there from the Redeemer jump pad, or the jump pads on the Body Armor or Shock Rifle sides of the temple. This also lets you quickly reach the Body Armor or the Shield Belt inside.

DEATHMATCH

This map is deceptive in Deathmatch. The inner area seems like the place to be, but there is really little of value inside the temple. The Rocket Launcher and the Shield Belt, and that's about all.

The interior *is* a good place to hunt targets who are traveling through it, but patrolling the rooftop and Body Armor sides gives you access to more health, and a positional advantage in combat.

A rather large map, Sanctuary is nonetheless quite simple to navigate, as the giant temple at the center dominates the terrain, and most of the space is taken up by its bulk.

You can fight inside, outside, and on top of the temple, though most of the action tends to flow in and out of the inner area, with conflict moving from the Body Armor and the Shield Belt to the nearby areas.

The roof of the temple is a great place to recharge and pick a target. It often sees less traffic, and you can usually quickly locate another player before dropping down to ambush them from above before quickly transitioning to the Health pick-ups on either side of the temple.

The Redeemer is located out on a platform at the edge of the map, beside a jump pad that conveniently deposits you on the roof of the temple, in a perfect position to blast anyone inside the temple with the nuke.

SPIRE FIRE

When the Redeemer is spawned, the spires around the Redeemer platform light up with blue flames.

Once you can see the lit spires, you know that the Redeemer has appeared. Be there *before* this happens, unless you want to be part of a mad rush for the super weapon.

TEAM DEATHMATCH

A tricky map to control, as with Deathmatch, the Body Armor and rooftop should be your targets, and you may also want to make an effort to soak up the Vials around the Bio Rifle side of the temple—two sets of five Vials add up quickly. There are more on the outer rings near the Link Gun and Shock Rifle, but they're not worth exposing yourself for the small benefit they provide.

Time the Shield Belt and the Redeemer carefully, grabbing the Shield Belt and getting out of the middle is advisable. Instead, you should have most of your team hopping around on the pillars and the rooftop hunting for targets. With only a few ways onto the roof, they are easily guarded, and you can hunt the opposing team easily, with a nice height advantage. The roof also gives you the fastest access to Health on both sides and the top of the temple.

1: INNER TEMPLE

WEAPONRY	Rocket Launcher, Flak Cannon
HEALTH & ARMOR	Vials, Shield Belt
POWER-UPS	None

The interior of the temple is a large flat ground level, broken up slightly by a fountain between the Shield Belt and the Rocket Launcher overlook. The Rocket Launcher is up on a ledge at the end of the temple towards the Bio Rifle, while the Shield Belt is near the Stinger side of the map.

There are two raised walkways on either side of the temple walls; each has two exits out of the temple. On one side, you can reach the Shock Rifle, and on the other, the Body Armor.

The Shock Rifle side gets you to two Health pick-ups quickly, and a jump pad leading to the roof, so it is the better exit of the two if you're going for health instead of armor, as well as a faster means of reaching the roof.

Both walkways slope from low (Stinger end) to high (Rocket Launcher side). Both lead to open doorways out to the Stinger as well, so you can quickly reach it from either side. That's handy, since the open area is a nice space for mowing down people.

The lower part of the Body Armor side walkway is ruined, so you can easily move from the walkway to the Shield Belt spawn point. However, the Shock Rifle side is intact. You *can* double jump up to reach it, but you need to shove yourself up against its edge at the lowest point on the walkway.

The Rocket Launcher ledge has a nice overview of the room, and you can quickly move from it out to the Bio Rifle end of the temple.

Below the Rocket Launcher platform are multiple routes in and out of the room, via cracks in the temple foundation. You can get out on the left or right (facing the Rocket Launcher), leading out to the Link Gun or Shock Rifle sides. The Shock Rifle hole also leads to a nice stash of five Vials, a useful health boost if you're at 100 already.

The "center" route out leads to the Flak Cannon, a useful weapon in the area below the Rocket Launcher.

The entire center floor is exposed to a gaping hole in the roof, so don't be surprised by the occasional sniper up in the rafters (or worse, a Redeemer through the hole).

2: OUTER TEMPLE, SHOCK RIFLE AND STINGER

WEAPONRY	Shock Rifle, Stinger
HEALTH & ARMOR	Health x2, Vials
POWER-UPS	Redeemer

The Shock Rifle area outside the temple is quite simple. A sizable raised platform houses the Shock Rifle. On either side of it, you can go around the temple grounds to reach the Bio Rifle or the Stinger.

If you're heading to the Stinger, make a point of traveling past the two Health packs that are beside the entrance to the temple. You can grab them, head inside briefly, then get out to the Stinger.

There's nothing wrong with going the outer route on the temple grounds, but it's a dead path. There are no pick-ups and no connectivity to other sections, so it's safer. However, there's usually no chance of picking up kills.

The jump pad beside the double Health pick-ups is the quickest way up to the roof, the only other means of

reaching it require climbing the Body Armor tower, or running out to the Redeemer platform.

The Redeemer is located out past a narrow walkway above the ocean below, just beyond the Stinger.

3: OUTER TEMPLE, BODY ARMOR AND BIO RIFLE

WEAPONRY	Bio Rifle, Shock Rifle, Link gun
HEALTH & ARMOR	Health x2, Vials, Body Armor
POWER-UPS	None

This side of the map has less accessible Health pick-ups than the Shock Rifle side, and the jump pad to the roof is slower to reach, but it does have more weaponry. The Bio Rifle, Link Gun and the Sniper Rifle are all located in or around the Body Armor tower.

The tower itself is fairly small, you can find Health pick-ups just below it, a trio Vials in its lower level, and the Body Armor itself on the upper level. From the Body Armor, a short walkway leads to the Sniper Rifle and a jump pad to the roof of the temple. The Link Gun is down below the tower on a separate staircase.

This area also stretches around from the Link Gun to the Bio Rifle at end of the temple just outside the Rocket Launcher on the interior. If you're heading that way, take the inner

the outer temple grounds—you can grab five Health Vials on the way.

The Bio Rifle in front of the temple is right near multiple ground level entrances to the inner temple, and more importantly, to the Flak Cannon in the halls beneath it.

ROCK HOPPING

It *is* possible to jump up on the rocks that are just below the Body Armor tower. This allows you to skip the stairs up to the Bio Rifle, useful if you're coming from the Stinger side of the temple.

Experiment with the jump, there are a few places where you can get up quickly and reliably, and a few where you're going to slide off the rocks, making an easy target for anyone nearby.

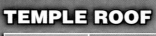

4: TEMPLE ROOF

WEAPONRY	Sniper Rifle
HEALTH & ARMOR	Health x2
POWER-UPS	None

The roof of the temple is a potent tactical location. Not only is it ideal for sniping distant targets, there are two Health pick-ups on the Stinger end of the roof.

Beyond that, you can reach a hole in the roof of the temple, an easy way to get down to the Shield Belt, or to attack players inside.

The roof also allows you to jump out onto the various pillars around the temple, and it isn't difficult to hop from one to another (which, beyond being bizarrely entertaining, is useful for ambushing targets from above).

You can also easily drop down to Health pick-ups on either the Body Armor or Shock Rifle sides of the temple, which makes the roof superb for restoring yourself to full health.

AVRIL

BIO RIFLE x1

FLAK CANNON x1

LINK GUN x1

ROCKET LAUNCHER x1

SHOCK RIFLE x1

SNIPER RIFLE x1

STINGER x1

SPECIAL PICK-UPS
UDAMAGE

ARMOR
BODY ARMOR
HELMET
SHIELD BELT
THIGH PADS

FLOOR 1

An ideal dueling map, Sentinel is small and tightly interconnected, with a few powerful items to fight over, and several areas to fight in.

The outer area holds the Shield Belt, while inside you can find the Body Armor and the UDamage. All three items are important in both smaller and larger games, and the abundant weapons and tight, multi-level nature of the map makes for fast and intense combat.

Sentinel also has an extremely distinctive feature: there are only three Health pick-ups on the entire level, and they're all located in one spot on the map. As a result, a huge amount of conflict is directed to that one specific area, since there is no other way to recover quickly from a battle.

DUEL

Perfectly suited for Duels, Sentinels multi-layered nature and interconnectivity make it perfect for matches if you enjoy close-range combat.

Controlling the Body Armor, Shield Belt, and the upper level Health pick-ups are all key. If power-ups are enabled, the UDamage is generally a better trap than it is a power-up. Given that you have to crouch to reach it, it is usually suicide to make an attempt to take it first unless you are certain your opponent is on the opposite side of the level.

The upper level where the Health is located also provides easy access to both the Body Armor and the Shield Belt, so you really need to lock that area down. And, if you're (forcefully) removed from your perch, expect a tough fight to get back up. Be careful about grabbing the Vials near the Rocket Launcher or below the Health, doing so instantly messages your opponent telling them exactly where you are.

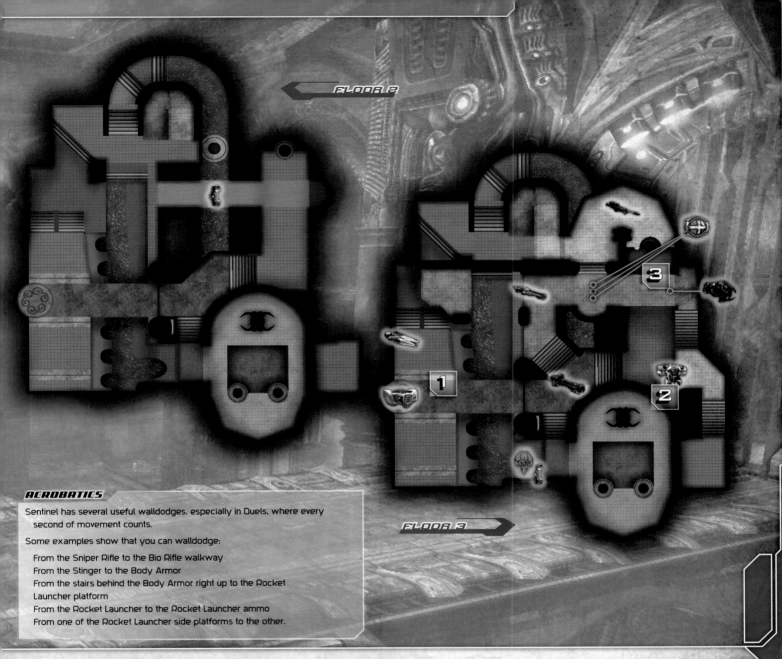

FLOOR 3

ACROBATICS

Sentinel has several useful walldodges, especially in Duels, where every second of movement counts.

Some examples show that you can walldodge:

From the Sniper Rifle to the Bio Rifle walkway
From the Stinger to the Body Armor
From the stairs behind the Body Armor right up to the Rocket Launcher platform
From the Rocket Launcher to the Rocket Launcher ammo
From one of the Rocket Launcher side platforms to the other.

DEATHMATCH

A fast paced and brutal map for even mid-size free for all, there's still enough separation between the areas to prevent this from turning into complete chaos.

Dominating the Health area is nearly impossible with many players, so you may want to try controlling areas with comfortable terrain, like the outer ledge overlooking the Health hallway and Shield Belt, or the Rocket Launcher room.

Going for the UDamage is inadvisable, kill the guy who *does* waddle under the overhang, and take it from his corpse.

TEAM DEATHMATCH

Sentinel can't support larger games, but again, 2v2 matches are solid on here, you can work very well as a team, guarding the Health pick-ups, roaming out to secure the Body Armor or Shield Belt, then returning while your partner does the same.

It is somewhat easier to go after the UDamage in this mode, having your teammate aggressively fight off the other team, but it is still very risky. If you have the enemy team confined to that side of the map anyway, you may be able to simply make a push just as they attempt to pick it up.

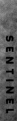

1: OUTER AREA AND FLAK HALL

WEAPONRY	Link Gun, Flak Cannon
HEALTH & ARMOR	Shield Belt
POWER-UPS	None

The outer portion of Sentinel consists of a large raised platform housing the Shield Belt. Nearby, a lower tunnel holds the important Flak Cannon, a powerful weapon in the narrow halls on the interior of this map.

There are only two ways in or out of the lower Flak Cannon hall (barring Impact jumping), so be careful about heading down there. You may want to avoid it entirely, and simply hope to acquire one from a dead enemy.

The Shield Belt platform looks into the center of the level by the Stinger through a grating that can be fired through, but not walked through.

Other than the grating, there are a few other paths in or out of this area, you can take the walkway over the Flak Cannon to reach the hall below the Bio Rifle, passing over several Vials, or you can head up on the other side to get in to the Stinger or Rocket Launcher rooms (again passing a few Vials on the way to the Rocket Launcher).

Part of the ruined level is a second floor platform that overlooks the Shield Belt, and as the upper hall near the Health also overlooks this platform, you can expect to take Sniper Rifle and Shock Rifle fire. Don't dawdle in this area; grab the Shield Belt and move on.

2: ROCKET LAUNCHER AND BODY ARMOR

WEAPONRY	Stinger, Rocket Launcher
HEALTH & ARMOR	Vials, Body Armor
POWER-UPS	UDamage

The Rocket Launcher room is a two level affair, with a lower level containing a pair of jump pads up to the Rocket Launcher itself, and a twin pair of walkways connecting the Rocket Launcher platform to its mirror on the opposite side of the room where the ammo for it rests.

The UDamage is beneath a low-sloped ledge on the bottom floor, only reachable by crawling in crouched. Worse, the UDamage is visible through a grating, allowing you to be shot at from either side while your movement is crippled. However, if all the advice above didn't sink in, here it is one last time: it is not safe!

Across from the exit to the outer Shield Belt area is a short hallway to the Body Armor. You can also get to the Body Armor by going around the other side to the Stinger, and then wall dodging across to reach it.

The ledge where the Body Armor is located has a set of stairs leading up to the Bio Rifle and triple Health walkway above, or you can take the

lower route below the armor to the jump pad or lift up to the Sniper Rifle or Bio Rifle. This also puts you beside the walkway with several Vials on it that is just over the Flak Cannon.

3: UPPER LEVEL AND VIAL WALKWAY

WEAPONRY	Bio Rifle, Shock Rifle, Sniper Rifle
HEALTH & ARMOR	Health x3, Vials
POWER-UPS	None

The most critical area on the map, three Health pick-ups on the upper walkway provide the only solid healing on the level.

In addition, you can find several useful weapons here. The Sniper Rifle is located on a recessed ledge, back from the Health walkway, while the Shock Rifle is right on the edge of the upper floor, looking out over the Shield Belt portion of the map.

You can grab the Bio Rifle on the upper walkway, and from this area, you can quickly reach the Body Armor, drop down to the Flak Cannon (or take the switchback ramp to the lower floor), or jump out to the Shield Belt or the second level ruined floor across from the Shock Rifle.

AVRIL

BIO RIFLE x1

FLAK CANNON x1

LINK GUN x1

ROCKET LAUNCHER x1

SHOCK RIFLE x1

SNIPER RIFLE x2

STINGER x2

SPECIAL PICK-UPS

UDAMAGE | JUMP BOOTS

ARMOR

BODY ARMOR | HELMET | SHIELD BELT | THIGH PADS

Shangri La takes place within an idyllic Izanagi setting, high atop a mountain where the training grounds appear serene—at least until the rockets start flying.

Despite initial appearances, Shangri La is only a medium sized map. There are three major areas connected to one another, with the large courtyard holding the UDamage dominating most of the combat space on the map.

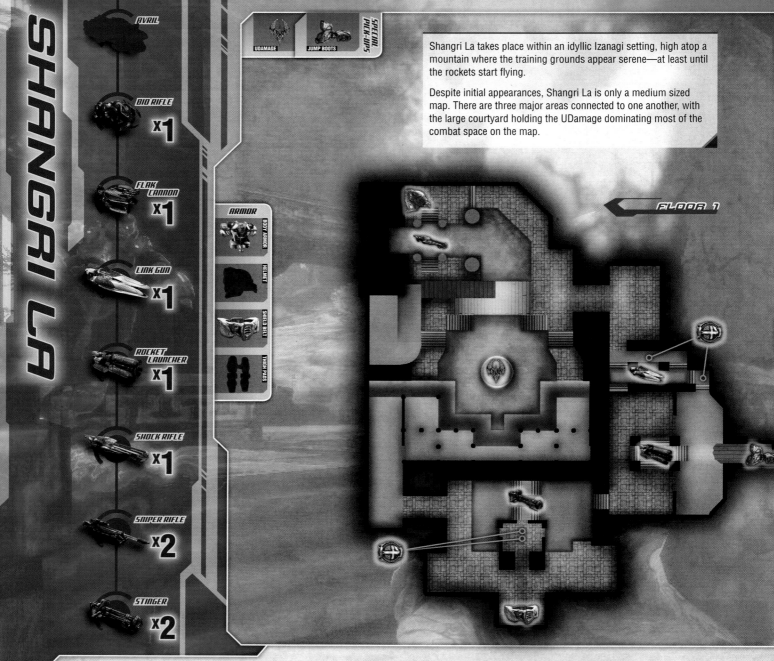

FLOOR 1

DUEL

This map is a bit big for duels, but the connectivity is just good enough that you can usually locate your opponent quickly. Dominating control of the Shield Belt and Body Armor are key for controlling the map, and if the UDamage is enabled, it needs to be timed relentlessly as well.

Staying on the upper floor and only dropping down to pick up Health or ammo is advisable, nearly every weapon can be used more effectively against an opponent below.

Be careful about spending too much time in the open courtyard area, particularly back by the Helmet and the Shock Rifle. It takes awhile to get back up to the upper floor, and you're dreadfully exposed out in the open, plus the Helmet is usually not worth giving up control of the Body Armor (and its pile of attendant Vials) or the Shield Belt room.

DEATHMATCH

Contrasting sharply with duels, free for all matches make great use of the open courtyard—for finding targets! Don't be the one out in the open. Instead, roam along the upper balconies overlooking the UDamage room, picking off targets below.

Camping out around the Body Armor area is usually worthwhile. You have easy access to Health and ammo down in the Link Gun hallway below, Vials and Armor to tank up, and *plenty* of targets nearby.

Other than the courtyard, two adjacent areas provide additional combat arenas, one holding the Rocket Launcher and Flak Cannon, the other with the useful Shield Belt.

Height is a significant factor in battles on most of the map, as nearly every part of the map can be attacked from a second floor, so controlling it (or avoiding players watching the ground level) is crucial for survival.

FLOOR 2

The Shield Belt room is a bit enclosed, and it exposes you to some dangerous combat. While both the Shield Belt and the two Health pick-ups adjacent to it are useful, there isn't a dominant position to fight from when there are so many entrances to the room.

If you do spawn out in the courtyard, try not to get wrapped up in battles, make your way to the adjacent areas, grab a useful weapon, then make your way back up to the second level.

The UDamage spawn tends to cause pandemonium. Depending on how confident you are, you may not want to go for it at all, instead trying to pick off anyone who *does* make an attempt at picking it up.

TEAM DEATHMATCH

Control of Shangri La depends on locking down the Rocket Launcher room and the Shield Belt. If both areas are controlled, your opponents are forced out into the courtyard—a perfect situation.

Patrolling the upper ledges while armed and armored gives you a serious combat advantage and it is tough to crack a defense that has both an elevation, and an armor advantage.

The UDamage is very important, so be sure to get players into position on the ledges above to quickly dodge over to reach it. If the other team manages to pick it up, damaged amped Shock Combos or Stinger fire are quickly lethal even to a heavily armored target.

Try to control the Health pick-ups as well. If your team is using up the Health in the Rocket Launcher and Shield Belt rooms, that only leaves a pair of Health pick-ups out in the courtyard on an awkwardly exposed ledge for the enemy team.

1: UDAMAGE COURTYARD

WEAPONRY	Shock Rifle, Stinger
HEALTH & ARMOR	Helmet, Health x2
POWER-UPS	UDamage

2: SNIPER BALCONY

WEAPONRY	Bio Rifle, Link Gun, Sniper Rifle x2, Body Armor
HEALTH & ARMOR	Vials
POWER-UPS	None

The focal area for Shangri La is the large open courtyard area, with the UDamage spawning atop a small sculpture at the center of the room.

The Helmet at the back of the room rests beside the Shock Rifle, and you can find the Stinger on a raised bridge beside the UDamage.

Up on a ledge near the Stinger, accessible via stairs from below is a pair of Health pick-ups.

All around the insides of the courtyard, touching the two other inner areas is a second floor ledge, which has a clear view of the entire courtyard. This ledge is only immediately accessible from the Health platform, where you can easily jump over to reach the low hanging roof nearby. It is also possible to Impact jump up if you absolutely have to get up to the second floor quickly.

From this room, you can exit through the open doors on the ground floor to reach the Shield Belt room, or through a doorway across from the Stinger bridge to reach the Flak Cannon room.

The terrain in the courtyard is ideally suited to both weapons present here, which makes this area dangerous to be in, since any freshly spawned player quickly becomes a threat.

The upper balcony area connects the inner and outer portions of the training grounds, and provides a clear view of the entire courtyard, as well as quick access to all parts of the map.

On the outer portion of the balcony, you can find a Sniper Rifle and a Bio Rifle, both useful for attacking targets below. Behind the outer Sniper Rifle is a walkway that leads past a bundle of Vials (9!), straight to a suit of Body Armor, perfect for getting buffed up.

The section of the ledge that overlooks the Shield Belt room holds the Link Gun, as well as a side chamber with a second Sniper Rifle. From here, you can jump straight down to reach the UDamage from above, important if you're carefully timing its respawn.

Sniping from the upper ledge is tempting, but don't get too focused on standing still and zooming in, you expose yourself to attack from behind. Take isolated shots, then move on— the balcony gets a lot of traffic, and there are too many ways to be attacked from behind, no matter where you're standing on the second floor.

3: ROCKET LAUNCHER AREA

WEAPONRY	Link Gun, Flak Cannon, Rocket Launcher
HEALTH & ARMOR	Health x2
POWER-UPS	Jump Boots

4: SHIELD BELT ROOM

WEAPONRY	Stinger
HEALTH & ARMOR	Health x2, Shield Belt
POWER-UPS	None

The Rocket Launcher side of the map has quite a few useful pick-ups. The Rocket Launcher itself rests on the ground level of the building, just outside a doorway leading to the Shield Belt room.

The Jump Boots rest on a narrow wooden walkway stretching out over the nearby stream. Grabbing them and then jumping straight up to the second floor Body Armor spawn is very useful, and they are helpful for getting to the second floor from any part of the map.

A pair of lifts beside the Rocket Launcher allows you to reach the second floor, where you can either go through another doorway to reach the Shield Belt room from above.

Travel back down the hall to come out near the Bio Rifle, up the stairs from the Flak Cannon.

The ground floor Flak Cannon is connected to the Rocket Launcher by a short series of halls, inside which you can find the second Link Gun and a useful pair of Health pick-ups.

Much like the courtyard, the Flak Cannon and Rocket Launcher work well in the narrow hallways around this area. Be careful moving through these rooms, walking into a face full of flak is never pleasant.

The Shield Belt itself is located out on a short wooden dock, behind a small building that contains the two Health pick-ups in the room.

Down on the ground level below the building, the Stinger sits on a slightly raised platform.

This room connects the Rocket Launcher room through two doorways (one low, one high), and through a large pair of slightly open wooden doors to the center courtyard area.

Above the room, on the opposite side of the Rocket doorways is an entrance to the upper Sniper Rifle, from which you can move out onto the balconies overlooking the courtyard area.

Generally, the lower route to the courtyard is the least safe way in or out of this room You're better served by taking the Sniper Rifle route out of the room, or heading over to the rocket area to get some close-range weaponry.

AVRIL

BIO RIFLE

FLAK CANNON x2

LINK GUN x2

ROCKET LAUNCHER x2

SHOCK RIFLE x2

SNIPER RIFLE x2

STINGER x2

SPECIAL PICK-UP
UDAMAGE

ARMOR
BODY ARMOR
HELMET
SHIELD BELT
THIGH PADS

FLOOR 1

FLAG ROOM ACCESS TWO ROUTES

Another classic returning map, Coret has been around in Unreal for quite some time. In this incarnation, Coret takes place high in the skies of the Liandri capitol city on Tayrd, Hyperion.

Coret is a tightly spaced, heavily enclosed map, almost cramped in some places, with many narrow corridors running between the two bases. The center of the map opens up somewhat, but with several routes for flag runners to travel between the bases, skirmishes in the midfield are somewhat rare (barring tussles over the UDamage in the center of the map).

Many locations on the map heavily favor close range weapons, so make a point of grabbing the Flak Cannon or Rocket Launcher for offense or defense. The frontal hallways in each base are one of the few spots you can exploit long-range weaponry, though the Shock Rifle can still use its combos to devastating effect in the corridors.

OFFENSE

The flag rooms are highly defensible, so getting out with the flag usually requires a concentrated assault to kill the defenders present in the flag room, or distract them long enough for a runner to get the flag and get out in one piece.

Getting armored up prior to a run is important; you must be able to take some hits on the way in and out of the flag room.

With only two ways in or out of the flag room, there isn't much you can do to fool flag room defenders. You're going to have to fight, either on the way in, or after you're spotted on the way out.

The "lower" route to the flag takes you past the Flak Cannon, and you can grab some Health on the way out, while the upper route takes you past the Body Armor (and a few Health Vials) on the way out.

Both routes intersect near the front of the base at the midfield, so you can choose your route across the midfield at that point, or have it chosen for you, depending on where the defenders are moving.

To gear up for a successful attack run, check your base's Body Armor, try to get Thighpads from the midfield, and possibly even grab the double Health Vials from the ramp leading up to the Rocket Launcher room.

The UDamage in the center of the map is key for breaking a defensive stalemate, so if you know it's spawning soon, hang out around the center. Ideally, guard both entrances to the UDamage hall with your teammates, so you're guaranteed to pick it up, even if one guard goes down.

Neither route into the flag room itself is safe from getting blasted in the face if the defenders are aware of your approach. If you *are* spotted by a midfield player on your way to the flag room and you're reasonably certain they reported your current path in, consider switching routes. It isn't much, but if the defenders are at least focused on the wrong entrance, you may have a split second to initiate the attack.

Assaulting a defended flag room solo is extremely difficult, so coordinate your pushes on the flag room with your teammates. Coming in from both entrances at the same time can give one of you a chance to get the flag and start running while the other distracts - or kills - the defenders.

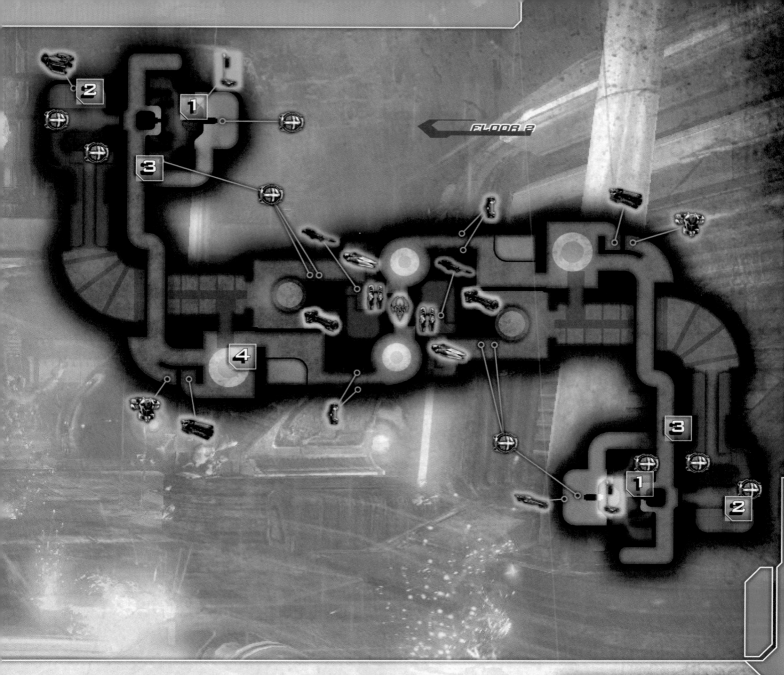

FLOOR 2

On your way back, you are initially constrained to the first route that you take out of the flag room, but as you approach the midfield, you can change your path. Generally, heading out through the Stinger/Health hall to the midfield is preferable, simply due to the presence of the Health, but the Rocket Launcher exit does provide Body Armor, and it is ever so slightly less vulnerable to pursuers shooting you in the back, due to the narrow and twisting corridors.

Hitting midfield, you may have a chance to pick up Thighpads, if you're not taking the UDamage hall across the middle, and from there, you can choose which path to take back into the base if you're still being pursued.

DEFENSE

Defense on Coret relies heavily on team communication. The flag room is blind to the approach of enemies from immediately inside, so it is vital that you have a forward defender guarding the lower hallway. From there, they can spot incoming enemies from both routes (due to the transparent glass in the upper hallway) and report the offensive approach to the inner flag room defenders.

It is also important that defenders regularly rotate from midfield duties to the flag room, This allows your defense to armor up, which is important. You don't want your flag room defense having 100 health and no armor against offensive players that are 100/80 (or higher with Vials).

Your offensive team must also rigorously hold the UDamage, and you may even want to have your front base defenders push forward when the UDamage spawn approaches, switching from defense to offense momentarily.

Be sure to have your own Body Armor checked regularly, either your offense or your defense should be taking it constantly, simply to deny incoming offensive players the armor boost.

In the midfield, you usually aren't going to find dedicated flag runners willing to stop and engage in battle, though it's worth taking shots at runners if you're in the area grabbing Health or Armor.

1: FLAG ROOM

WEAPONRY	Shock Rifle
HEALTH & ARMOR	Health x2
POWER-UPS	None

The flag room is extremely small and defensible. There is one lower entrance from the Flak Cannon room, and one upper entrance from the Body Armor hallway.

Both entrances can easily be covered by a single defender, and if you know which route an attacker is approaching from, you can adjust your position accordingly. The flag itself is located on the bottom of the room and a Shock Rifle is behind it and up a bit.

A jump pad is to the right of the flag. Runners can use it to get back up to the upper hallway, or to reach the ramp with the Shock Rifle before walldodging across.

The lower Flak entrance is a split left/right hallway, a short branch that merges in the Flak Cannon room. This adds a tiny bit of guesswork to a defender's job, but the halls are so short, that it isn't hard to simply wait for an attack to emerge and go for the flag.

The upper route is generally preferable when attacking the room, since coming in low immediately puts you at a disadvantage against defenders on the upper ledges. There is so much Health near the flag room that it's easy to restore full combat effectiveness to a damaged defender: two Health pick-ups here, and two adjacent in the Flak Cannon room.

2: FLAG ROOM ANNEX

WEAPONRY	Flak Cannon
HEALTH & ARMOR	Health x2
POWER-UPS	None

The Flak Cannon room is important simply for providing the defenders with quick access to another lethal weapon, but it cuts both ways. Attackers can grab it on the way in from the lower route. Expect to face this weapon no matter which side you're on.

Other than the Flak Cannon, there is little in this room, and the winding ramp path out delays a flag runner just long enough for an out of position flag defender to catch up with translocation. Expect to be firing backwards on your way out. You can grab Health on the way, which helps a bit. Expect to run into resistance when you emerge from this room, as it connects to the front of the base,

and a large, open area, where you are exposed to long-range assailants.

The hallway connecting the Flak Cannon room to the midfield passes *under* the upper hallway—the second path into the flag room.

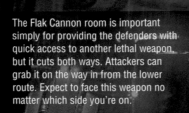

This hallway is the preferred way to tackle the flag room, as it provides a handy Body Armor pick-up, tucked away in a corner just before the hall leading to the flag room.

However, potential flag runners should be wary that the hall crosses over the front of the base, and its glass walls leave you open to the gaze of defenders watching the hall. Translocate through it as quickly as possible to give defenders little time to respond to your attack.

CORE7

4: ROCKET LAUNCHER ROOM

WEAPONRY	Rocket Launcher
HEALTH & ARMOR	Vials
POWER-UPS	None

The front of the base connects the open hallway to the Flak room with the small chamber containing the Rocket Launcher. It's possible to exit to the midfield either from the Rocket Launcher room (passing through a hall with some Health Vials in niches on either side of the hall), or to go down a short ramp through the door to the Stinger area of the midfield.

You can also translocate from the upper hall overlooking the Stinger, though this isn't relevant as a flag runner. You have to decide which route to take ahead of time, since you can't get through the blocking fence separating the two routes.

5: MIDFIELD

WEAPONRY	Sniper Rifle, Stinger, & Link Gun
HEALTH & ARMOR	Thighpads
POWER-UPS	UDamage

The midfield consists of a central lower area with Thighpads tucked away towards each base, and a hallway passing over the center area containing the UDamage.

A small ledge is outside the UDamage exits and it can only be reached via Translocation. The Sniper Rifle is resting on it and the Link Gun and Thighpads are below it. A few health pick-ups are just down the hall from the Sniper Rifle area are, and the doorway to the flag room annex area.

From the lower center, you can head up ramps to either the Rocket Launcher room, passing the Vials on the way, or towards the Stinger, which also connects to the annex room.

It is possible to translocate between the Stinger and Rocket areas, but you have to pass around a dividing wall to get to the Link Gun/UDamage corridor.

Excepting the lower area with the Thighpads, all of the halls here are quite narrow, so most weapons become more lethal due to the limited maneuvering room. If you're focusing on running the flag, translocate through the midfield with an eye to avoiding conflict, you're unlikely to come out of a fight unscathed, and you need your armor for the assault on the flag room.

HYDROSIS

AVRIL

BIO RIFLE x2

FLAK CANNON x2

LINK GUN x2

ROCKET LAUNCHER x2

SHOCK RIFLE x2

SNIPER RIFLE x4

STINGER

SPECIAL PICK-UPS

ARMOR

BODY ARMOR

HELMET

SHIELD BELT

THIGH PADS

Hydrosis is a traditional CTF map, with an extensive midfield area, and a sizable base that has two sections leading in and out of the base.

While the dual flag room access is similar to Coret, the midfield (and overall map) is considerably more open. In the center, mirrored bunkers provide ready made sniping posts, proving a constant hazard for your offense.

Within the base, the two distinct routes in and out of the flag room force a choice for flag runners on offense, going in and coming out of the flag room. One route is faster, but considerably harder to escape while carrying the flag with alert defenders, the other is longer, but has two armor pick-ups along the way, giving the potential to suit up on the way in or out of the base.

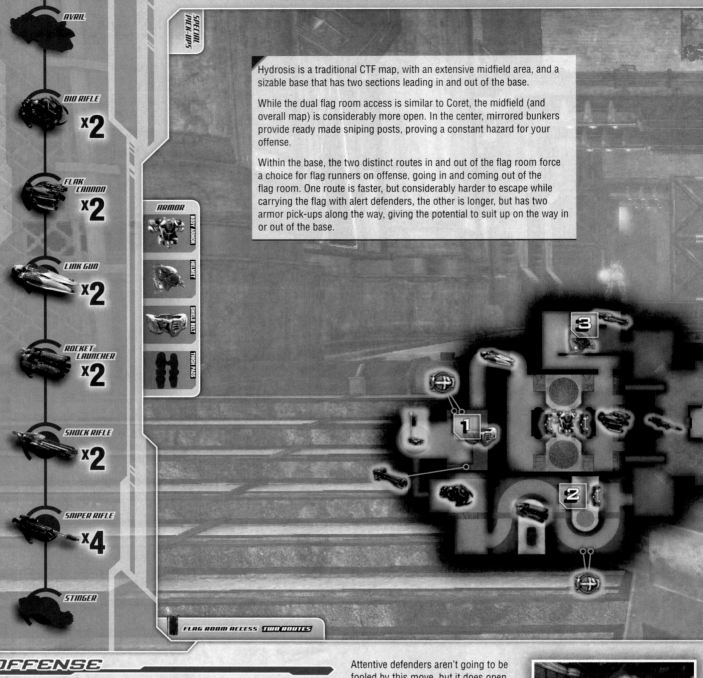

FLAG ROOM ACCESS TWO ROUTES

OFFENSE

Playing offense on this map is complicated by the danger of snipers in the midfield. There isn't a completely safe way to cross the center, though you can minimize risks by using the limited cover, and choosing your translocation targets carefully. Better to slow your approach to the enemy base slightly than to zip across in a straight line and either go down on the way, or arrive at the enemy base barely standing.

Once you reach the enemy base, you have several options. You can go in the quick route, through the Rocket Launcher hall, or the slightly longer route, via the Thighpad/Shock Rifle room, giving the possibility of armoring up a bit. The last option is to translocate in through an open vent shaft at the front of the base. This skips the Shock Rifle room, dropping you by the Flak Cannon in the Body Armor room. Unfortunately, you can't take that particular shortcut on the way out, but it is a good way to go in if you're looking for armor.

The flag room itself has only two routes in, though you *can* sneak in slightly by coming from the Rocket Launcher side. Next to the Bio Rifle just outside the flag room is a small vent shaft that drops out right by the flag itself.

Attentive defenders aren't going to be fooled by this move, but it does open the possibility of having a coordinated attack getting the flag out. Have one player come in from the Link Gun side of the room, get the attention of the defenders, then quickly drop down from the vent shaft, grab the flag, and head out via the Rocket Launcher route.

Heading out from the flag room, you have to decide whether to go back through the Rocket Launcher room (faster) or the Flak Cannon route (slower, though more armor on the way). There are two Health pick-ups on the Link Gun side of the flag room, which you can use if you head towards the Flak Cannon, and there are also two Health pick-ups on the way out via the Rocket Launcher.

The Flak Cannon route is marginally safer—that is, you're still going to engage in combat on the way, but at least you can fight on level ground. If you take the Rocket route out, defenders can stand on top of the Rocket Launcher platform and fire down at you with impunity, and there is little you can do to retaliate.

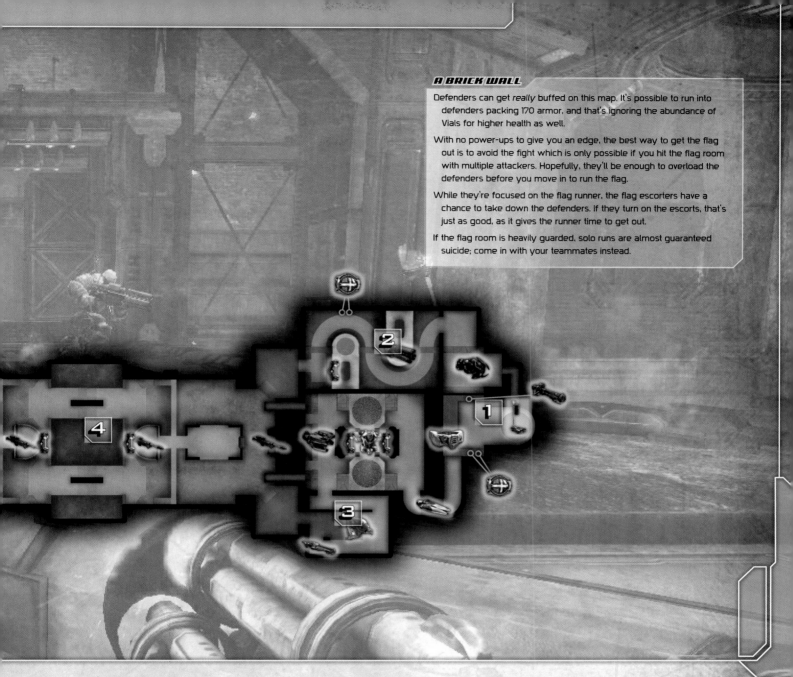

Defenders can get *really* buffed on this map. It's possible to run into defenders packing 170 armor, and that's ignoring the abundance of Vials for higher health as well.

With no power-ups to give you an edge, the best way to get the flag out is to avoid the fight which is only possible if you hit the flag room with multiple attackers. Hopefully, they'll be enough to overload the defenders before you move in to run the flag.

While they're focused on the flag runner, the flag escorters have a chance to take down the defenders. If they turn on the escorts, that's just as good, as it gives the runner time to get out.

If the flag room is heavily guarded, solo runs are almost guaranteed suicide; come in with your teammates instead.

Crossing the midfield is murderous; you usually need assistance from your teammates. You *must* walldodge the entire way to speed up your movement, you're at enough risk from snipers and translocating defenders who can catch up to you quickly, its even worse if you're moving slowly.

Once you get back to your side of the map, the Rocket route is usually preferable, as you get back into the flag room quickly, and you can pick up health on the way in while your defenders use the rooms geography to your benefit.

DEFENSE

Defense on Hydrosis can become extremely solid; there is a Shield Belt located right in the flag room! In combination with a midfield defense that softens or kills incoming attackers, and warns of their approach route, it is easy to gain the upper hand against attackers.

Because there is Body Armor and Thighpads located near the flag room, it's worth trading off flag room defense to sweep the armor. This is also important, because you don't want attackers coming in and grabbing both pieces of armor before they hit the flag room.

Inside the flag room, you have a convenient ledge to watch the flag from an elevated perch, two Health pick-ups in the corner, and more Health just around the corner in the Rocket room. Abuse the defensive advantage. You may be able to get away with less defenders who are more heavily armored, giving your offense an extra body or two to crack the enemy team's defense.

Some of your defenders should be playing midfield defense, as the sniping potential is too potent to ignore, plus your midfielders can alert interior defenders of which route attackers are approaching from.

The Rocket Launcher room is easily defended from flag runners, as you can translocate up to the Rocket Launcher, or the platform holding the ammo and Vials. Both positions provide superb line of sight on the narrow channel between the platforms, making it easy to take down runners. You may also be able to nail translocating players, they don't have a lot of room to maneuver.

The Flak Cannon area must be defended from the Body Armor area, rather than the Shock Rifle room, if you want to stop offensive players translocating behind you and getting to the flag room. On the way out, if they take that route, you can still catch them, since they can't translocate back out from the Body Armor room to the midfield.

1: FLAG ROOM

WEAPONRY	Bio Rifle, Link Gun
HEALTH & ARMOR	Health x2, Shield Belt
POWER-UPS	None

The flag room is a fairly large open area, making midrange weapons quite effective.

Convenient for the defense, since the Link Gun is located nearby, and the Stinger is on a ledge overlooking the flag itself. The Bio Rifle is on the Rocket hallway side of the room, along with the small vent shaft that connects it to the flag. The Shield Belt is slightly hidden, located on a pipe *above* the Stinger, you need to translocate up to reach it.

There are two Health pick-ups in the corner of the room, and more around the corner in the Rocket room if you need to recharge. Now, this may not be the safest route, but it is possible to Impact Jump out with the flag.

2: BASE ENTRANCE, ROCKET LAUNCHER SIDE

WEAPONRY	Rocket Launcher
HEALTH & ARMOR	Health x2, Vials
POWER-UPS	None

By far the fastest way in and out of the flag room, it is also the most dangerous to run *out* of, as it has two raised platforms that can only be reached via translocation, and provide a superb platform for launching rockets down on the head of the flag carrier.

On the upshot (at least for the offense), the two Health pick-ups on the way out can help to recover from a battle in the flag room (or on the way out), but getting out in one piece with an alert defense usually requires an escort to clear the Rocket Launcher platform and provide cover.

3: BASE ENTRANCE, SHOCK RIFLE SIDE

WEAPONRY	Shock Rifle, Flak Cannon
HEALTH & ARMOR	Body Armor, Helmet, Vials
POWER-UPS	None

The winding passage from the midfield to the flag room goes through the Shock Rifle room first, which has a Helmet, and then through a *very* narrow hallway to the Body Armor room, which also has the Flak Cannon, and some Health Vials on either side of the Body Armor platform.

You can translocate in or out of the base through a vent just above the Flak Cannon.

HEADSHOTS!

The Helmet is particularly significant on this map, as it can save you from an ignominious death in the midfield from a single Sniper Rifle round.

If you're playing offense and you spawn anywhere near this room, make a point of checking to see if it is up.

4: BASE FRONT AND MIDFIELD

WEAPONRY	Sniper Rifle
HEALTH & ARMOR	Vials
POWER-UPS	None

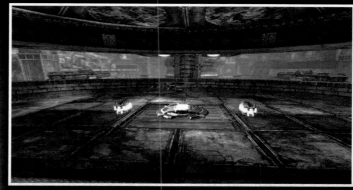

The immediate front of the base has an easily accessible Sniper Rifle, the three entrances to the base (Shock Rifle/Rocket Launcher/and Flak Cannon teleport), and the large bunker that dominates the midfield.

The large bunker has Health Vials at the front of it, though these aren't really a major concern. Of great significance is the cover the bunker provides, and the conveniently sized sniper slits at the front, ideal for covering the enemy side of the map.

At the very center of the map, two bridges cross over a (deadly) waterway below, watch your step on the way across.

A few columns and walkways on the sides of the bunker provide the only cover from enemy snipers, make use of them when running the flag through the midfield.

Constant sniper wars in the midfield are likely, since counter-sniping is one of the few ways you can suppress the enemy team's snipers. If your team is greatly outmatched by the enemy snipers, you may want to recall your sniper to assist with interior defense—or to go on offense and simply try to translocate across the midfield as quickly as possible.

OMICRON DAWN

AVRIL

BIO RIFLE x2

FLAK CANNON x2

LINK GUN x2

ROCKET LAUNCHER x2

SHOCK RIFLE x2

SNIPER RIFLE x2

STINGER x2

SPECIAL PICK-UPS

ARMOR

BODY ARMOR

HELMET

SHIELD BELT

THIGH PADS

A tiny (and perilous) midfield connects two complex bases that have multiple routes in and out of the flag room, as well as plenty of crossover for the offense to choose their route in and out of the base.

The midfield consists only of two narrow bridges crossing the yawning gulf of space below—don't slip!

Each base front has a sniper chamber that can watch the midfield bridges and the opposing sniper, so you may want to launch some projectile fire up into the perch if you're moving through the center, to keep any potential snipers occupied.

Inside the bases, there are many potential routes for attackers to use, and for flag runners to use on their escape run. As the only choke points occur at the front of the base, expect a lot of conflict inside the flag room, and more near the bridges as a flag runner leaves the base.

FLAG ROOM ACCESS THREE ROUTES

You can reach a pretty sturdy armor level if you sweep your base before heading across the bridges connecting the bases, though you must expose yourself to pick up the Helmet. However, armoring up deprives your defenders of the added protection, and it takes time.

Generally, picking up at least one piece on the way, and then checking on a second piece on the way through the enemy base gives you at least some armor before you hit the flag room.

As far as actually reaching the flag room, you have quite a few options. Crossing the midfield, your only real danger is an enemy sniper watching the bridges, but you can translocate across so quickly, you shouldn't be exposed for more than a few seconds.

Inside the base, you can take the lower route through the Rocket room, the middle route past the Health *or* the Thighpads, or the upper route past the Flak Cannon (and more Health).

Of the three, the upper route is usually the safest way to get to the flag, and the lower route the least safe. However, it is easily covered by defenders. The safest route is usually one of the two middle paths, which lead to the gallery overlooking the flag room. With several pillars blocking line of sight, you're somewhat less exposed to instant attack than the other approaches.

The flag room is very likely going to be guarded, and with its distinct sloping terrain, you're at a significant disadvantage if you're fighting from the lower part of the room.

Once you do manage to pick up the flag, you need to quickly decide which way to get out of the base. The fastest way out is the middle level, and it has the advantage of taking you past two Health pick-ups.

The lower level also takes you past two Health pick-ups, but only if you're willing to expose yourself to fire from behind while in the flag room.

Finally, it is possible to get back to the upper route past the Flak Cannon. If you quickly move over to the column flanking the stairs at the back of the room, you can actually double jump against it, then dodge off the column to reach the upper ledge out of the room. This move may surprise defenders expecting you to move out of the room the more usual lower or center routes.

Note that you can easily dodge or double jump to the center level, into any of the three openings facing the flag.

Once you exit the flag room, you can change courses again at several points. From the Rocket room, you can double jump up to the same path as the mid-level exit from the flag room, and from the Flak Cannon, you can either drop down to the right exit from the base, or continue into the Sniper Rifle chamber and go down either side to reach the central bridges.

Defense on Omicron is tricky, while defending the flag room is fairly straightforward, and guarding all possible entrances to the room is difficult. Few rooms have line of sight to other areas of the base.

In addition, the extremely short midfield does not take long to traverse, and even if you have a sniper watching incoming players, they can only tell you the initial direction from which the enemies entered your base. Once inside, they can easily translocate to a different route.

Because there are two pieces of armor in the base, as well as plentiful health, you may want to have a few defenders constantly roaming and picking up armor. This has several benefits, including denying the enemy offense armor in your base, intercepting the occasional attacker, and armoring up your defense.

If you have players who are comfortable switching roles, a very effective strategy is to have your fully armored defenders switch to offense. If they can grab a Helmet on the way across the midfield, they can enter the enemy base with a full suit of armor, giving good odds for a successful flag run.

From the flag room, if the flag is taken, successfully returning it requires fast and accurate communication. Give constant updates on the flag runner's position, so that outlying teammates can translocate to intercept on the proper route. Around the center of the base, the carrier can change directions several times, so you need to make sure your teammates are heading in the right direction.

While having both flags out isn't a desirable situation, one nice thing about the base layout is that it is quite easy for your own flag carrier to move about in the base to different positions, all of which have either armor or health nearby.

WEAPONRY	Shock Rifle
HEALTH & ARMOR	Health x2
POWER-UPS	None

The flag rooms inside the base are fairly large, with a large semicircular walkway around the flag located at the center of the room. The flag is on a round platform, with a pair of stairs that wind down to the bottom level of the base.

On the upper level, a long circular ledge surrounds the room, with the Shock Rifle on one side. From these ledges, it is easy for defenders to watch the entire room, all three entrances to the flag, and have a nice height advantage against incoming enemy players.

Offensive players can easily transition from the flag room to the central or lower levels of the base, or get back out via the upper route with a little tricky jumping, or the more mundane method of walking up the steps at the back of the room to the upper level.

There are two Health pick-ups at the bottom of the room, helpful for restoring defenders to fighting trim after an engagement.

WEAPONRY	Rocket Launcher
HEALTH & ARMOR	Body Armor
POWER-UPS	None

The lower Rocket Launcher room is a simple circular chamber, though it holds a rather well hidden Body Armor that is not immediately apparent.

Make your way over to the exit from the room that leads to the Link Gun and look up. A pair of panels are directly above and they can be shot through (though not translocated through) revealing an open area leading to the Body Armor up on a ledge. Translocate up to grab it.

If you want to, you can actually camp out up on the Body Armor ledge, looking down through the transparent panels. Since you can shoot through them, you may be able to land a pre-emptive hit on an incoming player from above. This isn't an ideal defensive position however, as the line of sight is restricted, and this is only one way for incoming players to attack.

3: MIDDLE LEVEL

WEAPONRY	Stinger, Bio Rifle
HEALTH & ARMOR	Health x2, Thighpads
POWER-UPS	None

The mid-level of the base is important, as it has both the Bio Rifle and the Stinger, but it also holds the Thighpads, and two Health pick-ups. This area has a clean line of sight to both the flag room, and to the outer part of the base, where you can watch for incoming players.

The Health pick-ups are located at the edge of this area, close to the Link Gun, while the Bio Rifle is off in a side chamber, just below the Flak hallway. The Thighpads are tucked away beside some crates in the Bio Rifle room.

Note that it is possible to translocate through the slim windows that provide a narrow line of sight to the Flak Cannon hall.

From the Bio Rifle room, a ramp leads up to a ledge overlooking the flag room and the Stinger. Beside the walkway is another of the transparent windows that can be fired through, this one looking down into the other side of the lower Rocket launcher room.

4: UPPER HALLWAY

WEAPONRY	Flak Cannon
HEALTH & ARMOR	Health
POWER-UPS	None

The upper hallway contains the Flak Cannon and a single Health pick-up. It also overlooks the Bio Rifle room, and you can translocate down there if needed.

There isn't much to this area, but it is important, as it connects the upper level of the flag room with the sniper chamber at the front of the base. Incoming attackers frequently use this route to even out the height advantage that defenders enjoy.

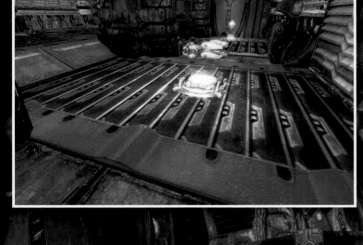

5: SNIPER RIFLE CHAMBER

WEAPONRY	Sniper Rifle, Link Gun
HEALTH & ARMOR	None
POWER-UPS	None

The Sniper Rifle is located in a large chamber at the front of the base, which has three open windows facing the midfield bridges.

Two staircases lead down to the two front base entrances, and a walkway passes out the back of the chamber to the Flak Cannon hallway.

Behind the chamber, just outside the lower Rocket Launcher room, is the Link Gun. The Link Gun is positioned right at the meeting point for all of the various routes into the heart of the base.

From this position, you can go down to the Rocket room, double jump up to get to the hall leading to the Stinger ledge, or translocate up to the walkway leading into the Flak hallway.

One handy trick for flag runners; you can actually Impact Jump up through the window into the sniper chamber, then drop out either window at the front to reach either bridge. If you can spare the Health, it can throw off chasers for a brief moment.

6: MIDFIELD

WEAPONRY	None
HEALTH & ARMOR	Helmet, Vials
POWER-UPS	None

The midfield area is extremely simple. Two separate bridges connect the two bases, and in front of each base, just below the sniper chambers, a mirrored pair of ledges holds Helmets and a few Health Vials.

REFLECTION

AVRIL

BIO RIFLE x2

FLAK CANNON x2

LINK GUN x3

ROCKET LAUNCHER x2

SHOCK RIFLE x2

SNIPER RIFLE x2

STINGER x3

ARMOR

BODY ARMOR

HELMET

SHIELD BELT

THIGH PADS

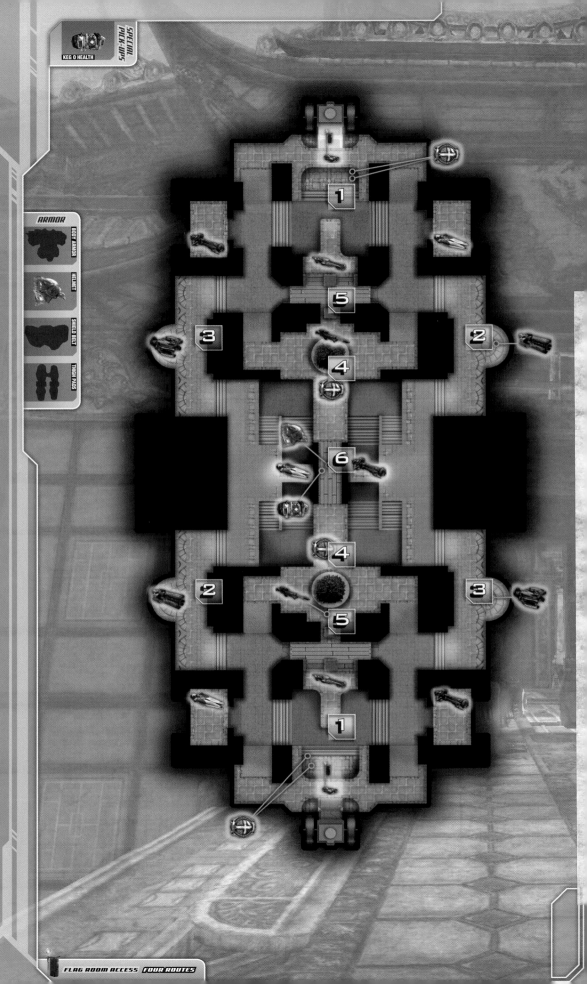

FLAG ROOM ACCESS   FOUR ROUTES

Reflection is a simple CTF map, with little vertical space, and a short midfield. However, the flag rooms are quite open, and have quite a few routes in and out, making defense rather difficult.

The small size of the map allows extremely rapid translocation between bases, as there is usually little action in the center of the map. Only a Helmet and the Health Keg are there to distract travelers and most offensive players zip through to swiftly arrive at the enemy base.

Each base has a platform facing the midfield, and *four* entrances to the main flag room area. Two lower side routes are to the left and right of the platform. They're identical, but one passes the Rocket Launcher, and the other provides access to the Flak Cannon on the way to the flag room. Just below the platform is a tunnel that leads to the Shock Rifle, which is located just below the flag itself in the flag room.

Inside the flag rooms, there is a lower lift that provides access from below to the flag platform (though of course, you can simply translocate up). The flag itself is on a raised bridge, accessible by frontal translocation, the ramp below it, or one of the side hallways.

The side hallways also have two small rooms that can be translocated into, one on each side of the center flag room. One contains the Link Gun, the other the Stinger. In the flag room itself, there's a Bio Rifle and two Health pick-ups below the flag—crucial for defenders.

The upper platform area leading from the flag room to the midfield is directly across from the flag room. Pick up the Sniper Rifle on the way.

There are two lifts on either side of the Sniper Rifle platform that can be used by escaping flag runners to transition from one of the side halls to the upper platform, or even to the other side hall. The ramps beside the lifts head right up to the front of the platform facing midfield.

HEAL ME!

Health is limited on this map, with no Vials to speak of, and with only a single Helmet in the center of the map, it is basically impossible to get seriously tanked up. This has a considerable impact on both offense and defense; offensively surviving a flag run is difficult with so little mid-field Health to recover from damage in the flag room.

Defensively, it is hard to get especially buffed up to resist a strong offensive push, making anticipation and communication of incoming flag runners critical. If you can ambush an unarmored attacker, the fight is usually going to go in your favor.

The midfield area of the map has a Helmet in the top center bridge, and the Health Keg just below it in a crosswalk. There is one Health pick-up in front of each base, on the lower level that leads to the Shock Rifle halls.

Crossing through the midfield can be done from the upper platforms (leading across the bridge containing the Helmet), or along the sides of the midfield (emerging either from the Rocket/Flak side passages, or the lower Shock Rifle hallway).

Below the side ledges are two narrow channels that dip down sharply, one holding a second Stinger, the other a second Link Gun. The Stinger is on the Blue Base Rocket Launcher/Red Base Flak Cannon side, and vice versa for the Link Gun.

OFFENSE

Before heading for the flag, determine which weapons are required to break the defenders and help you escape, then take the shortest route from your spawn point through those weapons. Ideally, grab one or two weapons on your way out of your base, then pick up any other weapon you feel you need while heading through the enemy base.

Because the midfield is short, you can usually get through it quickly. The biggest danger from dedicated defenders is snipers. The raised platforms in front of each base make for decent sniping platforms (with the Sniper Rifle close at hand for them to pick up), and there is little cover through the middle if you're translocating across quickly.

If you know there is an active sniper, be careful about teleporting through the upper bridge. The enclosed space in the bridge makes for a perfect tunnel for any sniper watching the midfield, and even if you're translocating, you and your ghost make an easy target.

If the midfield isn't being watched closely, you can generally take whatever route you feel most comfortable with. Wherever you last ran into defenders inside their base, take an alternate route. Ideally, you don't want them spotting you until you're ready to engage.

You have a couple of choices for going after the flag. While getting to the flag is easy, getting back out is considerably less so. The fastest way to and from the flag is via the upper platform or lower Shock Rifle hall, and then to rush out again through the same hall. However, this route is also commonly trafficked on the upper floor, and the lower route is easy for defenders to watch.

The other option is to take one of the side routes. From there, you have the additional choice of taking one of lift entrances to the upper platform, or continuing to attack the flag room from the left or right.

Before you enter the flag room, decide if you're going to go straight for the flag, or engage the defenders. If you are going to fight, have your chosen weapon out and ready. The brief second it takes for you to switch from the translocator isn't a long time, but you don't want to give up any edge if you are going in seeking combat.

Depending on the current map situation, you should usually go for a straight translocator run on the flag if the defenders were either recently killed, or had to chase a flag runner out and have just returned the flag. Going for the flag while defenders are in place and ready for you is usually a waste of time, since they'll get free shots, and are plenty ready for anyone heading for the flag itself.

Whether you fight in or translocate in, once you have your hands on the flag, you need to quickly decide which route to take out. Pick a route, and have your teammates translocate ahead of you to clear the way, or stay to engage any freshly spawned defenders who are coming after you.

BEATDOWN

The upper platform is one of the better routes in if you're planning on taking the fight to the defenders. It puts you on even ground with any defenders already there, removes some sniper pressure from the midfield, and gives you a nice elevated vantage point when you reach the flag room.

It isn't perfect though. Defenders in the Shock Rifle hall can't be seen, nor can defenders who are hiding out in the side halls to the left and right of the flag room.

Deal with the visible threats first, but don't ignore the ones you can't see when you do finally make a run on the flag.

If you can manage it, the straight route out through the Shock Rifle can take you past both the Health below the flag, and the Health as you emerge from the hall. The other direct option is double jumping from the flag platform, then walldodging over to the Sniper Rifle platform, which gets you out just as fast - or faster than the Shock Rifle hall - though you won't be in line to pick up the midfield Health on the way.

Otherwise, you need to pick one of the side routes. Both are identical, so the only consideration should be which weapon you'd rather *not* run into, the Rocket Launcher, or the Flak Cannon.

You can also divert from the side routes by taking the lifts or the ramps up to the center platform, then running through the upper bridge once you hit the midfield.

If you come out up top, you might get lucky and snag the Helmet on the way, but wherever you emerge, scan the Keg quickly; picking it up on the way can increase your chances of a successful capture.

Passing through the midfield on the sides makes walldodging a bit easier. You can't pick up a lot of momentum on the upper route, but you can hug a wall and bounce off of it the whole way across the center on either side.

Once you reach your base, you again have to pick a route, with preference to the Shock Rifle hall or the upper Sniper Rifle platform, as those two routes are the most direct. If you take one of the side routes, you may return only to find that your flag has been taken by their offense while you took a detour.

Naturally, if you have heat on your tail, you may not have a choice. Dodging and fighting backwards while trying to avoid the closest enemies may force you down a particular route. That's fine, just make sure your team knows where you are at all times, and which route you are taking.

DEFENSE

Defense on Reflection is difficult. Your forward defense is limited to some sniping across the midfield from your side of the map, and the small size of the midfield allows offensive runners to quickly reach your base.

Successful defense on Reflection depends on good communication between your midfield players and your interior base defenders, because there are so many potential routes in and out of the flag room, it is critical that your defenders aren't getting hit "blind" by attackers who translocated in without being spotted.

You need to have at least one defensive player on midfield duty at all times however, because even if they aren't stopping the runners, you need to know exactly which route they are coming in. Call out incoming targets with simple directional (upper, left) or weapon (Rocket Launcher side, Shock Rifle hall) indications, and your inner defenders can deal with them as they arrive (and they're hopefully injured).

Choose your defensive position carefully. The upper platform around the Sniper Rifle is a great vantage point, but the enclosed hallways make it a dangerous place to fight without taking at least *some* damage from any offensive player with a mind to engage you.

The side halls, or the flag platform itself, give you somewhat better lines of sight, but both are restricted in what they can immediately cover. If you're on the left or right, the other side is slightly open, and if you're on the center flag platform, you are guaranteed to be targeted by every incoming player.

Unless you're grabbing health, avoid the ground floor below the flag platform. You don't have a good line of sight, and you're at a disadvantage to any opponent arriving from any route except the Shock Rifle.

It is fairly easy to recover from an attack by scooping up the two Health pick-ups below the Flag, and teleporting down the Shock Rifle hall briefly to grab the other Health pick-up in the center.

The midfield player can continue to harass other incoming players, steal the Helmet and Keg, and if necessary, fall back to intercept a flag runner should the interior defense fall. Should your midfield player manage to get both the Helmet and Keg, or even just the Keg, he should switch to offense while another player rotates to midfield defense.

For the flag room defense itself, your fresh defenders should quickly scoop up all weapons around the base, and gather ammo while idle. If there is very little pressure, an extra defender can switch to offense, but never leave the flag room undefended, it is too short of a trip for a runner if he is unchallenged.

Be careful with leaving the flag room to procure the Rocket Launcher or the Flak Cannon, if you're going to get them, make sure you have a defender who can cover the flag while you translocate out and back. The brief gap in your defenses can be breached by a strong offensive push.

1: FLAG ROOM

WEAPONRY	Bio Rifle, Link Gun, Stinger
HEALTH & ARMOR	Health
POWER-UPS	None

2: ROCKET HALLWAY

WEAPONRY	Rocket Launcher
HEALTH & ARMOR	None
POWER-UPS	None

The flag room in each base consists of a large floor area, overlooked by the flag itself, and the platform with the Sniper Rifle. From here, you can translocate into the side rooms to pick up the Link Gun or the Stinger.

On defense, the side halls are difficult to cover at the same time as the flag room itself, so you must either constantly patrol to each side, or position yourself centrally and rely on your teammates to warn you of incoming targets. Standing on the flag is the easiest way to cover the room, but it makes you a prime target for all offensive players.

The two health pick-ups below the flag are critical for restoring defenders (or rarely, returning flag runners). If you're feeling especially confident, you can even injure yourself to grab the health in advance of an approaching enemy push, simply to deny them even the chance of picking up the health on the way in or out. Naturally, this is a risky tactic.

The Bio Rifle below the flag stand can be used to hose down one of the approaches to the flag room if you know where an enemy player is coming from. With early warning from a midfield defender, this is easy to accomplish.

Beware of fighting from the ground floor, coming into the room, attack from either the side halls, or the upper platform. Fighting from the Shock hallway or the ground is usually unsafe.

The Rocket Launcher is located off to the side of the main base area, requiring a detour to acquire. The area is comfortable for fighting with it, though most players moving through here are either translocating rapidly to reach the flag, or to return to defending it.

You can monitor the midfield from here slightly, though without the superior lines of sight from the upper platform in front of the base.

The Rocket Launcher hall is located on the same side (left, facing OUT from the flag) in each base, with the Link Gun room on the same side.

3: FLAK HALLWAY

WEAPONRY	Flak Cannon
HEALTH & ARMOR	None
POWER-UPS	None

The Flak Cannon hall area is identical to the Rocket Launcher area, just located on the opposite side of the base. Whichever weapon you are more comfortable with, you should make an effort to pick up—or to avoid fighting if you're running with the flag on the way out.

Remember that the Flak Cannon hall is located on the same side (right, facing OUT from the flag) in each base, with the Stinger room on the same side.

4: SNIPER PLATFORM

WEAPONRY	Sniper Rifle
HEALTH & ARMOR	None
POWER-UPS	None

This whole area is important for both defense and offense, as it provides a dangerous platform for sniping incoming players, and close range halls for offense that does break through.

On the midfield side, this platform provides a useful sniping vantage point, and on the flag side, it can easily be used to defend or to reach the flag in either base.

When running the flag or defending, remember the two side lifts and ramps that reach this area, they can be used by a flag runner to completely switch sides as they move from the flag room.

Similarly, on offense and defense, remember that flag runners can walldodge from the flag platform to this platform, allowing quick egress from the flag room.

5: SHOCK HALLWAY

WEAPONRY	Shock Rifle
HEALTH & ARMOR	Health
POWER-UPS	None

The lower Shock hall usually gets traffic to reach the single Health pick-up near the midfield side. On the flag side of the hall, you can also quickly get to the two Health pick-ups under the flag itself.

It is possible to play defense from this hallway fairly easily, as you can both watch the incoming enemies from the midfield, and get back to the flag in a flash if necessary.

This hall is similarly important on offense, as it provides the shortest route in and out of the base. It is also usually the most dangerous, as it emerges on ground floor below the flag. Translocate quickly, or expect to get gibbed before you even touch the flag.

6: MIDFIELD

WEAPONRY	Stinger, Link Gun
HEALTH & ARMOR	Helmet, Keg O Health
POWER-UPS	None

The midfield area between the bases is quiet small, and consists of a simple tower-like structure in the center of the map. The upper level has a bridge stretching between the two bases, containing the Helmet, and just below it is a crossways room that holds the Health Keg.

On each side, walkways run between the front of the bases, and between the walkways and the center tower, lower channels can be traversed to acquire some ammo on the way in or out of the bases, at the risk of considerable exposure from above.

Barring sniper wars between the two bases sniper platforms, the midfield usually only sees significant fights between players going for the Health Keg.

The Helmet is generally too minor a boost to be concerned with, though defensive players can usually grab it more often than offensive players, unless they happen to get lucky while translocating through the center.

Note that you *can* teleport from the Health Keg crosswalk up to the Helmet with a bit of careful aiming from below. Similarly, you can drop a Translocator beacon down into the Health Keg room from the Helmet.

From the midfield, all of the entrances to each base can be quickly reached via the Translocator, so choosing your route into the base carefully is as important on offense as spotting the incoming flag runners is on defense.

On foot with the flag, the fastest way across the center is walldodging on the side walls, or double jumping and wall dodging across the channels beside the tower.

SPECIAL PICK-UPS

AVRIL	
BIO RIFLE	x2
FLAK CANNON	x2
LINK GUN	x2
ROCKET LAUNCHER	x4
SHOCK RIFLE	x2
SNIPER RIFLE	x2
STINGER	x4

ARMOR

- BODY ARMOR
- HELMET
- SHIELD BELT
- THIGH PADS

Strident is a small CTF map with rapid access to both bases possible in a matter of a few seconds. The midfield is blocked off completely in terms of visibility from each side of the map with a large wall separating the two bases. The flag room is an immense area, with multiple floors, and two side areas (containing the Rocket Launcher on the lower level, the Stinger on the upper).

The flag itself is located on a moving flag stand that periodically raises and lowers. As a result, flag runners need to be aware of its position. If you come in along the bottom route and the flag is raised, you have to take the jump pad up, or teleport to reach it. Usually this doesn't have much of an impact, but it can foil a last second flag capture. The safest method is always coming in from above, as you can drop down to the flag is lowered, but this exposes you to more defenders.

In front of each base, between the midfield wall, there are quite a few weapons along with the only Health pick-ups, two on each side. The Shock Rifle and Link Gun are both on the ground level, and the Sniper Rifle is up on a ledge overlooking the front of the base areas.

STRIDENT WAVE

Periodically, a massive machine (visible through the transparent edges of the map) passes over the battlefield.

Each time it does so, it emits a lifegiving field, healing every player it touches for 10 health, up to and beyond 100, all the way to 199.

This constant health boost, in combination with the plentiful Vials located around the map, raise the average toughness of all players. This is especially true for flag defenders, who have time to grab Vials in the flag room.

This may throw off your normal combat rhythm. Expect your opponents to take more shots than usual to kill.

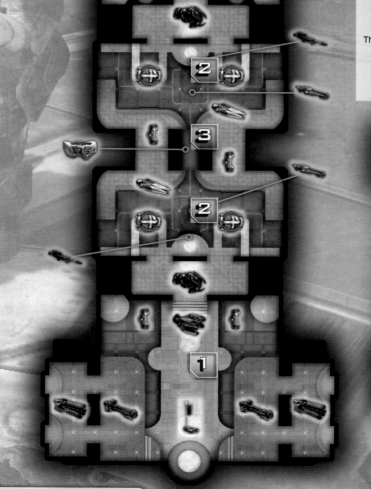

FLAG ROOM ACCESS **THREE ROUTES**

OFFENSE

Getting between the bases is a snap, your primary consideration should be whether to head into the flag room from one of the lower side routes, or take the upper path directly to the flag platform.

The lower side routes have the advantage of a small health boost (three Vials located on each side as you enter the flag room), and you are slightly less exposed to fire from the opposite side of the flag room.

From the lower route, you can reach the Flak Cannon and the flag, and once you do, getting back out is the tricky part. Leaving via the upper route is usually unsafe, as you are easily visible from any of the upper platforms in the room, or any defenders on the flag walkway itself.

Taking one of the lower routes also has the advantage of taking you past Vials again, and to the Health pick-ups in the midfield. There's also a chance you may hit the Shield Belt on the way back through the middle.

Traveling through the midfield wall, the lower route past the Shield Belt is the quickest. Otherwise, you must make your way up one of the ramps that passes through the wall on the upper level. There are a few Vials to be picked up on the way through the upper passage, though not enough to save you from heavy firepower.

Taking the upper route is usually a worse option, as it slows you down enough for translocating enemies to easily catch up to you, and you're exposed to any sniper perched on the sniper platform.

Due to the layout of the level, it is possible to walldodge virtually the entire way between the two bases. Doing so greatly speeds up your return trip if you bounce off the halls out of the flag room, the pillars by the Health pick-ups and the Shield Belt tunnel. Repeating the pattern on your side of the map is also a benefit.

DEFENSE

Most of your defense needs to be concentrated in the flag room, as the midfield does not have a clear line of sight to the enemy base, preventing pre-emptive long range engagement. It is worthwhile to have one sniper waiting out on the Sniper Rifle platform in the front of the base, as he can easily call out incoming targets, and take a few shots while they translocate their way in.

Inside the flag room, you have quite a few options. The holograms in the corners of the flag room are resting on fairly sizable platforms that you can stand on. These corner platforms have a clear view of the flag from above, and each one can see incoming players from the center route, or the side route directly below them.

You can wait on the flag walkway itself, usually the upper level. This lets you intercept incoming flag runners from any direction, though you're also going to be targeted immediately in return.

Finally, you can stand up on the upper level, where the Stingers are located, on either side. This gives you a clear view of the entire flag room, and you're just a short drop away from the flag platform. Waiting up here with a Shock Rifle, Stinger, or Sniper Rifle is reasonably effective.

If the flag does get taken, you don't have much time to recover it. Your best chance is having anyone on offense immediately attempt to intercept the carrier, while your defense translocates out in an attempt to catch up to the runner.

Once the flag passes midfield (unless you have an offensive player nearby), it's almost a guaranteed capture.

If you manage to get the flag out and you're holding it in your base, the safest place to wait is generally up on the Stinger platforms. You can bounce between the two, gathering up Vials on both sides of the base, and you have clear line of sight to incoming enemies. Periodically change your side if you aren't standing in clear view, to mix up any enemies that do spot you, but are taken down by you or your defenders.

1: FLAG ROOM

WEAPONRY	Bio Rifle, Flak Cannon, Rocket Launcher x2, Stinger x2
HEALTH & ARMOR	Vials
POWER-UPS	None

The flag room is quite a large area. The flag is located at the back of the room, on a moving platform that periodically raises and lowers.

While lowered, the flag is located in an enclosed hallway that contains the Flak Cannon, and a jump pad leading to the upper level of the hall, where the flag rests when it is raised.

The flag platform leads straight out of the base to the Bio Rifle, which quickly wraps around to the Sniper Rifle platform just outside the front of the base.

On the left and right sides of the flag platform, mirrored side areas contain a large flat space below, with a side hallway holding the Rocket Launcher, and a ramp up to the flag platform.

At the center of the flag platform are a pair of jump pads, which can be used

to get to the large upper platforms on each side of the room.

Each platform holds the Stinger, as well as a side hallway containing four Vials that can be used for buffing up your defenders (or your flag carrier).

In addition to the upper route out of the base, there are short hallways on the left and right, each with several Vials beside them.

At the front of the flag room, in the upper left and right corners (above the left and right hallways) are two platforms, each with a floating hologram. These platforms can be reached via translocation, and are decent vantage points for defenders, not immediately visible to any offensive players coming into your base. Just be careful about stepping into the hologram, it blurs your vision, which can mess up your aim.

2: FRONT OF BASE

WEAPONRY	Sniper Rifle, Shock Rifle, Link Gun
HEALTH & ARMOR	Health x2
POWER-UPS	None

The front of each base holds the important Sniper Rifle on the upper central platform, and the only Health pick-ups on the map. One is located on each side of the area, bracketed by a pair of pillars.

The Shock Rifle is located on the ground level in the center of this area, with the Link Gun on the left side (this is reversed as you enter the enemy base, so the Link Gun is on your right).

This area is wide enough to have medium range battles, though you aren't likely to get dedicated offensive players to stop and engage you before they translocate into your base. If you're defending, waiting on the sniper platform is usually the best you can do to delay the enemy team's offense.

3: MIDFIELD CENTER

WEAPONRY	None
HEALTH & ARMOR	Shield Belt, Vials
POWER-UPS	None

The center of the map is simply a barrier to line of sight, as a large wall divides the map into the Blue and Red sides.

There is a lower hallway through the wall, containing the Shield Belt. This should be timed by your forward defender, and once acquired, used on offense, shifting a different defender forward to watch the midfield.

On the upper level, the left and right sides of the wall have hallways connecting the two sides of the level. These halls are accessible from the ground easily by translocating, or for flag runners, by ramps that are considerably slower to ascend.

In addition, there is one curious feature of this wall. On the left and right sides, just above the ramps, are small holes in the wall. These holes are *just* big enough to toss a Translocator disc inside.

Do so, and the disc is shot through the hole to emerge on the other side of the wall. If you don't want to expose yourself to fire by an enemy defender watching their side of the map at all, you can translocate through the hole to reach the other side of the map.

VERTEBRAE

AVRIL

BIO RIFLE x2

FLAK CANNON x2

LINK GUN x2

ROCKET LAUNCHER x2

SHOCK RIFLE x2

SNIPER RIFLE x2

STINGER x4

SPECIAL PICK-UPS

BERSERK   REDEEMER

ARMOR

BODY ARMOR

HELMET

SHIELD BELT

THIGH PADS

Initially one of the more confusing maps in the game, Vertebrae is a heavily vertical CTF map, with a huge drop from the flag rooms to the lower midfield area.

With a bit of practice and exploration, Vertebrae's smooth connectivity from upper flag room to lower midfield allows for extremely rapid flag running from the base to the midfield, though getting up to the flag room in the first place requires some fancy translocation, and usually a fight against determined flag room defenders.

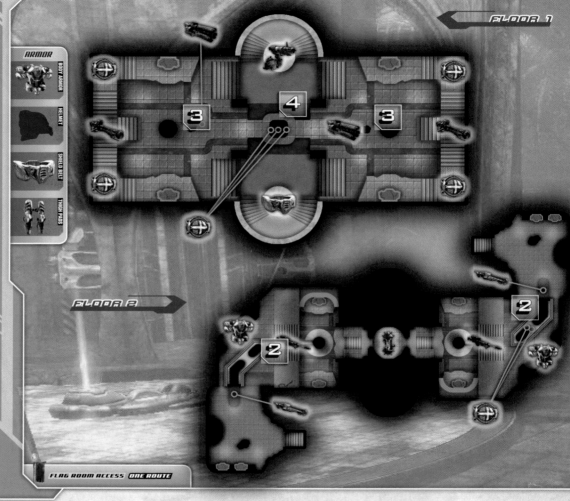

FLOOR 1

FLOOR 2

FLAG ROOM ACCESS ONE ROUTE

OFFENSE

There is some serious heavy firepower on this map in the form of the Berserk power-up and the Redeemer, and a fair amount of armor.

In addition, the Berserk power-up is located in the center of a fast route between the bases, can easily be picked up and then taken into the enemy base to clear out entrenched defenders.

At the bottom of the map (what serves as the "midfield" on Vertebrae), the Shield Belt, Redeemer, and several Vials provide more fuel for an offensive push. Because the trip between the bases usually necessitates passing through the midlevel of the base anyway, you should always check the Body Armor on the way out.

Down below, on the bottom level, there is a pair of Thighpads somewhat hidden up on a Nanoblack tentacle. Look up from the Stinger and translocate up to grab them, along with a few Vials. If you move really quickly, you may take a bit of falling damage moving from your base to the lower area, but there's so much health in the bottom of the level, you can recharge easily.

The quick way between the bases is definitely going through the Berserk chamber, though if your offense uses this route regularly, you're essentially surrendering the Shield Belt and Redeemer to the enemy team.

The Redeemer in particular is helpful for clearing out the flag room, as the flag room chamber is open, ideal for piloting the Redeemer in for a quick kill of any nearby defenders. Assaulting the enemy flag room favors mid and long range weaponry, as the area is quite open, and it is possible to hang back and pick away at flag defenders in the open.

Once you have the flag, you can drop down to the mid level through the hole leading to the Bio Rifle, and then from there down to the bottom level quickly, though this skips the health and Body Armor, it is a bit faster.

Traveling through the lower level, you may want to drop to the bottom of the center area to pick up the triple Health pick-ups. As you approach the lower area of your base, you can actually Impact jump up to the Health located on either side of the Stinger. Take the right side to get up close to the Body Armor, then make your way back to the flag room.

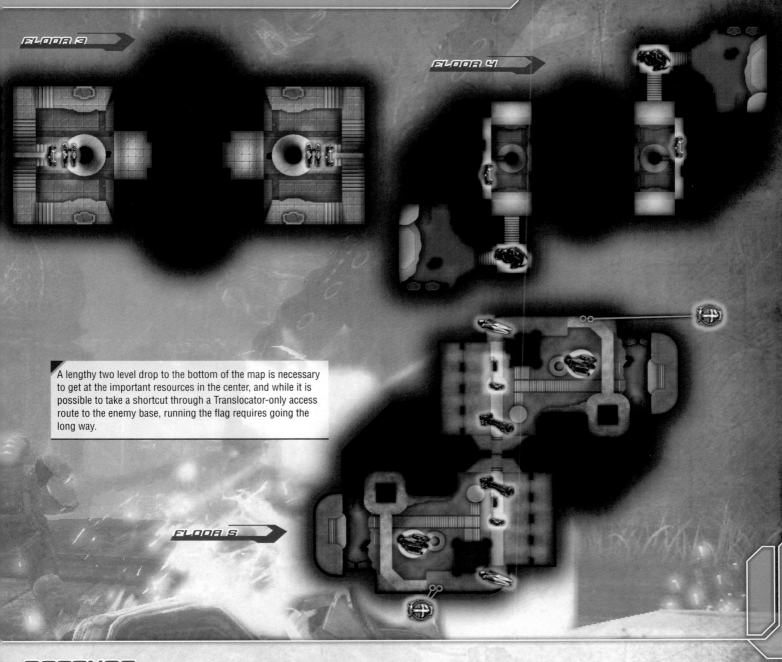

FLOOR 3

FLOOR 4

A lengthy two level drop to the bottom of the map is necessary to get at the important resources in the center, and while it is possible to take a shortcut through a Translocator-only access route to the enemy base, running the flag requires going the long way.

FLOOR 5

DEFENSE

Defending the flag room is relatively straightforward, as attackers can only come from one direction. Your decision is largely where in the flag room to situate yourself. No matter where the enemy offense comes in, you have several seconds to engage them before they can reach the flag.

It is definitely worth dropping down to the mid level of the base to pick up the Shock Rifle and Sniper Rifle (and possibly the Body Armor). Both can be put to good use in the flag room.

Conveniently, the Stinger and Link Gun are both in the flag area, and both are useful for fighting at midrange in the open ground around the flag. The Flak Cannon is only somewhat useful here, unless you want to force an engagement at close range with the flag carrier.

Having a midfield (in this case, lowerfield) defense is important, as there is so much ground to cover between the bases, rapid translocators may run their charges dry, just long enough to be engaged by a forward defense.

Just be careful of fighting below the mid level of the base, because enemy offense can come through the Berserk room, essentially invisible to players down in the Stinger area.

WEAPONRY	Link Gun, Stinger, Flak Cannon
HEALTH & ARMOR	Health x2
POWER-UPS	None

The flag room is a large open space, with large ledges, crosswalks, a back hallway and gallery, and a small gazebo down the slope from the flag. All this terrain provides plenty of options for flag defenders to set up shop, so choose your position based on your favored combat range after you've picked up the weapons you need.

Coming into this area is only possible from the mid-level of the base below, either from one of the two lifts from the center floor, or by double translocating up from the Bio Rifle through the small hole next to the Flak Cannon in the gazebo.

The Stinger and Link Gun are both located near the flag, and both are quite useful on the terrain around the flag.

One peculiarity of this room: due to the layout (a sort of twisted 'U' shape) of the entire map, the flag rooms are actually adjacent to one another. More relevant to their proximity is the fact that they are visible to one another, at least slightly. There is a Nanoblack shield between the two flag stands, and it *is* possible to shoot through.

Generally, this has little bearing on engagements, but it is occasionally possible for flag room defenders to offer some fire support to flag runners. Communicate when you are heading for the flag and flag defenders can spray some fire through the screen, possibly helping against enemy flag defenders.

Otherwise, the shield is easily avoided, so you don't need to worry about eating shots while defending the flag, as it only has a limited line of sight to the entire flag room, which is quite large.

OBNOXIOUS TACTICS 101

If you happen to be ahead of a returning flag runner, and you know they are close to reaching their flag room from the mid level, *use their lifts.*

The only way back up to the flag room is to take one of the two lifts from the mid level of the base, and if you hop on one, then drop to the other, you can keep the lifts busy.

While this isn't going to stop nearby teammates from engaging you (flag defenders are almost certain to investigate mysteriously bouncing lifts), it just might delay the flag runner long enough to score a kill.

Stepping on and off the lifts is very fast, but it takes a few seconds for them to come back down. You can even bounce the descending lifts off your head, moving between them to prevent them from ever hitting the ground floor.

2: MID-LEVEL BASE

WEAPONRY	Bio Rifle, Shock Rifle, Sniper Rifle
HEALTH & ARMOR	Body Armor, Health x2, Vials
POWER-UPS	Berserk

The center floor of the base is quite important, connecting the bottom midfield area and the upper flag room. In addition, the Berserk chamber is accessible from this floor, allowing translocation from the Red

3: BOTTOM FLOOR

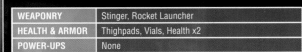

WEAPONRY	Stinger, Rocket Launcher
HEALTH & ARMOR	Thighpads, Vials, Health x2
POWER-UPS	None

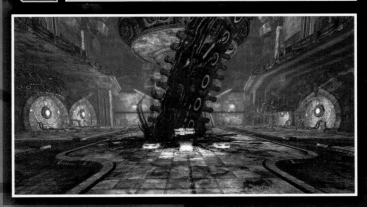

Down below the midlevel is the Stinger, and the Thighpads, up on a Nanoblack tentacle, which must be translocated to reach.

The Rocket Launcher is located closer to the bottom center of the map, and both are useful for fighting in the bottom area, though most players traveling through here on offense tend to be translocating rapidly.

The bottom floor area has a single staircase that leads up to the Stinger, then splits into a left and right ledge, each leading to a lift. Both lifts lead up to the middle level, but the left lift (facing the Stinger) deposits the user just below the Bio Rifle chamber.

As a result, it is possible to lift jump right up into the Bio Rifle room, and from there, double translocate up into the flag area—the fastest way there, potentially avoiding some mid level defenders who are out of position.

There are two Health pick-ups on either side of the Stinger, and it is worth noting that you can Impact jump up to the ledge right where the Health is, before moving onto the nearby lift. Thanks to the Health, this maneuver is fairly safe for a flag runner, and it can save precious seconds by avoiding the run up the stairs to the Stinger (and more importantly, enemy fire directed at that singular route to the lifts).

4: LOWER MIDFIELD

WEAPONRY	Redeemer
HEALTH & ARMOR	Health x3, Shield Belt, Vials
POWER-UPS	None

The very bottom center of the map has the very important Redeemer and Shield Belt, each located in a small gazebo-like structure on the left and right of the center walkway through the middle.

Below that center walkway is a short, tight hallway that contains *three* Health pick-ups. Very handy for restoring a flag carrier, or recovering from a battle nearby.

Indeed, with the Health below the center, and on each sides Stinger ledge, you can actually roam this area fairly safely, grabbing the two Thighpads on each side, along with the Vials in the area to tank up a bit. If you're camping out waiting for the Shield Belt or Redeemer, you can do so reasonably safely.

The Berserk can *only* be reached via translocation, so flag runners can't take advantage of the shortcut.

The mid level holds the Bio Rifle, Shock Rifle, Sniper Rifle, two Health pick-ups, *and* the Body Armor, all within a short distance of each other, making it a solid area for arming and resupplying.

The back of this level holds two lifts that are the only regular means of accessing the flag area. The lifts can be used to lift jump over to the large walkway that overlooks the flag room, or simply to propel the rider into the air to throw off flag defender aim.

The Bio Rifle is located just beneath a narrow vertical shaft that leads to the flag room. By translocating straight up, teleporting while the disc is at its apex, then translocating vertically again, you can manage to get out of the shaft and up into the flag room, handy, since you can get to the Bio Rifle from one of the lifts that leads to the midlevel area, without passing through the larger chamber to the normal lifts that lead to the flag room.

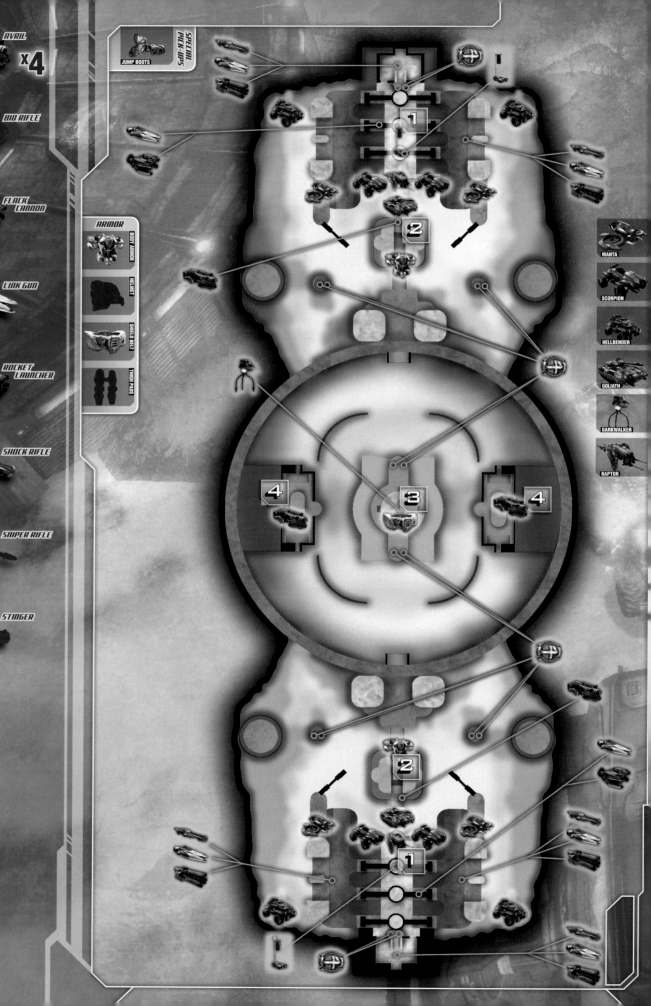

CONTAINMENT

AVRIL **x4**

BIO RIFLE

FLAK CANNON

LINK GUN

ROCKET LAUNCHER

SHOCK RIFLE

SNIPER RIFLE

STINGER

SPECIAL PICK-UPS
JUMP BOOTS

ARMOR
BODY ARMOR
HELMET
SHIELD BELT
THIGH PADS

MANTA

SCORPION

HELLBENDER

GOLIATH

DARKWALKER

RAPTOR

Getting out with the flag is *slightly* easier on this VCTF map than some of the others, as once you have the flag past the base and into the midfield, it becomes substantially harder for respawning defenders to catch up with you. Plus, there are abundant Health pick-ups on the way out of the base, and in the midfield.

The fastest and safest way to bring the flag home is to be carried through the Raptor tunnels leading to the midfield, though any travel through the center is hazardous if the enemy team holds the Darkwalker.

Otherwise, you have to pass through one of the ground exits from the base, though fortunately, there are jump pads on the outskirts of the flag area that lead right to double Health platforms a short distance from the exits to the midfield.

In terms of setting up an assault on the enemy flag area in the first place, you have plenty of options. With multiple Mantas, Scorpions, and Hellbenders in your base, in addition to the Goliath and Raptor, you can cross the midfield quickly, or with heavier firepower.

The side routes through the midfield area are inaccessible to vehicles, so you can zip through on your Hoverboard with some degree of safety, though generally you only want to be doing this if you have to (you're already carrying the flag).

The Shield Belt located atop the Darkwalker prison is key for running the flag, as is the lone Body Armor located at the front of each flag area. If possible, while you're hanging out in the midfield guarding the Darkwalker, camp out atop the center prison with an AVRiL. Because there is no Sniper Rifle present on the map, it is difficult to remove you from your perch, and you can deal serious damage to incoming vehicles while you wait for the Shield Belt (or Darkwalker) to spawn.

There is little of value in the midfield other than the center Shield Belt. The side passages hold AVRiLs and Health on each side of the Darkwalker prison, but otherwise, the open ground is mostly just for vehicles to drive through, so stay off the road if you aren't in one!

For the approach to the flag, you can either come up from the Body Armor tower, or one of the side ramps. The Body Armor tower is marginally safer, as it avoids all of the vehicles on the sides and front of the base. Up at the flag area, you may need to contend with a camping Manta or Hellbender nearby, so be sure to bring an AVRiL along.

Depending on how heavily the enemy is guarding the flag area with vehicles, you may have to come in with multiple vehicles of your own, or several players packing Longbows to take down the armor. A Goliath that decides to camp out instead of going on offense can be a real threat.

Defending the flag on Containment is peculiar, as the flag area is nicely separated from the midfield, but there is no "base" to speak of for the flag, it's sitting right out in the open!

On the bright side, the barricades on the edges of the flag platform prevent some vehicles from getting up to it, and you have a lot of vehicles to choose from for defense. The Hellbenders and Goliath are highly effective. Mantas and Scorpions can be used, but they're so effective for transport (and vulnerable to AVRiL fire) that they're generally better left to your offense to get through the midfield quickly.

One point about the Mantas: due to the way this level is laid out, they are *highly* effective for squashing flag carriers, just watch out for AVRiL fire. Bail out if you hear a lock-on; you can't take the hit.

As for the midfield, the Darkwalker at the center of the map is actually a key defensive weapon, not an offensive weapon. Holding it allows you to easily fry the enemy offense, and tie up their attention while your own offense heads through the center unimpeded.

Make sure you have at least one dedicated defensive player camping the Darkwalker, when it gets destroyed, they can camp out at the Shield Belt with the AVRiL, waiting for the Darkwalker to respawn. If the Shield Belt does spawn, you may want to have that player transition to offense with the belt, and have someone else take over on the Darkwalker, at least temporarily.

Warning of incoming players to the flag area isn't really vital, as all the front entrances to the flag area can be easily monitored by anyone up on the flag stand. Barring someone Impact jumping from the midfield center route and coming up the Body Armor tower from the blind side, the side routes are easy to cover.

Don't hesitate to use the teleport up to the Raptor to lurk up in the rafters. You can fire AVRiL shots at incoming vehicles (or the enemy Raptor) from the heights, and drop down to engage anyone getting near your flag. This works even better if you have the Jump Boots, to avoid falling damage.

WEAPONRY	Lockers only
HEALTH & ARMOR	Health x2
POWER-UPS	None
VEHICLES	Manta x2, Hellbender x2, Scorpion x2, Raptor, Goliath

The flag area holds several tons of vehicles, all of which should be fully exploited by your offense and defense.

The flag itself rests in the center of a raised platform, accessible via side ramps (with small vehicle barricades), or from the front of the base via a bridge to the Body Armor tower.

The back of the flag stand holds a small building with a teleporter within. The teleporter takes you up to the platform above the flag, where the Raptor rests.

Both sides of the flag area have jump pads that launch the user out to the double Health platforms at the front of the base area. Expect flag runners to make use of these regularly.

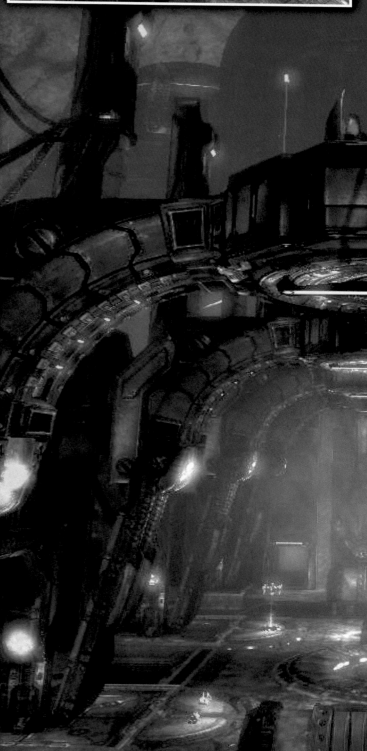

2: BASE FRONT

WEAPONRY	AVRiL
HEALTH & ARMOR	Health x4, Body Armor
POWER-UPS	Jump Boots
VEHICLES	None

The front of each base has a large tower which holds a Body Armor, and the only AVRiL in the base area. It is important for defenders to pick it up, or for offensive players to stop by here if they aren't planning on going through the side passages in the midfield area.

The Jump Boots can be used to quickly get up to the AVRiL from below, bounce up to the flag platform, or simply as an asset for flag runners.

There are double Health pick-ups on each side of this area, both reachable via jump pads from the flag area. These are a boon for flag runners, but they can also be used by flag defenders to recharge quickly.

From the frontal base area, there are four ways in and out of the middle on the ground, and the single upper tube that can be flown through with the Raptor. The two routes on the far left and right can be dropped through by players in lighter vehicles, though even the Goliath can fit through.

The center route splits to the left or right on the base side, but merges into one exit to the midfield. You can also drop down to that center route from the base on a Hoverboard, but you can't get back up from the midfield side (short of Impact jumping, or using the Jump Boots).

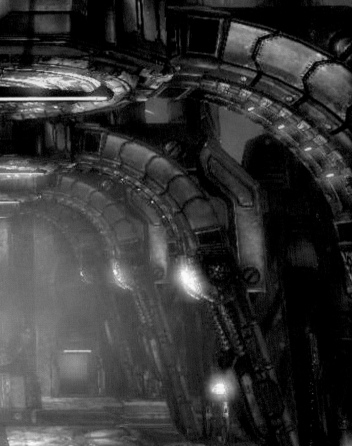

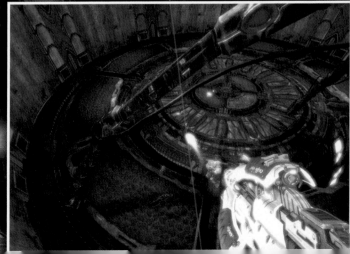

3: MIDFIELD, CENTER

WEAPONRY	AVRiL
HEALTH & ARMOR	Health x4, Body Armor
POWER-UPS	None
VEHICLES	Darkwalker

The center Darkwalker prison is the focus of the entire midfield area. A giant walled container holds the Darkwalker, but the transparent walls can be fired through, both by the Darkwalker within, and by players outside to damage and eventually destroy it. Holding the Darkwalker is very important for controlling the midfield.

Both sides of the Darkwalker prison have double Health pick-ups, making this a great area to recharge if your team controls the Darkwalker (or it is in the process of respawning after being destroyed).

To the left and right of the prison, open icy fields provide a ready route for vehicles to drive quickly through the center of the map.

On top of the Darkwalker prison is the Shield Belt, reachable via jump pads at either side of the midfield, or with the Raptor. Note that you can drop down into the Darkwalkers prison from either side (with jump pads inside to get back out), or from above where the Shield Belt is located.

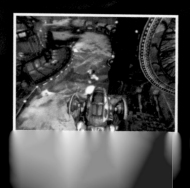

4: MIDFIELD, SIDES

WEAPONRY	AVRiL x2
HEALTH & ARMOR	None
POWER-UPS	None
VEHICLES	None

The side areas don't hold much in the way of goodies, but they do provide a safe route for Hoverboarders (that means, usually, flag carriers). Both side routes around the circular midfield have barricades slightly blocking line of sight from the icefields in the center, helpful for screening you from enemy fire.

In addition, the side buildings on each edge of the midfield have barricades preventing all larger vehicles from getting inside.

Within the buildings, you can find AVRiLs, a bit of ammo, and the useful jump pads that hop up to the top of the Darkwalker's chamber.

CORRUPTION

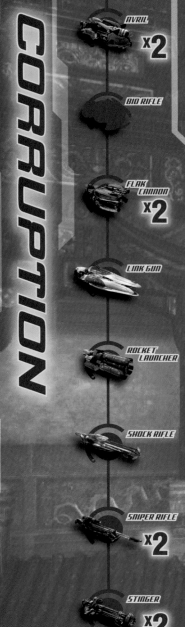

AVRIL x2

BIO RIFLE

FLAK CANNON x2

LINK GUN

ROCKET LAUNCHER

SHOCK RIFLE

SNIPER RIFLE x2

STINGER x2

SPECIAL PICK-UPS
- BERSERK
- UDAMAGE

ARMOR
- BODY ARMOR
- HELMET
- SHIELD BELT
- THIGH PADS

A curious mix of peaceful Izanagi structures and Nanoblack infection, Corruption is one of the few asymmetric maps in the game (though only slightly so), with the Blue and Red bases having ever so slightly different frontal areas.

While the actual gameplay differences between the two sides are slight, the appearances are radically different, with the Blue Necris side completely corrupted by Nanoblack, while the Red Izanagi side of the map is still pure.

Corruption pits the Axon forces against the Necris, allowing for Goliath vs. Darkwalker showdowns in the middle of the map.

The presence of both the UDamage and the Berserk in the midfield allow for easy Juggernaut action, and with a bit of coordination, a Juggernaut equipped heavy vehicle can lay waste to the entire midfield area.

- MANTA
- SCORPION
- HELLBENDER
- GOLIATH
- VIPER
- SCAVENGER
- NEMESIS
- DARKWALKER

OFFENSE

With an extensive midfield area, getting across it in one piece to reach the flag is a bit tricky. The faster vehicles (Viper, Manta, & Scorpion) can all get through the mill area the quickest, or you can head through the caves on the other side of the midfield, possibly picking up the Thighpads on the way.

The Body Armor is helpful for flag running, but it is located in a *very* unsafe position, right in the middle of the path that most heavy vehicles tend to take.

Just getting to the enemy base is the first obstacle, once you arrive, you need to get through any defenders around the flag, which is fairly defensible by a player on foot, or someone hanging out inside the flag area in a vehicle—bring an AVRiL.

Once you have the flag, the safest route back is generally running out the center window in the flag room, dropping down to the jump pad, and hopping up into the rocks around the Sniper Rifle.

From there, you can jump down and over to the caves, where only the smallest vehicles can chase you, then (hopefully) surviving the run across the midfield to the opposite cave.

If you can manage it, grappling to a fast vehicle is a great way to get home, and coordinating a multi-person assault on the enemy base is the best way to break through a vehicle blockade in any case. Because the AVRiLs on the map are located outside the main base, you have a decent chance of surviving the trip back to the midfield, which is where you're at the greatest risk of eating a Longbow missile.

If you aren't strictly on flag running duty, focus on controlling the power-ups in the midfield, as well as the Redeemer. Locking down the UDamage and Berserk gives your team a powerful advantage, and the Redeemer can have a devastating effect on flag defenders in the small flag room.

DEFENSE

Defending the flag room itself is straightforward. The larger vehicles have a hard time getting inside the constrained space, and since your team respawns literally right outside the flag area, any offensive teammates downed can rejoin the flag room defense if any attackers happen to be in the area.

Other than protecting the flag room itself (possibly with a vehicle or two), you may want to have a sniper up on the Sniper Rifle ledge at the front of the base area watching the midfield. Since the AVRiL is right near the rifle, they can serve double duty as infantry snipers and vehicle snipers both, as well as warning of any players that do slip past.

The middle of the map is largely a battleground for the offense, there is little to be gained by pushing forward so far from the flag, but if you want to armor up at least a bit, you can get to the Thighpads and back to the flag room (or to the sniper perch) fairly quickly.

It is also worthwhile to have your flag area defenders swap guard duties temporarily so that everyone can pick up the AVRiL, it is useful to have on hand should a vehicle get past the midfield and enter your flag room area.

1: FLAG ROOM, RED SIDE

WEAPONRY	Stinger, Flak Cannon
HEALTH & ARMOR	Health x2
POWER-UPS	None
VEHICLES	Manta, Scorpion x2, Hellbender

2: FLAG ROOM, BLUE SIDE

WEAPONRY	Stinger, Flak Cannon
HEALTH & ARMOR	Health x2
POWER-UPS	None
VEHICLES	Viper, Scavenger x2, Nemesis, Darkwalker

The flag room area consists of a large building with two sides, each side holding several vehicles. The spawn rooms (and their weapon lockers) are above the two sides.

Both sides can get into the flag room itself, which has access routes on both sides of the base, as well as a front entrance, through a window at the front of the base.

Inside, the flag room is quite simple, with a weapon locker up on the upper ledge near the window, and the flag situated at the back of the base.

The room is too small for larger vehicles to get inside, but smaller ones can do so easily, so defenders must have AVRiLs ready to deal with vehicular interlopers.

Two Health pick-ups are the only restorative items in the area, making extended flag room defense difficult for the same player.

The Blue flag room is identical to the red, with the only difference being the presence of the Necris vehicles.

3: BASE FRONT, RED SIDE

WEAPONRY	AVRiL, Sniper Rifle
HEALTH & ARMOR	Health, Vials
POWER-UPS	None
VEHICLES	None

The front area of the base has two roads that lead out from the two sides of the flag area, and a central rocky area that is only easily passable by infantry.

The rocky outcropping holds the Sniper Rifle and a single health pick-up, and more importantly, just beyond the Sniper Rifle, the AVRiL rests on the ground outside the rocks.

There are two ways up to the rocks, one being a jump pad in front of the base, the other being a small ramp on one side of the rocks.

This is an ideal area for playing forward defense, and it is also useful for flag runners trying to avoid large vehicles on the way in or out of the base.

Note that just outside the Red base, there is a bridge that cross over to reach the ledge leading up to the mill area in the midfield. This is distinct from the blue side, which has no bridge.

BASE FRONT, BLUE SIDE

WEAPONRY	AVRiL, Sniper Rifle
HEALTH & ARMOR	Health, Vials
POWER-UPS	None
VEHICLES	None

The front of the blue base is mostly identical to the red side, the exceptions being a large open area on the left route into the flag area, providing slightly more space for vehicles to maneuver, and the lack of a covered bridge at the front of the base.

The two routes out of the flag area head to the midfield, but on the left side, you can travel up a sloping pathway to head towards the mill.

MIDFIELD, MILL

WEAPONRY	None
HEALTH & ARMOR	Health x2
POWER-UPS	Berserk, UDamage
VEHICLES	None

The large waterwheel at the center of the building in the midfield marks the location of the very important power-ups in the midfield.

On each side of the structure, one power-up is tucked away in a small niche, open and visible from the midfield, so you can easily tell when the power-ups are spawned.

The waterwheel in the center of the building is actually a hazard, as you must pass between its spokes to get from one end of the building to the other, a feat only possible by the smaller and more agile vehicles (or a player on a Hoverboard).

There is also ammo and health present in the building, handy for recharging before grabbing the power-ups.

The Berserk is on the Blue side of the building, with the UDamage on the Red side.

6: MIDFIELD

WEAPONRY	Redeemer
HEALTH & ARMOR	Vials, Health x4, Body Armor, Thighpads x2
POWER-UPS	None
VEHICLES	None

The extensive midfield area consists of a large pool of water just below the waterwheel (which the Darkwalker, Manta, and Viper can all cross), a small bridge over the pool (infantry only), and a small pond with the Body Armor at its center.

The pond drops off into a small waterfall at the edge of the map—drop off of the waterfall to find a hidden ledge with the Redeemer tucked away behind the waterfall. A jump pad allows you to get back up to the midfield, though you can easily fire the Redeemer and guide it to a worthwhile target from the concealment offered by the ledge.

At each end of the midfield, on the Body Armor side, a pair of Thighpads and two Health pick-ups allow passing players to gain some armor and recover. Both Thighpad areas lead into small caves that come out on one of the pathways into the base, as well as close to the rocky area holding the Sniper Rifle.

There are basically only two ways through the midfield—either you're going up through the mill, or you're coming across the Body Armor in the middle of the map.

The pool is too deep to be crossed by most vehicles, though a few have the unique abilities necessary to cross it.

The entire midfield tends to be a constant vehicle battleground, so be very careful about traveling through the area on a Hoverboard unless you absolutely must do so.

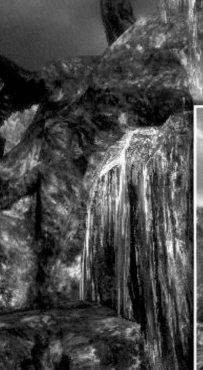

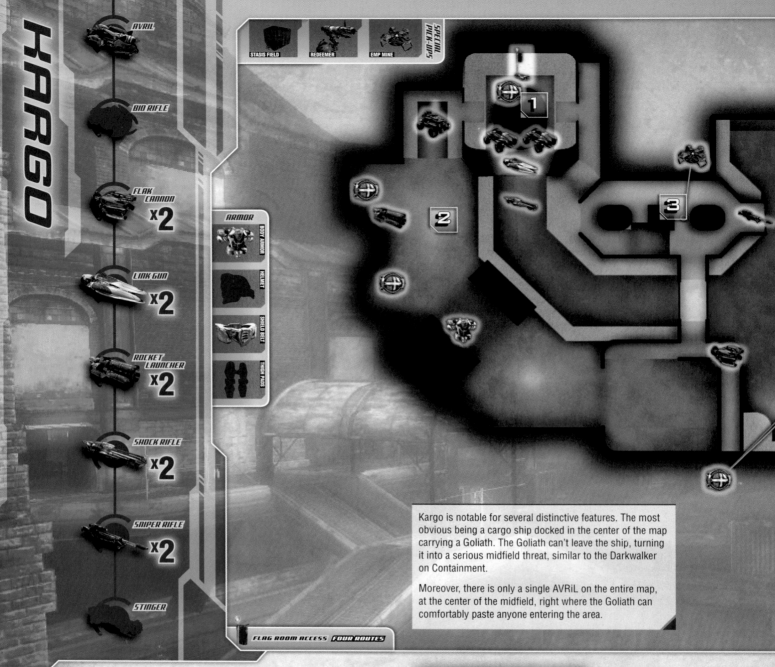

AVRIL

BIO RIFLE

FLAK CANNON **x2**

LINK GUN **x2**

ROCKET LAUNCHER **x2**

SHOCK RIFLE **x2**

SNIPER RIFLE **x2**

STINGER

SPECIAL PICK-UPS

| STASIS FIELD | REDEEMER | EMP MINE |

ARMOR

BODY ARMOR

HELMET

SHIELD BELT

THIGH PADS

1

2

3

Kargo is notable for several distinctive features. The most obvious being a cargo ship docked in the center of the map carrying a Goliath. The Goliath can't leave the ship, turning it into a serious midfield threat, similar to the Darkwalker on Containment.

Moreover, there is only a single AVRiL on the entire map, at the center of the midfield, right where the Goliath can comfortably paste anyone entering the area.

FLAG ROOM ACCESS | **FOUR ROUTES**

OFFENSE

Pressuring the enemy team on Kargo consists of two stages, the first being seizing the midfield Goliath to suppress the enemy team's vehicle advance, and the second actually attacking the flag room and going for a capture. Though holding the Goliath is actually a defensive operation, it is important to make sure it is secure before running the flag, or you're in for an unpleasant surprise on the way back.

Flag runners traveling through the midfield can get through in several ways. The lower Scorpions below the flag room are a fast means of transport, and they can be used as bombs against the Goliath in the midfield if necessary.

The Hellbender makes a good multi-person transport for a group assault on the flag room, just make sure the Goliath is destroyed or in your team's hands before you go driving a loaded Hellbender in to the midfield.

It is also possible to take the halls from the flag area through the midfield fairly safely, as you can stay above the ground level, and any vehicles moving through the area.

Snipers may be an issue, and though their sight lines are somewhat restricted from the sniper bunker and hallway that faces the midfield, if you do have a serious problem with one, either get your own counter-sniper, or traverse the midfield in a vehicle to avoid the problem.

Once you hit the enemy flagroom, avoid going in the front door (Shock Rifle) every time. You can also come in from either side, or even from down below. Going in below also gives you a chance to blast the enemy Scorpions, slowing down their offense slightly.

Making your way back across the map on a Hoverboard is quite a trek. Having a Scorpion around to grapple onto is the best way to get back; otherwise, you're going to have to take the long way.

You may want to go through the tunnels beside the flag area, you're considerably less exposed to enemy fire on the way back, just be aware that it extends the trip, giving more time for defenders to catch up in vehicles, or even on Hoverboards using the direct route.

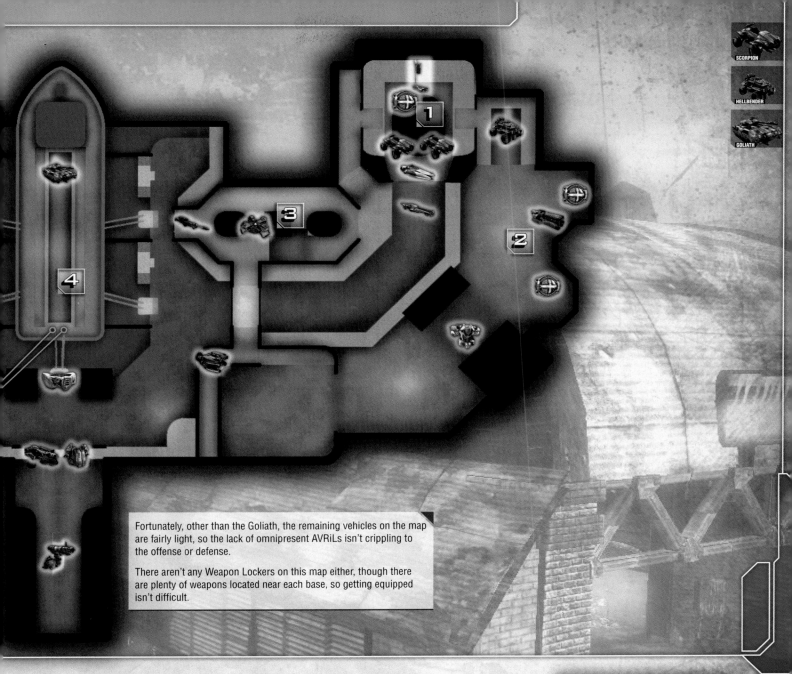

1

3

4

2

Fortunately, other than the Goliath, the remaining vehicles on the map are fairly light, so the lack of omnipresent AVRiLs isn't crippling to the offense or defense.

There aren't any Weapon Lockers on this map either, though there are plenty of weapons located near each base, so getting equipped isn't difficult.

DEFENSE

Your defense of the flag should consist of actual flag room defense, a midfield sniper, and a few players dedicated to holding down the Goliath in the center of the map.

The Goliath can inflict heavy damage, particularly if two teammates work in tandem to man the Goliath and the turret, occasionally having one hop out to repair the Goliath with the Link Gun.

A midfield sniper can be useful if the enemy has more players than vehicles, otherwise, you may want to have your midfield defender make their way to the AVRiL area, where both the Redeemer and the Shield Belt provide extra resources that can be used on offense, shifting a respawning runner to defense while the armed or armored midfielder makes a flag run.

The Stasis Field located in the center of the map is very handy on defense, you can use it to block off either main route to the flag area, or drop it in the flag room to create a serious obstacle for attackers. Just try to avoid placing it on the flag itself, the flag counts against the Stasis Field's timer, and it will dissipate considerably faster if it is touching the flag.

The EMP Mine in the tunnels is also useful on defense, and it is close enough to easily pick up. You may want to deploy it in the midfield to catch vehicles moving through the AVRiL area, but you can also stick it on one of your own vehicles and use it as an offensive tool instead.

1: FLAG ROOM

WEAPONRY	Link Gun, Shock Rifle
HEALTH & ARMOR	Health
POWER-UPS	None
VEHICLES	Scorpion x2

The flag room is nicely defensible, located inside a large building. Though there are multiple routes inside, it is difficult to get vehicles within the building (not impossible, just almost entirely impractical), so you only need to worry about threats on foot for the most part.

With Body Armor and a handful of Vials just outside the base, it isn't hard to get solidly armored in advance of enemies hitting the base.

Attacks approaching the flag room should take advantage of the multiple routes in to hit the defenders from different angles each time they attempt to grab the flag.

With the Link Gun, Shock Rifle, and Rocket Launcher all nearby, it's not hard to get well-equipped with a weapon you're comfortable with, and all three are useful around the flag area.

The Scorpions on the map are largely for transit to the opposite side, but they can be used as bombs against the Goliath if necessary.

2: BASE FRONT

WEAPONRY	Rocket Launcher
HEALTH & ARMOR	Vials, Health x2, Body Armor
POWER-UPS	None
VEHICLES	Hellbender

The area immediately outside the flag room consists of two distinct areas, a lower channel for the Scorpions to drive to the center of the map, and an upper area, which contains the Hellbender, a Rocket Launcher, and two Health pick-ups.

A short distance down the road from the front of the base is an open building that holds the Body Armor. On the ledge beside the Body Armor

building that overlooks the Scorpion channel, you can find several Health Vials to aid in a flag run, or, more frequently, to buff up a defender.

This area is quite friendly to the defense, since it is so easy to spot incoming attackers who aren't using the tunnels to reach the flag area, and if they've managed to pick up an AVRiL from the midfield, they can cause serious damage to an incoming attacker on foot or in a ride.

MIDFIELD TUNNELS

WEAPONRY	EMP Mine, Sniper Rifle, Flak Cannon
HEALTH & ARMOR	None
POWER-UPS	None
VEHICLES	None

The tunnels are very important, as they provide cover from the vehicles on the map, and contain several useful weapons. The Sniper Rifle can be used to cover the midfield, or taken back to the flag area to cover the outside of the base.

The Flak Cannon is highly useful when fighting in the tunnels, or inside the flag room. Finally, the EMP Mine can be used in several places on the map

to block incoming enemy vehicles, shut down the Goliath, or on a friendly vehicle as a mobile EMP device.

There is a "hidden" exit from the tunnels immediately adjacent to the flag area down into the Scorpion tunnel. Check the walls just below the EMP Mine spawn point, you can crouch and crawl through a vent shaft to reach the channel, handy as an alternate escape route for flag runners.

MIDFIELD

WEAPONRY	AVRiL, Stasis Field, Redeemer
HEALTH & ARMOR	Health x2
POWER-UPS	None
VEHICLES	Goliath

The midfield area is quite extensive on Kargo, and traveling through it is a challenge with the Goliath parked comfortably on the cargo ship at the center of the area.

Directly across from the Goliath, you can find two Health pick-ups, and a recessed room on the other end of the map. That are holds several very important items, including the only AVRiL on the map, the Stasis Field, and the Redeemer.

The Stasis Field is a powerful flag room defense tool, but it can also be used on the Goliath "track" on the ship to suppress it's movement nicely, or right in the center of the map to block off enemies chasing your own flag carrier.

The Redeemer can be used to quickly remove the Goliath, but it is also valuable for devastating the flag room defenders from outside before going in for a flag run attempt.

The Shield Belt is highly useful on offense as well, though its position is rather exposed, located up on a platform that is in line of sight to the Goliath, as well as every Hellbender and Scorpion driving through the center of the map.

The upper walkway that holds the AVRiL and the Stasis Field is reachable via jump pads, and it stretches from base to base, connecting the two tunnel networks to the midfield. While walking

along the wall towards either base, you are dreadfully exposed to the Goliath.

The ship that holds the Goliath has convenient ramps on either side that can be used by a boosting Scorpion to propel itself into the Goliath, or across the ship entirely to reach the other side of the map quickly.

NECROPOLIS

AVRIL **x4**

BIO RIFLE

FLAK CANNON

LINK GUN

ROCKET LAUNCHER **x4**

SHOCK RIFLE **x4**

SNIPER RIFLE **x2**

STINGER **x2**

SPECIAL PICK-UPS

| UDAMAGE | KEG O HEALTH | REDEEMER |

ARMOR

| BODY ARMOR |
| HELMET |
| SHIELD BELT |
| THIGH PADS |

VIPER

NEMESIS

SCAVENGER

DARKWALKER

NIGHTSHADE

Necropolis is a fast-paced VCTF map, with a long narrow midfield, perfect for Vipers to fly through at full speed, and with a long bridge connecting the two bases for Hoverboarders; it is possible to get between the two bases with considerable speed.

In addition, there are heavier vehicles around for both defense and offense. The Nemesis and Darkwalker can provide devastating midfield fire support, or powerful flag defense.

FLAG ROOM ACCESS **FOUR ROUTES**

The Nightshade is very useful for defending the flagroom against Vipers rushing into the area. Using its deployables can help to clamp down the flag room against constant vehicle rushes.

For the Scavenger, you can best use its mobility by bouncing around in the midfield using the bridge for cover, or hiding out inside your base, crushing players on foot trying to go for your flag. The Scavenger can easily jump up to the flag platform in either base, but on offense, your lack of durability and speed makes you a dead easy AVRiL target.

The flag room area is quite large, with plenty of space on the ground for vehicle battles. The flag itself is located on a raised platform, accessible either through the large palace building, by one of the jump pads located on either side, or by jumping or climbing up to it in a Scavenger, Viper, or the Darkwalker.

Other than the flag platform itself, there is little tactical value to the rest of the room on defense, with one exception. The open room to the back of the flag area contains the only two Health pick-ups on the ground level. Other than the single Health pick-up inside the palace area, this is the only quick way for defenders to quickly heal.

There are four routes into the flag room area, two through the palace (upper and lower) and two from the side passages out of the base, on the left and right side.

The side passages are important both offensively and defensively, as they allow rapid access for Viper pilots (even the Scavenger can come down them quickly

while rollixxNemesis while lowered), so they must be defended to ease the pressure on the flag. You really don't want a constant stream of self-destructing Vipers rushing your flag defense.

The Nightshade can bottle up the channels nicely by deploying a Spider Mines, a Slow Field, or an EMP Mine. The Energy Shield is somewhat harder to use effectively. Unfortunately, the Nightshade can't get up to the flag platform itself, so there's no way to deploy the shield around the flag.

In addition, the readily available AVRiL at the flag stand and the AVRiL ammo down both side channels gives you plentiful ammunition for defending against incoming vehicles—and quick access to the useful pick-ups on each side.

NIGHTSHADE VILLAINY

The spawning areas on each side of the flag room hold little of interest beyond the weapon lockers. However, they *are* ever so slightly raised off the ground level.

This is important because they're *just* high enough for you to park the Nightshade on, and *just* high enough for a Viper or crouched Nemesis to get below the Nightshade.

Once in place, you can drop any of the deployables other than the Slow Field onto the waiting vehicle, transforming it into a mobile mine layer, shield, or roaming EMP.

Racing into the enemy base dropping Spider Mines or disabling their vehicles with mobile EMP blasts is always a blast—and effective.

The UDamage and Health Kegs located on each side of the bases should be used for your offensive team. The UDamage combined with any strong vehicle can blast a hole in the flag room defenses, and the Health Keg is helpful for a flag runner.

The palaces in front of each bases flag rooms are two story structures, accessible from the flag room via an upper or lower path. The lower path contains the useful Jump Boots and the Scavenger, while the upper path has a Health pick-up, and the Sniper Rifle and another AVRiL.

From the midfield side, the palace floors are accessible via lifts. The lifts take you to the lower level of the palace, but you can easily lift jump up to the upper level. It's useful both on offense and defense for misdirection, and to quickly get up to the Health if needed.

The midfield consists of a large bridge that connects both bases palaces on the upper floor, and two sunken areas flooded with water on each side of the bridge. One side has the lone Darkwalker, the other the Body Armor. Naturally, of the two, the Darkwalker is the rather more important resource (though the Body Armor can be helpful to a flag carrier).

There is also plenty of Health in the midfield. However, getting to it is time consuming, as each of the four Health pick-ups is located in a small tunnel behind the waterway, requiring precious time on foot to pick up. You're usually better off respawning than taking the time to pick up more than a single Health pick-up from the midfield.

The central bridge is a snipers dream platform, and with the Sniper Rifle *and* an AVRiL conveniently located right on the bridge's end points at each palace, you can expect frequent sniping. At the center of the bridge, the Redeemer spawns

periodically, and it is accessible either by walking the bridge directly, or taking one of the two jump pads up from the center of the midfield on either side of the bridge.

Getting in and out with the flag can be *really* easy, or *really* hard, depending entirely on how well the flag defense is set up. Left alone, or with a single defender on foot, you can zip in and grab the flag through the upper floor of the palace, and get back out very quickly.

However, if both side passages are covered by Nightshade traps, and they have the Darkwalker on defense covering the flag platform, there is *no* easy way to get in, and you're going to have to break through with some brute force.

The Darkwalker is actually rather more useful on defense than offense, due to its speed (and the superior manner in which it can cover all but one entrance to the flag room), but you *can* use it on offense if you manage to acquire it. Just expect to eat a lot of fire slowly stomping your way up one of the side passages to the flag room.

Otherwise, your best options are using the Vipers to get in quickly, and their suicide to destroy defending vehicles (or infantry). In addition, you can use the aerial boost provided by detonating the Viper to land yourself safely on the flag platform, and (hopefully) get out in the confusion.

The Scavenger can get up to the flag platform easily enough, and roll to the enemy base fairly quickly, but it is just as fragile as the Viper, and even easier to hit, so it isn't the best option for attacking.

The Nemesis works well on offense or defense. If you can swing it, coming into the enemy base armed with UDamage in the Nemesis is a devastating assault, and your only real danger is players on the flag platform ducking in and out of sight firing Longbow missiles at you, but if you paste the ground defense and vehicles, you can usually manage to eject before you take critical damage, leaving you to fight with at least parity on foot.

If you're going to go for a straight flag run, rather than trying to deal with the defense in the flag room, you need to come in through the upper floor of the palace. Your best chance of doing so successfully is grabbing the Health Keg, and possibly the Body Armor on the way to the enemy base.

Tanked up, you have a good chance against any defenders on foot, and the only vehicle threats you should have to deal with are the Darkwalker and the Scavenger, if they are on defense. Of the two, you can survive the Scavenger fairly easily if you're alert to its location and have your AVRiL ready.

The Darkwalker is more problematic. If it's present, you may be able to get off a few shots ducking in and out of sight with the AVRiL; otherwise, you need your team to push in and take it down before you can go for the flag. Running out onto the flag platform while the Darkwalker covers it is pure suicide.

You may also need to watch out for a sniper; an enterprising sniper who grabs the Jump Boots can get up to a beam on the upper level of a large chamber at the back of the flag room, which has a perfect line of sight to the flag platform. Bring your own Sniper Rifle if you happen to get taken down by this threat (easy enough, since you can pick it up on the way in or out of the palace).

Once you have the flag, the safest way back is through the upper or lower floor of the palace. On the upper route, you can pick up a single Health pick-up on the way, and once you're out, you can drop down from the bridge, bounce back up

to it with the center jump pads, grab Health from the waterlogged pits, and possibly grab the Body Armor on the way.

The lower route gives you access to the Jump Boots, which can be very useful for throwing off pursuit.

When you get close to your base, you can either use one of the side paths, or go in through the palace, possibly using the lifts to lift jump up to the upper floor for a fast cap (and access to another Health pick-up).

The least safe way back across is generally hoverboarding right across the bridge. You make an incredibly easy sniper target, and any angry defender chasing you picks up the Sniper Rifle just as they come into line of sight of the bridge.

If you can manage it, grabbing the flag and then hopping down and grappling onto a friendly Viper makes for a *very* fast trip back to your base, though this requires some coordination, and it's risky, given how exposed the Viper is to AVRiL fire.

DEFENSE

While most CTF and VCTF maps encourage playing a strong midfield defense, doing so here is rather difficult. Because the flag is situated so close to the upper and lower exits through the palace, even a moments inattention can result in the flag at *least* getting to the midfield, and possibly all the way back to the enemy base.

Instead, you should have at least a few players dedicated to flag room defense. Take the Nightshade and block off easy access from the bottom routes, using the EMP Mine, Spider Mines, and the Slow Field. With the lower routes impeded, you can then utilize the Nemesis, Scavenger, and (ideally) the Darkwalker for vehicular defense.

In addition, at least one player on foot should be guarding the palace entrance. Ideally your best sniper, positioning them just outside the palace on the midfield side gives early warning for incoming enemies, and ample time to take long distance shots with the Sniper Rifle or AVRiL.

Landing shots with the AVRiL in the midfield can be difficult if they use the bridge for cover, but with so much AVRiL ammunition in the side passages, wasting shots isn't really a concern.

If your offense isn't periodically sweeping the side passages, be sure to have one person doing this regularly. Having the Health Keg loaded on your defensive players is helpful, but more important is denying the enemy offense the use of either the extra health or the UDamage to break your flag room defense.

Remember the fire traps over the power-ups can be used in a pinch. You can watch the power-up rooms from a distance, and if you spot an enemy going in, shoot the switch from a distance to incinerate them.

The lower palace route out of the base also has a trap, a pressure pad you can stand on to raise a gate, blocking exit from the lower route. Most of the time, players grabbing the flag are going to be leaving either through the upper palace halls, or through one of the side passages (usually grappled to the back of a speeding Viper), but every now and then, you can block someone from going out or coming in by using the gate pressure pad.

Weaponry is a problem on defense. The weapon lockers only provide a Link Gun and a Flak Cannon, hardly a diverse set of equipment. The Shock Rifle available just inside the palace from the flag stand is helpful, as is the AVRiL on the flag stand, but you may want to venture out to pick up the Stinger, Rocket Launcher, or Sniper Rifle before returning.

Remember that the Jump Boots are very useful for attackers to leap up to the flag stand (or to aid their escape), so periodically sweep them and pick them up. Even if you're going to burn them off immediately, it's still better than letting the other team use them.

You can use the boots to jump up to a sniping perch inside the large chamber behind the flag stand, but this perch is usually more useful for hiding *with* the flag, rather than protecting the flag, simply because if you miss (or they're armored enough to survive a non headshot hit or two), they're on their way with your flag, and you're sitting a good room away looking simple.

1: FLAG ROOM

WEAPONRY	AVRiL
HEALTH & ARMOR	Health x2
POWER-UPS	None
VEHICLES	Nemesis, Nightshade, Scavenger, Viper x2

The flag room in each base is expansive, providing lots of ground for vehicles to move around in, which is good for the offense, not so much for the defense.

The flags themselves are located on raised platforms, accessible from the second floor of the palace, via the jump pads on either side of the platform, or using another method (Jump Boots or a vehicle).

The corners of the room contain the spawn points, and they are far enough away that if your immediate flag defenders are killed, you aren't likely to get back in time to stop a flag runner, unless you luck out and a Viper is spawned. You may be able to catch them in the midfield.

From the flag room, there are four routes leading to the center of the map. Immediately in front of the flag are the upper and lower routes through the palace. The upper floor leads to several weapons and to a Health pick-up, the lower to a Scavenger and the Jump Boots.

On each side of the palace, two narrow streets provide easier vehicle access to the bases. Both passageways must be watched by the defense, and abused by the offense.

At the rear of the flag room is a large chamber that contains the only two Health pick-ups in the room. On the upper part of the chamber is a narrow beam that can be reached with the use of the Jump Boots. From this narrow walkway, you can hide out with the enemy flag, and snipe through the grating with a clear line of sight to the flag platform.

The flag room contains nearly all of your vehicles, and all of them should be utilized on both offense and defense. The Nightshade is powerful defensively, the Vipers provide rapid transport for your flag runners, and the Nemesis can be used either offensively or defensively.

Should you manage to bring the Darkwalker back for defense, remember that the Nightshade's laser turret functions like a Link beam, and you can use it to heal the Darkwalker. In combination with your deployables, this can be a *real* hassle for the offense to break through. A constantly repaired Darkwalker is an enormous threat. It is likewise possible to take this combination on offense. The slow-moving Darkwalker is easy to keep pace with the Nightshade, even while cloaked.

2: PALACE

WEAPONRY	Sniper Rifle, AVRiL
HEALTH & ARMOR	Health
POWER-UPS	Jump Boots

The gorgeous palaces that act as the front of each base have several frontal entrances to the midfield. The bridge that spans the center of the map runs from the top of one palace to the other, and at each end, a Sniper Rifle and an AVRiL provide plenty of long range firepower.

In addition, ramps on each side of the palace (one next to each side street leading to the flag room) provide quick access to the lower floor of the palace. It is also possible to lift jump up from the lifts to the second floor with a well timed double jump while the lift rises.

The lower floor holds a Scavenger, the Jump Boots, and a pressure pad that raises a blocking gate, preventing passage through the lower route to the midfield. Curiously, although there are several holes in the upper level floor that can be used to drop down, you can't *quite* reach them with the Jump Boots to get up to the second floor—you must use the front of the palace instead.

The Scavenger is generally best used for flagroom defense to crush impertinent infantry trying to grab you flag. You *can* use it on offense; the trick is surviving the run across the midfield. If you do make it, it's a simple matter to either roll along one of the side streets to reach the flag room, or preferably, to jump up into the palace and then make your way directly to the flag (hopefully squishing any defenders inside the palace).

The upper floor has a single Health pick-up, another set of weapon lockers holding Link Guns and Flak Cannons to reload, and the Shock Rifle.

The palace is very important for both offense and defense, and knowing when enemies are coming through it is critical for the defenders. Usually having one player stationed at the front of the palace around the Sniper Rifle warning of incoming players is sufficient.

WEAPONRY	Stinger, Rocket Launcher, AVRiL Ammo
HEALTH & ARMOR	
POWER-UPS	UDamage, Big Keg O Health

WEAPONRY	Rocket Launcher, AVRiL, Shock Rifle, Redeemer
HEALTH & ARMOR	Body Armor, Health x4
POWER-UPS	None
VEHICLES	Darkwalker

The twin streets that run around the palace to the flag room are the easiest way for vehicles to get into the flag room (and the only way, for the Darkwalker, Nemesis, and Nightshade).

The right side (from the flag room) has a Rocket Launcher, and the vital UDamage power-up. The left side has the Stinger and the Health Keg. Both sides have *two* AVRiL ammo pick-ups, and a few Health Vials. The abundant AVRiL ammunition is helpful for defenders, as you can afford to poke your head out to the midfield briefly and unload shots without worrying about running dry.

Both streets can be easily covered by Nightshade deployables, so you can expect to run into them frequently while on offense. If the passages are blocked up, you may instead need to either use the palace (on foot), or take the Viper or the Scavenger and jump inside the palace to get in with a vehicle.

Because there are four power-ups in total, one is nearly always up, so it is very important that you are timing at *least* the UDamage spawns, and ideally the Kegs as well. Keeping a stranglehold on the power-ups (or at least, tripping the traps when an enemy tries to pick them up) can give your team a considerable advantage.

The streets are usually very unsafe for infantry to travel, as offensive vehicles frequently take these paths, and getting run down by an incoming Viper is no fun. You can hide out in the AVRiL ammo niches a bit, popping out to take long distance shots at incoming vehicles, just be careful out in the open.

The midfield area on Necropolis is large, but due to its topography, vehicle movement is highly restricted. This actually makes it somewhat safer for infantry to move through, as the central bridge provides plenty of cover, and you can get down into the waterway that runs through the center of the map on the east or west side.

Both sides have Health pick-ups, a Shock Rifle, and in the center of the water, either the Body Armor or (rather more importantly!) the Darkwalker. Getting to the Darkwalker immediately should be a huge priority, securing it for offense or defense is very helpful.

The Body Armor is more useful for flag runners than anyone else. It's a bit far out for defenders to roam safely. The Health pick-ups and their attendant Vials tucked away in the small water pits are inconvenient to reach, so you usually shouldn't waste time going for more than one on your way to either base.

The large bridge that dominates the center of the map has narrow passages on either side that allow all of the vehicles to pass by them, but the bridge supports obstruct line of sight, and restrict mobility considerably.

The pair of jump pads on either side of the middle of the bridge allow infantry to quickly reach the bridge from the middle of the map, and the lifts on the front of each palace allow them to get up to the bridge from either end of the bridge.

The Redeemer spawns in the center of the bridge, and it is a very important weapon for dealing with the Darkwalker. A heavily defended Darkwalker on defense can be a royal pain to take out, even with the UDamage, and distracting it with an assault then blasting it with a remotely piloted Redeemer can clear the way for your offense.

There are Rocket Launchers *and* AVRiLs located just under the bridge in front of each palace, so if you happen to be out in front on foot for whatever reason, you can pick these up.

When moving through this area as a flag runner, you should take advantage of all of the terrain as much as possible. You can, for example, emerge from the enemy base on the top level of the palace, drop down to the Body Armor water pit, leap on the Hoverboard and dismount to pick up the armor, double jump across the water and remount, coast up to the lift, hop off again, double jump up from the lift to reach the upper level of your palace, and in to grab another Health pick-up on your way to the flag.

You can also use the jump pads in the center to throw off a pursuer, head out across the bridge, drop down, run under to the other side. If they chase, use the jump pad to get back up, then drop down on the other side, closer to your base, before using a lift to get to the lower level of your palace.

Covering the midfield with your vehicles is generally somewhat difficult, since so many AVRiLs and ready cover make it easy for infantry to take potshots from concealment at a distance. Generally focusing your efforts on pushing vehicles through the midfield quickly is more effective, rather than trying to control it.

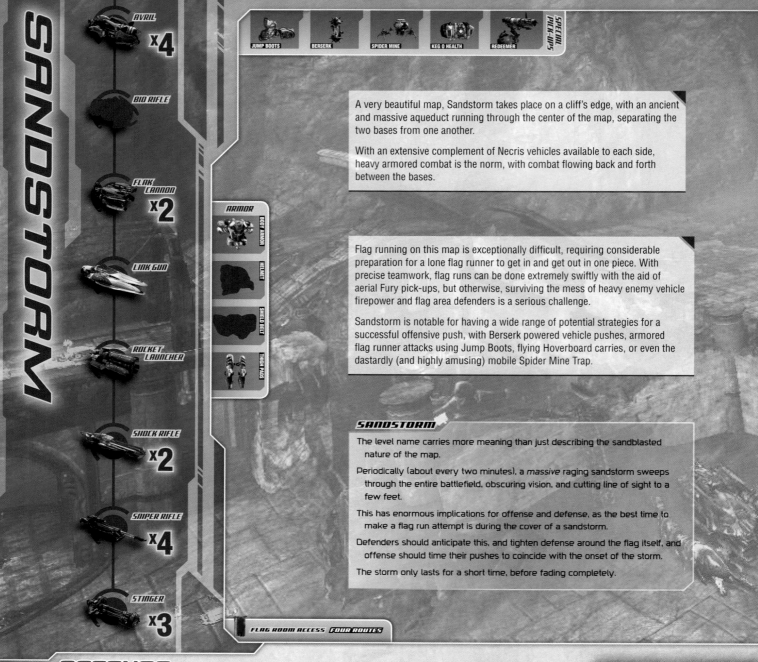

AVRIL x4

BIO RIFLE

FLAK CANNON x2

LINK GUN

ROCKET LAUNCHER

SHOCK RIFLE x2

SNIPER RIFLE x4

STINGER x3

JUMP BOOTS | BERSERK | SPIDER MINE | KEG O HEALTH | REDEEMER | **SPECIAL PICK-UPS**

ARMOR

BODY ARMOR

HELMET

SHIELD BELT

THIGH PADS

FLAG ROOM ACCESS *FOUR ROUTES*

A very beautiful map, Sandstorm takes place on a cliff's edge, with an ancient and massive aqueduct running through the center of the map, separating the two bases from one another.

With an extensive complement of Necris vehicles available to each side, heavy armored combat is the norm, with combat flowing back and forth between the bases.

Flag running on this map is exceptionally difficult, requiring considerable preparation for a lone flag runner to get in and get out in one piece. With precise teamwork, flag runs can be done extremely swiftly with the aid of aerial Fury pick-ups, but otherwise, surviving the mess of heavy enemy vehicle firepower and flag area defenders is a serious challenge.

Sandstorm is notable for having a wide range of potential strategies for a successful offensive push, with Berserk powered vehicle pushes, armored flag runner attacks using Jump Boots, flying Hoverboard carries, or even the dastardly (and highly amusing) mobile Spider Mine Trap.

SANDSTORM

The level name carries more meaning than just describing the sandblasted nature of the map.

Periodically (about every two minutes), a *massive* raging sandstorm sweeps through the entire battlefield, obscuring vision, and cutting line of sight to a few feet.

This has enormous implications for offense and defense, as the best time to make a flag run attempt is during the cover of a sandstorm.

Defenders should anticipate this, and tighten defense around the flag itself, and offense should time their pushes to coincide with the onset of the storm.

The storm only lasts for a short time, before fading completely.

OFFENSE

Offense is a complicated matter on Sandstorm, due to the extremely open area around the flag. There is no flag room per se, but rather, simply a flag located at the "back end" of the enemy base.

Since the bases on this map consist of little more than a few ruined buildings, there is a lot of open ground to cover.

Generally, straight frontal approaches to run the flag are doomed to failure. Even assuming you survive the approach from the narrow channel through the aqueduct, once you're on foot carrying the flag, getting back across the map is difficult at best, since there is so much heavy vehicle firepower present.

On foot, your best recourse is the Jump Boots, and a bit of armor. Generally, grabbing the Body Armor and Thighpads on your side of the map, then picking up the Jump Boots on your side or the enemy side and making an attempt works.

Doing this prep work for every run is time consuming, but throwing yourself against the enemy defenses repeatedly is even worse.

If you do take the Jump Boots from your side of the map, head to the tunnel through the aqueduct. If you're lucky, you may be able to snap up the Health Keg and the Spider Mine Trap both. Then take one of the lifts up to the top of the aqueduct.

From up top, you can Hoverboard down the aqueduct until you're close to the enemy flag. Wait for a sandstorm to roll in, then drop down (the boots will shield you from falling damage). Quickly grab the flag, and then make your way over to the triple 'steps' that go up the side of the aqueduct.

If (and only if) you have all three charges on the Jump Boots still, you can jump up each step, drop down the other side of the aqueduct, and quickly cap the flag!

The other option requires rather more brute force. If possible, secure the Berserk power-up, on either side of the map, then hop in a vehicle and lay waste to the enemy's vehicles. The Darkwalker and Nemesis are best suited to this task.

While you are busily devastating the enemy's heavy armor, a teammate can sneak in through the south end of the aqueduct near the Redeemer. The Viper or the Fury can be used to get there quickly, or the Scavenger can jump over the aqueduct to reach it. If the Redeemer is up, so much the better.

VIPER

NEMESIS

SCAVENGER

DARKWALKER

NIGHTSHADE

In either case, while a Berserked heavy vehicle (and some other lighter craft) are distracting the defense, you have a good chance to pick up the flag. Getting out is still difficult, your chances are improved if you have a friendly teammate in another vehicle to grapple on to.

Speaking of grappling, the easiest way back with the flag is to grapple onto a friendly Fury, even better in a Sandstorm.

DEFENSE

Defense is peculiar on this map, with a *lot* more emphasis on vehicular combat than some of the other VCTF maps. ALL of your vehicles that aren't being used on offense should be used on defense.

Balancing offense and defense with your vehicles is tricky, as all of the powerful vehicles are important for cracking the enemy defense. The Fury in particular is vital for flag running, as it provides the easiest means of carrying a flag runner out of the enemy base.

The Vipers are also important on offense, as they can leap up to the Redeemer area, possibly carrying a flag runner. The Scavenger can do the same on the

'steps' up to the aqueduct, but it is so fragile, doing so and surviving with a flag carrier in tow is difficult.

The Nemesis and Darkwalker however, are ill suited to flag running, and should be used to keep the lighter enemy vehicles at bay, and to maintain parity with the enemy's heavy vehicles.

Sniping is highly effective on defense, as you can assassinate flag carriers, and anyone foolish enough to come into your side of the map on foot.

The periodic sandstorms that sweep the map are hellish for defenders, as they cut visibility to nothing. It is important that you always maintain a few defenders near the flag (even squatting on it with a vehicle) during a sandstorm to prevent stealthy flag runs.

Be sure to make use of your AVRiLs on defense to support your vehicle defenses if you aren't in a vehicle yourself. Doing so can keep the enemy vehicles at bay, even if you've lost some of your heavy vehicles. This is especially important against the enemy Fury, which you want out of the sky as quickly as possible to keep it from helping with a flag capture.

Keep an eye on the Redeemer ledge, enemies can sneak across from their base, and if your team isn't timing the Redeemer itself, you can be sure you're going to eat an occasional incoming Redeemer. If you're quick, you may be able to shoot it down before it devastates your flag defenders.

WEAPONRY	AVRiL, Sniper Rifle, Stinger
HEALTH & ARMOR	Health, Body Armor
POWER-UPS	None
VEHICLES	Viper, Scavenger, Fury

WEAPONRY	AVRiL, Shock Rifle, Flak Cannon, Sniper Rifle
HEALTH & ARMOR	Health, Thighpads
POWER-UPS	Jump Boots
VEHICLES	Darkwalker, Nemesis

The area around the flag holds the Body Armor, and quite a bit of Health up on the walkways connecting the various building skeletons in the area.

The building just behind the flag also holds the very useful Sniper Rifle and an AVRiL on the upper floor, providing a superb platform for flag area defense against infantry or vehicle threats from a great distance.

All of the vehicles around the flag are useful for flag running, as they are too light to really battle the heavier vehicles. Instead, the Scavenger should be used to jump over the "steps" leading up the side of the Aqueduct. The Viper can go up the steps, or up to the Redeemer, and the Fury of course, can be used to reach any point on the map swiftly. It should be used to check the Berserk power-up, the Redeemer, and for flag runner transport.

The Vipers self destruct is useful in a pinch against the enemy Nemesis or Darkwalker, as you can get to them quickly and launch a self destructing Viper to deal serious damage. Useful, if your own heavy vehicles have been taken down.

The front end of the base has the heavy vehicles, and quite a few important pick-ups. The Flak Cannon is only of middling utility on this level, given how much combat is at long range or in vehicles, but the Shock Rifle is handy, as are the forward AVRiL and Sniper Rifle.

Picking up the Thighpads if you already have the Body Armor can give you some extra durability for attempting a flag run, but don't fool yourself into thinking a bit of armor will help you against heavy enemy vehicles.

The Jump Boots are critically important, as they can be used to reach the Redeemer, cross the aqueduct with the flag, or perform a boosted lift jump in the northern sniper tower to get to the Berserk on its rooftop.

Otherwise, the Berserk is only accessible with the Fury, and given its power in an offensive vehicle, it is important to secure every time it spawns. If possible, stealing the enemy Berserk can also help your cause. Even dropping down with the Fury, grabbing it, and then flying *away* can be helpful, you don't want to die in enemy territory in the lightly armored Fury and hand them the Berserk you were trying to steal.

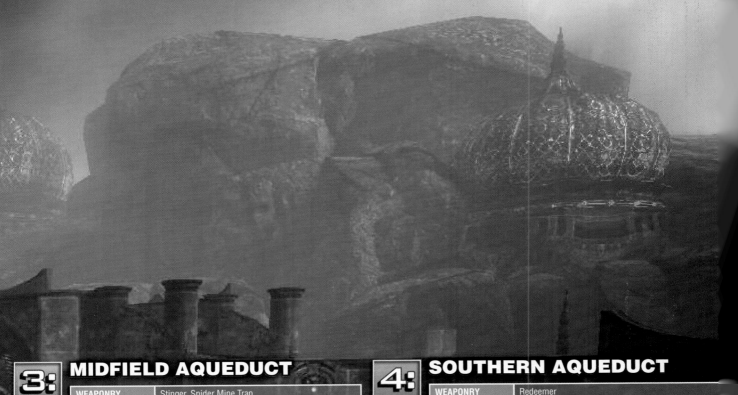

3: MIDFIELD AQUEDUCT

WEAPONRY	Stinger, Spider Mine Trap
HEALTH & ARMOR	Big Keg O Health
POWER-UPS	None
VEHICLES	None

4: SOUTHERN AQUEDUCT

WEAPONRY	Redeemer
HEALTH & ARMOR	None
POWER-UPS	None
VEHICLES	None

VEHICLE LIFT

The large lift platform in the tunnel through the aqueduct can be used to get the Nemesis up on top of the aqueduct, where it can then open fire on the enemy team below.

The immense aqueduct runs north south along the map, splitting up the map between the two bases. Other than flying or jumping over it, the only way between the two bases on foot (or in the heavy vehicles) is through a small tunnel at the north end of the aqueduct.

The tunnel holds the Health Keg, a very handy Spider Mine Trap, and several lifts that can be used to get atop the Aqueduct on foot or in a smaller vehicle.

Remember that you can attach the Spider Mine Trap to a friendly vehicle, and then drive around dispensing mines on the move automatically, an amusing and effective offensive or defensive tactic.

This tunnel tends to be a constant combat zone, but you shouldn't be going through here on foot or in the lighter vehicles if you can cross the aqueduct via other means.

Midway along the aqueducts sides are three giant steps that reach the top of the aqueduct. You can scale the steps by leaping with a Scavenger, jumping with a Viper, or jumping up with the aid of Jump Boots to reach the top of the aqueduct.

The broken ledge at the south end of the aqueduct is accessible via a small shaft from the top of the aqueduct, or from either base using several of the vehicles or the Jump Boots.

This is a very quick way between the two flag areas, and as the Redeemer spawns here, it is important for both offense and defense to be mindful of this location. Zipping between the two bases on a Viper and detonating the enemy flag area defenders, or carrying a flag runner out can help your offense considerably.

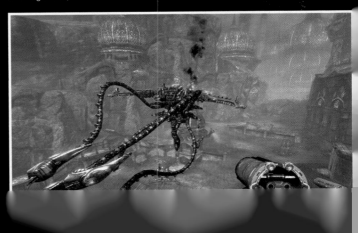

				SPECIAL PICK-UPS
UDAMAGE	KEG O HEALTH	REDEEMER	BERSERK	

AVRIL x2

BIO RIFLE

FLAK CANNON

LINK GUN

ROCKET LAUNCHER x4

SHOCK RIFLE x2

SNIPER RIFLE x4

STINGER x2

ARMOR

BODY ARMOR

HELMET

SHIELD BELT

THIGH PADS

Suspense takes place on the border of Axon and Izanagi territory on the planet Taryd. One of the few passage points for heavy vehicles, the massive suspension bridge here is the focus of conflict between the two bases.

In addition to the primary (and most dangerous) route across the bridge itself, it is possible to take a detour down to the river below, where you can quickly zip to the other side (generally a much safer route when Goliaths and AVRiL snipers are camping out on the bridge).

FREEFALLING

Pick up the Jump Boots from the side of the bridge before you make a flag run. On your way out, instead of going towards the slope leading below the bridge, go up past the enemy SPMA balcony, then along the side of their base building.

From here, you can drop right down to the narrow wooden walkway far below in the river. With the Jump Boots active, you won't take any falling damage, and you can then Hoverboard across the center quickly.

Since you only need one charge active for the boots to work their magic, use the other two to either grab the Body Armor quickly, or to help with your escape from the flag area if you're spotted on the way out.

There is some serious vehicle firepower available on this map, with the Goliath, Raptor, and SPMA all available for use. The Manta, Scorpion, and Raptor all provide rapid transit, and the Raptor in particular is key for providing an aerial extraction of a flag runner.

The bridge is usually the site of massive vehicle battles, with snipers (both Sniper Rifle and AVRiL varieties) hanging out in the upper expanses of the bridge.

With UDamage and Berserk both present, it is possible to get some unreal firepower with any of the stronger vehicles. A little coordination with your team to get a Goliath in place, or using the Raptor yourself, and you can lay down a withering barrage of fire on the enemy team while in Juggernaut mode with both power-ups active.

This map is peculiar in that the flag room itself is nearly indefensible, but the bridge provides the major chokepoint. The only other way across is going beneath the bridge, or flying across in the Raptor.

FLAG ROOM ACCESS THREE ROUTES

OFFENSE

Offense actually serves two roles here, the first being actually going for the flag, and the second, tying up the *enemy* offense, largely to prevent the heavy duty vehicles from being brought to bear on your flag carrier.

One Goliath shot is all it takes to end a potential flag run, so you need to make sure that the Goliath isn't around to do that in the first place.

The SPMA can be used from its spawn point, or at the back of the base to shell the center of the map. With lots of vehicle activity there, you're almost guaranteed to score kills, or at the very least, make it a real pain for the enemy to move through the area safely. You can also do this to shell the Berserk and make it a very hazardous area for the enemy team to camp around.

The Goliath is a key part of your offense, but be careful about driving it straight onto the bridge. If possible, hang back and zoom all the way in to take shots from a great distance. You can still be lethal even at great range, and you're less exposed to enemy fire.

The Scorpion, Manta, and Raptor should all be used for rapid transit, but with the Raptor, you have to decide if you're going to use it to combat the enemy team's Goliath (and Raptor) or to ferry yourself or another flag carrier across the map.

When it comes to flag running, there's no better way in and out of the base than clinging to the bottom of an aerial vehicle, and if possible, you can move from the flag room to the SPMA ledge, grab the Big Keg, then grapple onto a friendly Raptor and make the journey back in style. You're exposed to rapidly reacting snipers, but other than that, it's a heck of a lot safer than making the journey across the bridge, and faster than going below.

Speaking of going below, generally, if you're Hoverboarding it, the lower route is the way to go to get out on your own. Ideally, a friendly Manta can show up to give you a grapple connection for a rapid trip out, but getting a Manta across the bridge and into the enemy base in one piece is a bit of a trick. A well-coordinated team may be able to bring up the Manta from below the bridge and wait just out of sight for a flag carrier to make the short run from the flag room to the slope down to the water.

The Berserk, UDamage, and Redeemer are all very important tactical assets on this map. Time them all, and deny the enemy team their use. If you can get a powered-up vehicle into the enemy's flag area, you can devastate their vehicle stock, and then pick off the hapless infantry while the flag is stolen.

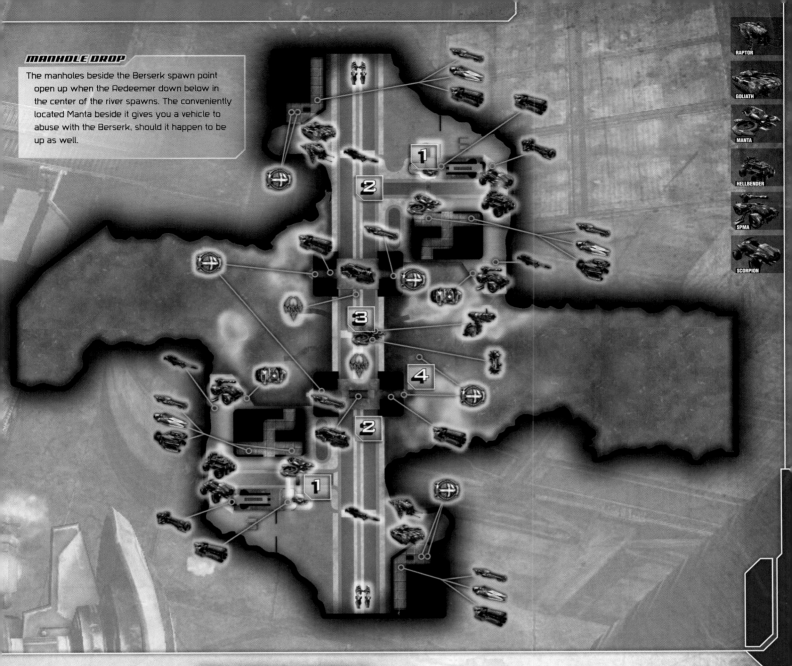

RAPTOR

GOLIATH

MANTA

HELLBENDER

SPMA

SCORPION

MANHOLE DROP

The manholes beside the Berserk spawn point open up when the Redeemer down below in the center of the river spawns. The conveniently located Manta beside it gives you a vehicle to abuse with the Berserk, should it happen to be up as well.

The Redeemer is usually most useful for quickly eliminating the enemy Goliath or SPMA from a distance, though it can be used to remove a troublesome sniper up in the bridge supports if you're feeling especially vindictive.

There is a fair amount of armor to be had, but with the abundance of vehicles, and the open terrain, trying to get tanked up is usually a bit of a waste. However, grabbing the Body Armor after picking up the Jump Boots is rather speedy, so that much at least is worth doing. If you happen to be doing long distance sniping of the bridge on the ground, there's no reason you can't back up to the end of your base and pick up the Thighpads on the way—just don't bother making an express detour to pick them up unless you're idle on defense, not pressing on offense.

DEFENSE

Defense on Suspense is difficult, as the flag room is little more than a small hut, open on both sides, and with a hole in the ceiling that attackers can drop through. Not the most defensible of locations.

However, to *get* to that easily assaulted building, the enemy flag runners must pass the suspension bridge, either by getting across it directly (which you can resist with fervent enthusiasm), or more frequently, by sneaking under the bridge.

Occasionally, an enemy may come across in the Raptor, so it is important that your own Raptor pilot, and any AVRiL, Sniper Rifle, or Shock Rifle armed players on your team quickly eliminate the Raptor before it has a chance to participate in any high flying flag heists (not to mention raining hot plasma death down on your team, always a downer).

As for the bridge itself, your own SPMA is a good defensive tool, as well as the Goliath. If you aren't planning on using the Goliath for offense, consider pulling it back to protect the flag room itself. By camping out of line of sight of the bridge, you can thrash any incoming light vehicles and infantry very easily. This does put your offense at a disadvantage though, so be sure they're aware the Goliath is out of commission.

Be sure to have a properly cozy camper with a nice campfire parked up in the upper levels of the bridge. The AVRiL is vital for defense, and you can only reach it by using jump pads (or the Raptor). The fact that the platforms make superb sniping perches is just an added bonus.

Because snipers are such a threat to the midfield, you may need a counter-sniper of your own. Since you are aiding your offense and protecting your base, this is a worthwhile defensive position, just be aware that it is blind to enemies passing under the bridge.

For those enemies that do bypass the bridge using the lower route, keep an eye on the slope that leads down to the water. Guarding the water route explicitly is usually a waste of defensive resources that need to be protecting the bridge and the flag room itself.

1: FLAG AREA

WEAPONRY	Rocket Launcher, Sniper Rifle, Stinger
HEALTH & ARMOR	Health x2, Vials, Thighpads
POWER-UPS	None
VEHICLES	Manta, Scorpion, Hellbender, Goliath, Raptor

The field around the flag room itself is quite extensive, though you *can* defend just inside the flag room itself. The Rocket Launcher is conveniently located just above it (as is the Stinger), and firing rockets down from the hole above down to the flag can stop incautious flag runners fairly easily.

The jump pad up from the flag room to the Stinger area may be used by flag runners to reach the SPMA section of the base for a getaway, so watch for carriers emerging from the top of the flag room if you're freshly spawned and you hear your flag taken.

As for the rest of the area, there is a large field, broken up only by the barricade in the center of the road that runs up to the bridge itself.

At the back of the road, you can find the Thighpads, then the Sniper Rifle, then a small bundle of Vials.

Opposite the flag room is the slope that leads down to below the bridge.

It is possible to hang back and snipe targets on the bridge from the back of the field, and it's also possible to climb up the suspension cables anchored in the area to reach the top of the bridge, either to get at the UDamage above, or simply to get some altitude to fire down at targets below.

There is very little health in the immediate area; the only two Health pick-ups in the vicinity are located inside the small building by the Goliath and Raptor spawn points.

The Manta, Scorpion, and Hellbender are all parked by the flag room itself, making for quick access from the spawn point nearby.

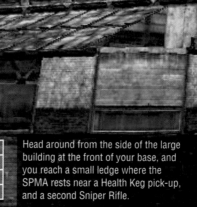

2: FRONT OF BASE

WEAPONRY	Sniper Rifle
HEALTH & ARMOR	None
POWER-UPS	None
VEHICLES	SPMA

Head around from the side of the large building at the front of your base, and you reach a small ledge where the SPMA rests near a Health Keg pick-up, and a second Sniper Rifle.

This platform is great both for sniping, and for long range bombardment with the SPMA. Carefully targeted, you can rain shells down on the enemy field area by their flag room, and on the center of the bridge.

There is also a narrow ledge on the front of the building that connects to the inside of the building (and a hall with several Health Vials), and can be used to drop down beside the jump pad that leads up to the bridge platform holding the AVRiL.

Going down from here is an option as well, though you'll take damage doing so if you don't have the Jump Boots, but you can get down to the center quickly if you must.

One very important point, for both offense and defense—using the Jump Pads, its possible to jump up to the ledge on the front of the base, so a careful attacker can get into the base from the SPMA platform (or the Vial hallway if he wants to risk running through your spawn area).

3: BRIDGE

WEAPONRY	Shock Rifle, Rocket Launcher, AVRiL
HEALTH & ARMOR	Health x2, Vials
POWER-UPS	None
VEHICLES	None

The bridge itself is fairly simple, a straight shot between the two bases with the Berserk located in the center. When the Redeemer is active below, the manholes beside the Berserk open up, allowing you to drop through to beneath the ridge.

At each end of the bridge a pair of structures on the left and right that support a central platform overlooking the bridge. On the left side (facing out of your base) bottom floor, inside is the Shock Rifle, and on the right side bottom floor, the Rocket Launcher. On the outside, both left and right sides have a Health pick-up next to a pair of Vials for a quick health boost.

Outside the ground level buildings to the left and right, jump pads lead up to the sniping platform above, where you can find Sniper Rifle ammo, more vials, and critically, the AVRiL.

If you carefully look down from the AVRiL platform to the jump pads below, you should be able to spot the narrow hall that runs through the building (a 'middle' level, between the ground and the AVRiL platform).

On the left side, it contains the Jump Boots, and on the right, the Body Armor. If you grab the boots, you can drop down onto the bridge again, then jump up to the Body Armor.

To reach the UDamage, you must climb the suspension cables to get above, or come in on the Raptor.

4: UNDER BRIDGE

WEAPONRY	Redeemer
HEALTH & ARMOR	Health x2
POWER-UPS	None
VEHICLES	Manta

The area beneath the bridge is quite simple, a Health pick-up, the Manta, and the Redeemer spawn point.

The river water is no good for Hoverboarding on, but as long as you stay on the dry land or the small wooden bridges crisscrossing the water, you can move at full speed through this area.

If you're chasing a flag runner down here, the Sniper Rifle or Shock Rifle are your best bets for knocking him off his hoverboard (or if you're really desperate, a carefully aimed Enforcer shot).

AVRIL ×4

BIO RIFLE

FLAK CANNON

LINK GUN

ROCKET LAUNCHER

SHOCK RIFLE

SNIPER RIFLE ×8

STINGER

SPECIAL PICKUPS

SHAPED CHARGE

ARMOR

BODY ARMOR

HELMET

SHIELD BELT

THIGH PADS

RED POWER CORE

1

2

RED PRIME

WEST

4

6

6

5

EAST

CENTER

6

BLUE PRIME

7

BLUE POWER CORE

An unusual asymmetric Warfare map, Avalanche has more distinct special Node features than most other Warfare maps, *and* it features Axon vs. Necris combat. Although the Node vehicles remain the same, the base vehicles at the Power Cores are not.

The Power Core areas are identical, but the terrain surrounding them is not. The Red Base features a large raised ledge area that can be approached from the west, or a set of ruined stairs up a slope to the east.

The Blue Base on the other hand, has two routes accessible from the Blue Prime Node, with the stairs leading to the Power Core on the east, and a large sloping area accessible from the west. Unlike the Red Prime Node, both routes can be reached from the Prime Node, whereas the ledge is only accessible from the Center Node on the red side.

To balance out the split paths to the Red Power Core, the Blue (Necris) team receives slightly heavier firepower at its Power Core in the form of a Nemesis, and support deployables from a Nightshade.

There are two special features on this map. The first is a typical support node function; by capturing both the East and the West Nodes (you must hold both), a Nanoblack Infection Tube is deployed from the sky onto the enemies Prime Node.

This tentacle continuously drains and damages the enemy Prime Node, *even if you do not have it linked*. That is, you can be pushed back to your Prime Node, but if you hold both the East and the West Nodes long enough, the tentacle will completely drain and destroy the enemy Prime Node, severing all of the Node connections.

Second, when you are pushed back to your Power Core (the enemy holds your Prime Node), the Shaped Charge can be taken from the Thighpad tower in the base over to the barricades on the side of the mountain. Drop the Shaped Charge to trigger a massive avalanche. The avalanche sweeps down the ice field, wiping out anything in its pass, and destroying both your Prime Node, and the East and West Nodes in the center of the map. This is a one-shot remedy, but it can help your team to bounce back if you get pushed back during the match.

MIXED GROUND

The area around each base is extremely open and exposed. It's prime territory for sniping incoming enemies and providing some support for your team as they push back to the Prime Node.

The center of the map is contained in an enormous cavern, accessible from each base through several routes.

Inside the cavern, there is a fair amount of room for even large vehicles to move around, and enough cover that sniping from one to the other is difficult.

Because the Goliath and Darkwalker both spawn in the center, the midfield tends to be a heavy duty vehicle battlefield. Don't hesitate to teleport to your base from a forward Node to bring an AVRiL into the fight.

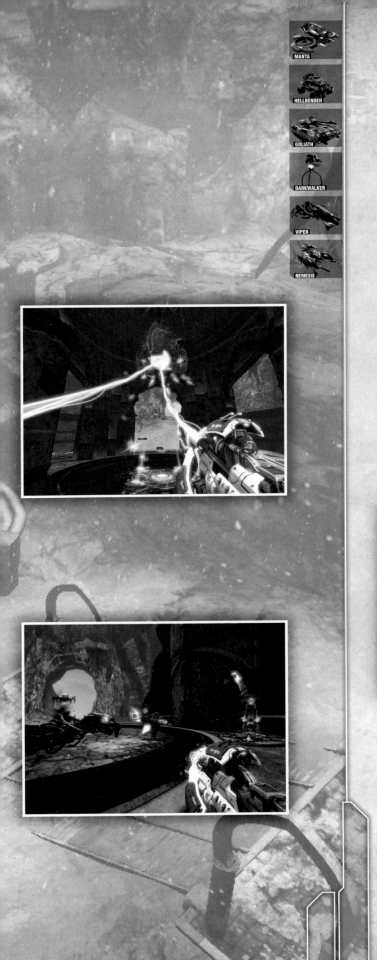

MANTA

HELLBENDER

GOLIATH

DARKWALKER

VIPER

NEMESIS

VEHICLES	Manta x2, Hellbender x2
PICK-UPS	AVRiL x2, Thighpads x2, Sniper Rifle x2, Health x4, Shaped Charge

VEHICLES	Scorpion x2
PICK-UPS	Health x2, Sniper Rifle

The Power Core area consists of the Power Core at the front of the base, slightly shielded from direct attack on the front, and two side towers containing Thighpads. One of the towers has the Shaped Charge, which can be used to trigger the last second avalanche.

There are *four* Health pick-ups at the back of the base, handy if you happen to be playing Power Core defense on foot.

The avalanche barricades are just outside the base area to the east. A bit farther east is a tower that has a Sniper Rifle and an AVRiL both, which can be used as a sniping perch for covering the Prime Node.

The western tower contains another Sniper Rifle, and a Beam Turret, helpful for defending against enemy vehicle assaults on the Power Core area.

The Red Prime Node is identical in appearance to the Blue Prime Node, but the terrain around it is slightly different. Two Health pick-ups and the Sniper Rifle are around the Node itself.

Securing the Node provides your team with two Scorpions, which are handy for quickly reaching (and detonating) any of the Nodes in the center of the map.

On the west side, a series of stairs half buried in snow lead up to the Red Power Core, and to the east, a smoothly sloping hillside leads up to the other side of the Power Core.

VEHICLES	Scavenger x2
PICK-UPS	Health x2

VEHICLES	Goliath
PICK-UPS	Sniper Rifle

Controlling the Center Node is necessary to push to the enemy base, though it offers little in the way of vehicle support, a pair of light Scavengers is the extent of the added firepower here.

The twin Beam Turrets are helpful for defending the Node and this is a decent Node to defend with your own Orb, as you can use the walls around the Node to protect yourself from distant vehicle fire, and the pair of Health pick-ups to recover from glancing hits.

The huge cavern around the Center Node encompasses the Center, East, and West Nodes, with three routes on each side leading out to the Blue or Red bases. There are small Hoverboard boosting jump pads on either side of the Center Node, allowing you to quickly propel yourself to the East or West Nodes.

Both the east and the east side Nodes have the same basic layout. That is, they provide no cover at all, just a Node and a Sniper Rifle. However, each Node supplies your team with a powerful vehicle, and each Node is half of the key to extending a Necris Infection Tube to damage or destroy the enemy Prime Node.

The West Node provides the Goliath, and has a nearby tunnel leading to the Blue Prime Node.

VEHICLES	Darkwalker
PICK-UPS	Sniper Rifle

VEHICLES	Viper x2
PICK-UPS	Health x2, Sniper Rifle

The East Node is identical in layout to the West Node, the difference being the Darkwalker present, and the tunnel leading to the Red Prime Node.

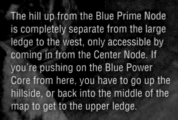

The Blue Prime Node is identical to the Red Prime Node in terms of the building around the Node itself, but the terrain around it is not.

The hill up from the Blue Prime Node is completely separate from the large ledge to the west, only accessible by coming in from the Center Node. If you're pushing on the Blue Power Core from here, you have to go up the hillside, or back into the middle of the map to get to the upper ledge.

'7: BLUE CORE AREA

VEHICLES	Viper x4, Nightshade, Nemesis
PICK-UPS	AVRiL, Thighpads x2, Health x2, Shaped Charge

The Blue side has Necris vehicles at their base, and while the front of their base is slightly more accessible from the front, they also have more vehicle firepower to compensate.

With *four* Vipers, you can afford to use them for suicidal detonation purposes on enemy vehicles (or the Node), though they are also very helpful for getting an early jump on the center of the map, given how fast they move.

The Nightshade should not be used immediately at the start of the map, as it is too slow to assist with offensive operations initially, and setting up defenses so early in the match is premature. It is quite useful when you *are* on defense, and you can bring it forward to block off the tunnels leading from the midfield with deployables.

The Nemesis is a powerful asset, as the Axon side has nothing to match its firepower initially. Bring it forward and use it to help in the battle for the Center Node.

As with the Red base, you can trigger an avalanche with the Shaped Charge in the base, and you have an AVRiL and Sniper Rifle tower to the west, as well as a sniper and Beam Turret tower to the east for defense.

MAP VARIANTS: TWO FRONTS

This variant links the Prime Nodes to the East and West Nodes, skipping the Center Node entirely.

As a result, it is very easy to be fighting an offensive and defensive battle at the same time, compared with the normal map which is usually a constant back and forth battle.

This also has the effect of making the Goliath and Darkwalker an even greater part of the battle, as players are spawning at the East and West Nodes very often.

One important point: While using this variant Node layout, the *Center* Node becomes the "Tentacle" Node, and controlling it causes the infection tube to damage your opponents Power Core. Because you only need to control the single middle Node to trigger the tentacle, it is necessary to occasionally stage a raid on it to destroy the Node if you aren't concentrating on holding it.

AVRIL **x7**

BIO RIFLE

FLAK CANNON

LINK GUN

ROCKET LAUNCHER

SHOCK RIFLE

SNIPER RIFLE **x2**

STINGER

SPECIAL PICK-UPS

BERSERK

REDEEMER

SHAPED CHARGE

JUMP BOOTS

ARMOR

BODY ARMOR

HELMET

SHIELD BELT

THIGH PADS

Downtown takes place in Oxida Nova, the capital of the Axon on Taryd. The cramped streets and plentiful cover afforded by the buildings in the area make for brutal combat, as vehicles have little room to maneuver, and the central Node between the two bases is hotly contested.

This map has one support node, the Tank Node, which provides access to the mighty Axon Goliath. This monster can be used to aid in a powerful offensive surge, or to help hold off an assault and push the enemy back from your own Prime Node.

Otherwise, the basic Node layout is very simple. From either base, the Prime Node is just up the street, and that is connected to the Center Node at the "top" of the map. The Tank Node is located directly between the Red and Blue bases, easily reached from either the Prime Nodes or the main bases.

The Power Core areas are highly defensible on the ground, and must usually be attacked from the nearby rooftops to have any chance of damaging the Core extensively.

The Prime Nodes are located inside buildings, and are brutally difficult to assault with vehicles. Small vehicles can get in, but they are extremely exposed to infantry fire once inside where they can't maneuver well. Hellbenders firing from outside have the best chance of assisting an assault.

The Center Node is the most exposed, located in the center of a large plaza. It has the benefit of a defensive turret, and the Berserk power-up spawning nearby. Notably, there are ramps around the periphery of the Node itself, which can be used by Scorpions to boost blast straight into the Node.

Just up the street from the Prime Nodes is a barricade that permits travel by vehicles only *towards* the Center Node. This barricade must be blown away to allow access for your vehicles while attacking the enemy Prime Node and Power Core (barring the Goliath, which is a threat to either, as it comes up the street from the opposite side).

The Tank Node is located in a large building, but it has restrictive terrain disallowing vehicles from getting inside (other than the Manta), meaning that assaulting or defending it is largely an infantry fight, and an important one, unless you are comfortable allowing the enemy team easy access to a Goliath.

MANTA

HELLBENDER

SCORPION

PALADIN

GOLIATH

A REALLY BIG BOOM

The Redeemer and the Shaped Charge are both extremely useful for taking out Nodes. Because the Shaped Charge respawns more quickly, it is up more frequently should you sweep by the area. If you're relentlessly timing it, you can keep heavy pressure on the other team by constantly dropping the Charge on their closest Node.

Save the Redeemer for clearing out defending infantry. Once a Node comes under attack, blast the area, and your team should be able to clear out anyone who managed to dodge the blast. The Redeemer is also much easier to use against the Prime Nodes, since you can guide it in easily, while the Shaped Charge requires getting inside and in close to the Node to use it effectively.

Just don't go firing the Redeemer while you're standing out in the sewage channel, you're begging to get shot. Ideally, use some nearby Jump Boots to hop on a rooftop and fire from there.

There is a Redeemer in the sewage channel that runs across the map between the Power Cores and Prime Nodes, the Redeemer itself is located in the very center of the map. Just to the south of the Redeemer there's a spawn for the Shaped Charge. It can also be reached quickly from the Tank Node if you control it.

Both the Redeemer and the Shaped Charge are useful for attacking the various Nodes, and blasting open the barricades when you are ready to push on the enemy's side of the map.

There are numerous pairs of Jump Boots scattered about, these are helpful for getting onto the rooftops of the Prime Nodes and Power Core areas, as well as getting around in the center of the map. You can find some in the alleys near the Power Cores, as well as in the alleys to the south of the Center Node.

The building just to the south of the Center Node has an upper floor that can only be reached with Jump Boots, and is a useful sniping vantage point.

Speaking of snipers, use of vehicles on the approach to the various Nodes is advisable, as the narrow streets are easily covered by a rooftop sniper, who has little to fear in retaliation, unless you have a Sniper Rifle of your own.

The Berserk power-up located at the Center Node is valuable for making a heavy push on the enemy Prime Node. A Berserk Hellbender can unleash a massive chain of Shock explosions, enough to thrash any enemy light vehicles, and definitely any infantry in the area.

The Paladin and Goliath are very heavy vehicles, and both can be useful for soaking up enemy fire. Of the two, the Goliath can inflict more damage and take down the Center Node very quickly indeed, but don't discount the Paladin entirely. One shot from its main cannon can destroy an annoying Manta, and it can provide shield coverage for your team when they push to the enemy side of the map.

1: POWER CORE

VEHICLES	Hellbender, Manta, Paladin, Scorpion
PICK-UPS	AVRiL x2, Jump Boots, Health x2

The Power Core is your main source of vehicles, and you shouldn't hesitate to teleport back to bring them forward, especially if you spawn forward and no vehicles are present.

The Power Core is conveniently located to quickly strike out at either the Prime Node or the Tank Node, and you can also get to the Shaped Charge or the Redeemer quickly. Since the Redeemer does not spawn immediately, your initial choice should be from one of the Tank Node, Prime Node, or Shaped Charge.

Defending the Power Core is fairly easy if the opposing team is sloppy about their assault. There is a Rocket Turret on the roof of the building around the Power Core, and it can be used to help defend against an enemy Goliath coming from the Tank Node, easily kill infantry on the ground inside, and throw some firepower up the street towards the Prime Node.

In addition, the building to the north of the Power Core can be reached via a jump pad inside the base, and it has an AVRiL on top of it, as well as a pair of Jump Boots.

If you're pushed all the way back to your base, you unfortunately won't have rapid access to the Sniper Rifle. The fastest way to reach it is to take the Jump Boots, drop down into the sewer channel, then jump on top of

the Prime Node from the south. There is a pipe running along the side of the building that can be used to reach the top—and the Sniper Rifle.

There is a second AVRiL in the back alley leading to the Prime Node, as well as a few Health Vials. If you aren't taking a vehicle (or the rooftop) for whatever reason, you can at least grab the Longbow on the way to the Prime Node. It is slightly quicker to hoverboard down the alley on the way to the Prime Node than it is to jump up to the rooftop and head for the Jump Boots.

Assaulting the Power Core is best done with the assistance of the Goliath, but you can also initiate a solid attack from the rooftop. Get onto the roof of the building to the north of the Power Core (there is an entrance on the street level), then make your way to the southern building rooftop that overlooks the Power Core area. From here, lob shots into the Power Core; respawning defenders must take the jump pad up to stop you. Even if you're taken out, you're pretty much guaranteed to get in some shots on the Core.

Unless you have the defenders *massively* suppressed, don't drive vehicles into the Power Core area unsupported, you're going to get blasted by every respawning player in an amazingly quick flash of death.

LEAPING TALL BUILDINGS

In addition to the double jump up to the top of the Prime Node building, the Jump Boots can also be used to quickly reach the Body Armor in the center of the map and the Shaped Charge (or the Redeemer, if it happens to be up).

Make a boot jump from the edge of the building and you can reach the building overlooking the center of the map. From there, you can grab the armor, either of the pick-ups, or head to the Tank Node or the Center Node.

You can get into the Tank Node from the second floor, which is helpful if it is in enemy hands, and if you proceed to the Center Node, you should have boot charges remaining to get up inside the large building just south of the Center Node.

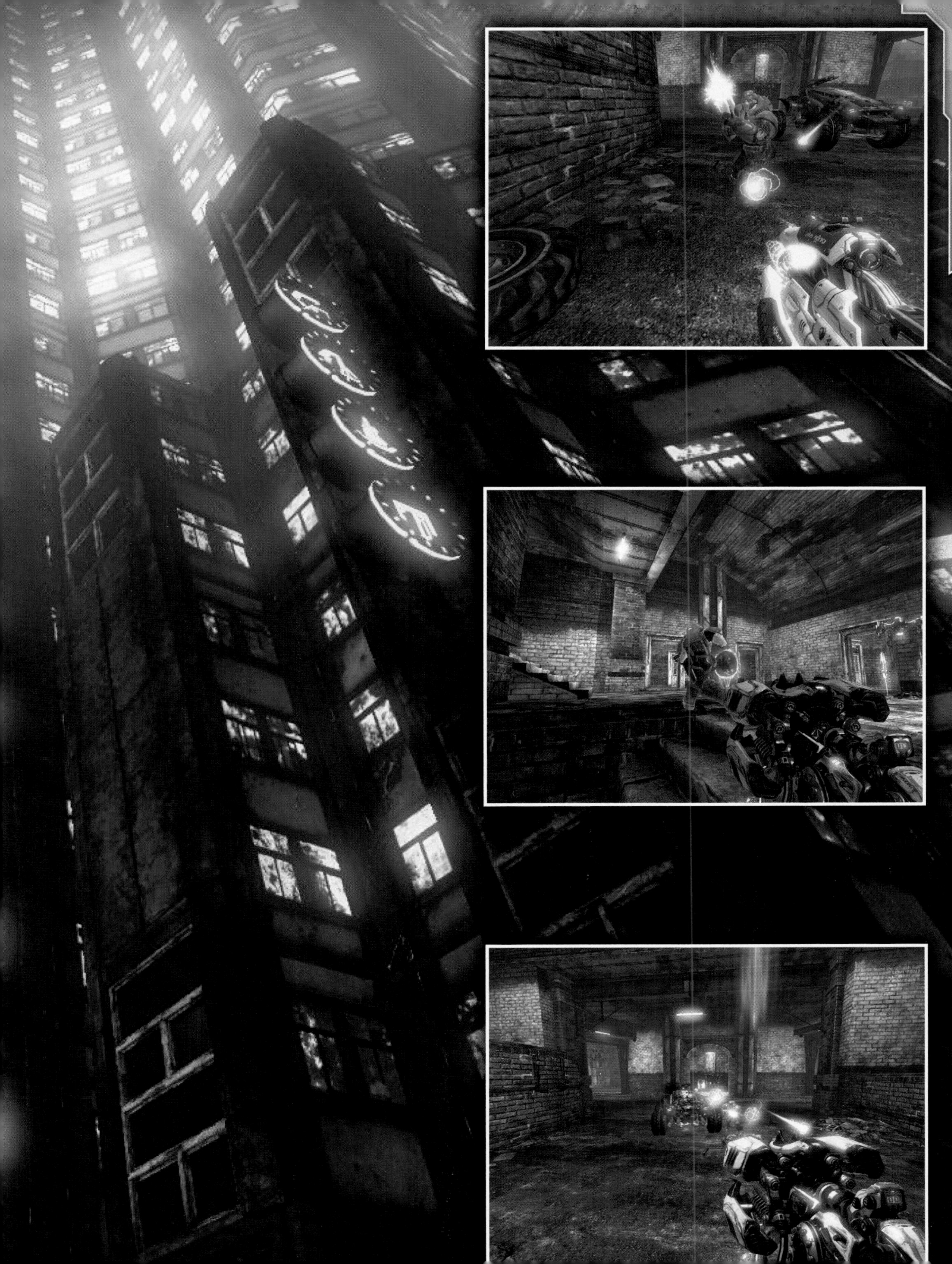

2: PRIME NODE

VEHICLES	Scorpion X2
PICK-UPS	AVRiL, Jump Boots, Body Armor, Health x2

The Prime Nodes are well-defended against large scale vehicle assault. Only the Manta can really get in and provide a serious threat to defenders, and even then, with so little room to maneuver, it is AVRiL bait for an alert defender.

The Prime Node is also easily defendable by an Orb carrier, as he must be rooted out inside, usually on foot. With Body Armor and two sets of Health Vials nearby (in the alley near the Body Armor and on the steps to the roof), it is possible to get somewhat beefy as an Orb holder.

The Prime Node has two Scorpions as vehicles, both useful for detonating on the Center Node to destroy it quickly.

Because the barricade is right outside the Prime Node, you shouldn't have to deal with Hellbenders camped outside—at least right away. The barricades are typically destroyed quickly, unless your team is *extremely* diligent about timing the Shaped Charge and the Redeemer.

It is possible for the enemy team to bring vehicles around via the Tank Node street, though this takes considerably longer, and if you are actually pushed back to your Prime Node and you have teammates spawning at the main base, they can be taken down before they ever reach the Prime Node.

The Sniper Rifle is located on the roof of the Prime Node building, and it is very helpful for attacking Center Node defenders, or in the defense of the Prime Node itself.

If you're assaulting the Prime Node, you may want to bring one of the heavier vehicles up and park yourself outside on the south side. Firing in with the Hellbender (especially Berserk) may net you some kills of

incautious defenders, and if you can damage the Node to prevent respawns, you should have an easier time when you do drive in.

Whatever you do, don't go charging into the Prime Node in a vehicle if you know there are active defenders inside. The Hellbender can take a few hits, but the Scorpion or the Manta cannot, and the AVRiL is located right outside the spawn points inside.

Coming down from the roof is possible, if you grab a pair of Jump Boots from either the Power Core roof, or the alleys in the center of the map. This is especially effective if you attack from the roof while a teammate distracts any defenders inside with a vehicle. Coming up behind the defense is a huge benefit, and can easily break the defenders.

The other safer route inside is the alley beside the Node, and this has the added advantage of supplying you with Body Armor (and a few Health Vials). The extra durability comes in handy once you engage in combat inside.

If your team is pushed back on its heels defending the Prime Node, you usually want to send the Orb forward to recapture the Center Node, as that is the fastest way to ease pressure. If you must use the Orb on defense, try to use the Shaped Charge or the Redeemer to quickly take down the Center Node. Generally, using the Orb on defense is more useful when you have captured the *enemy* Prime Node, rather than holding your own.

Locking down the Prime Node with the Orb while the enemy Power Core is exposed gives plenty of time for your offense to push the advantage and cement a victory.

The Center Node is easily the most exposed of all the Node locations, fitting for its role as the prime battleground on the map. The open square that the Node rests in is exposed from all sides. Both Prime Node streets reach it quickly, and barricades on both sides allow all vehicles to reach the Center Node. In addition, it is exposed to snipers in the skyscraper to the south, and to snipers on the east and west gallery ledges.

As if that wasn't enough, there are convenient ramps on each side of the Node that are perfect launching points for Scorpions rushing in to boost detonate on the Node.

The Center Node does have a few defensive advantages; specifically, the Beam Turret located just to the north of the Node is helpful (at least until it gets blown to pieces), the Berserk power-up spawns here, and the spawn point for the Node is inside the building on the second floor, a good vantage point for firing down on attackers. You may actually want to venture out to pick up Jump Boots and a Sniper Rifle and AVRiL, then return and jump back up to resume defending the Node.

The Berserk power-up is key for assaulting the enemy Prime Node, any of the vehicles with Berserk active becomes a killing machine. The Hellbender is usually the best target for it, as the Manta and the Scorpion are considerably more fragile. The Goliath would be nice—but bringing it to the Center Node is fairly impractical.

You *can* use it with the Paladin for some benefit, but again, it must be brought all the way up and survive combat until the Berserk spawns.

If you're under light assault at the Center Node due to your team pushing the enemy back heavily, make a point of repairing the turret (and/or your Hellbender, if you're using it on defense). Between pushes, you can at least restore the turret to full health, giving you a few extra seconds of survivability.

Watch out for Shaped Charges and the Redeemer, both are likely to be used continuously against the Node, as it is so exposed. Of the two, the Shaped Charge is slightly easier to stop, though canny attackers will come in with Jump Boots and drop it from the sky onto the Node.

When attacking the Center Node, you can apply enormous pressure by using all of your vehicles, going after the Shaped Charge and Redeemer, and attacking with weaponry from a great distance, either from inside the skyscraper to the south, or from the east and west galleries.

Be careful about approaching the Node prematurely—try to damage it first to shut down respawns, then pick away at the turret first, any vehicles, then any infantry in the area. Once the Node is clear, you can usually take it down swiftly before reinforcements show up.

VEHICLES	Goliath, Manta X2
PICK-UPS	Big Keg O Health, Health x2, AVRiL, Sniper Rifle, Shaped Charge, Body Armor, Redeemer

The Tank Node is completely optional, but very useful. In addition to the titular Goliath that the Node provides, it also gives the Stinger and Flak Cannon from its weapon lockers, and a pair of Mantas, useful for quickly joining the fight in a vehicle if the Goliath isn't up.

The Health Keg and Body Armor also provide a bit of sturdiness for either defense of the Tank Node itself (important in larger games), or for making a push on the Prime Nodes. Getting armored up for the Center Node fights is usually a bit of a waste, since the area is so exposed and you're likely to die in seconds from vehicle fire regardless of your armored status.

The extra Sniper Rifle here is helpful, you can bring it to bear from the rooftops in the area, picking off a few targets while you wait for the Goliath, Shaped Charge, or Redeemer to show up.

It is very easy to strike out from the Tank Node in any direction, though one of its primary uses is putting intense pressure on the Power Core once the enemy Prime Node has been seized. Assaulting the Power Core from the south with a Goliath, and a team push from the north simultaneously is very hard to stop.

One point about the Goliath, *don't* go driving it right into the Power Core area. You're begging to get taken out before you can inflict any real damage. Instead, hang back a bit and fire in, blasting vehicles and killing any exposed infantry. If the Power Core's tracked Rocket Turret is being manned, you can blast it from a distance as well.

The Goliath can also be brought up to attack or defend the Prime Node, as needed, and it is useful for shutting down vehicle access to the north south street that stretches from the Power Core to the Prime Node. This can be very helpful for preventing enemy reinforcements from reaching your Prime Node if it is under attack, or hitting the enemy Prime Node from the south when their attention is on the Center Node.

If you do want to bring the Goliath up to the Center Node, it is usually safest to do so by driving it around on your side of the map, the distance is the same, and you're less likely to eat attacks from the rear while doing so.

MAP VARIANTS: TWO FRONTS

This variant links the Tank Node to both Prime Nodes, as a result, it gives considerably more importance to the Tank Node for the offense, as it provides both a link to the enemy Prime Node, and the Goliath.

Shutting down enemy access to your Prime Node is very difficult with this layout, so you may want to have a dedicated Orb defender protecting the Prime Node while your offense pushes out from (preferably) the Tank Node to the enemy Prime Node.

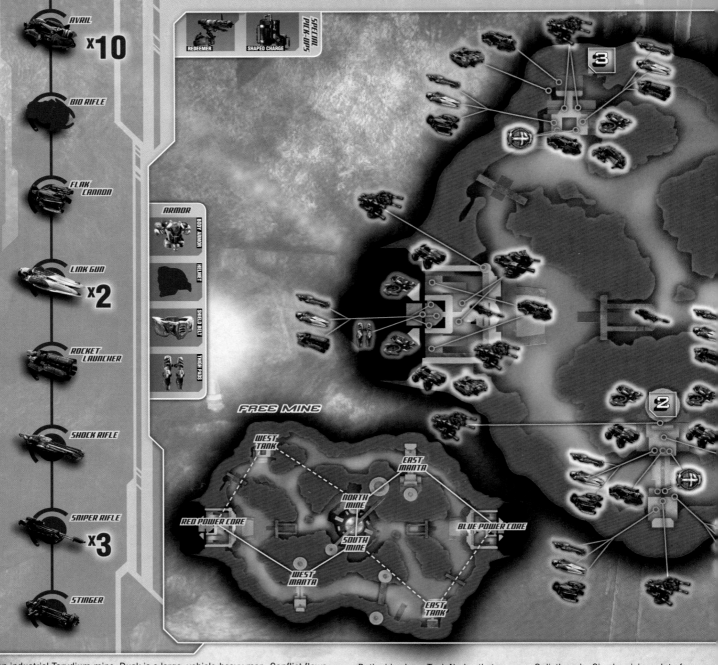

AVRIL x10

BIO RIFLE

FLAK CANNON

LINK GUN x2

ROCKET LAUNCHER

SHOCK RIFLE

SNIPER RIFLE x3

STINGER

SPECIAL PICK-UPS

REDEEMER

SHAPED CHARGE

ARMOR

BODY ARMOR

HELMET

SHIELD BELT

THIGH PADS

FREE MINE

WEST TANK

EAST MANTA

NORTH MINE

RED POWER CORE

SOUTH MINE

BLUE POWER CORE

WEST MANTA

EAST TANK

3

2

An industrial Tarydium mine, Dusk is a large, vehicle-heavy map. Conflict flows between the two bases via two different routes on the North and South, with two Nodes linking to the Power Cores.

The center of the map holds a pair of Mine Nodes that, if claimed for the same team, unlock a vault containing a Cicada and a Shield Belt.

Both sides have Tank Nodes that spawn a Goliath and a Cicada, giving a lot of heavy firepower when combined with the Goliath back at the main base, and the Cicada in the center of the map. It is possible to have *three* Goliaths on your team, and four running around on the map.

Initially, a pair of barricades blocks easy access from the Tank Nodes to the enemy side of the map. These must be taken down with the Shaped Charges located near the Mine Nodes, or with the Redeemer, located high above the center of the map on a narrow walkway.

With so many vehicles at the home bases and at the various Nodes, traveling on foot is highly inadvisable. Find a ride and use it to get to your destination. The Tank Node has some cover for fighting (or defending) on foot, but the Prime Node is quite exposed.

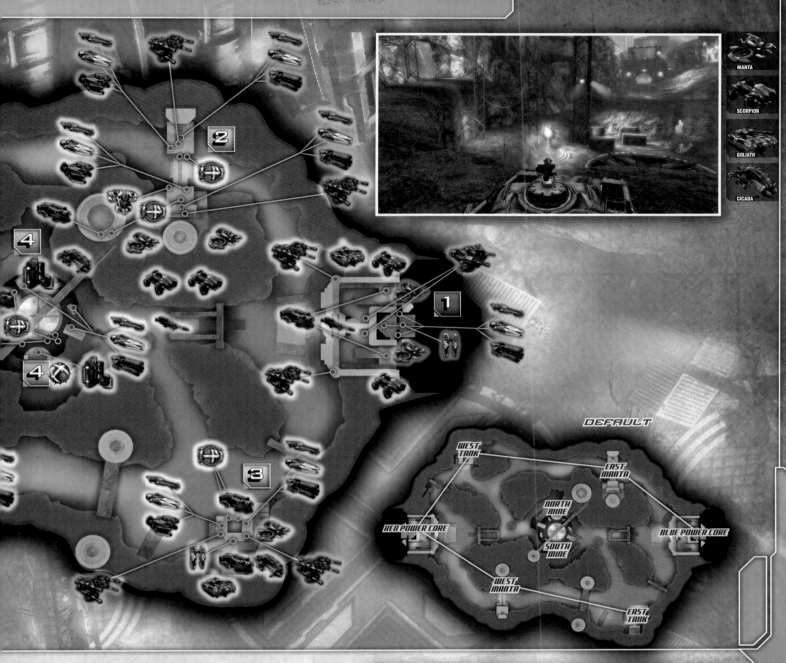

MANTA

SCORPION

GOLIATH

CICADA

DEFAULT

WEST TANK

EAST MANTA

NORTH MINE

RED POWER CORE

SOUTH MINE

BLUE POWER CORE

WEST MANTA

EAST TANK

Every non-secondary Node on the map has turrets to assist in the defense against the abundant vehicles, though they can be taken down from a great distance extremely quickly by the heavier vehicles. Still, they are helpful for cutting down on the number of light vehicles zipping about near the Nodes.

Assaulting the Power Cores requires the use of all the heavy armor available on the map. Buried as it is in a defensible base, destroying the Core is a brutal task.

VEHICLES	Manta, Scorpion x3, Goliath
PICK-UPS	AVRiL x2, Sniper Rifle, Thighpads

Both Power Cores are situated inside sturdy fortified bases, armed with twin Rocket Turrets on the interior ground level, and twin Beam Turrets mounted up on the walls to repel incoming light vehicles and aerial Cicadas.

The base is loaded with vehicles, with a Manta and three Scorpions providing rapid transit to Nodes, and the Goliath giving you some heavy muscle to begin your push on the enemy.

From the Power Core, you can quickly strike out to any of the other Nodes on the map, so carefully choose your initial destination for the Orb. Securing one of the side Nodes allows you to begin the assault on the enemy side of the map, while holding the center Mine Nodes provides access to an extra Cicada.

Be sure to grab all AVRiL from the upper floor before you set out, if your vehicle gets heavily damaged, you can still hop out and get off a shot or two before going down, hopefully destroying or crippling an opponent's ride.

Assaulting the Power Core area is difficult, generally all of the turrets must be destroyed, and the Goliath as well. Once that is done, you can drive your own Goliath into the base, or bombard the Core from above with the Cicada. No matter how you go after the Core though, you're going to be exposed to respawning defenders. There's no tricky method of accomplishing this; brute force is the only way to get in and pummel the Core.

2: PRIME NODE

VEHICLES	Manta x2, Scorpion x2
PICK-UPS	Body Armor, Health x3, AVRiL, AVRiL ammo x2

The Prime Node is extremely open and exposed, though it has a pair of Beam Turrets for defense, the vehicles spawning here are light transports: two Mantas and two Scorpions.

If you're trying to hold off enemy Cicadas or Goliaths, make the best use of the turrets and extra AVRiL ammunition present here, fighting out in the open or in a Scorpion against either is either useless or dangerous, depending on the target.

Don't hesitate to use the Scorpion's Self Destruct, with so many present on the map, they're effective as Node or Goliath bombs.

There are multiple Health pick-ups here, along with the Body Armor, so if you use the limited cover available, you can provide some very useful on-foot defense of the Node, especially against lighter vehicles, even if the turrets are all destroyed.

The Red Prime Node is located in the southwest of the map, with the Blue in the northeast.

TANK NODE

VEHICLES	Goliath, Cicada
PICK-UPS	AVRiL, Thighpads, Health x2

As with all of the other primary Nodes on the map, the Tank Node has two Beam Turrets mounted on the roof of the Node building, providing additional anti-vehicle defense.

Inside the building, you can find Thighpads and some Vials, and the roof has a pair of Health pick-ups, so you can get a little extra protection from light vehicle fire if you're defending the Node with an AVRiL.

The main attraction at the Tank Nodes is the presence of the Goliath and the Cicada. Both are powerful weapons on this map, as the Goliath can deal lethal damage to light vehicles and punish Nodes from a distance, while the Cicada can take advantage of the numerous rocky mountains to duck in and out of sight while bombarding Node defenses from a distance.

At both the Red and Blue Tank Nodes, there is a barricade present that initially prevents the Goliath from driving straight to the enemy Prime Node. To remove it, you must recover a Shaped Charge or the Redeemer from the Mine Nodes at the center of the map—otherwise, you can drive the Goliath back around to the front of your base, and from there, to the center of the map, or the long way across your own Prime Node.

The Red Tank Node is located in the northwest, with the Blue in the southeast.

4: MINE NODES

VEHICLES	Cicada
PICK-UPS	Shield Belt, Redeemer, Jump Boots, AVRiL, Sniper Rifle x3, AVRiL Ammo x2, Shaped Charge x2

The center of the map is a sprawling area, with the focus being the deep mining pit at the very middle of the map. A pair of spiraling ramps provides access for vehicles from the surrounding roads between the Tank and Prime Nodes on the north and south of the map, while vehicles can also access the middle of the map by driving straight out from either base.

When you are coming to the middle of the map from the bases, there is a large structure that looks something like a gate. You can get on top of this structure to find a Sniper Rifle, which provides an ideal perch for sniping targets down around the Mine Nodes, or firing AVRiLs at vehicles mixed up in a melee around the Nodes. The upper level is accessible via a jump pad on the Power Core facing side of the gate.

Down in the center of the pit, two unlinked Nodes, the north and south Mine Nodes provide several useful resources. There is an AVRiL and a Sniper Rifle at the bottom of the pit, as well as additional AVRiL ammunition, and some Health pick-ups for infantry combatants.

If both Nodes are held by one team, the center blast doors open up, revealing a deep mining shaft that contains a Shield Belt, and another Cicada.

The mining shaft is something of an unnecessary perk for securing victory on the map, as you can get a Cicada from the Tank Nodes, and the Shield Belt is not especially critical either, given the massive numbers of vehicles present on the map.

Still, you can use the Cicada here (or from one of the Tank Nodes) to fly up to the walkway located far above the center pit. On this walkway, you can find the Redeemer, and a pair of Jump Boots, should you need to get back down after your Cicada is blown away.

The primary reason for coming to the Mine Nodes is to secure access to the Shaped Charges and the Redeemer. Blowing open your Tank Node barricade is helpful, but being able to constantly teleport here and pick them up, then take them to the enemy Nodes or, even better, the enemy Power Core gives your offense a nice boost. Helpful, when the enemy Power Core is in such a defensible location.

Don't spend too much time wrestling over the Mine Nodes though, keep your focus on attacking (and defending) the Nodes that connect to the Power Cores.

MAP VARIANTS: FREE MINE

This variant removes the Tank Nodes completely, leaving only the Mine Nodes linked to each other, and to the Prime Nodes.

As a result, this map turns into a massive brawl over the center of the map—make good use of the sniper platforms that overlook the mine area, you can fire AVRiLs and sniper shots at targets down in the pit, while your team struggles to control the mine area.

If there are more than 8 players present when the map is started, the Tank Nodes are activated, and linked to both each Power Core, and to the closest Mine Node (dotted lines on the map). This added firepower makes the combat on the map even more hectic, and rather than the straightforward linear connectivity with less players, you can now reach the enemy Power Core via either a purely south or north route using the Tank Nodes. The crisscrossing connectivity also forces constant offense and defense on multiple paths—it is entirely possible to be hitting the enemy Core while your own is under attack.

AVRIL x3

BIO RIFLE

FLAK CANNON

LINK GUN

ROCKET LAUNCHER

SHOCK RIFLE x2

SNIPER RIFLE x6

STINGER

SPECIAL PICKUPS
REDEEMER

ARMOR
BODY ARMOR
HELMET
SHIELD BELT
THIGH PADS

1 RED POWER CORE

2 RED PRIME

3 CENTER

4 FLOOD GATE

2 BLUE PRIME

1 BLUE POWER CORE

Set deep beneath the Necris city of Absalom, the ruined floodgate presents a dark and decayed battlefield for the mirrored Necris forces to battle.

This is one of the more extensive, Necris-only Warfare maps in the game, with a critical secondary Floodgate Node in the center of the map providing an alternate route to victory.

When held, the Floodgate Node starts a 60-second countdown timer. If it is not destroyed or recaptured with an Orb, it floods the enemy Power Core, dealing 20% damage. The Floodgate Node can *always* damage the enemy Core, regardless of the current Node control situation.

As a result, the battle on this map flows between the normal Prime and Center Node fights, and a constant struggle to either control the Floodgate Node for the full duration, or to occasionally break enemy control of it long enough to reset the countdown.

Otherwise, Floodgate is a mix of heavy-duty exterior vehicle battles, and more intimate close range fighting—every Node on the map is located within a ruined Necris building, giving infantry a fighting chance against vehicles.

Outside, the mighty Darkwalkers and the Nemesis tanks can slug it out on the wide open ground between the Nodes, making travel via Hoverboard rather dangerous. Taking a Viper or Scavenger to reach most Nodes is usually safer.

I'm not swimming in THAT

While the Floodgate Node triggers a Nanoblack flood of the enemy Power Core, it also causes the level of the Nanoblack in front of the enemy base to rise. This actually raises the water level high enough to hamper movement, or shut down a Hoverboard. Keep this in mind if you happen to be travelling through the open field while a flood is in progress.

Your team should decide early if you're going to pursue the Floodgate trap aggressively, or if you'd rather focus your attentions on the normal push to the enemy Power Core.

Because you can break the Floodgate countdown by running an Orb to it, you may be able to tie up enemy players by occasionally attacking the Floodgate Node to draw their attention, then shifting the attacker to the Center or Prime Node fights.

On the other hand, if you're going to actively hold the Floodgate Node, you need to have defenders in place to stop an enemy Orb carrier, and to prevent an enemy push from destroying the Node completely. Be careful about fighting to a stalemate over the Floodgate Node, you don't want to go into overtime if you can help it.

NIGHTSHADE DEFENSE

The Nightshade *can* get into the area around the Floodgate Node, and by dropping its deployables around the entrances and using its beam to heal the Node, you can greatly increase your team's chances of holding the Node for the duration of the countdown.

1: POWER CORE

VEHICLES	Viper x2, Nightshade, Darkwalker
PICK-UPS	AVRiL, Sniper Rifle

The Power Core area is more exposed than the Nodes on the map, making enemy vehicles a serious threat if you are pushed back to your Core. There is a single tracked Beam Turret on the north side of the Core that can be used to aid in defense, though it isn't likely to stand up long to a serious offensive push.

The Core area has a solid stock of initial vehicles, the twin Vipers can be used to quickly reach the Prime Node or the Floodgate Node, and the Nightshade is excellent for defending the Core area. However, you need to be sure to set up the defenses when the Prime Node is threatened, not when they're already at your doorstep.

The Darkwalker is a powerful tool for controlling the open spaces between the Prime Node and the Center Node, but it is too slow to participate in an early rush. Consider moving out to secure Nodes first, then teleporting back to move it forward.

Both an AVRiL and a Sniper Rifle can be procured here, helpful for fighting in the open expanses outside, as well as defending any of the Nodes, or the Core itself.

NIGHTSHADE ABUSE

The conveniently varying height levels on here provide the perfect setup for dropping EMP Mines, Spider Mines, or the Energy Shield on top of a friendly Viper (or the Nemesis, with a bit of work).

Ignoring the fun of mobile EMP bombs, once the map situation stabilizes a bit, if you secure the Center Node, bring the Nightshade forward to defend it. You can really ruin an attacker's day by planting deployable traps all around the critical middle Node.

2: PRIME NODE

VEHICLES	None
PICK-UPS	Sniper Rifle, Shock Rifle

The Prime Node is situated within a large building that runs north-south, connected to the Floodgate Node building via a small bridge near the center of the building.

Inside the building, the hollowed out chamber has two floors, with an upper ledge running around the interior of the building. In some places, you can shoot out through windows or duck out onto an exterior ledge to take shots at distant vehicles or infantry, a task aided by the presence of the Sniper Rifle near the Node.

The Shock Rifle isn't in an immediately obvious location, you need to go outside the Node towards the center of the map, and the Shock Rifle is tucked away on the south side of the building. Shock Combos make a useful tool for defending the Nodes inside the buildings, so it's worth picking up if you're staying in the area.

There are numerous ground level entrances to the Prime Node building, though they are too small for the larger vehicles to penetrate. Don't be surprised to see a Viper or Scavenger squeeze inside though, have an AVRiL ready to deal with them if they do so.

The south side of the building has a drop into a tunnel that passes from the Power Core side of the map into the center area. You can also jump up from the tunnel via a jump pad. This is usually the quickest way to reach the Node from your base, but it can be useful to assault the enemy Prime Node as well.

The only healing available here is a six-pack of Vials; it's not much, but if you're defending on foot, take what you can get.

VEHICLES	Scavenger, Nemesis
PICK-UPS	Sniper Rifle, Health X2

The Center Node is located in a medium sized building at the north edge of the map, just at the edge of the massive Nanoblack lake that dominates the landscape.

The Center Node has three entrances, a narrow tunnel with stairs leading up to the Node from the south, and two larger tunnels on the east and west side, accessible to most vehicles.

Inside, the Node is situated up on a slightly raised platform, and a pair of Health pick-ups provide some much needed restorative power to an otherwise health-poor map.

The area around the Node is fairly constrained, close range weaponry

and vehicle fire can have a devastating effect on defenders. Generally, if you're going to defend the Center Node, you need to do it from outside, before attackers get close.

Fortunately, the building is well-suited to just this sort of defense. You can pick up yet another Sniper Rifle here, and there are three upper ledges accessible via jump pads and a short flight of stairs. Each ledge looks out over a different area of the battlefield, so you can easily cover approaching vehicles or infantry. Bring an AVRiL to complement your Sniper Rifle, and you can damage or destroy attackers before they get anywhere near the Node.

FLY BY WIRE

The Redeemer can easily be flown in with its secondary fire to either of the Prime Nodes, making it a great tool for busting the enemy's Node, or saving your own Power Core from attack.

Make a point of timing the Redeemer, there are precious few special pick-ups on this level, and any edge can help your team.

4: FLOODGATE NODE

VEHICLES	None
PICK-UPS	Body Armor, AVRiL, Rocket Launcher, Sniper Rifle, Health x2

The Floodgate Node unleashes a torrent of damaging Nanoblack on the enemy Power Core (as well as raising the water level on the north end of the map) if you can manage to capture and hold it for 60 seconds after it is fully constructed.

Once the Floodgate has flushed the enemy Core, it reverts to neutral, so it must be recaptured and fully rebuilt before it begins another flood countdown.

The Node area itself is a very sizable building, similar in construction to the Prime Node buildings. On the far north end of the building, you can find a suit of Body Armor, and by taking a lift up from the armor, an

Following the walkway north leads directly out of the Floodgate Node, passing a Rocket Launcher to reach a small raised building near the center of the map. Inside, you can find the Redeemer, an extremely useful tool for aiding in the offensive push on the enemy Prime Node, or eliminating a frustrating defensive Darkwalker.

Back inside the Floodgate Node, you can find a Sniper Rifle, Health pick-ups, and even some Vials to help with interior defense. The raised ledges on the upper floor are usually the safer place to guard the Node, if you're trying to hold it for the full countdown timer (or to assault it, for that matter).

The Floodgate building can be reached

AVRIL
x3

BIO RIFLE

FLAK CANNON

LINK GUN

ROCKET LAUNCHER

SHOCK RIFLE

SNIPER RIFLE
x3

STINGER

SPECIAL PICKUPS

SHAPED CHARGE

REDEEMER

ARMOR

BODY ARMOR

HELMET

SHIELD BELT

THIGH PADS

RED POWER CORE

1 2 WEST

3 AIR

Islander is one of the smaller Warfare maps, but it is also quite distinct in that it is one of the few completely asymmetrical maps. Indeed, more than even a bit of variance in the terrain, Islander has a completely unique layout for the Red and Blue bases.

Rather than a traditional Warfare Node battle, Islander plays out more like a siege mission. The Blue team receives a fortified base protected by multiple turrets and barricades, and the Red team receives heavy vehicles.

The single Prime Node on the map is located right in front of the Red Power Core, making Orb protection and recapture easy, forcing the Blue team to make constant Orb runs to capture the Node, and damage the Red Power Core slightly before falling to respawning defenders and trying again.

4

BLUE POWER CORE

Conversely, Red attackers must first penetrate the Blue base's barricades to allow heavy vehicles a route into the Power Core area, all while destroying the turrets that can easily shut down isolated attackers.

Finally, an unlinked Air Node throws a wrinkle into the conflict, as either team can claim it, and the twin Raptors that it provides give either team a serious advantage, both in terms of aerial firepower, and by allowing flight out to the small structure located off the southern coast of the island. It holds the Redeemer, which can be extremely useful for pounding one of the Cores, or clearing out defenders.

Despite the small size of the map, Islander packs a lot of unusual tactical challenges, a nice change of pace from the more "normal" Warfare battles.

1: RED POWER CORE

VEHICLES	Hellbender, Paladin, Goliath x2
PICK-UPS	None

2: PRIME NODE

VEHICLES	None
PICK-UPS	AVRiL, Health x2

The Red Power Core area is housed in an abandoned building, and the Red team's vehicles all spawn in the building here.

With a Paladin, Hellbender, and *two* Goliaths, the Red team has the advantage of some serious firepower, but the vehicles are only useful for defense (or exterior turret destruction) at the Blue base until the barricades are blown.

Doing so is not difficult, it's more a matter of how long the Blue team can prevent you from doing so, rather than if they can stop you completely, which is almost never, unless you're playing with incredibly unbalanced teams.

You can (and should) drive a heavy vehicle up to the Air Node to provide defense, the Hellbender works well for this task, as it can get up more quickly than the heavy Paladin or Goliath, and easily defend against enemy infantry from the Blue side.

Defending the Power Core itself is usually a matter of using your Orb to defend the Prime Node while your offense pushes on the blue base. The Blue offense must take down the Orb defender first before they can even begin to work on the Prime Node, giving you time to respawn and re-engage.

At least one of your vehicles can also be used on defense, the Paladin works reasonably well for this role, as it can park itself in front of the Node, shield incoming projectiles, use its close range blast against infantry nearby, and take slow but lethal shots at Blue team attackers coming through the midfield.

The Prime Node is located inside a small building just outside the Red base area, and immediately outside the Power Core enclosure.

Just below the Prime Node on the north side is a pair of Health pick-ups and the AVRiL, otherwise, there's not much to the Prime Node room itself. It's an open space for (largely) infantry battles to take place.

The Red team can defend the Prime Node from the front by parking a heavy vehicle in front of the jump pads up from the AVRiL to the Prime Node building, restricting access fairly easily, at least until the vehicle is taken out.

Defending the Prime Node with an Orb is the easiest defensive technique, as the Orb is only needed otherwise to capture the Air Node quickly. Its proximity to the Red base makes it considerably more difficult for the Blue team to capture, plus the Blue team usually needs to use their Orb to capture this Node fast enough to deal a bit of damage to the Red Power Core.

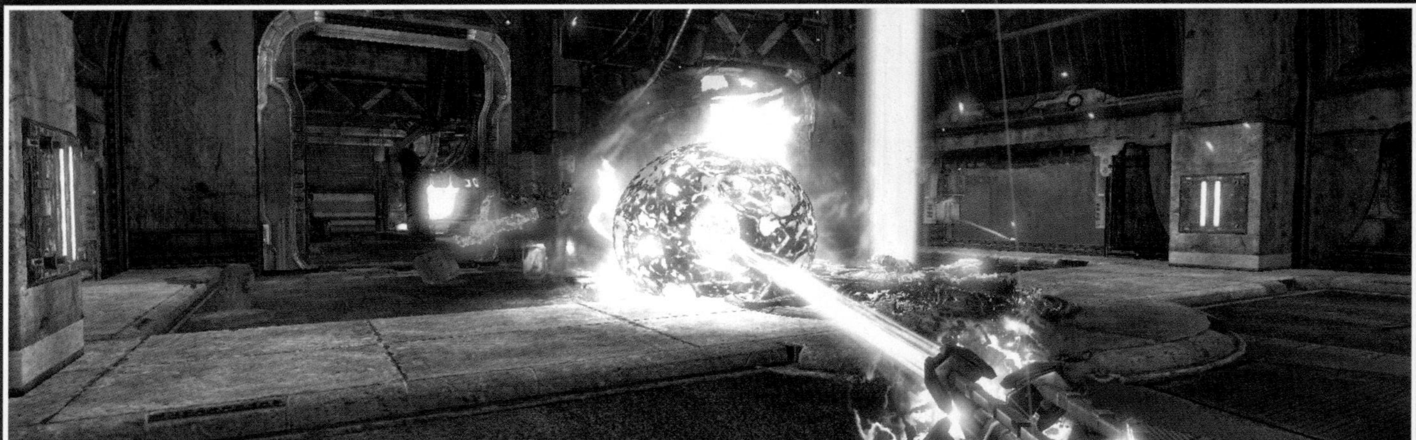

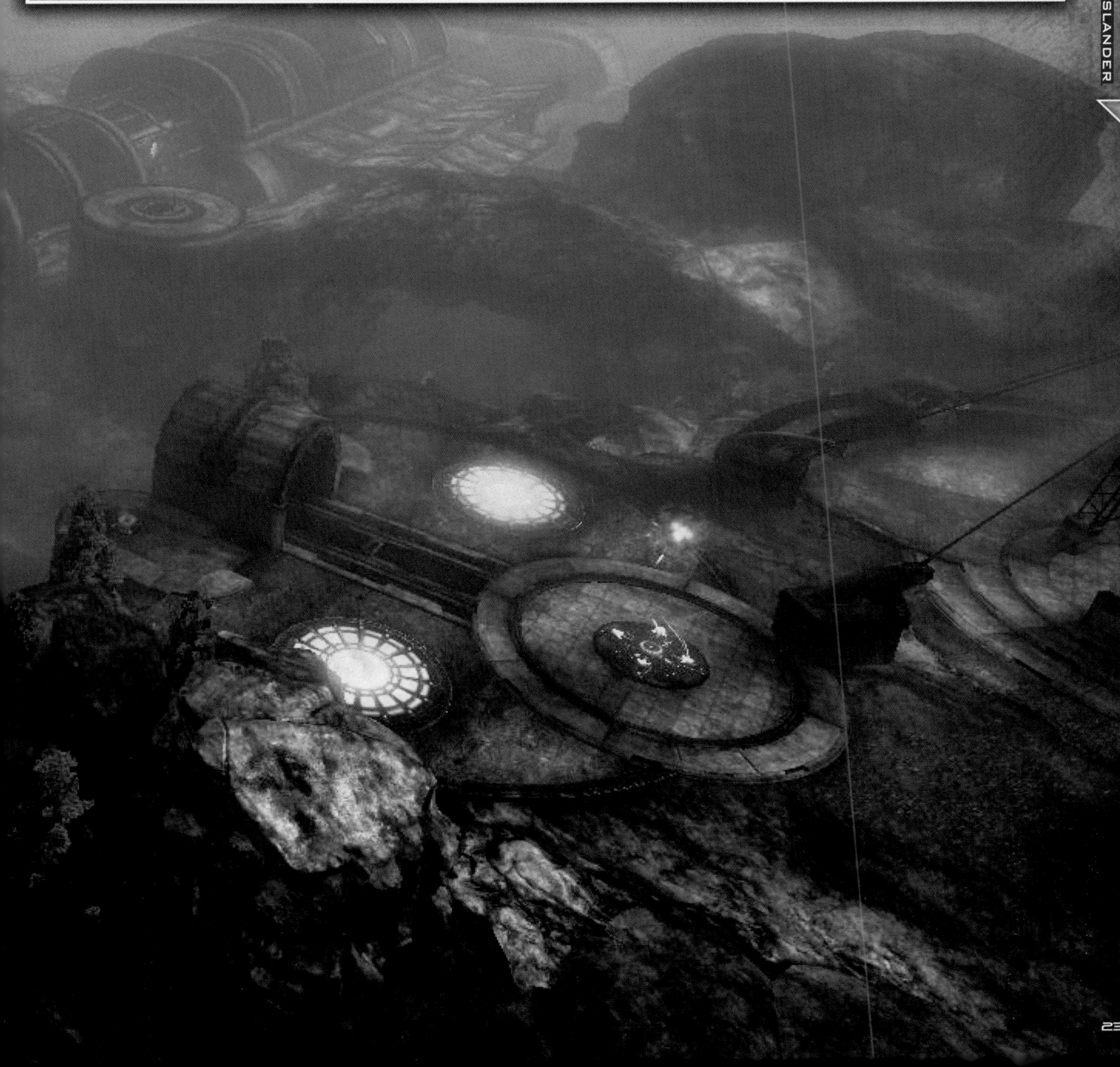

AIR NODE

VEHICLES	Raptor x2
PICK-UPS	AVRiL, Sniper Rifle

The Air Node is an important support node for both teams, though it is somewhat easier for the Red team to capture and hold.

It is located up atop a high plateau on the north side of the map, accessible from below via a jump pad, or from a sloping ramp closer to the Blue base.

The ramp entrance also has a Sniper Rifle and an AVRiL, both handy pick-ups on the way up to the Node, as the AVRiL can be used against the Raptors if they are already spawned, and the Sniper Rifle can be used to good effect from the lofty vantage point offered by the area around the Node.

Capturing the Node causes two Raptors to spawn, highly useful

transport for the Red team to penetrate the Blue base and attack the turrets and Power Core within.

For the Blue team, the Raptors are less useful for assaulting the Prime Node and Power Core, but securing them as a defensive measure is useful.

Both teams need to use the Raptors to reach the Redeemer, located as it is on an otherwise inaccessible structure just off the edge of the island, almost directly across from the Air Node.

The Redeemer is extremely valuable to either team. It can crack the Prime Node instantly, or better still, used in conjunction with an Orb push, can be used to hammer the Power Core in either base.

There are two jump pads up at the Air Node, and both are useful. The one closer to the Red base launches you to a platform above the Prime Node building, where the sole Body Armor on the map rests. From here, it is a short hop down to the Prime Node, helpful both for Blue attackers and Red defenders.

Taking the pad closer to the Blue base deposits you on the Shaped Charge platform, very useful for assaulting the Blue base.

4: BLUE POWER CORE

VEHICLES	None
PICK-UPS	Sniper Rifle, AVRiL

The Blue Power Core area is actually a heavily fortified base. With two Beam Turrets at the barricaded entrance to the base, and two more Rocket Turrets inside overlooking the Power Core, the Blue team does not suffer from the lack of vehicles when it comes to defending their turf.

Up on the walls, you can also acquire a Sniper Rifle and an AVRiL, both useful for defending the base.

The entrance to the base is blocked by a pair of barricades, as is the eastern road route, initially restricting the heavy Red team vehicles from getting inside the base at all.

Just outside the base, a small raised platform holds a Shaped Charge that can be used by either team. The Red team needs the charge to blast the

barricades to gain vehicle access to the Blue base, and the Blue team can use it as a very effective Power Core bomb. Break the Prime Node with the Blue Orb, then hammer the Power Core before the defenders can recapture the Node.

The Shaped Charge platform also holds two AVRiL ammo packs, very handy for the Blue team defenders to help handle the push of Red team vehicles.

There isn't a lot of complicated terrain inside the base. A thick outer wall runs around the base forming a circle, the area inside the walls is open enough for vehicles to get through, and the very center houses a large structure, at the base of which is located the Blue Power Core.

The Blue Power Core is resting in coolant tank, lethal for infantry, so it cannot be approached directly on foot. Red team attackers must fire at it from a distance, preferably with a vehicle.

The easiest way in to the base to assault the Core is with a Raptor, so the Blue team must be vigilant, and quickly destroy any Raptors that set off

from the Air Node, or recapture the Air Node as quickly as possible, possibly burning an Orb run to snatch the Raptors. The Raptors are very useful against the Paladin and the Goliaths, and help to ease the pressure on the Blue base itself.

MAP VARIANTS: NECRIS

Another map that takes place during the Necris invasion of Taryd, this variant replaces the Axon forces with Necris vehicles, and changes the appearance of the map slightly.

The overall flow of the map does not change, though the Nightshade provides some additional defensive muscle for the Blue (Necris) Team.

Strangely, the Blue Team becomes offense on this map, with the Red Team holding the base.

The Necris team possesses a Nightshade, two Nemeses, and the mighty Darkwalker to begin with.

Note that the Air Node still provides Raptors to either team.

AVRIL

BIO RIFLE

FLAK CANNON

LINK GUN

ROCKET LAUNCHER **x2**

SHOCK RIFLE **x2**

SNIPER RIFLE **x2**

STINGER **x2**

SPECIAL PICKUPS

UDAMAGE   JUMP BOOTS

ARMOR

BODY ARMOR

HELMET

SHIELD BELT

THIGH PADS

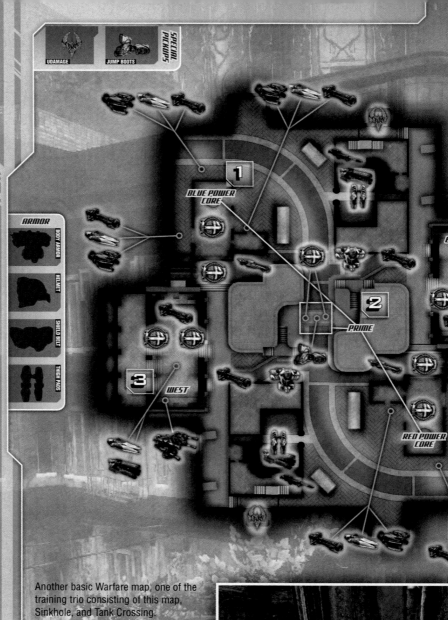

BLUE POWER CORE 1

EAST 3

2 PRIME

WEST 3

RED POWER CORE 1

Another basic Warfare map, one of the training trio consisting of this map, Sinkhole, and Tank Crossing.

This map teaches some of the basics of using secondary, unlinked Nodes for special effects. In this case, capturing both support nodes raises the enemy Power Core out of their base, exposing it to attack from a distance.

Otherwise, the map is fairly simple. There are actually no vehicles present at all—an oddity for Warfare. You *do* still have the Hoverboard for transit, and since this map is fairly small, you can zip between Nodes quickly.

1:8 POWER CORE

VEHICLES	None
PICK-UPS	Health x2, Thighpads, Shock Rifle, Rocket Launcher, Sniper Rifle, UDamage

The Power Core area is a large building, with the Power Core nestled safely within the walls, protected from attack by its position, and respawning defenders appearing close by.

You can find a Health pick-up inside the building near the Core, and another in the alley outside, near the Shock Rifle.

It is possible to get up onto the roof of the building, either from a jump pad inside, or if you really had to, by Impact jumping up from near the Shock Rifle.

This is handy for attackers and defenders, as the elevation gives a good line of sight to the alley leading to the closest side Node, and to the midfield near the Prime Node.

Should the Power Core become raised and exposed (due to the enemy team holding both support nodes), you may need to protect it from the roof while your team scrambles to break one of the side Nodes or the Prime Node with your Orb. You really don't want a turret from one of the side Nodes blasting away at your Core unimpeded.

Outside the Power Core, there is a large building and alley network that contains the Sniper Rifle and the Rocket Launcher, as well as the important UDamage power-up. This area is southwest of the Red Core, northeast of the Blue Core.

The Rocket Launcher is easily accessible from the Core area, the Sniper Rifle is located up inside a building that has a decent line of sight to the open ground around the Core.

are proficient snipers. There are also a few Vials down below the Sniper Rifle, which, if you're camping out sniping anyway, you may as well gather to get buffed up a bit.

The UDamage is tucked away in the alley leading to the Core, blocked by a fence. On the UDamage side, you can get out to the Core area with a jump pad, but you have to take a longer path in (again, short of Impact jumping).

The UDamage is critical for attacking the enemy Core, so if you happen to have a sniper on patrol in the building near it, be sure they're timing its respawn, denying the enemy the ability to get to your core while damage amped is a valuable support role.

2: PRIME NODE

VEHICLES	None
PICK-UPS	Jump Boots, Health x2

The Prime Node is located on a small raised bridge area at the center of the map, not far from either Core. A pair of stairs on either side allows for quick access to the Core.

Generally, this Node changes hands constantly throughout the match, as both teams use their Orb to break the Node, then hold it. As long as an Orb defender is present, you're forced to deal with them first before you can damage the Node.

This is good training for other Warfare maps, as Orb defense is an important skill, and with no vehicles here, your best DM players have a chance to shine, much like they do on Warfare maps where the Nodes are in protected interior areas.

Just below the Node, you can find a pair of Health pick-ups to recharge, and the Jump Boots. The Boots are useful both for quickly leaping up to the Node, and perhaps even more for reaching either the Body Armor nearby, or the UDamage at either base.

3: SIDE NODE

VEHICLES	None
PICK-UPS	Body Armor, Health x2, Stinger

The unlinked side Nodes are not necessary for securing a victory on this map, as only the single Prime Node in the center of the map is required to expose the enemy Power Core to attack. However, by securing both side Nodes for your team, you cause the enemy Power Core to rise from its position inside the enemy base, exposing it to attack from a great distance.

While there are no vehicles on the map, both side Nodes *do* provide access to a tracked Beam Turret. The track on this turret actually extends into the midfield, and it has several uses. You can protect the side Node from attack, reach into the midfield enough to harass players moving around the Prime Node, and perhaps most importantly, one of the turrets can be used to attack the enemy Power Core when it is raised and exposed.

The Beam Turret is accessible via a jump pad from the ground level, and the track that it rests on can be used by a player to walk out into the center area of the map.

This is important, because even if the turret has been destroyed, you can still walk out and drop down to a ledge holding Body Armor. This is very helpful, given the infantry combat focus on this map. The only other way to get up to it safely is with Jump Boots, or if you don't mind some damage, with an Impact Jump.

Note that the turret itself can't fire directly at the Prime Node, only the Power Core if it is exposed. There are large shielding walls protecting the Prime Node—you can use it to suppress incoming infantry or the enemy Orb Carrier of course.

The area around the Node itself is a largely open warehouse, with a few boxes on one end providing some cover, and behind them, the Stinger. Two Health Pick-ups provide useful restoration, especially if you're traveling through the area to reach the back alleys near the enemy Power Core.

ONYX COAST

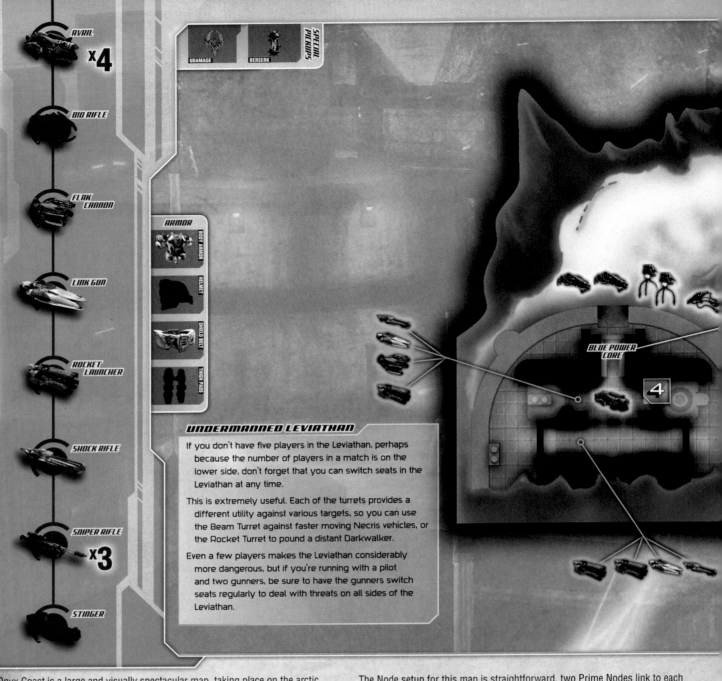

AVRIL x4

BIO RIFLE

FLAK CANNON

LINK GUN

ROCKET LAUNCHER

SHOCK RIFLE

SNIPER RIFLE x3

STINGER

SPECIAL PICKUPS
- UDAMAGE
- BERSERK

ARMOR
- BODY ARMOR
- HELMET
- SHIELD BELT
- THIGH PADS

BLUE POWER CORE

4

UNDERMANNED LEVIATHAN

If you don't have five players in the Leviathan, perhaps because the number of players in a match is on the lower side, don't forget that you can switch seats in the Leviathan at any time.

This is extremely useful. Each of the turrets provides a different utility against various targets, so you can use the Beam Turret against faster moving Necris vehicles, or the Rocket Turret to pound a distant Darkwalker.

Even a few players makes the Leviathan considerably more dangerous, but if you're running with a pilot and two gunners, be sure to have the gunners switch seats regularly to deal with threats on all sides of the Leviathan.

Onyx Coast is a large and visually spectacular map, taking place on the arctic coastline. Jagged rock formations dominate the landscape, providing cover and breaking up line of sight near the two bases.

It's notable for being not only an asymmetrical map, but also for presenting a unique tactical challenge to both teams. The map is Axon vs. Necris, which is not unique, but the vehicles involved are.

The Node setup for this map is straightforward, two Prime Nodes link to each other and to the two Power Cores. The only support node however, is critical to the battle. The Bridge Node, as you might expect, controls a large bridge in the center of the map. The bridge passes over an artic river below, and it is the only way for the Leviathan to pass from the Red (Axon) side of the map to the Blue (Necris) side.

As a result, the combat on this map is a constant battle to secure and defend the Bridge Node by the Axon forces, against the urgent need to destroy the Node before the Leviathan can cross the bridge.

The Axon forces only receive a pair of Mantas—and the devastating Leviathan! In contrast, the Necris are heavily loaded with vehicles, giving them an edge, but only if they can manage to take down the Leviathan first.

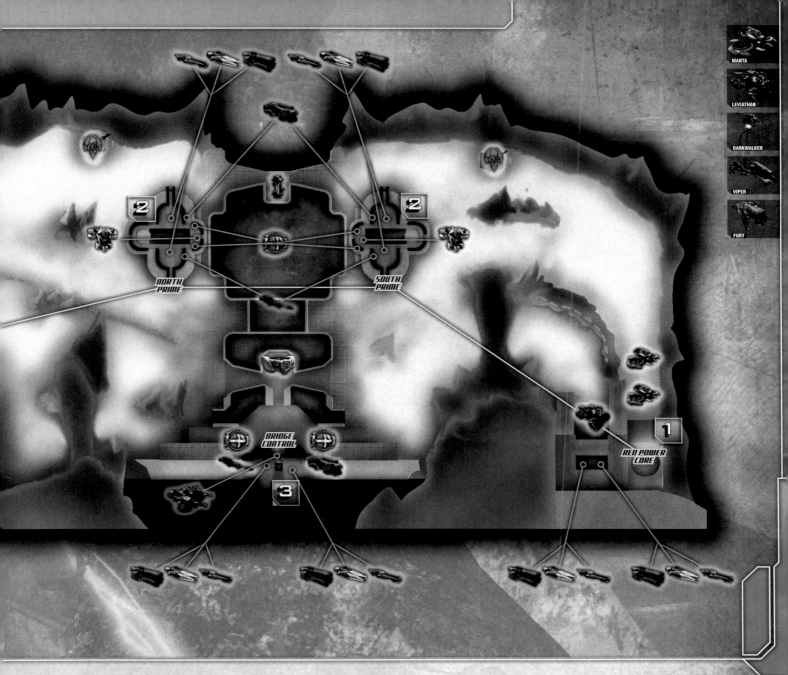

MANTA

LEVIATHAN

DARKWALKER

VIPER

FURY

NORTH PRIME

SOUTH PRIME

BRIDGE CONTROL

RED POWER CORE

If the Leviathan *does* manage to get across the bridge and the Necris forces do not have their vehicles present, their Power Core is in critical danger of being rapidly destroyed.

If the Necris can hold on to the Bridge Node, they must still contend with a parked Leviathan blasting at either Prime Node. As a result, it is difficult or impossible to attack the Red Core while the Leviathan is active.

Once it is destroyed however, the lack of vehicles on the Red team's side becomes telling, and the Necris can usually manage to push into the Red base to deal damage before the Leviathan respawns.

While the Leviathan is downed, Axon forces must make use of the AVRiLs located at each Node, stay under cover, and attempt to take down the Necris vehicles before they can push through the Nodes and siege the Red Power Core.

ONE PIECE AT A TIME

Fighting the Leviathan if it is fully loaded is a dangerous and messy operation, there's no easy way to deal with that much firepower.

However, remember that all four turrets on the corners of the Leviathan *can* be destroyed, and they are far more fragile than the Leviathan itself.

Take down the turrets, and you remove a lot of the danger, rendering it highly vulnerable to attack from the flanks or above with the Vipers or the Fury, and make it safer for AVRiL armed players to pound away.

1: RED POWER CORE

VEHICLES	Leviathan, Manta x2
PICK-UPS	None

The Red Power Core is located around a bend in the terrain from the midfield, shielded from immediate view by large rock formations. This is the last line of defense the Core area has however, as the base itself is actually quite exposed. Players spawn inside, but outside, there is a large docking bay for the Leviathan, two Mantas on top, and that's about all.

The Power Core is located up the "lower" road to the base, but incoming Necris forces can easily attack it from either direction, or even from atop the base. Two Mantas usually aren't enough to dissuade them from pushing in with their greater vehicle complement.

Being pushed back to the Red Power Core is a dire situation for the Axon team, and they should make it a priority to recapture the Prime Node immediately, or risk suffering serious or critical damage to the Core.

2: PRIME NODE

VEHICLES	None
PICK-UPS	Body Armor, Health x2, Sniper Rifle, AVRiL, UDamage

Both Prime Nodes are situated in identical structures, one on each side of the river that separates the Red and Blue sides of the map.

At the front of the Node buildings, facing the Bridge Node, a lift can be used to reach the upper floor. This is useful, as the Node itself is located on the second floor of the building.

Note that it is possible to lift jump with the lift over the "cages" that surround the lift on the way up. If there are active defenders near the Node, you don't want to be forced to walk out from the lift and right into their fire if you can help it.

A lift at the rear of the building provides similar access, but deposits its rider on a more open area on the second floor, rather than the narrow channel of the other lift.

The lower floor of the base is accessible through several small doorways. Inside, you can find a suit of Body Armor conveniently located next to a pair of Health pick-ups, great for restoring and suiting up for protecting the Node.

The upper floor has good visibility to the rest of the map, and with both an AVRiL and a Sniper Rifle present, you can protect the Node against infantry or vehicle threats. There is good cover too, so even enemy Darkwalker or Leviathan fire can be avoided. (Well, everything except the Leviathan's singularity cannon at least…).

One last and very important note: a UDamage power-up is just outside each Prime Node, a short distance down the coast. This is crucial both for assaulting the Prime Nodes and for powering up a vehicle to participate in midfield combat, even more so for the Necris than the Axon. It is close enough to reach the Berserk on the central bridge as well, allowing for a player to achieve lethal Juggernaut status.

3: BRIDGE NODE

VEHICLES	None
PICK-UPS	Shield Belt, Berserk, Sniper Rifle, AVRiL, Health x2

Located directly between the two Prime Nodes, the Bridge Node is situated on a small platform above the icy river below. It is accessible from both sides of the map, and from a narrower bridge across the water in front of it (too small for the Leviathan to cross).

If the Red team holds the Bridge Node, it extends a bridge across the center of the river, large enough for the Leviathan to cross.

As a result, when the Leviathan is up, the Red team tends to focus most of their energy on capturing and holding this Node long enough for the Leviathan to cross. The Blue team must do everything in their power to prevent this from happening, lest a fully loaded Leviathan lay waste to their team and their Power Core.

The area around the Node has several useful goodies, you can find a Shield Belt out on the bridge in front of the Node, and in the immediate vicinity, a pair of Health pick-ups.

A jump pad is behind the Node and it leads up into the building beside the Node. The jump pad deposits you on an upper ledge, from there you can drop down to two lower ledges, one holding the AVRiL, the other the Sniper Rifle.

In addition, there is a Rocket Turret mounted on the upper level of the building overlooking the Bridge Node. This is useful for either team trying to hold (or destroy) the Node, though its line of sight is somewhat restricted by the abundant bridge cables and rocky formations on either side of the map.

Travel from the Bridge Node to either Prime Node is simple, even on foot. There are a pair of jump pads beside the Shield Belt spawn that drop you right in front of one of the Prime Nodes.

In addition to the narrow bridge that passes in front of the Bridge Node, there is another one on the other end of the river near the shore—this bridge also connects the two Prime Nodes to one another, but more importantly, it is the spawn point of the Berserk power-up.

Keep an eye on this, in combination with the two UDamage power-ups, you can cause some serious damage, especially since there are two jump pads beside the Berserk, just like the Shield Belt. A Berserk Leviathan is *not* a friendly sight.

4: BLUE POWER CORE

VEHICLES	Viper x2, Fury, Darkwalker x2
PICK-UPS	None

The Blue Power Core area is similar to the Red base in that the base itself, while sizable, holds little of value for the defenders in terms of pick-ups.

The Blue base *does* have an abundance of vehicles, something the Red team does not enjoy. With two Vipers, the Fury, and *two* Darkwalkers, you have all the equipment you need to battle against the Leviathan, and press home your advantage once the Leviathan is destroyed.

The Vipers are particularly notable, as they can be used to self-destruct bomb any of the Nodes, since they can jump high enough to reach the exposed Prime Nodes, or easily get across the water to the Bridge Node.

The Fury is handy for harassing the Red team when the Leviathan is down, just be careful about flying it around in the open when the Leviathan is active. Its Beam Turret can shred you, and that's ignoring all the other turrets if they are manned.

The Darkwalkers are your heavy assault vehicles, though they can't stand up to the Leviathan's main cannon, they can do solid damage if you use the rocks for cover. Once the Leviathan is destroyed, they can stomp across the midfield, blasting the Nodes and clearing the way for your team to siege the Axon base.

POWER SURGE

AVRIL x5

BIO RIFLE

FLAK CANNON

LINK GUN

ROCKET LAUNCHER x2

SHOCK RIFLE x3

SNIPER RIFLE x2

STINGER x2

SPECIAL PICKUPS
BERSERK | INVISIBILITY | JUMP BOOTS | REDEEMER

ARMOR
BODY ARMOR | HELMET | SHIELD BELT | THIGH PADS

EAST TANK

4 PRIME

2

4 PRIME

3

WEST TANK

One of the larger and more complex Warfare maps, both in terms of size and terrain, and in the possible assault and defensive tactics, Power Surge takes place underground, inside an immense Tarydium mining operation.

A monstrously huge digging machine dominates the center of the map. It's a huge earthmover used for processing the massive amounts of Tarydium that the corporations on Taryd battle over. The digger serves as the critical support node in this mission.

CAVERNOUS

The winding pathways between the various parts of the map are surprisingly open, in spite of the rock and Tarydium formations scattered about the level.

You can generally get from any Node to any other Node with a minimum of hunting for a route, this is particularly useful for the faster vehicles. Flying in with a Scorpion bomb from an unexpected angle is always a nice treat for the other team.

Likewise, the Manta can make good use of its maneuverability to zip through the various channels to intercept an enemy Orb carrier, attack the enemies Tank Node, or get to the Mine Node quickly.

On foot, make good use of the rock formations to provide some cover from enemy vehicles, while you dodge in and out between AVRiL shots. The distances aren't excessive with your Hoverboard, just don't go boarding around the level in the open near contested Nodes, you make a juicy target for the abundant vehicles.

MANTA

HELLBENDER

SCORPION

PALADIN

GOLIATH

BLUE POWER CORE

[1]

[1]

RED POWER CORE

Similar to the special Node on Floodgate, when the Mine Node is fully constructed for one team, it triggers a 60 second countdown. When the timer elapses, the enemy Power Core is blasted with the titular power surge from the miner, dealing 20% damage each time, then reverting to neutral, uncontrolled status.

In addition to the support node, the Prime Nodes on this map are linked directly to one another, and to an additional Tank Node that provides some heavy Goliath firepower.

The total lack of armor and abundant vehicles on this map make fighting on foot around the primary Nodes dangerous, but the central Mine Node has terrain favorable for battling on foot, as well as a very useful sniping perch for using the Sniper Rifle or AVRiL from elevated cover.

1: POWER CORE

VEHICLES	Manta x2, Scorpion x2, Hellbender
PICK-UPS	AVRiL, Sniper Rifle, Stinger, Redeemer

The Power Core bases are sizable structures, surrounding the Power Core within with a ringed outer wall, and an upper walkway on the outside that holds the Sniper Rifle.

The upper ledge is accessible via jump pads all around the Power Core building, and you can reach the Core within by walking through one of the doorways to get below the Core.

Inside, the Power Core is suspended in the center of the building, and four jump pads on the floor below allow quick travel between the ground level and the upper ledges.

On offense, attacking this room must be done on foot, and bouncing between the upper and lower floors constantly works well to buy extra time while angry defenders chase you.

Outside the Core room, each Power Core base has plenty of vehicles present for transit and combat. Two Mantas and two Scorpions provide rapid transport, and the Hellbender is helpful for assaulting any of the Power Cores, as well as moving two players about the battlefield.

An AVRiL located just outside the base near the Orb spawner is an important asset, given the amount of open terrain on the map. Despite the presence of numerous rocky walls breaking up the ground between the Nodes, the space around the Nodes (particularly the Prime Nodes) is quite open, giving plenty of room for vehicle warfare.

From the Power Core, you can strike out to either your Tank Node, your Prime Node, or the Mine Node at the center of the map.

The Mine Node route is notable, because if you take a path directly towards the enemy Power Core, just as you reach a narrow channel leading up to the Mine Node, you can find a Redeemer resting on the path. This Redeemer is critical for destroying the Mine Node at the last second before it hurts your Power Core if the enemy has claimed it, and it can also provide some firepower for your offense.

Because it is located so far away from the main battle around the Prime Nodes, try to time its respawn and teleport back to the Power Core to reach it quickly.

On either side of the Redeemer, up on the rocky ledges overlooking the path to the Mine Node, you can find a pair of oddly placed Stingers, one closer to each teams' Power Core.

2: MINE NODE

VEHICLES	None
PICK-UPS	AVRiL, Jump Boots, Invisibility, Shock Rifle

The Mine Node rests on the back of the immensely huge digging machine that dominates the center of the map.

The Node itself is located beside a pair of small rooms with lockers inside, important as they provide cover from incoming enemies. An AVRiL beside the Node is also helpful for defense.

Holding the Mine Node is important, as it triggers the 60 second countdown to damage the enemy Power Core. You must decide if you are going to focus your efforts on holding the Mine Node, while only defending your Prime Node, or if more of your forces will be used in a traditional assault on the enemy Power Core.

There are plenty of goodies located around the Mine Node. Down below the huge treads of the machine, there is a pair of Jump Boots on each side, as well as the Invisibility in the very center beneath the machine.

Jump pads on either side of the machine provide quick access to the deck where the Node is located, and towards the front of the machine, you can find a Shock Rifle, and a jump pad that deposits you out on the huge arm that hangs over the battlefield below.

The walkway on the arm is ideal for sniping (and indeed, there is Sniper ammo at the end of the walkway), both with the Sniper Rifle from your main base, and with the AVRiL. It has a clean line of sight to both Prime Nodes.

There is one final pair of Jump Boots in the area. They're a short distance down the path to the Redeemer (near the area where you can see the little Mining Robots moving Tarydium into the processor once the Node is active).

TANK NODE

VEHICLES	Goliath
PICK-UPS	Shock Rifle, Rocket Launcher

The Tank Node provides a powerful offensive asset in the form of a Goliath, and for fighting on foot; grab the nearby Shock Rifle and Rocket Launcher.

An extended raised walkway stretches from this Node all the way to the Mine Node in the center of the map, and half way along the walkway, a small building holds the Rocket Launcher.

Simply due to the location of the Tank Node (off to the "edge" of the map), it is frequently possible to reach this Node and attack it unimpeded, simply because the enemy is often too busy

fighting over the more critical Prime Node or the Mine Node to send anyone to deal with an attack on the Tank Node.

The fastest way to do this is by hitting it from the Mine Node, where you can simply Hoverboard along the walkway connecting the digger to the Rocket Launcher tower. From there, you can lob rockets at the Node until it drops.

This is particularly useful when you're fighting a battle to claim the enemy Prime Node, as denying the enemy their Goliath weakens their defense considerably.

Be sure to have a player periodically teleport to your Tank Node to bring the Goliath forward after it is destroyed, you want it on offense as often as possible. If you're serious about defending the Mine Node as your means of attack, you may want to use the Goliath there instead of attacking the enemy Prime Node, but in any case, it is an important weapon.

4: PRIME NODE

VEHICLES	Hellbender, Paladin
PICK-UPS	Berserk, AVRiL

The Prime Nodes are the primary battleground on this map; each is situated within a rocky grotto, recessed into the rocky terrain. Outside the Prime Node, sloping ground rises up in a hill towards the earth mover at the center of the map. Once up the slope, the terrain essentially amounts to a wide open plain. It's dangerous for players on foot, and ideal for vehicular combat.

The Paladin and Hellbender here should both be used along with the Goliath from the Tank Node and your speedy vehicles at the Power Core to press the assault on the enemy Prime Node.

To aid with defense, an AVRiL is present, and up on the top of the rocky area, a Rocket Turret provides some additional assistance.

You can get up onto the rockets either from farther behind the Node, or via jump pads near the Node itself.

There is one other critical pick-up in the area, and that is the Berserk, located up on a ledge near the Node itself. Grabbing the Berserk and then hopping in a vehicle makes for a deadly offensive push. What vehicle you use is important, because the slower Goliath or Paladin get less time to use it as you get close to the enemy Prime Node, but a faster vehicle is more vulnerable to enemy AVRiL fire (or heavy weapons for that matter).

Should you lose your Prime Node, you may still have access to your Goliath at the Tank Node to assist in reclaiming it. If it is clear that the Prime Node is going to fall, make sure that someone checks the Tank Node for an advance enemy trying to clear it quickly. Losing both Nodes is dangerous, and worse still if the enemy actually captures the Tank Node to use your own Goliath against your base vehicles.

Defending the Prime Node with the Orb is useful both on offense and defense, another reason holding the Orb spawner at the Mine Node is helpful even if you aren't aiming to use the Mine Node's countdown. The closer Orb can help to lock down the enemy's Prime Node.

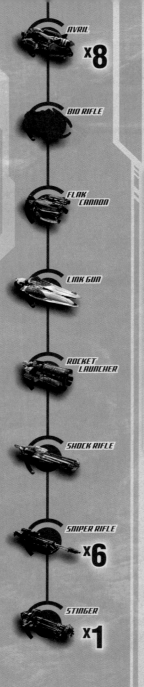

SERENITY

AVRIL	x8
BIO RIFLE	
FLAK CANNON	
LINK GUN	
ROCKET LAUNCHER	
SHOCK RIFLE	
SNIPER RIFLE	x6
STINGER	x1

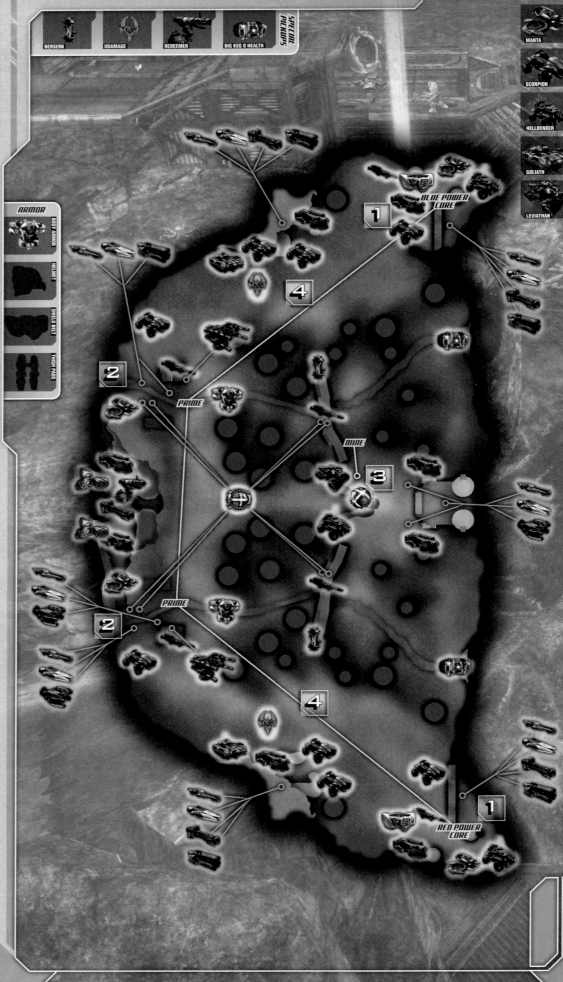

SPECIAL PICKUPS

BERSERK　UDAMAGE　REDEEMER　BIG KEG O HEALTH

ARMOR

BODY ARMOR　HELMET　SHIELD BELT　THIGH PADS

MANTA

SCORPION

HELLBENDER

GOLIATH

LEVIATHAN

BLUE POWER CORE

PRIME

MINE

PRIME

RED POWER CORE

Serenity is a beautiful forest of massive trees, with peaceful streams flowing through the map. The forest rarely remains peaceful for long, the massive firepower of the Leviathan that can be constructed here is quite loud indeed.

Despite Serenity's size, the basic Node layout and flow of the map is straightforward. The complexity arises not from the layout or size of the map, but rather, dealing with the secondary Mine Node, and the Leviathan that it spawns.

There are no additional Nodes on this map for the main linkage between the bases. The Prime Node links to the Power Core on each side, and that's the extent of the connectivity. The only other Node present is the Mine Node at the center of the forest.

The sprawling forest interferes with vehicle movement for all but the most nimble, and frequently blocks line of sight at great distances. Traveling through the forest is useful for staying in cover, particularly if you're hunting for the abundant power-ups.

Both bases have Berserk and UDamage power-ups located not far from the Power Cores. They're close enough to the Power Cores and the Prime Nodes to be used on either, and with proper timing, it is possible to have Juggernaut enabled vehicles storming the enemy defenses.

Because the Leviathan spawned from the Mine Node is so central to the map's flow (literally and figuratively), you may occasionally be able to pull a victory by pushing *hard* against the enemy defenses, and ignoring the Mine Node initially. Rather than burning manpower on fighting for the Leviathan, use them on pushing to the enemy Prime Node and taking the fight into the enemy base.

When the countdown timer on the Leviathan's construction grows near, send in an Orb carrier to break the Node and reset the Leviathan timer. Even if the Node is immediately reclaimed, you save a lot of time that can be used to press the attack on the enemy base.

The Prime Nodes are located on tricky rocky terrain on the edge of a massive cliff, just outside the boundaries of the forest proper.

The two Prime Nodes are joined by more rocky terrain, at the center of which lies the Redeemer. It provides another method of knocking out the Mine Node, should you lose control of it, or simply wish to stop the Leviathan from being built. If the Leviathan *is* completed (and more pertinently, rolling towards your Power Core with murderous intent), use the Redeemer to inflict grievous damage on it from a distance.

Dealing with the Leviathan if it does fall into enemy hands is critical, because it can park itself between the Prime Nodes and unleash devastating firepower, easily cracking your node while defending its own. If your Prime Node is then claimed (or worse, locked down by an Orb carrier), the Leviathan then has time to ponderously move towards your Power Core, a dire situation indeed. If the Leviathan manages to get in range with turret gunners in place, it can level the Core in seconds.

Fighting the Leviathan while it has a full complement of turret gunners is suicide, your best bet is to attack it from a distance and attempt to blow off the turrets before you get close to it with any vehicles.

1: POWER CORE

VEHICLES	Manta, Hellbender, Scorpion x3, Goliath
PICK-UPS	AVRiL x2, Shield Belt, Sniper Rifle, UDamage

The Power Core area is extensive, with several vehicles located in two areas. Immediately outside the Power Core, you can find a Manta, Scorpion, and Hellbender. A short distance away, the ponderous Goliath is parked with a pair of Scorpions.

All the vehicles are extremely useful on this map, both for transport, and for combat. The Manta in particular can get around in the forest really well, which is super handy for reaching the goodies on the streams, and the power-ups on each side of the map.

The rough road leading from the Core to the Prime Node is easily defensible by vehicles, or on foot with AVRiLs (of which there are two conveniently close at hand).

With so many Scorpions present, don't hesitate to use boost detonation to take down enemy vehicles, or to go after the Prime Nodes (particularly your own, should it be claimed by the enemy).

The greater distances on this map translate into an increased time while traveling with the Orb. If possible, hitch a ride with a Manta or Scorpion to speed up your travel time.

Be wary of the UDamage located just down the road from the Core, it can be used against your Core easily if you aren't diligent in picking it up every time it spawns, and the same goes for the nearby Berserk, located on the end of the bridge closest to your base.

2: PRIME NODE

VEHICLES	Scorpion, Manta
PICK-UPS	Health x2, Sniper Rifle, AVRiL, Jump Boots, Redeemer

The Prime Node is located in some interesting terrain, situated as it is on the edge of a huge cliff wall, just beyond the fringes of the forest proper.

The Node itself is nestled in the rocky terrain, reasonably concealed from long distance shots from the forest, but the upper part of the Node is *just* exposed enough to be boost detonated by enterprising Scorpion drivers who use the nearby ramp that just happens to conveniently face the Node.

Thankfully, with both an AVRiL and a Sniper Rifle close at hand, vehicles and infantry threats approaching the Node can be dealt with at a distance.

If that's not enough, the Beam Turret mounted atop the Node area is a great help against enemy incursion. As such, it is a prime target for long distance destruction. If you're taking light fire and guarding the Node,

repairing the turret periodically is worthwhile (or even better, having a teammate repair you while you fire on threatening vehicles).

Between the two Prime Nodes, a narrow ledge holds the Redeemer (and curiously, a Stinger). Timing this powerful asset is helpful (have at least one player set their preferred mode to Special Ops to get a voice over assist on the timer, but keep track of it as a team whenever possible).

The Manta and the Scorpion present at the Node are helpful both for quickly reaching the enemy Prime Node, and for heading into the forest, either to reach the Mine Node, gather power-ups, or get the goodies located on the streams.

3: **MINE NODE**

| VEHICLES | Hellbender, Leviathan |
| PICK-UPS | Health x2, AVRiL x2 |

4: **BRIDGE**

| VEHICLES | None |
| PICK-UPS | Health x2, Berserk, Body Armor, Big Keg O Health |

A minute after the Mine Node is fully claimed by a team, the Leviathan is constructed, appearing just to the west of the Node. From here, the Leviathan can be driven up the cleared road area to a junction between the two Prime Nodes.

Worth noting is that the Leviathan can actually deploy right there at the T-junction in the road and blast either Prime Node from a distance.

Otherwise, it's a lengthy but clear journey to either Power Core. Taking the Leviathan through the forest isn't really feasible, its sheer bulk prevents it from passing through the narrow spaces, so you have to take the long route.

This is good for the defenders, as it gives them time to deal with the behemoth, so if you're going to use the Leviathan as part of your offensive strategy, be sure to load it up with turret gunners. The Leviathan is *vastly* more dangerous with a full complement of active turrets, shielding the Leviathan from some damage and dishing out punishment in every direction.

Other than the Leviathan, the Mine Node has little tactical value, removed from the Prime Nodes as it is, and with only a Hellbender to provide transit for spawning players. Having an Orb location a bit closer than the Power Core can be slightly helpful, but the Prime Nodes are so close together this is rarely an issue.

Stretching north south, a lengthy bridge in the depths of the forest crosses a stream on both sides of the map, just to the north and south of the Mine Node.

At the end of each bridge structure is the Berserk power-up, and just across from the Berserk is the UDamage. The close proximity of these power-ups allows for the easiest Juggernaut acquisition of any map, so both power-ups must be rigorously timed by your team, or you risk facing some *really* unpleasant enemy vehicles (and infantry for that matter).

The bridges also have Sniper Rifles atop them, and provide just enough elevation to get a good line of sight on enemy infantry moving through the forest, near the Mine Node, or on the upper levels of the Prime Nodes.

The streams that pass beneath the bridges are important, as they hold two Health pick-ups each, and at the beginning of the river, a Health Keg. Following the river down towards the Prime Node provides Body Armor, so you can quickly tank up by sweeping the rivers.

Given the number of vehicles on the map (and the presence of the Leviathan), getting buffed up to fight on foot is only marginally useful, but you can make yourself into an annoyingly resilient AVRiL/Sniper Rifle pest in the trees, or provide sturdy Orb defense of your Prime Node (or better still, the enemies).

MAP VARIANTS: SERENITY NECRIS

The Necris variant of Serenity is substantially different, not only is the map much darker and grimmer with the advent of the Necris corruption, and the vehicles are changed, with Necris vehicles present.

The Blue Team uses (mostly) Necris vehicles on this map. Their Power Core has a Viper, Scorpion, and Nemesis present. The Goliath is replaced by a second Nemesis.

The Prime Node gives you a Viper and a Scorpion, and the Mine Node still provides the Leviathan and a Hellbender.

While the Node layout remains unchanged, with a constant battle over the Prime Nodes and the Leviathan being the focus, the addition of the Nemesis and Vipers gives the Blue Team more self destructing vehicles, and powerful long ranged firepower—the Nemesis can be used to great effect in the open spaces of Serenity, even with the trees providing some cover to Axon vehicles.

SINKHOLE

AVRIL **x4**

BIO RIFLE

FLAK CANNON

LINK GUN

ROCKET LAUNCHER

SHOCK RIFLE

SNIPER RIFLE **x4**

STINGER

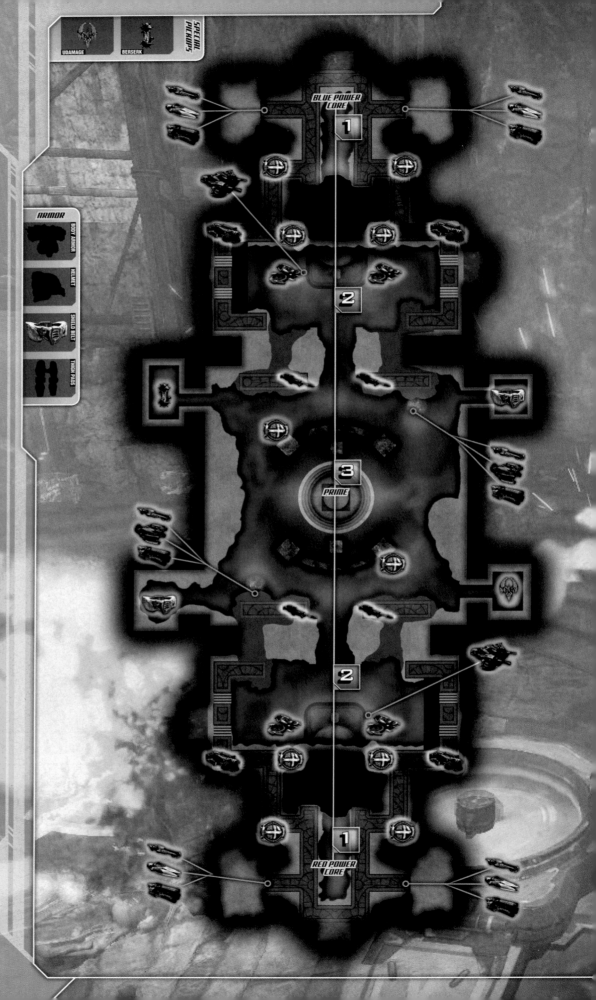

SPECIAL PICKUPS

UDAMAGE

BERSERK

ARMOR

BODY ARMOR

HELMET

SHIELD BELT

THIGH PADS

BLUE POWER CORE

1

2

3

PRIME

2

1

RED POWER CORE

This is another of the three simple Warfare maps. It's actually one of the early training maps for Warfare in the single player campaign. Sinkhole has only a single Prime Node in the center of the map between the two bases.

There aren't any elegant tactics to be executed on this map. It comes down to using your Orb to grab the Center Node, then having one player guard the Node with your Orb to give you extra time on offense.

It is possible to become a Juggernaut, as both UDamage and Berserk are present, and with Shield Belts as well, and plenty of Vials on each side, becoming quite sturdy *and* getting a power-up makes for a strong push to the enemy Power Core.

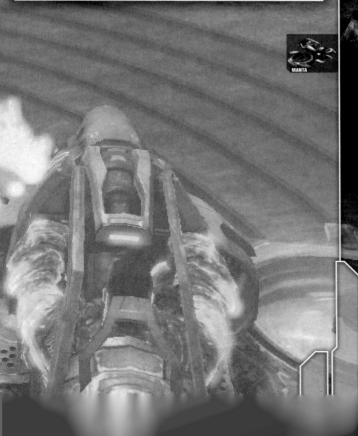

MANTA

1: POWER CORE

VEHICLES	None
PICK-UPS	Health x2

The Power Core area is a two-story affair, with the Core down on the ground level recessed slightly into the ground, and a lift at the back of the room leading up to the second floor. If it becomes necessary to defend the room, fighting from the second level is preferable.

On offense, you can reach the upper ledge inside the Power Core room by coming up the lift at the front of the base (on the opposite side of the room from where the Mantas spawn). From above, you can rain flak or rockets down on the Core, just watch out for players spawning nearby.

2: BASE FRONT

VEHICLES	Manta x2
PICK-UPS	Vials, Health x2, AVRiL x2

The front of the base contains both Mantas, the only vehicles present on the map. They are both highly valuable for attacking the Prime Node, and the enemy base for that matter. It's quite easy to pancake opponents in the constrained hallways on this map.

The Rocket Turret here is helpful for defending against enemy pushes if you lose the Prime Node for a moment. Wipe out their offense, then push back to the middle.

Don't forget to grab the AVRiL on the upper level here, it is a one shot kill on the Mantas, and the most important tool you can have for holding the Prime Node with the Orb.

The plentiful Vials here can actually add up to a sizable amount of health, useful in conjunction with the Shield Belt to get tanked up.

3: MIDFIELD

VEHICLES	None
PICK-UPS	Sniper Rifle x2, Health x4, Shield Belt x2, UDamage, Berserk

On the upper ledge from the base front, you can find a Sniper Rifle, and the ledge it is perched on is a decent spot for sniping players running around in the midfield near the Prime Node. Plus, you can fire Longbow shots down at Mantas below more safely than on the ground level.

Down on the ground floor, each side has a pair of Health pick-ups, and on the sides of the room, two chambers. The Red Base side has the UDamage, and the Blue Base side the Berserk. Both sides have a Shield Belt tucked away in the opposite chamber.

All of these pick-ups are important, timing them is critical for maintaining an offensive edge, since there is so little finesse involved in the fighting here, having an edge with power-ups and Shield Belts is important.

The Prime Node rests in the very center of the map, defending or attacking it with the Orb from your base is advisable. If you're guarding the Node with the Orb, have an AVRiL ready, a Manta squashing you is the most serious threat you can face.

TANK CROSSING

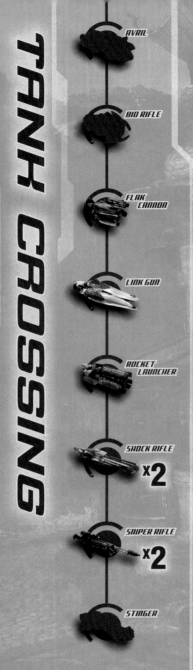

- AVRIL
- BIO RIFLE
- FLAK CANNON
- LINK GUN
- ROCKET LAUNCHER
- SHOCK RIFLE **x2**
- SNIPER RIFLE **x2**
- STINGER

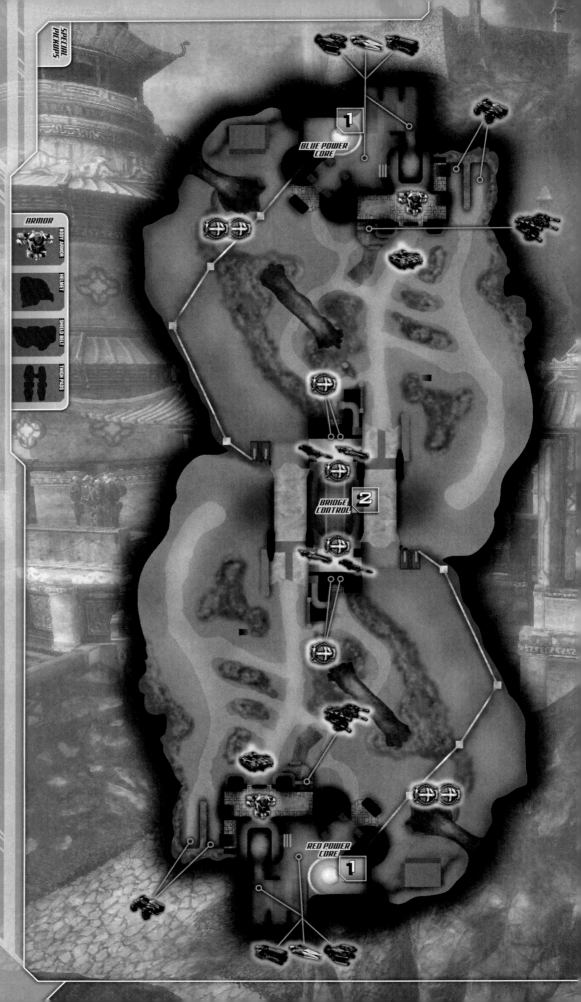

SPECIAL PICKUPS

ARMOR
- BODY ARMOR
- HELMET
- SHIELD BELT
- THIGH PADS

BLUE POWER CORE

1

BRIDGE CONTROL **2**

RED POWER CORE **1**

SCORPION

GOLIATH

This is the third simple Warfare map. There is only a single central Prime Node to battle over. However, victory on this map cannot be won solely by controlling the Prime Node. Damaging the enemy Power Core is slightly more involved on Tank Crossing.

The Prime Node has a special function on this map; it adjusts the movable bridges that cross over the Prime Node.

This is critical, as the *only* way to damage the enemy Power Core is to drive your Goliath across the bridge, and park it on a large pressure plate located just outside the enemy Power Core.

Doing so opens the blast shields protecting the Core, allowing the Goliath (and anyone nearby) to pound away at the enemy Core.

Destroying the Prime Node raises both bridges, and capturing it lowers yours but keeps the enemies raised.

There is no AVRiL on this map, so about the best you can do against the enemy Goliath if it *does* cross the bridge is pounding away at a distance with flak or rockets. You may get some shots off with your Scorpions or the Beam Turret near the base, but there isn't a quick and easy answer for the massive tank. You can usually destroy it before it kills your Core, but expect to take a pounding before it goes down.

ALERT!

When the pressure pad is activated by an enemy Goliath, warning alarms are triggered in the base. If you hear the alerts, or see the flashing lights at a distance, you need to pay attention to the warning and deal with the enemy Goliath before it can devastate your Power Core

POWER CORE

VEHICLES	Scorpion x2, Goliath
PICK-UPS	Body Armor, Health x2

The bases at each end of the map are simple affairs, with a few weapon lockers inside, a pair of Scorpions outside, and of course, the Goliath.

You can find a suit of Body Armor at the front of the base, and a nearby Beam Turret provides some last ditch defense against an incoming enemy Goliath (or any overzealous enemy Scorpions)

Otherwise, your attention should be focused forward. Unlike most Warfare maps, you can't directly defend your Power Core from your base, you must proactively prevent the enemy Goliath from crossing the bridge, and destroy it if it does manage to get across.

The enemy can't touch your Core without the Goliath, so your efforts must be aimed at controlling the Prime Node, and damaging the Goliath whenever it comes into view.

There are two ways to fight the enemy Goliath, should it get across the bridge. For one, the road that leads to the pressure plate beside your Power Core is exposed through a small window next to the pressure plate. This window is visible from just outside the base, and it is conveniently located next to a pair of Health pick-ups.

From here, you can lob flak or rocket shots at the Goliath, and dodge over to the Health if the gunner takes an interest in you.

The other is to use your Hoverboard and hit the Hoverboard boost pad on the Scorpion side of the base, just down the road. It propels you clean across the midfield, dropping you down on the enemy team's Goliath road. This isn't a safe move to get in *front* of the Goliath, but if it has already crossed the bridge, you can get behind it and attack it while its attention is focused on your Core.

When it comes to attacking the midfield, the front of the base has essentially three routes, the far left (by the Scorpions) leads down a road to the Prime Node. The center road is used by the Goliath, and terminates at the (initially raised) bridge, and the right path deposits players on foot inside the small bunker that overlooks the Prime Node.

2: PRIME NODE

VEHICLES	None
PICK-UPS	Shock Rifle, Sniper Rifle, Health x6

The Prime Node is located in a ravine below the two bridges above, exposed to fire from above, from the Scorpion roads on either side, and from the small bunkers built into the rock face on either side of the Node.

This is truly as bad as it sounds. The Prime Node is *constantly* under attack and holding it is difficult. This is deliberate, as once the Goliath is across the bridge, the Core does not tend to last long, even if your team is quick about going after it.

Using the Orb to defend the Node is hard, as there's no great place to stand, the closest thing to cover is the ledges with Health on either side of the Node, and even there you can be pasted from above by a sniper, or from a Scorpion's energy bombs. Not to mention that boost detonating Scorpions can pound the Node.

The quickest way down to the Prime Node is via Scorpion, helpful both for transport and for protecting the Node once it is built.

The small bunker buildings beside the Node are very useful as well, as the Sniper Rifle on the upper floor and the Shock Rifle on the middle level can both be used to fire at enemy infantry in the area, protecting the Node from a safe distance.

There are several Health pick-ups for bunker dwellers as well, two on the inside, and one out on the ledge overlooking the Node, as well as a trio of Vials inside by the Shock Rifle.

A lift provides quick travel between the middle floor by the Health, and the upper deck where the Sniper Rifle is located.

AGGRESSIVE DEFENSE

Pushing towards the enemy base is not at all a bad idea on this map. There are a lot of benefits for bottling up the other team before they can get anywhere near the Prime Node.

Generally, sending in a strike team to take out their Scorpions and (especially!) their Goliath is quite helpful.

If you can get your Scorpions across the center of the map, you can even drive onto their Goliath path—catching up to their Goliath from behind and boost detonating into it is a quick way to save your Core from getting pounded.

If you have idle defenders around the Prime Node, it's better to have them stopping an incoming Orb carrier before it ever gets near the Prime Node. Setting up shop in their bunker can work too, as you can snipe the front of their base just as easily as the Prime Node area or the enemy bunker.

TORLAN

AVRIL **x4**

BIO RIFLE

FLAK CANNON

LINK GUN

ROCKET LAUNCHER

SHOCK RIFLE

SNIPER RIFLE

STINGER

SPECIAL PICKUPS

BERSERK | REDEEMER | JUMP BOOTS

ARMOR

BODY ARMOR

HELMET

SHIELD BELT

THIGH PADS

A classic UT Onslaught map, Torlan returns, with more variants than any other Warfare map, a new basic setup, and all the carnage you'd expect from a large scale, vehicle-heavy battlefield.

More than many other Warfare maps, Torlan is focused on vehicular combat, with tons of wide open terrain for maneuvering vehicles. The distances involved makes getting from place to place in a vehicle the safest way to travel.

WHERE'S MY TANK NODE?!

The base version of Torlan in *UT3* has East and West Nodes linked to the Prime Nodes, with the Tank Nodes inactive (though you can grab a Weapon Locker there containing Link, Stinger, and Rocket weaponry).

By default, the Prime Nodes are already captured when the map begins, allowing for quick assault on the East, West, or Center Nodes using your Orb.

If you want your Goliath back, load up the Torlan Classic variant!

If you are playing Torlan with 10 or more players, the Tank Nodes *are* enabled in the default Node layout.

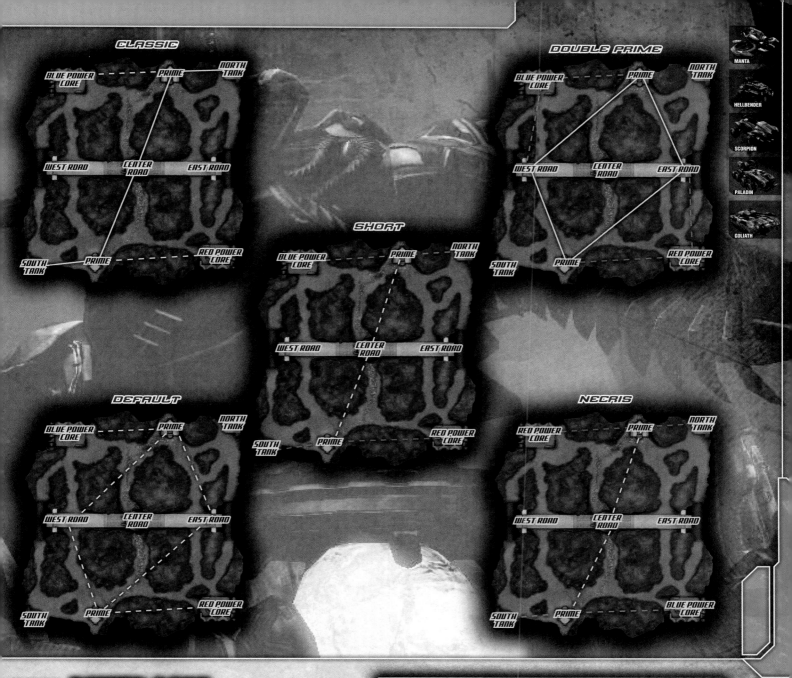

CLASSIC

BLUE POWER CORE · PRIME · NORTH TANK
WEST ROAD · CENTER ROAD · EAST ROAD
SOUTH TANK · PRIME · RED POWER CORE

DOUBLE PRIME

BLUE POWER CORE · PRIME · NORTH TANK
WEST ROAD · CENTER ROAD · EAST ROAD
SOUTH TANK · PRIME · RED POWER CORE

SHORT

BLUE POWER CORE · PRIME · NORTH TANK
WEST ROAD · CENTER ROAD · EAST ROAD
SOUTH TANK · PRIME · RED POWER CORE

DEFAULT

BLUE POWER CORE · PRIME · NORTH TANK
WEST ROAD · CENTER ROAD · EAST ROAD
SOUTH TANK · PRIME · RED POWER CORE

NECRIS

RED POWER CORE · PRIME · NORTH TANK
WEST ROAD · CENTER ROAD · EAST ROAD
SOUTH TANK · PRIME · BLUE POWER CORE

MANTA
HELLBENDER
SCORPION
PALADIN
GOLIATH

1:8 POWER CORE

VEHICLES	Manta, Hellbender, Raptor
PICK-UPS	AVRiL, Sniper Rifle, Jump Boots, Health x2

The Power Core areas are both rather sizable base structures, with a Beam Turret on the outer wall providing some extra defense.

The Power Core has a Manta and Hellbender for quick transport, and a Raptor which is vital for: 1) air-to-air combat against the enemy Raptor and Cicada 2) stalking Mantas on the ground, and 3) hunting SPMAs bombarding your base.

The elevated sniper tower in the center of the base has a clean line of sight to much of the map facing your base, which is handy if you're pushed back on defense.

The inside of the base consists of a central raised platform, with two routes around it that descend to the Power Core, lowered in a depression at the back of the base. Enemies seeking to damage the Core must penetrate all the way inside the base area, either driving a vehicle in, or bombarding the Core from a great distance with the Cicada or SPMA.

Be sure to pick up the AVRiL here, there is *not* an AVRiL located at the Prime Node.

HEAL ME!

There is little health available on Torlan. The two Health pick-ups in the main base and the single Health pick-up down at the Prime Node are all you get. Consequently, restoring yourself after a battle is rather difficult, giving more weight to spending your time in vehicles, rather than on foot. It's better that your armor takes damage than your health, which you can easily repair using the Link Gun.

2: PRIME NODE

VEHICLES	Manta, Scorpion
PICK-UPS	AVRiL ammo, Jump Boots, Body Armor, Health

3: WEST NODE

VEHICLES	Manta, SPMA
PICK-UPS	AVRiL

MAP VARIANTS: CLASSIC

Mirroring the version from Onslaught, Classic removes the East and West road nodes in favor of activating the corner Tank Nodes. In this version, the Prime Node is *not* immediately captured when the map begins.

The Tank Node holds a Manta and a Goliath.

Note that you can still grab the AVRiL's located where the East/West Nodes were.

Without SPMAs, and with only the central Node linking the two Prime Nodes, constant battles over the Central and Prime Nodes become the norm. Use the Tank Nodes to give your team added firepower for taking down the enemy Nodes.

MAP VARIANTS: DOUBLE PRIME

No Tank Nodes present in this variant, but the main difference is that the Prime Node *and* the East Node function as Prime Nodes for the Red Power Core.

Similarly, the Blue Prime Node and the West Node act as Prime Nodes for the Blue Power Core.

As a result, it is considerably easier to reach the enemy's Power Core, as you can choose which Node to go after. Defense is tricky, requiring constant use of your Orb to reclaim Nodes.

Capturing the Center Node is still just as important as it is on the normal map, giving you easy access to a second Orb spawn location, plus the Cicada to assist in offensive or defensive operations.

Curiously, the Prime Node is captured initially at the start of the battle, so you can quickly turn your attention to the midfield battle. Deciding which Nodes you are going to pursue initially (especially with your Orb) is an important decision. Going for one of the side road Nodes provides a link to the enemy Prime Node for direct offense, but the Center Node holds numerous goodies—great for supporting your attack.

The Prime Node is a fairly open structure, with jump pads on the sides that can be used to get up on the roof, or by using the Jump Boots located below.

The Manta and Scorpion here are helpful for quickly reaching the other Nodes.

Because there is no AVRiL here, you may want to teleport back to the main base to pick it up if you happen to spawn here, the extra ammo here is useful if you're hunting any of the numerous vehicles moving about the map.

A Beam Turret at the front of the Prime Node provides excellent defense against the various light vehicles present on the map.

The West Node holds little in the way of supplies, but like its twin on the east side of the map, it provides the extremely powerful SPMA, and a Manta for quick transport. The nearby AVRiL is also helpful for defending the Node against light vehicles coming up from the enemy base or Prime Node.

The SPMA from here is exceedingly useful for bombarding the enemy Nodes, and it can even hit the enemy Power Core from a hilltop.

Because the SPMA can do so much damage out of line of sight, it is important for defenders to shoot down the SPMA's targeting camera, easily done with a Sniper Rifle, or in a pinch, with the Shock Rifle.

4: EAST NODE

VEHICLES	Manta, SPMA
PICK-UPS	AVRiL

The East Node is a mirror of the west, the only distinction being proximity to the Blue Base, rather than the Red.

Note that both east and west Nodes have a bridge area behind them that passes above and behind the actual Node area, which can be useful for traveling across the map. You can also drop down from this upper road area to the Node below through a few holes in the side of the bridge.

5: CENTER NODE

VEHICLES	Scorpion x2 (lower), Cicada (center)
PICK-UPS	Sniper Rifle, Berserk, Jump Boots, Redeemer, Shield Belt x2

The Center Node is *loaded* with goodies. The bottom area, where the Node itself is located has a Shield Belt and a pair of Scorpions for quick transit to either Prime Node.

On the center level, where the bridge crosses the water below, the Sniper Rifle, Berserk, and Jump Boots are all right next to each other.

The Jump Boots are handy for dropping down from the center level to the bottom without taking much damage, and the jump pad on the bottom level can be used to return to the middle.

Finally, far above the ground on the top of the tower above the center bridge is the Redeemer and another Shield Belt. The Redeemer is quite handy, but as you can only reach the top with a flying vehicle, be careful not to get stranded. Grab the goods and get back to ground level before your ride is toasted by an alert enemy.

As if all the pick-ups weren't enough, the Center Node also spawns a Cicada on the middle level, and with the Berserk nearby, it can be a devastating source of firepower, especially if the Berserk is up. Bring a teammate along to provide turret fire, and flares to avoid AVRiL shots. Use the terrain to exploit the Cicada's lock on secondary fire, and you can blast Nodes from cover without exposing yourself to long distance fire.

If you find yourself pushed back to your Prime Node, it's worth sending a player to the Center Node—the Orb spawner can be used to quickly break one of the side Nodes, and the Cicada is a useful offensive asset, as well as providing quick access to the Redeemer, a helpful Node reset button.

MAP VARIANTS: NECRIS

Like the other Necris variant maps, this comes right out of the single player campaign after the Necris invasion of Taryd. Not only are the Blue Team vehicles replaced with Necris craft, the map itself bears the signs of Nanoblack corruption.

The Node layout is similar to the Short variant, with the Prime Nodes linked to one another, but *all* Nodes are active in this version, East, West, and both corner Tank Nodes.

There is a *lot* of heavy vehicle firepower available here. Don't go running around on foot if you can help it, you're so much meat for the behemoths on patrol.

The Blue base holds a Viper, Nemesis, and Fury.

The Prime Node has a Viper and a Scavenger.

The East and West Nodes provide a Nightshade and a Viper.

Finally, the Center Node gives two Scavengers (below) and a Darkwalker (on the center bridge).

Note that unlike Avalanche or Serenity, when the Necris or Axon team captures a Node in this variant, the vehicles are swapped completely—the Necris always have Necris equipment, and vice versa.

MAP VARIANTS: SHORT

Just like it sounds—short! Not only are both Prime Nodes active at the start of the map, the Tank Nodes are present, there are no East or West Nodes, and the Prime Nodes are linked to each other!

You can still go for the Center Node to get some added firepower, and using your Orb to protect the Prime Node is advisable on offense or defense.

UNREAL TOURNAMENT® III
OFFICIAL STRATEGY GUIDE

Written by Phillip Marcus

©2007 DK Publishing, a division of
Penguin Group (USA), Inc.

BradyGames® is a registered trademark of
Pearson Education, Inc.

BradyGames Publishing
An Imprint of DK Publishing, Inc.
800 East 96th Street, 3rd Floor
Indianapolis, Indiana 46240

ISBN: 0-7440-0955-3

Printing Code: The rightmost double-digit number is the
year of the book's printing; the rightmost single-digit number
is the number of the book's printing. For example, 07-1
shows that the first printing of the book occurred in 2007.

10   09   08   07   4   3   2   1

Manufactured in the United States of America.

BRADYGAMES STAFF

Publisher
David Waybright

Editor-In-Chief
H. Leigh Davis

Licensing Manager
Mike Degler

Director of Marketing
Debby Neubauer

Creative Director
Robin Lasek

CREDITS

Sr. Development Editor
Christian Sumner

Screenshot Editor
Michael Owen

Designer
Dan Caparo

Production Designer
Bob Klunder

Contributing Designer
Colin King

Map Illustrators
Argosy Publishi...

BRADYGAMES ACKNOWLEDGEMENTS

The creation of this book was a difficult process, but also an immensely satisfying one. As a fan of the series from the very first game, writing about *UT3* was a remarkable experience.

Thanks must go first and foremost to the team at Epic Games. They graciously gave of their time, and answered my most obscure questions with good humor, even in the midst of the final crunch to completion. If you've ever wondered if the guys who release so much neat stuff freely for the Unreal series are just as cool in person as they are to their fans, the answer is yes.

To Jeff Morris, for giving a warm welcome, and for providing anything I requested at incredible speed.

A special mention must go to Jim Brown, for his invaluable assistance with the Necris campaign.

For the level designers and programmers, a thank you for putting up with fiddly queries about every aspect of the game.

To David Wright, for helping to capture the stunning visuals of the Unreal world.

Finally, this book is not the result of a single writer. The creative design staff at Brady are responsible for turning raw text into the guide you hold in your hands. My editor, Christian Sumner, had to wade through a ridiculously large manuscript, I have to thank him for cleaning up my mess (but if there are any mistakes, blame him, not me, hah!).

SPECIAL THANKS

This is my first project with Epic, and I have to say that I'm simply blown away. Everyone over there is truly fantastic to work with and you can sense their passion for their games within a heartbeat of meeting them. An especially big thanks goes out to Jeff Morris, whom I had the pleasure of meeting and the luck to work with.

Phil destroyed himself for this one. However, the biggest challenges bring out the best in him and I can't possibly be more pleased. Thanks for everything Phillip.

The BradyGames design team was phenomenal. Colin jumped in to help out, and I want to thank him for it. Dan's design and Bob's hard work brought this thing to life. It couldn't have been done without them.